Working in the Family Justice System

The Official Handbook of the Family Justice Council

Third Edition

Elizabeth Walsh LLB
Solicitor and Mediator

Gillian Geddes LLB
Barrister

Family Law

Published by Family Law
A publishing imprint of Jordan Publishing Limited
21 St Thomas Street
Bristol BS1 6JS

British Library Cataloguing-in-Publication Data

A catalogue record for this book is available from the British Library.

ISBN 978 1 84661 112 4

Typeset by Letterpart Ltd, Reigate, Surrey

Printed and bound in Great Britain by Antony Rowe Limited, Chippenham, Wiltshire

Working in the Family Justice System

The Official Handbook of the Family
Justice Council

WITHDRAWN

DEDICATION

This book is dedicated to all those working selflessly in the family justice system.

ACKNOWLEDGEMENTS

Special thanks are due to the Family Justice Council for making this book possible. Individuals who have given generously their advice and support are, in alphabetical order:

Paula Adshead (Family Justice Council)

Alex Clark (Family Justice Council)

Bruce Clark (Cafcass)

Charles Geekie QC

Members of the Family Justice Council

Laura Newhofer (Legal Services Commission)

Keith Revoir (Senior Social Worker)

Lord Justice Thorpe

Lord Justice Wall

Joanna Wilkinson (Family Justice Council)

Greg Woodgate (Jordans)

Jane Worsey (Legal Services Commission)

Gillian Wright

FOREWORD

My experience of family law and practice now stretches back almost 50 years. As a young barrister defended divorces and defended cases in the magistrates' court provided the arena for embittered and embattled spouses and families. Wardship proceedings were still conducted in Chancery.

The Divorce Reform Act 1969 and the Matrimonial Proceedings and Property Act 1970 revolutionised the law and the practice. We practitioners entered into a new and vibrant scene in which we rapidly learned the complexities of ancillary relief litigation. Disputes as to children were generally within the framework of the divorce proceedings (the fashion for co-habitation being yet in its infancy) and in wardship, now transferred to the newly created Family Division. Those essential reforms gave us practitioners a new sense of commitment to professional practice which was so evidently and increasingly vital to sustaining public confidence in social and family justice.

The final enduring reform was, of course, the Children Act 1989 which modernised, rationalised and consolidated the previous position into a uniform code of law and practice for the protection and for the welfare of all children, whether born in or out of wedlock, and whether the subject of private or public law proceedings. The Government's commitment to achieve excellence by sufficiently resourcing specialist practitioners and experts within an inter-related and inter-disciplinary collaboration introduced a decade in which the importance of family justice was acknowledged, often by its prioritisation over competing justice systems. Into this world the first edition of Working in the Family Justice System was born.

Its second edition was promoted by the newly created Family Justice Council, then confidently developing as the focus of policy and practice debate within the family justice system.

Sadly, much of its advice and exhortation to Government has gone unheeded over the course of the last two years and I now survey a family justice system in crisis. Never has the morale of the specialists from every discipline been so low. In such a climate the only hope is to avoid self interest and faction. We must work together and we must support each other through the difficult times that will undoubtedly lie ahead. It is therefore particularly timely that the third edition of Working in the Family Justice System arrives to facilitate communication and a sense of a professional community united in adversity. In writing the third edition Elizabeth Walsh has been joined by Gillian Geddes, a practicing children proceedings barrister with great experience. I am encouraged to hear that a fourth edition is on their future agenda.

The Rt Hon Lord Justice Thorpe

CONTENTS

`

TABLE OF STATUTES

References are to paragraph numbers.

TABLE OF STATUTORY INSTRUMENTS

References are to paragraph numbers.

TABLE OF EC AND INTERNATIONAL MATERIAL

References are to paragraph numbers.

INTRODUCTION

THE FUTURE FOR FAMILY JUSTICE

Since the second edition of this book was published in 2006 there have been many changes in the operation of the Family Justice System, most of which the authors hope have been included in this edition. However, practitioners in the field of family law are dismayed that certain issues have remained unchanged. The Rt Hon Lord Justice Thorpe spoke, during the inauguration of the Family Justice Council in 2004, of many of the contributing professions at the time feeling 'besieged or undervalued', of 'legal practitioners having seen such radical reduction in the level of fees for publicly funded work that they are quitting, or considering quitting, the field', of 'a marked shortage of front line social workers', and of 'misfortunes and misjudgements that have dogged the creation of the Children and Family Court Advisory and Support Service Cafcass'. To practitioners, it is deeply disturbing that these observations are still relevant and the concerns now even more acute.

In his keynote address to the Annual Conference of the Association of Lawyers for Children in 2009, the Rt Hon Lord Justice Wall spoke of the 'parlous state of family law in 2009' and of three particular issues currently the focus of professionals' concern: an ongoing general lack of funding for the system, the crisis that Cafcass now faces, and the need for and process of transparency of the system to the general public.

As the system creaks and lurches under its current restrictions, Lord Justice Wall echoes what most professionals in the system still believe, and in 2010 what the professional organisations have striven to demonstrate to those holding the purse strings, that the need for a powerful and properly resourced family justice system (particularly in the field of children's cases), peopled by specialist practitioners who are properly remunerated cannot be over-emphasised, and that without proper funding the system will implode and children will suffer most.

Professionals working in the family justice system are physically and emotionally exhausted from striving to achieve the best possible outcomes from the system at a time when resources are being pared to the bone and especially in the aftermath of the flood of children's cases in 2009 that followed the tragic case of Baby Peter. Lord Justice Wall observed that 'the proper presentation of a difficult child case is a highly skilled process requiring an approach which is different to almost every other area of law and practice', that specialist representation for children, parents, family members and local authorities is 'very difficult work requiring a special and very high level of expertise', and that what 'those who control the court's purse strings simply do not – or will not – understand is that competent legal representation not only saves time . . . but that it also saves money'.

Cafcass is now under such economic strain that guardians are not allocated when they should be and important decisions are, at the beginning of 2010, having to be made about children in both private and public law cases without a guardian's input. 2009 has seen a high number of care cases in which a guardian had not been allocated, and the current insistence on a Cafcass monopoly has inevitably meant that guardians currently cannot timeously be allocated. The President of the Family Division, in the 2009 Hershman Levy Memorial Lecture, ran into criticism when he announced a system of 'duty' guardians to plug the deficiencies in the system. In Lord Justice Wall's opinion, 'an inadequately funded Cafcass, which is unable to work with parents and children outside the courtroom, is a bitter disappointment to those who believed that they were being promised change for the better when Cafcass was brought into being'. The role of the guardian in care proceedings is of the person who gets to know the child, who provides continuity for the child, and who acts as the protector of the child against inappropriate or shoddy practice by the local authority: this role is critical. The guardian makes an individual assessment of the child's needs and circumstances and in tandem with the child's solicitor presents the child's case to the court. His or her statutory duty is to safeguard the interests of the child and the appointment of an individual guardian for individual children is 'pivotal to the system'. Certainly, all professionals working in the child care system believe it is of fundamental importance in ongoing child care proceedings that representatives for all the parties concerned are able to share their views with the individual guardian and his or her solicitor as the case progresses, and to put forward each party's case for the guardian's consideration as he or she forms a final view upon the evidence put before the court. As Lord Justice Wall stated, the 'tandem model' of a named, identifiable and contactable guardian and solicitor throughout proceedings is of pivotal importance, and the current 'duty system', intended to be only a temporary measure during the difficulties which Cafcass is facing, must be remedied.

Clauses in the Children, Schools and Families Bill published in November 2009 build on changes announced in April 2009 that allowed the media to attend most family proceedings for the first time. The changes are to be introduced in phases to allow the government to assess their impact before potentially moving to a greater degree of openness. As press headlines accuse the system of 'secret justice' and of utilising experts who are in the pay of those who instruct them, in particular local authorities and guardians, all in the profession agree that greater transparency of the family justice system is needed and that a wider and more informed public appreciation of the work that is done within the system is important. In the light of the publication of the Bill, the Government's intentions nevertheless remain unclear. Some professionals feel that the wrong mechanism is being offered and that perhaps a system of court open days, trialled for the first time in 2009 to great success, would be of greater use in rendering the system more user-friendly. Journalists comment that s 34(2) of the Bill only allows them to report information that has been obtained by 'observing or listening to the proceedings when attending them . . .' and that this is unworkable as very few journalists are able and available to attend hearings, and would in fact be unwilling to do so in 'run-of-the-mill' cases. What is crucially needed at this point is a sensible dialogue between the government and those directly affected by the proposed changes, including the press, leading perhaps to an agreed protocol.

Giving journalists the right to see sensitive documentary evidence in cases is a matter which requires the most careful consideration. Danya Glaser, Psychologist at Great Ormond Street Hospital for Children, says that it is inconceivable that clinicians should be put in the position of having to warn the patient (ie the child) that what is being discussed, almost invariably highly personal and often distressing and already being included in a clinician's report, will also be read by the media. However, the piloting of the anonymisation and publication of judgments is welcomed, together potentially with press releases in cases of complexity and controversy.

As for the canard of experts allegedly being in the pay of those who instruct them, the public needs to be aware that there is a very strict code for experts to follow and for the instruction of experts. Appendix C to the Protocol for Judicial Case Management in Public Law Children Act Cases, now replaced by the Public Law Outline (the PLO) and the 2008 Practice Direction on Experts set out that code in considerable detail. The duty which the expert owes is to the court, not to the party instructing the expert, and the process is subject to judicial control.

With the effects of under-resourcing now biting hard, and perhaps with Lord Justice Wall's strong advice still resounding down corridors, the Ministry of Justice announced at the beginning of 2010 a fundamental and wide-ranging review of the family justice system, a part of the cross-government Families and Relationships Green Paper. Battle-weary practitioners wonder exactly what reforms this will herald.

Change is uncomfortable and it is not always welcome. But change is often the forerunner to valuable results. The Family Justice System works well when team work and inter-agency co-operation are at their most effective. For the Family Justice System to change in ways which would assist families most in need, team work and co-operation between those in charge of drafting legislation, those in charge of the purse strings, and those at the coal face of the system itself is vital. As Lord Justice Wall said in his speech, 'Please talk to us. We know what we are talking about'.

LIST OF ABBREVIATIONS

ACMD	Advisory Council on Misuse of Drugs
ACP	Association of Child Psychotherapists
ACPO	Association of Chief Police Officers
ADHD	Attention Deficit Hyperactivity Disorder
ADR	Alternative Dispute Resolution
ADSS	Association of Directors of Social Services
AFT	Association of Family Therapists
ALC	Association of Lawyers for Children
ALSG	Advanced Life Support Group
ASBO	Anti-social Behaviour Order
BAAF	British Association for Adoption and Fostering
BACCH	British Association for Community Child Health
BMA	British Medical Association
BPC	British Psychoanalytic Council
BPS	British Psychological Society
CAB	Citizens Advice Bureau
cafcass	Children and Family Court Advisory and Support Service (England)
CAFCASS CYMRU	Children and Family Court Advisory and Support Service (Wales)
CAIU	Child Abuse Investigation Unit
CAMHS	Children and Adolescent Mental Health Service
CDRA	Children's Dispute Resolution Appointment
CEOP	Child Exploitation and Online Protection Centre
CFM	College of Family Mediators
CFLQ	Child and Family Law Quarterly (published by Jordans)
CICS	Criminal Injuries Compensation Scheme
CLA	Community Legal Advice
C-MEC	Child Maintenance and Enforcement Commission
CMO	Chief Medical Officer
CPD	Continual Professional Development
CPO	Case Progression Officer
CPS	Crown Prosecution Service
CRB	Criminal Records Bureau
CROA	Children's Rights Officers and Advocates
CSA	Children's Services Authority
CSA	Child Support Agency
CSCI	Commission for Social Care Inspection
CVAA	Consortium of Voluntary Adoption Agencies
CVS	Councils for Voluntary Service
DAT	Drug Action Team

DCS	Director of Children's Services
DCSF	Department for Children Schools and Families
DOH	Department of Health
DWP	Department for Work and Pensions
DVU	Domestic Violence Unit
ECHR	European Convention on Human Rights
ECtHR	European Court of Human Rights
EPO	Emergency Protection Order
ESRC	Economic and Social Research Council
Fam Law	Family Law (published by Jordans)
FCO	Foreign and Commonwealth Office
FCBC	Family Court Business Committee
FDR	Financial Dispute Resolution
FGC	Family Group Conference
FJC	Family Justice Council
FLBA	Family Law Bar Association
FMA	Family Mediators' Association
FMC	Family Mediation Council
FPI	Family and Parenting Institute
FPC	Family Proceedings Court
GMC	General Medical Council
GSCC	General Social Care Council
HMCS	Her Majesty's Courts Service
HMIC	Her Majesty's Inspectorate of Constabulary
HMICA	Her Majesty's Inspectorate of Court Administration
HMRC	Her Majesty's Revenue and Customs
HRA 1998	Human Rights Act 1998
ICACU	International Child Abduction Contact Unit
ICO	Interim Care Order
IFL	International Family Law (published by Jordans)
ILEX	Institute of Legal Executives
ISA	Independent Safeguarding Authority
IRO	Independent Reviewing Officer
JAR	Joint Area Review
JR	Judicial Review
JSB	Judicial Studies Board
LA	Local Authority
LAC	Looked After Child
LFJC	Local Family Justice Council
LSC	Legal Services Commission
LSCB	Local Safeguarding Children Board
MAPPA	Multi-Agency Public Protection Arrangements
MDP	Multi Disciplinary Practice
MDT	Multi-Disciplinary Team
MOJ	Ministry of Justice
MRC	Medical Research Council
NACCC	National Association of Child Contact Centres
NACRO	National Crime Reduction Charity

NAGALRO	Professional Association for Children's Guardians and Children and Family Reporters
Napo	Trade Union and Professional Association for Family Court and Probation Staff
NCH	National Children's Homes
NGO	Non Governmental organisation
NICE	National Institute for Clinical Excellence
NFM	National Family Mediation
NRP	Non Residential Parent
NSF	National Service Framework (for Children)
NSPCC	National Society for the Prevention of Cruelty to Children
NYAS	National Youth Advocacy Service
Ofsted	Office for Standards in Education
ONS	Office for National Statistics
OPSI	Office of Public Sector Information
PCT	Primary Care Trust
PHCT	Primary Health Care Team
PII	Public Interest Immunity
PLP	Private Law Programme
PPP	Pre Proceedings Protocol
PR	Parental Responsibility
PSHE	Personal Social Health and Economic Education
PWC	Parent With Care
RCP	Royal College of Psychiatrists
RCPCH	Royal College of Paediatrics and Child Health
SCIE	Social Care Insititute for Excellence
SEN	Special Educational Needs
SENDIST	Special Educational Needs and Disability Tribunal
SFC	Specialised Family Courts
SHA	Strategic Health Authority
SPA	Special Health Authority
TSO	The Stationery Office (formerly HMSO)
UASC	Unaccompanied Asylum Seeking Children
UNCRC	United Nations Convention on the Rights of the Child
UKCP	United Kingdom Council for Psychotherapy
VC	Video Conferencing
YCW	Youth and Community Worker
YJB	Youth Justice Board
YOT	Youth Offending Team

CHAPTER ONE

THE FAMILY JUSTICE COUNCIL

INTRODUCTION

Family Justice
Council
Tel: 020 7947 7333/
7974/7950
www.family-justice-
council.org.uk

1.1   Launched in 2004, the Family Justice Council
(FJC) provides a much needed strategic steer to the
development of family justice in England and Wales. It
is a non-departmental public body fully funded by the
Ministry of Justice and is essential to the development
of interdisciplinary practice in the family justice system
in England and Wales.

The Council's terms of reference are to facilitate the
delivery of better and quicker outcomes for families and
children by:

- promoting improved inter-disciplinary working
  across the family justice system through inclusive
  discussion, communication and co-ordination
  between all agencies;

- identifying and disseminating best practice
  throughout the family justice system by facilitating
  a mutual exchange of information between local
  committees and the council, including information
  on local initiatives;

- consulting with government departments on
  current policy and priorities;

- working to secure improvements consistent with
  current government policy and priorities, and
  securing best value from available resources;

- providing guidance and direction to achieve
  consistency of practice throughout the family
  justice system and submitting proposals for new
  practice directions where appropriate;

- promoting commitment to legislative principles
  and the objectives of the family justice system by
  disseminating advice and promoting inter-agency
  discussion, including seminars and conferences as
  appropriate;

- promoting the effectiveness of the family justice
  system by identifying priorities for, and
  encouraging the conduct of, research;

- providing advice and making recommendations to government on changes to legislation, practice and procedure that will improve the workings of the family justice system.

ROLE OF THE FAMILY JUSTICE COUNCIL

1.2 The FJC's primary role is to promote an inter-disciplinary approach to the needs of family justice and, through consultation and research, to monitor the effectiveness of the system and advise on reforms necessary for continuous improvement. The Ministry of Justice is responsible for delivering civil, criminal and family justice systems in England and Wales. Delivery is facilitated by consultation with stakeholders and, in the family justice system, by active co-operation between the wide range of stakeholder disciplines and agencies.

Ministry of Justice (formerly Department for Constitutional Affairs)
Tel: 020 3334 3555
www.justice.gov.uk

The Council's core activities are as follows:

- a business plan is agreed with Ministry of Justice ministers for each year's activities;

- the Council is expected to meet four times a year;

- the Council is supported by a dedicated secretariat;

- the Council has authority to appoint sub-committees or working groups to do detailed work where needed;

- the Council is required to publish a yearly report.

THE VISION

1.3 The Rt Hon Lord Justice Thorpe said the following during the Council's inauguration in 2004. It is just as true in 2009.

'We must acknowledge the government's faith in investing in the Family Justice Council. We must ensure that it inspires a revival of inter-disciplinarity amongst all the professions contributing to the family justice system, both nationally and locally and especially wherever it has faltered since the enthusiasm that marked the advent of the Children Act 1989.

Many of the contributing professions feel besieged or undervalued. Legal practitioners have seen such radical reduction in the level of fees for publicly funded work that they are quitting, or considering

Cafcass
Tel: 020 7510 7000
www.cafcass.gov.uk

quitting, the field. Social workers undoubtedly feel bruised and unfairly criticised. This perception is reflected in a marked shortage of front line social workers. Cafcass officers and children' guardians have been sorely tried by the misfortunes and misjudgments that have dogged the creation of the Children and Family Court Advisory and Support Service (Cafcass). Medical experts, and particularly paediatricians, are currently under intense pressure, to the extent that leading consultants are being vilified and some threatened with all too real earnestness in their private and family lives. Even judges have grown used to intrusive demonstrations into their privacy the like of which would have astounded our predecessors.

Of course we are all fallible and where we fail we merit criticism to which we must respond positively. But much of the abuse is characterised by ignorance and disturbed emotion. In present times mutual support is valuable and to give it we must know and understand each other's work, expertise and problems. We must alert government and public opinion to dangers revealed to us by our experience and specialist understanding. If we do not we will only find that those that have no obligation to contribute to family proceedings will cease to do so. Whatever be the problems and shortcomings of the family justice system they will never be solved or resolved unless family justice is truly recognised to be an inter-disciplinary system with a need to find and to adopt only those remedial measures that have gained inter-disciplinary support.'

TASKS OF THE FAMILY JUSTICE COUNCIL

1.4   The Council aims to improve co-operation between the various professions that work in the family justice system (judges, lawyers, health professionals, social workers, guardians, mediators and others) and to promote a greater understanding between the professionals and the users of the family courts, namely parents and children.

An additional task is to secure effective and secure communication and collaboration between the FJC and the 39 Local Family Justice Councils (LFJCs) (see **1.15**).

MEETINGS OF THE FAMILY JUSTICE COUNCIL

1.5   The full Council meets quarterly. Its spring meeting is usually linked to a conference for representatives of the LFJCs (see **1.18**). Summaries of meetings are available on the Council's website.

A biennial interdisciplinary residential conference is held at Dartington Hall in Devon.

THE FAMILY JUSTICE COUNCIL COMMITTEES

1.6   The FJC has several committees. An executive committee undertakes a management role. There are three main committees.

Children in safeguarding proceedings

1.7   This committee looks at safeguarding children, principally but not exclusively under the public law aspects of the Children Act 1989; that is, proceedings relating to the safeguarding of children initiated by local authorities, through care and supervision proceedings which are in some cases followed by adoption.

Children in families

1.8   This committee brings together representatives from every profession concerned with children and families in order to ensure better outcomes for parties and children in private law proceedings under the Children Act 1989.

Money and property

1.9   This committee looks at the law and procedures for the distribution of money and property on the breakdown of relationships. It advises and assists the Family Procedure Rules Committee on matters referred by that Committee in relation to the making or amendment of rules relating to financial property proceedings or directions about practice and procedure.

Other committees

1.10   In addition, there are cross-cutting committees and working groups on:

- Experts
- Education and training
- Diversity
- Voice of the child
- Alternative dispute resolution
- Domestic violence
- Parents and relatives

The committees and working groups include co-opted members, who are not members of the full Council, as well as relevant Council members.

THE FAMILY JUSTICE COUNCIL WEBSITE

1.11   The FJC website is an excellent source of information about the ongoing work of the Council such as:

- news and events
- meeting summaries
- papers and publications
- membership of the Council

www.family-justice-council.org.uk

The website is also a valuable resource for families trying to find their way around the family justice system. A guide (click on 'Family Justice System') helps families to access those services dealing with relationship breakdown and its consequences. It was written by members of the Council and includes information for children and young people. The information includes:

- aims of the family justice system;
- advice and information on legal matters, mediation and therapy;
- information for children and young people including advice sources for children and young people;
- issues dealt with in the family justice system such as divorce, dissolution, property, domestic violence, children and care;
- organisations in the family justice system such as courts, lawyers and Cafcass.

FAMILY JUSTICE COUNCIL RESEARCH AND PUBLICATIONS

1.12   The FJC website is an invaluable aid in developing knowledge and understanding of the working of the family justice system for professionals and users, bringing together publications from various sources as well as papers from the Council itself.

Reports on the website include:

- Using Family Group Conferences for children who are, or may become, subject to public proceedings: a guide for courts, lawyers, Cafcass officers and child care practitioners, October 2008.
- Care Profiling Study and Research Summary, March 2008.
- A Mapping Exercise on Inter-disciplinary Training, March 2009.

MEMBERS OF THE FAMILY JUSTICE COUNCIL

1.13   The Members of the Council represent the wide range of bodies who have an interest in the family justice system, including the world of the law, healthcare, social care, parents groups and academics. The FJC is chaired by the President of the Family Division and the Deputy Chair is The Rt Hon Lord Justice Thorpe. Other members also appointed by the Secretary of State are:

- Deborah Ramsdale (Assistant Director of Children's Services)
- Alison Russell QC (Family Barrister)
- Jane Craig (Family Solicitor)
- Dr Elizabeth Gillett (Child Mental Health Specialist)
- Katherine Gieve (Family Solicitor)
- Mark Andrews (Justices Clerk)
- Bridget Lindley (Consumer Focus – Parental View)
- Professor Judith Masson (Academic)
- Dr Heather Payne (Paediatrician)
- Ms Khatun Sapnara (Family Barrister)
- Beverley Sayers (Family Mediator)

Judicial members, appointed by the Lord Chief Justice, in consultation with the Secretary of State are:

- The Honourable Mrs Justice King (High Court Judge)
- Martyn Cook (Magistrate)
- District Judge Nick Crichton (Magistrates' Courts)
- District Judge Marilyn Mornington
- Her Honour Judge Lesley Newton (Circuit Judge)

Advisory members are also provided by the government departments and agencies, which work within the family justice system.

CONTACT THE FAMILY JUSTICE COUNCIL

1.14 The Family Justice Council can be contacted at:

The Family Justice Council
E201, East Block
Royal Courts of Justice
Strand
London
WC2A 2LL
Tel: 020 7947 7333/7974/7950
Web: www.family-justice-council.org.uk
Email: fjc@justice.gsi.gov.uk

LOCAL FAMILY JUSTICE COUNCILS

Tasks of Local Family Justice Councils

1.15 Local Family Justice Councils (LFJCs) were established in 2005 to underpin the work of the national FJC at local level. There are 39 LFJCs in England and Wales. The three key roles of LFJCs are to:

- highlight and address local issues to improve the delivery of family justice securing best value from available local resources, including local training events and conferences;
- respond to key issues raised by the national FJC, highlighting any local problems and detailing any local initiatives which address those difficulties; and
- create a reciprocal exchange of information and ideas between the LFJCs and the national FJC.

Membership of Local Family Justice Councils

1.16   Local Family Justice Councils are chaired by a designated family judge and, as with the national FJC, members are drawn from a wide range of disciplines working within the family justice system. They are supported by a part-time administrator usually drawn from the local Courts Service staff. Membership is expected to reflect the needs of the local area and commonly consists of:

- a district family judge;
- a family magistrate;
- a Cafcass officer;
- a local authority children's services representative;
- a police representative;
- a paediatrician;
- a mental health expert;
- an education representative;
- a barrister or solicitor;
- a mediator;
- an academic member;
- a court manager;
- a voluntary organisation representative;
- a consumer representative.

Membership is not prescribed and a wider range of members from varying disciplines is encouraged. Local Family Justice Councils are free to co-opt additional members for specific pieces of work.

Generally, four meetings a year are held. Their objectives mirror those of the national FJC but on a wider or narrower basis depending on local circumstances. LFJCs also set up sub-committees to deal with ongoing issues such as the Public Law Outline, alternative dispute resolution, court users and education and training in addition to specific issues that may require more detailed consideration, for example working with the police in domestic violence matters. Each of the sub-committees consists of members with a specific expertise in that particular area.

Interdisciplinary events and training

1.17   The national Council asks LFJCs to undertake the responsibility for managing inter-disciplinary events and training. All the local Councils have organised annual conferences and training events covering a variety of subjects. The national Council can advise on topics but is not too prescriptive as LFJCs have their own local concerns to consider in addition to national issues. Recent topics have included mental health and learning disabilities, domestic violence, the voice of the child, expert witnesses and court skills. A number of Councils also hold regular short training forums on various topics.

In addition, many LFJCs have in place mini-pupilage schemes to assist medical practitioners, and other experts, to gain experience of court proceedings in family cases by sitting with a judge at hearings in which relevant expert evidence is expected to be given.

The Family Justice Council has put together a chart which highlights the elements of interdisciplinary training that the key professional groups in the family justice system undertake as part of basic training, post qualification training and continuing professional development. The chart can be viewed at http://www.family-justice-council.org.uk/docs/ MappingExercise_Chart.pdf.

National conference

1.18 A day conference takes place annually. A representative from each LFJC attends, as well as members of the national Council and government representatives. The stated chief purpose of the conferences is to assist Local Councils to foster joint participation in processes and an interdisciplinary approach to family justice.

Local Family Justice Council newsletter

1.19 Sharing information and best practice, not only between the national FJC and LFJCs but between the LFJCs themselves, is of paramount importance and it is important to exchange ideas and working practices. Published on a quarterly basis, the Local Family Justice Council newsletter contains a summary of the latest news from the FJC, including an update on the sub-committees' work and forthcoming business; it also signposts readers to sources of further information. The newsletter provides an opportunity for LFJCs to exchange information and ideas.

Sponsorship

1.20   Sponsors are members of the national FJC and its Secretariat who 'adopt' one or more LFJCs in order to provide a further link between the organisations including:

- offering support to Local Councils;
- taking back issues of concern to the national Council;
- providing advice and guidance to resolve local problems;
- providing a conduit for sharing good practice;
- helping to raise the profile of the Councils both nationally and locally.

Contact the Local Family Justice Councils

1.21   There follows a list of the LFJC administrators' contact details, as at January 2010.

Avon, Somerset, Gloucestershire	rebecca.cobbin@hmcourts-service.gsi.gov.uk
Bedfordshire	russell.ward@hmcourts-service.gsi.gov.uk
Cambridgeshire	jo.hart@hmcourts-service.gsi.gov.uk
Cheshire	Margaret.Eccleston@hmcourts-service.gsi.gov.uk
Cleveland	wendy.brown1@hmcourts-service.gsi.gov.uk
Cumbria	Lisa.Moorby@hmcourts-service.gsi.gov.uk
Derbyshire	georgina.cope@hmcourts-service.gsi.gov.uk
Devon & Cornwall	admin@pfjc.org.uk
Dorset	Sandra.Megrin@hmcourts-service.gsi.gov.uk
Essex	David.Tyler1@hmcourts-service.gsi.gov.uk
Hampshire	Rebecca.Smith@hmcourts-service.gsi.gov.uk
Hertfordshire	yvonne.mckenna-young@hmcourts-service.gsi.gov.uk
Humberside	fiona.large2@hmcourts-service.gsi.gov.uk
Kent	margaret.newey@hmcourts-service.gsi.gov.uk

Lancashire	Lisa.Moorby@hmcourts-service.gsi.gov.uk
Leicestershire	justine.blackwell@hmcourts-service.gsi.gov.uk
Lincolnshire	Jackie.Tween2@hmcourts-service.gsi.gov.uk
London	eloise.emanuel@hmcourts-service.gsi.gov.uk
Manchester (Greater)	barbara.stone@hmcourts-service.gsi.gov.uk
Merseyside	Margaret.Eccleston@hmcourts-service.gsi.gov.uk
Norfolk	samantha.scott2@hmcourts-service.gsi.gov.uk
Northamptonshire	heather.morrison@hmcourts-service.gsi.gov.uk
Northumbria	Anne.Chapman@hmcourts-service.gsi.gov.uk
Nottinghamshire	vicky.denton-jones@hmcourts-service.gsi.gov.uk
Staffordshire	lesley.gyte@hmcourts-service.gsi.gov.uk
Suffolk	carol.flatres@hmcourts-service.gsi.gov.uk
Surrey	lucia.wheeler@hmcourts-service.gsi.gov.uk
Sussex	lucy.bennett@hmcourts-service.gsi.gov.uk
Thames Valley	Geraldine.henley@hmcourts-service.gsi.gov.uk
Wales (Mid & West)	stephen.whale@hmcourts-service.gsi.gov.uk
Wales (North)	laura.edwards@hmcourts-service.gsi.gov.uk
Wales (Sth East)	mike.farr@hmcourts-service.gsi.gov.uk
Warwickshire	lucy.coyle@hmcourts-service.gsi.gov.uk
West Mercia	rosemary.darby@hmcourts-service.gsi.gov.uk
West Midlands	helena.bridgett@hmcourts-service.gsi.gov.uk
Wiltshire	HellywellyP@aol.com
Yorkshire (North)	janet.allsopp@hmcourts-service.gsi.gov.uk
Yorkshire (South)	philippa.young@hmcourts-service.gsi.gov.uk
Yorkshire (West)	Michelle.Dunderdale2@hmcourts-service.gsi.gov.uk

CHAPTER TWO

THE PROFESSIONALS

INTRODUCTION

2.1 Workers in the family justice system are professionals who:

- have technical competence acquired through long training;
- adhere to a set of professional norms which include a service ideal;
- show objectivity, impersonality and impartiality;
- possess a colleague-oriented reference group;
- have autonomy in professional decision-making; and
- have self-imposed control based upon knowledge, standards, and peer review;
- are usually subject to a regime of continual professional development (CPD).

Working in the family justice system also means that professionals must be able to communicate with, as well as respect the work of, other professions.

SOLICITORS

2.2 The Law Society represents solicitors in England and Wales. It negotiates with and lobbies the profession's regulators, government and others: it offers training and advice: it helps, protects and promotes solicitors in England and Wales.

The Solicitors Regulation Authority deals with all regulatory and disciplinary matters and sets, monitors and enforces standards for solicitors across England and Wales. Formerly known as the Law Society Regulation Board, it acts solely in the public interest.

The Legal Complaints Service is for members of the public wishing to make a complaint about solicitors. Formerly known as the Consumer Complaints Service, the Legal Complaints Service is independent and impartial. A Legal Services Complaints Commissioner (an Ombudsman) has responsibility for working with the Law Society to improve its complaints handling.

To practise in a firm, solicitors must have a current Solicitors Regulation Authority practising certificate. But a solicitor does not need any compulsory specialised training to practise family law and it is not a compulsory subject on the mandatory post-graduate legal practice training course. However, many solicitors specialise in family law and undertake specialised training as part of their continuing professional education (CPD) requirements. There are also family law and children law accreditation schemes run by the Law Society and membership is a good way of assessing a solicitor's competence, as is accreditation from Resolution (see **2.13**).

Much of family law work is private law divorce work, a small part of which is obtaining the divorce decree – generally straightforward paperwork. The bulk of the task is the negotiations between the couple's solicitors about the division of the joint assets and securing maintenance for the children and perhaps (usually) the wife. This is called ancillary relief (as regards maintenance for children, the Child Maintenance and Enforcement Commission (C-MEC) or Child Support Agency (CSA) can become involved if there is no agreement between the couple). Having negotiated these arrangements the solicitors will present the 'deal' to the court, called a consent order. Some couples (not generally their solicitors) want to fight the matter out at a court hearing, although even in these cases the matter is often agreed at the door of the court to avoid incurring additional costs.

Another area of private law work is applications for residence and contact orders in respect of children – that is, deciding with whom the children will live and how often the non-residential parent will have contact with the children after separation or divorce. These applications are made under s 8 of the Children Act 1989 whether the parents are married or not. Again, solicitors may negotiate these arrangements or refer parents to a mediator. The government and judiciary have been actively dissuading court proceedings as regards children for some time.

The third main area is obtaining injunctions (eg occupation and non-molestation orders) in the wake of incidents of domestic violence in order to prevent further abuse, for example, preventing one of the couple from entering the home.

A rapidly growing area of work involves settling financial and property disputes on the ending of cohabitation (ie living together).

Some solicitors specialise in public law child care work. Many solicitors are now trained as family mediators. A few have set up solely mediation practices; most practise mediation as an adjunct to their legal work.

Private law

2.3   As regards children, the Children Act 1989 places greater emphasis on the private ordering of family life, preferring parents to make their own arrangements without the necessity for court orders. The high cost of litigation and the stringencies of legal aid provision encourage divorcing and separating couples to negotiate their own arrangements (with or without lawyers) about property, finance and children. Mediation and other forms of dispute resolution can provide more satisfactory outcomes. Such activities are defined as 'private law'. In cases where children are represented, their solicitors should normally be members of the Children Panel (see **2.7**).

Public law

2.4   'Public law' means that the state, in the form of local authority children's services intervenes in family arrangements because there is believed to be a risk of significant harm to children. In these cases, solicitors representing children should be members of the Children Panel. There is no specialist knowledge required for solicitors representing parents or other parties, although some parents, grandparents and adult parties will be represented by Children Panel solicitors. The expected standards of all solicitors representing adult and other parties are set out in a guide called *Good Practice in Child Care Cases* (Law Society, 2004).

Quality assurance

2.5   The assurance of the quality of many family law solicitors comes from the Legal Services Commission which is responsible for the provision of legal aid. Only practices holding a contract with the Commission are entitled to provide publicly funded services. These

solicitors can be located via
www.communitylegaladvice.org.uk (tel 0845 345 4 345).
There is no quality assurance for non-legally aided
clients apart from the control of the Solicitors
Regulation Authority and The Law Society whose
accreditation scheme is voluntary and subject to an
ongoing review. Resolution (a voluntary organisation to
which most family solicitors belong) has a membership
of over 5,000 family solicitors who subscribe to a Code
of Practice. Resolution also has a private law
accreditation scheme which is also voluntary.

Organisations such as Citizens Advice Bureaux, Relate
and Mediation Services will provide names of local
solicitors but will not recommend individual firms. The
best assurance of quality is personal recommendation
and/or a solicitor's membership of a specialist
accreditation scheme.

The Law Society

Accreditation

Family Law Accreditation Scheme

2.6   The Law Society runs a Family Law Accreditation
Scheme. Only solicitors and legal executives who meet
certain requirements are permitted to join. Members of
an Advanced Family Law Accreditation Scheme can
provide advice and assistance to clients in more
complex family law cases.

Children Panel Accreditation Scheme

2.7   A Children Panel Accreditation Scheme for
solicitors involved in children cases is provided by the
Law Society. There are three types of scheme members:

- Children representatives, who act for children in all
  proceedings under the Children Act 1989, the
  Adoption Act 1976 and the Adoption and
  Children Act 2002. They can also represent
  parents, grandparents and other adult parties in
  public law proceedings under the Children
  Act 1989.

- Adult party representatives, who represent adult
  parties in public law proceedings under the
  Children Act 1989. They can also represent
  parents, grandparents and other adult parties in

public law proceedings under the Children Act 1989. They also have experience in private law proceedings under the Children Act 1989 and the Adoption Act 1976.

- Local authority representatives, who represent local authorities in public law proceedings under the Children Act 1989.

To be considered for membership, solicitors must have sufficient expertise to demonstrate familiarity with the range of work commonly encountered in the field, must have been practising for at least 3 years, and must have completed a 3-day training course. Solicitors are admitted to the panel for 5 years.

Panel lists are widely circulated among family proceedings courts, Cafcass, local authorities and libraries. All members of the Children Panel Accreditation Scheme are required to apply for an enhanced check with the Criminal Records Bureau (CRB).

Family Mediation Accreditation Scheme

2.8   Members of the Family Mediation Accreditation Scheme are solicitors who have to meet a set of detailed criteria designed to demonstrate competence and experience in family mediation. There are two levels of membership:

- General membership of the Family Mediation Accreditation Scheme is for a one-off, 2-year period. It is a stepping stone to practitioner membership for solicitors and legal executives who lack the experience required to apply directly for practitioner membership.

- Practitioner members are trained and experienced family mediators who can take the lead in all-issues mediations.

Family Mediation Accreditation Scheme members are bound by the Law Society's code of practice for family mediation which has been adopted by the Solicitors Regulation Authority. All Family Mediation Accreditation Scheme members must undertake continuing professional development (CPD) training in each year of their period of scheme membership.

Partnerships

2.9 New rules allowing solicitors' firms to take non-lawyers on as partners came into force in 2009. The new entity will be a legal disciplinary practice (LDP), and allows non-solicitors to become partners up to a maximum of 25% of the ownership. From a date yet to be determined by the Legal Services Board, alternative business structures with external investment and ownership, will be permitted. The Legal Services Board is the new, independent body responsible for overseeing the regulation of lawyers (solicitors and barristers) in England and Wales.

Legal Services Board
Tel: 020 7271 0050
www.legalservicesboard.org.uk

Solicitors can practise as family mediators within their firms but cannot act as mediators in relation to family issues which their firm has dealt with before.

Information

2.10 The Law Society holds a database of all solicitors in England and Wales. All information about solicitors can be sourced from this database. It includes the solicitor's practising details and any qualifications or accreditation.

The Law Society's *Directory of Solicitors and Barristers* draws information from its database of solicitors holding a practising certificate and is published each July. Each solicitor's entry includes where they practise, their date of admission, categories of work and whether they offer legal aid. Other details include foreign languages spoken and membership of accreditation schemes. Copies of the *Directory* are available in libraries and most advice centres.

Community Legal Advice provides information about solicitors contracted with the Legal Services Commission to undertake publicly funded work: www.clsdirect.org.uk or 0845 345 4345. It also offers free, confidential and independent legal advice for residents of England and Wales.

Local authority legal advice

2.11 Local government lawyers (employed solicitors and barristers) advise local authorities about the legal position when problems may arise and may conduct cases in court for the authority (which includes opening the case and conducting cross-examination). Local authority lawyers advise on the law relating to children, in particular the legal options available and the strength of the evidence. In partnership with children's services departments, they institute and conduct legal proceedings where appropriate, and many have considerable expertise in child law. The primary role of lawyers acting for local authorities is as follows:

(a) to ensure the proper conduct of cases;

(b) to ensure scrutiny of the local authority's case;

(c) to safeguard the integrity of the local authority before the court: for example, to ensure through appropriate preparation and presentation that all relevant information is before the court and other parties;

(d) to assist the court in its investigation and undertake all necessary steps to arrive at an appropriate result in the paramount interests of the welfare of the child.

The local authority lawyer's 'client' is the local authority but the day-to-day working relationship is with the Director of Children's Services, acting through managers and social workers.

Legal executive lawyers and paralegals

2.12 Legal executive lawyers specialise in a particular area of law which means the everyday work of a legal executive lawyer is similar to that of a solicitor. Legal executive lawyers may, for example, advise husbands and wives with matrimonial problems. A legal executive lawyer is normally an employee and currently cannot be a partner in a firm of solicitors, although it may be possible to become an associate in a law firm and Fellows can go on to become advocates. Legal executive lawyers may be self-employed and provide legal services to solicitors and unregulated legal work to the public. With extended rights of audience in family proceedings, those Fellows who train and qualify as legal executive advocates can represent their clients in the county courts and family proceedings courts.

Institute of Paralegals
Tel: 020 7887 1420
www.instituteofparalegals.org

Time-consuming business in a family law office may also be done by 'unqualified' personnel called paralegals, for example, preparation of bundles of documents for court and sitting behind barristers in straightforward cases in court. The Institute of Paralegals now offers a certified qualification.

Many firms of five or more partners employ at least one paralegal and/or legal executive. While the primary conduct of proceedings involving children and all related contested advocacy should be carried out by Children Panel accredited lawyers, the contribution made by the skills and competence of non-lawyers has to be recognised.

Trainee solicitors, formerly known as articled clerks, do a good deal of the routine work in solicitors' offices. For example, they may attend solicitors' appointments before the district judge or prepare instructions to counsel.

Resolution

2.13   Resolution's 5,000 members are family lawyers committed to the constructive resolution of family disputes. Members follow a Code of Practice that promotes a non-confrontational approach to family problems and encourage solutions that consider the needs of the whole family – and in particular the best interests of children. Resolution also campaigns for improvements to the family justice system.

Resolution supports the development of family lawyers through its national and regional training programmes, through publications and good practice guides and through its accreditation scheme. Resolution also trains and accredits mediators and is the only body providing training and support for collaborative lawyers in England and Wales.

The cornerstone of membership of Resolution is adherence to the Code of Practice, which sets out the principles of a non-confrontational approach to family law matters. The principles of the code are widely recognised and have been adopted by The Law Society as recommended good practice for all family lawyers. The code requires lawyers to deal with each other in a civilised way and to encourage their clients to put their differences aside and reach fair agreements. Members of Resolution are required to:

- conduct matters in a constructive and non-confrontational way;
- avoid use of inflammatory language both written and spoken;
- retain professional objectivity and respect for everyone involved;

- take into account the long term consequences of actions and communications as well as the short term implications;
- encourage clients to put the best interests of the children first;
- emphasise to clients the importance of being open and honest in all dealings;
- make clients aware of the benefits of behaving in a civilised way;
- keep financial and children issues separate;
- ensure that consideration is given to balancing the benefits of any steps against the likely costs – financial or emotional;
- inform clients of the options eg counselling, family therapy, round table negotiations, mediation, collaborative law and court proceedings;
- abide by the Resolution Guides to Good Practice;
- the Code works in conjunction with the Law Society's Family Law Protocol and all solicitors are subject to the Solicitors Practice Rules.

Mediation

2.14   Resolution pioneered mediation training exclusively for family lawyers. Many members have been trained as mediators. Resolution mediators help couples to resolve issues in dispute, including financial issues, by facilitating and guiding discussions and ensuring that negotiations take place on an equal footing. Mediation often results in an agreement which can then be converted into a court order. Using mediation can help couples resolve disputes more quickly.

Accreditation scheme

2.15   Resolution has a specialist accreditation scheme through which members demonstrate a high level of skill in family law as well as a specialist knowledge of two or more specific family law subjects.

Collaborative family law

2.16   The collaborative family law process is a relatively new way of dealing with family disputes. Each person appoints their own lawyer but, instead of conducting negotiations between each person by letter or phone, couples meet together to work things out face to face. Through collaborative law, couples, their lawyers and other professionals work together in round-table meetings to negotiate agreements to resolve financial and other issues without the involvement of the courts. All collaboratively trained lawyers join a local practice group called a 'pod'. This group meets up around once a month together with collaboratively trained members of other professions to discuss practice issues.

Affiliate membership

2.17   Resolution membership is open to family law solicitors, legal executives and paralegals. Family justice professionals who support Resolution's aims can become affiliate members. Affiliate status gives many benefits of membership and is also open to a wide range of related professionals such as independent financial advisers, mediators, guardians, family therapists and counsellors.

Association of Lawyers for Children

2.18   The Association of Lawyers for Children (ALC) is a national association of lawyers working primarily in the area of public child care law. It has over 1,000 members, mainly lawyers who act for children, parents, other adult parties or local authorities, as well as other legal practitioners and academics. It also has associate members such as children's guardians, social workers and other professionals such as medical staff.

The Association of Lawyers for Children www.alc.org.uk

BARRISTERS

2.19   Barristers are specialist legal advisers and courtroom advocates. Solicitors instruct them to help represent their clients because of their court-based training and experience. Barristers are trained to give advice on the strengths and weaknesses of a case. They can provide a fresh perspective.

Family proceedings should be non-adversarial. Barristers can assist in settling cases before a hearing. 'Door-of-the-court' negotiations and settlements when clients can be put under pressure from lawyers and judges to settle are to be avoided when husbands and wives are in dispute about the re-arrangement of finances after divorce (called ancillary relief). Barristers are also instructed in Children Act 1989 and similar proceedings.

Barristers are frequently selected by reputation or recommendation but, theoretically, they cannot refuse to take a case. This is known as the 'cab rank' rule – they must take the next passengers whoever they are. Solicitors should instruct barristers who specialise in family law. This does not, unfortunately, avoid a last-minute substitution of barrister where a first choice is unavailable.

Barristers have two overriding duties: a duty to act in the best interests of their clients; and a duty to the court to ensure that justice is properly administered, which means that they must not knowingly or recklessly mislead the court. In family proceedings, barristers also have the same duty as solicitors to the Legal Services Commission to ensure that public money is not wasted.

The barrister's duty towards his client is:

- to act competently and diligently;
- to deal with the work in a reasonable time;
- to inform the solicitor immediately if, for any reason, the barrister becomes unable to do work within a reasonable time or attend court on the client's behalf;
- to keep the client's affairs completely confidential;
- to deal with the client courteously;
- to advise to the best of his ability and act in the client's best interests;
- not to discriminate on grounds of colour, ethnicity, sex, nationality, sexual orientation, political persuasion, marital status, disability or religion.

The Bar Standards Board can be contacted on Tel: 020 7611 1444 www.barstandardsboard. org.uk

The General Council of the Bar's independent regulatory board, the Bar Standards Board, publishes a Code of Conduct and also has a complaints system. As regards training and development, in some respects barristers are very much alone. Unlike psychotherapists, psychologists, teachers, lecturers or mediators, who have regular supervisions or appraisal by their peers, most barristers, despite the introduction of Continuous Professional Development (CPD), rely on less structured discussion with colleagues.

There is no accreditation available for barristers who specialise in family law, although the Bar Council runs a mandatory continual professional development (CPD) scheme. Many barristers specialise in family law. Even though there are no special or different qualifications required to practise family law, a pupillage in family law chambers is recommended for new barristers.

Members of the public can now approach certain barristers for legal advice directly. In order to undertake public access work, barristers must attend a one day course held by the College of Law. The Bar Council runs a public access directory of such barristers.

Family Law Bar Association

2.20   The Family Law Bar Association (FLBA) is the specialist bar association for family barristers. With 2,300 members, it organises conferences, seminars, meetings and social events throughout the country via its regional network and often in conjunction with Resolution. It produces a newsletter, *Family Affairs*, three times a year to keep its members up to date with events around the country and the more important changes in the law and procedure. Annually since 1992 it has published and sold *At A Glance*, a 90-page ready reckoner for use in financial cases. *At A Glance* is widely used by practitioners and the judiciary. In matters of law and procedural reform the FLBA is frequently consulted by government departments, including the Ministry of Justice. Barristers who work in the family law field are encouraged to join the FLBA, an association of around 2,000 practising barristers who specialise in family law. The FLBA consults with the Department for Constitutional Affairs, the Law Commission and others in all areas of family law and practice and is strongly represented on the Family Justice Council.

Full membership is open to the following category of barristers:

- those in independent practice in England and Wales;

- those employed in a firm of solicitors in England and Wales;

- those employed in the Government Legal Service or for a Local Authority in England and Wales;

- those working in academia in England and Wales;

- any other Barrister approved by the Committee.

Associate membership is also available.

Further information from:
Family Law Bar Association
www.flba.co.uk

JUDGES AND JUSTICES' CLERKS

Judiciary of England
and Wales
www.juduciary.gov.uk

2.21   Judges, justices' clerks and justices' legal advisers are either barristers or solicitors. Family magistrates do not have a legal professional qualification. The Lord Chief Justice of England and Wales is Sir Igor Judge. An official judicial website – Judiciary of England and Wales – contains a wide range of information about the judiciary including the roles, responsibilities and powers of the different members of the judiciary. There is also information on the history of the judiciary and the importance of judicial independence.

PAYING FOR LEGAL SERVICES: PUBLIC FUNDING (LEGAL AID)

Summary of the Legal Aid Scheme

2.22   The Legal Services Commission (LSC) runs two schemes – the Community Legal Service, which provides advice and legal representation for people involved in civil cases; and the Criminal Defence Service, which provides advice and legal representation for people facing criminal charges. Legal aid is now known as public funding, although the term legal aid is still widely used. Under the Community Legal Service the LSC has an important role in coordinating and working in partnership with other funders of legal services, such as local authorities. The LSC also directly funds legal services for eligible clients.

To make it easier to find quality legal help and information the LSC has launched Community Legal Advice. It is possible to call 0845 345 4 345 to speak to a qualified legal adviser about benefits and tax credits, housing, debt employment, education or family problems or to find local advice services for other types of problem, including family issues. The Community Legal Advice website (www.communitylegaladvice.org.uk) can be used to search for a legal adviser or to find links to other sources of online information and help. There is also an online eligibility calculator and it is possible to print or view legal information leaflets which include divorce, domestic violence, living together and separation as well as child care law (public law Children Act 1989 proceedings). Clients who need to sort out residence and contact arrangements for children can look at

parenting plans which may help them reach an
agreement at www.cafcass.gov.uk/publications.aspx.

Only suppliers (including solicitors) with a contract
with the LSC can provide advice or representation
funded by the LSC – that is, public funding or legal aid.
Those firms and agencies which are contracted will
display the Community Legal Service logo. For family
cases the contract held by the supplier must be one
which covers family work.

The different types of Legal Aid

2.23   The LSC funds a range of legal services.
Currently the different levels of service in family
matters are:

- **Legal Help**

   Legal Help provides initial advice and assistance
   with any legal problem. This level of service covers
   some of the work previously carried out under the
   advice and assistance or 'green form' scheme.

- **Help at Court**

   Help at Court allows for somebody (a solicitor or
   adviser) to speak on the client's behalf at certain
   court hearings, without formally acting in the
   whole proceedings. This is not available in family
   cases as other family levels of service cover this
   work.

- **Family Mediation**

   This level of service covers mediation for a family
   dispute, which means trying to reach an agreed
   settlement with the help of an independent
   mediator.

- **Family Help**

   This level of service provides help in relation to a
   family dispute including assistance in resolving
   that dispute through negotiation or otherwise. It
   does not include the provision of mediation
   services but covers help and advice in support of
   Family Mediation. Family Help does not cover
   preparation for or representation at a contested
   final hearing or appeal. It can be:

   - *Family Help (Lower)* which is limited to
      exclude issue of proceedings or representation
      in proceedings other than help in obtaining a
      consent order following settlement of a
      family dispute; or

– *Family Help (Higher)* which is Family Help other than Family Help (Lower). It can therefore cover the issue of, and representation in, proceedings which are anticipated to be contested but not preparation for or representation at a contested final hearing or appeal.

- **Legal Representation**

  This level of service provides legal representation – so that the client can be represented in court including at a final hearing.

Different criteria apply to each level of service. These are imposed by a Funding Code which has statutory force. It is also possible for Legal Representation to be granted on an emergency basis where the matter is urgent and meets the applicable criteria (see below).

A low-cost interview

2.24 In addition to the above levels of service, some solicitors are prepared to give a free or low-cost initial interview whether or not the client qualifies for public funding. Solicitors offering these interviews are part of local referral schemes and details are available from local CABx, law centres or other advice agencies. The directory search on www.communitylegaladvice.org.uk can also be used by searching for local solicitors and then check under 'charges' to see whether they offer this service. These schemes are not available in some areas.

How the LSC administers the funding schemes

2.25 England and Wales are divided into a number of regions. Each region has a regional office which provides a locally based outward facing presence but, increasingly, administrative work (decision making and cost assessment) is carried out at processing centres based in South Tyneside, Liverpool and Nottingham. Independent lawyers consider applications for review of decisions in individual cases made by the processing centre. Most solicitors/legal advisers are authorised, under 'devolved powers', to decide whether funding should be granted for the following types of service:

- Legal Help and Help at Court;
- Family Help (Lower);
- representation in emergency cases (see below);

For other levels of service, the solicitor will normally apply on the client's behalf to the LSC whose staff will decide whether the application meets the criteria for LSC funding. The LSC (or solicitor where he/she is authorised) can either grant or refuse the application.

If an application is refused because the client does not qualify financially, or because the client has applied for an emergency certificate but does not meet the criteria for an emergency grant, the client can ask for the decision to be reviewed by the LSC. If the application is refused because it does not meet any other criteria applied to that type of case then there will also be a right to an independent review. This will be initially by the LSC and if the refusal is confirmed by the Commission, then by independent lawyers.

Financial eligibility limits usually change annually each April.

Statutory provisions

2.26   The provisions of the civil scheme are contained in the Access to Justice Act 1999, and the Funding Code, guidance, regulations, directions and orders made under the Act. More detailed information is on the LSC website at www.legalservices.gov.uk and in the LSC's four-volume loose-leaf manual (published by The Stationery Office).

Legal Help

What does Legal Help cover?

2.27   Legal Help can cover advice, writing letters, negotiations, getting a barrister's opinion and preparing a written case. Assistance with divorce proceedings is available under Legal Help. However, the solicitor or legal adviser will be unable to represent the client in court under Legal Help. The client must satisfy a financial eligibility test for these levels of service. Legal Help is available in England and Wales and applies only to questions of English law.

How to apply for Legal Help

2.28   Contact a solicitor or legal adviser who holds a contract with the LSC to provide these levels of service. The solicitor or adviser will tell the client at once whether he qualifies financially. The client will not have to pay a contribution, but the statutory charge may apply (see below). A solicitor or adviser can refuse to give Legal Help.

Children

2.29 Children are eligible for Legal Help. In most cases where a child under school-leaving age (16) requires the help of a solicitor, a parent or guardian should apply on his behalf. A solicitor can advise a child directly in certain cases. The parents' or guardian's means will be taken into account in assessing the financial eligibility of the child except in certain circumstances – for example, a conflict of interest between the child and parent.

The statutory charge

2.30 Where money or property is 'recovered or preserved' under Legal Help in a family matter this is called the statutory charge. If a family dispute is resolved under Legal Help, the statutory charge does not arise. However, if the dispute proceeds to a certificate for Family Help (Higher) or Legal Representation and property is 'recovered or preserved' the costs of all earlier levels of service, including Legal Help, count towards the charge. The statutory charge does not apply if the money or property recovered consists of maintenance payments.

Family mediation

What does family mediation cover?

2.31 The LSC provides funding for the mediation of a family dispute for couples and family members who qualify financially. Mediation can help with disputes relating to children, money and property and is provided by family mediators contracted to the LSC. A mediator does not make decisions or provide legal advice on the client's own legal position, but helps clients to reach their own decisions in a neutral environment. It is an alternative to reaching agreements or obtaining court orders entirely through solicitors and does not replace legal or other advice. For more information on mediation, see the section on mediation and the Community Legal Service Advice leaflet 'Family Mediation'.

Those financially eligible for mediation can obtain legal advice and assistance from a solicitor to support them during mediation. Publicly funded family mediation is provided by family mediators contracted to the LSC; eligible clients do not have to pay a contribution and the statutory charge does not apply to the cost of the mediation. This is to encourage the use of mediation, which can involve no costs at all for publicly funded clients.

How to apply for family mediation

2.32   Community Legal Advice can give details of local LSC contracted family mediators.

General Family Help

What does this level of service cover?

Family Help (Lower)

2.33   Family Help (Lower) (Level 2) is available in both private law cases and in public law cases where written notice has been given by a local authority.

In order for a private law case to progress to Family Help (Lower) the case must satisfy a cost benefit test and must be in relation to a significant family dispute. A significant family dispute is one which, if not resolved, may lead to family proceedings and for which legal advice and assistance is necessary to enable the client to resolve the issues.

In public law work Family Help (Lower) is available when advising a parent or person with parental responsibility for a child and where the local authority has given written notice of potential care proceedings. There is no eligibility test and this level of service is available where the client requires advice and assistance with a view to avoiding proceedings or narrowing and resolving any issues with the local authority. No application to the LSC is required. Solicitors can grant funding immediately.

In private law cases a client may be granted Family Help (Lower) for both children and finance issues. Applications to court under Family Help (Lower) can be made to obtain a necessary consent order following settlement of part or all of the dispute. When a client is actually participating in family mediation or has successfully reached an agreement or settlement as a result of family mediation and is in need of legal assistance, this may be provided under Family Help (Lower).

Family Help (Higher)

2.34 Family Help authorises help in relation to a family dispute including assistance in resolving that dispute through negotiation or otherwise. This includes the services covered by Legal Help or Legal Representation other than preparation for or representation at a contested final hearing or appeal.

Family Help (Higher) requires an application to the LSC for a certificate before help can be provided although solicitors have devolved powers enabling them to grant applications immediately. Family Help (Higher) is not available in public law proceedings.

Family Help (Higher) will only be justified where it is necessary to issue proceedings (other than merely for a consent order), all other reasonable avenues having been pursued, or where proceedings are already in existence. Family Help (Higher) will be refused unless mediation has been considered and may be refused if a mediator has determined that mediation is suitable for the particular case.

Legal Representation

What does Legal Representation cover?

2.35 'Full Representation' is the main form of Legal Representation. Although the LSC may impose limitations and conditions on the extent of funding, in principle Full Representation can cover all work needed to take legal proceedings to final hearings and beyond. Full Representation is available in both family and civil cases, but there are different merits criteria and financial criteria for different types of case. Solicitors who undertake publicly funded work will be able to explain the different merits criteria to clients, but they are intended to ensure that the limited Community Legal Service Fund is most appropriately applied.

Application for Full Representation will in most cases be assessed by the LSC which will decide whether the

criteria for funding are met. The LSC can either grant
or refuse the application. Any funding certificate issued
may be limited in terms of the work which the solicitor
can undertake and will be limited to an amount of
costs which can be incurred. The statutory charge may
apply to any money or property recovered or preserved
using this level of service.

What kinds of courts and cases are covered?

2.36   Legal Representation is not available for all cases
nor for all courts and tribunals, but it is available for
most family proceedings including appeals. Legal
Representation is not available for cases outside
England and Wales, except where a case is referred by
the court to the European Court of Justice.

How to apply for Legal Representation

2.37   Clients apply through a solicitor. Most
applications will need to be submitted to the LSC for a
decision. In every case the solicitor will need to
complete an application form on the client's behalf. The
majority of applications to the LSC are processed
within 2 weeks. Clients may be sent a further form to
fill in asking for more information about their finances.
They should complete and send it back immediately as
otherwise the application may be delayed or refused.
The LSC assessment officer will work out whether the
client qualifies financially. The LSC will also decide
whether the application satisfies the relevant merits
criteria for funding. Solicitors will usually not be
prepared to deal with or continue to deal with a case
until a funding certificate is issued by the LSC which
confirms that the client has got public funding. This is
because a certificate does not cover the solicitor for any
work done before it is issued.

A certificate will not be backdated but in some cases
involving children the solicitor can act immediately.
This is where the proceedings are Special Children Act
Proceedings, ie some child care proceedings, and Legal
Representation is free and not subject to a full means or
merits test. These special arrangements reflect the
nature of the proceedings and involvement of the local
authority. Special Children Act Proceedings are
applications for funding in cases where an application is
made for a care or supervision order, a child assessment
order, an emergency protection order or for the

extension or discharge of an emergency protection order and the applicant is a parent of the relevant child or has parental responsibility for the child or is a child who may be the subject of a secure accommodation order but is not already legally represented. In some other public law proceedings, a means test and a less strict merits test than usual are applied. This is the case in relation to public law proceedings concerning the welfare of children other than Special Children Act Proceedings or related proceedings but including:

- appeals (whether interim or final) from orders made in Special Children Act Proceedings;
- other proceedings under Part IV or Part V of the Children Act 1989;
- adoption proceedings, including placement orders;
- proceedings under the inherent jurisdiction of the High Court in relation to children (formerly wardship).

What happens if the case is urgent?

2.38   If the case is urgent, the solicitor can consider emergency Legal Representation. This can be granted at once. If the solicitor is authorised to do so by the LSC then they will be able to make the decision to grant emergency Legal Representation without applying to the LSC beforehand. Emergency Legal Representation covers limited urgent steps and lasts only until the LSC has taken a decision on the full application for Legal Representation. When the client applies for emergency Legal Representation they must agree to co-operate with the assessment officer in his enquiries into their financial position and to pay any contribution that is assessed. The client also has to agree to pay the full costs of their case if it is found that they do not qualify for Legal Representation or refuse it when it is offered to them (for example because they are asked to pay a contribution).Clients must:

- qualify financially (see below);
- meet the merits criteria relevant to the type of case.

(Note that in some cases between local authorities and individuals involving the protection and care of children there are no means or full merits criteria. These are called Special Children Act proceedings – see above.)

The LSC assessment officer will work out if the client qualifies financially for Legal Representation and if they have any contribution to pay. The finances of both the client and their partner must be added together if they live as a couple unless:

- the relationship is at an end and they live apart; or
- there is a conflict of interest between them.

Eligibility

2.39 Eligibility limits can be checked on the CLA eligibility calculator at www.communitylegaladvice.org.uk. Note that all the limits can be waived where the client needs to apply for an order to protect the person, including a domestic violence injunction although the client will still have to pay any assessed contribution. Note also that disposable income and capital which are used to test eligibility are calculated by applying only those allowances/disregards which are set out in the applicable Regulation. Note that the figures were correct in June 2006 but are subject to change.

Clients in receipt (either directly or indirectly) of income support, income based jobseeker's allowance or guarantee state pension credit are eligible on income and capital for all levels of service. Other types of benefit, such as Working Tax Credit and Child Tax Credit, do not give automatic ('passported') entitlement.

Capital: does the client qualify?

2.40 If the client's disposable capital is, (as at December 2009) £8,000 or less the client will qualify for all levels of service relevant to family cases. If the client's disposable capital as assessed is £3,000 or less, or the client is receiving income support or income based jobseeker's allowance or guarantee state pension credit, they will not have to pay a contribution from capital.

Capital includes:

- the market value of the client's home in excess of £100,000, after allowing for any outstanding mortgage but only up to £100,000;
- all land and buildings other than the client's home, including interests in timeshares;

- a maximum of £100,000 is allowed in respect of all mortgages on all the client's properties;
- money in the bank, building society, Post Office, premium bonds, National Savings certificates etc;
- investments, stocks and shares;
- money that can be borrowed against the surrender value of insurance policies;
- money value of valuable items, for example, boat, caravan, antiques, jewellery (but not wedding or engagement rings or usually the client's car);
- money owing to the client;
- money due from an estate or trust fund;
- money that can be borrowed against business assets.

There are some disregards, the most important of which are savings, valuable items or property, the ownership of which is the specific subject of the court case; this exception is limited to £100,000 for Legal Representation and Family Help.

If the client's disposable capital is assessed at more than £3,000, the client will have to pay a contribution; this will be required at once. The client will be asked to pay all of his disposable capital over £3,000. The calculation of disposable capital is different for pensioners. Men and women of 60 or over may benefit from an extra capital allowance if their disposable income is low.

Income: does the client have to pay a contribution?

2.41   If the client's disposable income exceeds (as at December 2009) £733 a month they will not qualify. Except for Legal Help, Help at Court, Family Mediation and Family Help (Lower), if the client's disposable income is more than £316 a month, the client will have to pay towards the cost of their case from their income. Disposable income is calculated by deducting certain fixed allowances from income. For further information see the eligibility calculator *Offers, re-assessments and discharge revocations*.

If the LSC decides that the case satisfies the merits criteria and also decides that the client qualifies financially, it will either issue a certificate if there is no contribution to pay or will send the client an offer of a certificate. The client does not have to pay anything until he accepts the offer. Once the client accepts, he must pay any contribution from capital straightaway and any contribution from income by monthly instalments, the first of which is paid when the client accepts the offer. A certificate will then be issued and the solicitor can deal with the case using LSC funding.

If the client's income or capital increases while the certificate is in force, he must immediately notify the LSC and the client's means may be re-assessed. If the client's income decreases, he may apply for his means to be re-assessed and his contribution may be reduced.

Funding may be withdrawn prior to the end of the case if the client's financial circumstances change so that he is no longer financially eligible for funding; for other reasons such as a failure to keep up payment of the monthly income contribution, failure to provide information to the LSC when requested to do so, or failure to fully disclose relevant information about financial circumstances.

If the certificate is discharged, funding stops from the date of the discharge notice. However, if the certificate is discharged as a result of a further assessment of capital, the client may be required to pay a contribution towards the costs previously incurred in the case.

If the certificate is revoked, ie cancelled, the client is deemed never to have been entitled to funding and the LSC may seek to recover all costs previously incurred. The solicitor is also entitled to recover the difference between their costs on a publicly funded and private client basis. Private client rates will be higher.

What does the client pay if he is successful?

2.42   The solicitor, as well as the barrister – if one is used – is entitled to be paid his reasonable costs. If the client is successful, the amount he will have to pay will depend on whether:

- the other party is ordered to pay their costs and in fact does so;
- the client is awarded or successfully holds on to any money or property which was in issue in the case. If the other party does pay the client's costs in full, the client may expect to be paid back the whole of any contribution paid.

If the other party does not pay the costs in full, the LSC must deduct from any money ordered by the court or agreed by the other party to be paid (and actually paid), the amount needed to cover the costs. This deduction is known as the statutory charge and it will apply to any property recovered or preserved in the case, whether by a court order or under a compromise or settlement of the case. Generally the statutory charge will include the costs of any injunction and private law proceedings concerning children where the client is funded for ancillary relief (money issues).

Maintenance is exempt from the statutory charge – and so are most state benefits. In some specific circumstances the statutory charge can be postponed, that is to say, not collected immediately. In these cases the money owed will be registered as a charge on the client's home like a mortgage, and it will be subject to payment of simple (rather than compound) interest. More information can be found in an LSC leaflet called 'Paying for Your Legal Aid'.

What costs does the client pay if they are unsuccessful?

2.43 If the client has received Legal Representation and loses the case then the most they will normally have to pay towards their own solicitor's and barrister's costs will be any contribution under the certificate. If the client is publicly funded the court will not normally order them to pay the other party's costs, but it may do so, including in some family cases. Even where the client is protected against costs through being publicly funded (and that is not the position in some family cases) the court decides how much they must pay. The amount will depend on the client's conduct in connection with the dispute. It will also take into account the other party's means and conduct.

Guide to assessing financial eligibility

Further information on legal aid generally, including financial eligibility, can be obtained from: www.legalservices.gov.uk Email: family@legalservices.gov.uk

2.44 Eligibility limits are usually changed annually. Up-to-date details can be found on www.communitylegaladvice.org.uk where there is also a step-by-step eligibility calculator. Note that eligibility is laid down by Regulations: there are fixed limits and very little discretion, in particular in relation to the expenses which can be taken into account.

SOCIAL WORKERS

2.45 Social workers' specific tasks are defined by legislation and by the agency in which they work, although they share an ethical code and approach to work acquired during their training (since 2004, an Honours degree). From April 2005 all social workers are required to register with the General Social Care Council (GSCC) and the title 'social worker' is protected, ie it is an offence for anyone who is not qualified and registered with the GSCC to describe himself as a social worker. This also means that service users can make a complaint against a social worker who can then be suspended or struck off the register (see GSCC Code of Conduct on www.gscc.org.uk).

Most social workers are employed by local authorities and from 2006, following implementation of the Children Act 2004, they work in separate departments headed by a Director of Children's Services (or Director of Children and Families) or a Director of Adult Social Care Services. The Director of Children's Services also heads up the local authority's local education authority (LEA) functions. These are statutory agencies responsible by law for the welfare of certain groups in their area, including children and young people, families under stress, people with disabilities, elderly people and people who are emotionally or physically chronically sick.

The Children Act 2004 and changes to the regulation of adult social care services require local authorities to set up strategic partnerships (in the child and family area sometimes referred to as 'children's trusts') to plan, co-ordinate and commission local authority, health and independent sector services within their areas. Voluntary social work agencies, such as the NSPCC, fill gaps in the statutory provision or provide specialist services, many of these employing full-time professional staff. Social workers also work in private sector agencies, mainly providing foster care or residential care. Children England (formerly the National Council for Voluntary Child Care Organisations) acts as a coordinating body and provides details of local and national voluntary organisations.

Children England
Tel 020 7833 3319
www.childrenengland.
org.uk

Children's services departments have legal investigative and protective functions in relation to children. Social workers employed by these departments may be engaged in assessing eligibility for services and negotiating with family members about the type of service which might be appropriate, providing services, or carrying out protective and investigative functions in relation to children.

The practical work of providing children's services and the day-to-day contact with the public is the responsibility of registered social workers and their managers. They can work in teams with family support workers. Some also work in multi-disciplinary teams with education and health professionals, e g child and adolescent mental health teams (CAMHS), youth offending teams (YOTs) or child development teams working with children with disabilities. Some social workers are based in hospitals, others work in day care settings such as family centres or 'Sure Start' children's centres, and others work within residential settings.

Social workers also work in specialist resource settings providing teams to recruit, assess, train and support foster carers, adopters or volunteers to support families in their own home (mainly through voluntary agencies such as 'Home Start').

The third broad grouping of social workers with children are those who prepare reports for the courts. Most are employed by Cafcass but some work as independent social workers, often providing direct services to children and families and also providing independent reports for the courts (see **2.64**).

Services

Fieldwork

2.46   The range of work carried out by social workers is varied and falls into several categories. Social workers' major client groups are:

- children: from unborn children to those up to the age of 18 who may be 'in need' as defined by ss 17 and 20 of the Children Act 1989;

- children and adolescents who may be suffering or likely to suffer significant harm;

- families whose children are assessed as being 'in need' including those where there are concerns that a child may be in need of protective services;

- adults and young people who are offenders or at risk of offending (although the probation service is now part of the criminal justice system and probation officers are no longer considered to be social workers). Social workers are increasingly employed by voluntary sector agencies such as Nacro (the crime reduction charity, see www.nacro.org.uk) and work in multi-disciplinary YOTs;

- people with learning, physical or sensory disabilities;
- adults and children with acute or chronic health problems;
- adults and young people with mental health problems and addictions;
- the elderly;
- adults and children who have caring responsibilities towards others.

As regards children and young people, the responsibilities of local authority social workers are set out in the Children Act 1989, the Children (Leaving Care) Act 2000, the Youth Justice and Criminal Evidence Act 1999, the Adoption and Children Act 2002, the Children Act 2004 and the Children and Young Persons Act 2008. They include assessment as to whether a child is 'in need', which services might be directly provided or commissioned to meet identified needs, coordinating the provision of services and directly providing some of them. They must also assess whether there is evidence that a child is suffering or is likely to suffer significant harm due to parental acts or omissions and whether the concerns are such that the formal child protection processes (as described in the Working Together guidance) should be followed. Social workers are usually the 'key workers' and coordinate the work of 'core groups' when a child is given a child protection plan. They also carry the lead role in initiating care proceedings and prepare the reports for the court, including the care plan to be followed if a care order is made. Approximately 61,000 children are looked after by local authorities, mainly in foster homes, although around 10% are in residential care at any one time; others remain in care but are allowed to live with their parents and some are in independent living situations. A small proportion of young people in care are in custody having committed offences. Although more than half start by being looked after under voluntary arrangements (ie they are accommodated), because those who start to be looked after via a court order tend to stay longer in care, the majority of children in care at any one time are there under the provisions of a care order.

Field social workers operate from area offices serving the local community which are run by local authority Children's Services departments or from family or neighbourhood centres or multi-disciplinary teams. As mentioned above, some are 'outposted' to schools or health care settings. They visit, or see in their offices, individuals and families and, after consultation with family members and assessment, provide or commission and coordinate a range of supportive or practical services. Some, more often in multi-disciplinary teams or in the independent sector, provide counselling or therapy. Because resources such as day care are much in demand, they have to decide on priorities. They generally work as part of a team (which may include welfare assistants, an occupational therapist, a home-help organiser and clerical staff) based in the district they serve and supervised by senior social workers/team managers who are directed by an area manager.

A field social worker has a case-load of clients who may include children at risk, young people in trouble with the law, families with financial or emotional problems and looked after children and those who care for them. When a social worker takes on a case, the first thing he or she must do is make an assessment – that is, decide on the appropriate course of action guided by the assessment framework (*Framework for Assessment of Children in Need and their Families* (DfES, 2000)). Some problems can be lessened with practical help, but social workers have to build a relationship of trust with clients. Among the fieldworker's responsibilities are:

- providing family support services to children in need and their parents;
- arranging accommodation for children whose parents are temporarily unable to look after them or respite for parents under stress or children with disabilities or damaging behaviour;
- investigating allegations of child ill-treatment and initiating care proceedings where children are at risk;
- arranging placement for children looked after by local authorities and safeguarding their interests;
- supervising children placed for adoption and arranging for children to be adopted if it is in their best interests;
- supervising children living apart from their parents in private foster homes.

Residential Care

2.47   Residential care is provided for children and
young people who need permanent or, more often,
temporary care. Residential homes are run by local
authorities and by voluntary organisations such as
Barnardo's and Scope, or by private organisations.
Where possible, children are placed in foster homes, so
those who remain in residential care tend to be
adolescents, children with special needs or behavioural
problems and children sent by the courts. Of children in
local authority homes, 70 per cent are aged over 13. The
homes can range from small family group homes for
children of mixed ages to more specialised homes or
observation and assessment centres for disturbed or
maladjusted children. There are also special schools for
disabled children and those with social and behavioural
difficulties. Residential social workers and support
workers have special roles which include:

- assessing the particular needs of children;
- providing respite care;
- helping provide family placements;
- preparing young people for independent living.

Their work also includes caring for the physical needs
of children, looking after their clothes, supervising their
day-to-day routine and organising recreational activities.

Day Services

2.48   Day services are provided in family centres,
children's centres, neighbourhood centres or, especially
for children with disabilities, child development centres.
They are often provided on an inter-agency and
multi-disciplinary basis and often by voluntary child
care organisations. They are an increasingly important
base for the provision of a range of family support
services and may be used as safe places where
containable contact between parents and children not
living with them can be arranged. There are also
specialist child contact centres, some specialising in
public and some private law contact work.

*Child and Adolescent Mental Health Services
(CAMHS)*

2.49   CAMHS are also known as child and family
consultation services/centres and used to be known as

child guidance clinics: they are occasionally known as child and adolescent psychiatry departments. These multi-disciplinary services are usually provided by health trusts, but may be run by education departments or jointly managed by education, health and social services. See below at **2.104**.

Youth justice

2.50   Youth justice teams are the responsibility of the local authorities, and are often managed directly from the local authority Chief Executive's office. They provide services to young people who have committed offences or are considered to be at risk of doing so and their parents or carers. The emphasis of the work is on helping young people to remain in their own communities but through care is provided for young people in custodial settings. Youth justice work focuses on changing the young person's attitude towards offending by formal and informal counselling, leisure activities, social skills teaching, group work and outreach work. The teams comprise social workers, teachers, probation officers, health staff and police officers.

Education Welfare Service

2.51   Education welfare officers (sometimes called education social workers) are now used less and less. Increasingly schools are employing child or family support workers, and social workers from area teams may be attached to or out-posted to schools. Social workers may also be employed in pupil referral units or as part of the school psychological service. Following the setting up of the Children's Services directorates, specialist education services for vulnerable children are likely to be co-located or amalgamated with other local authority services for vulnerable children.

Training and the Social Work Task Force

2.52   The General Social Care Council (GSCC) has statutory authority in England. (There are separate Care Councils for Wales, Northern Ireland and Scotland.) Its role is to accredit and quality assure social work training in England and to promote education and training for work in personal social services. The qualification is now an Honours degree, although many registered social workers (of whom there are now more than 70,000) have lower level qualifications. There is also a system of GSCC accredited post qualifying training provided by universities and all social workers must complete 15 days (90 hours) of post-registration training and learning (PRTL) if they are to continue on the Register.

A Social Work Task Force was set up by the Department of Health and the Department of Children, Schools and Families (DCSF) in 2008, following the death of Baby Peter, to undertake a comprehensive review of frontline social work practice and to make recommendations for improvement and reform of the whole profession across adult and children's services. In July 2009, the Task Force published its interim report *Facing up to the Task* which set out proposals for the comprehensive reform needed. In its final report published in December 2009 the Task Force set out 15 recommendations for improving and reforming social work, namely:

- reforms to initial training;
- a new 'licensing' system which will introduce an assessed probationary year in employment for new social work graduates;
- a revamped framework for continuing professional development;
- a career structure so experienced practitioners can progress in front line roles as well as in management;
- a new standard for employers to ensure all employers put in place high quality supervision time for continuing professional development and manageable work loads;
- pay reform;
- a new and independent College for Social Work led and owned by the profession.

The Government has accepted all the recommendations. A Social Work Reform Board will be set up to take forward the recommendations and to work alongside the Government in delivering change to the profession. In early 2010, the Government will set out an implementation plan for the social work reform programme, to be overseen by the Reform Board, working in partnership with the profession. This will include setting out how reform will be resourced and changes to legislation that will be needed.

Information about relevant university courses is available on university websites

Skills

2.53 Social workers are skilled in the basic areas of understanding human growth and development and the impact of socio-economic factors on human behaviour and perception. In relation to children and families they have to possess the following skills.

(1) **Communicating with, interviewing and providing therapist services to children**

Social work assessments should always take account of children's needs and wishes. If there are court proceedings ongoing, the court needs to know how firmly and consistently a child's view might be held; how much that view might have been influenced by immediately preceding events (or even by cues given inadvertently by the interviewer); and how appropriate it might be for a child of that age to hold a particular view.

(2) **Working in partnership with parents**

Parents need to be consulted and their views must be ascertained. Placements of children are generally defined by written agreements which have to be negotiated and recorded. Social workers need to be skilled negotiators and advocates, since there are often disagreements between family members and carers about the best course of action to take. It is sometimes appropriate (e g in contested adoption proceedings) for different social workers to be allocated to the child, the parents and the foster or adoptive parents.

(3) **Sensitivity to diversity**

It is unlawful not to consider race, culture, religious affiliation and language when providing any service under Part III of the Children Act 1989. It is equally important with regard to fostering and transracial placements.

(4) **Multi-agency, inter-disciplinary working**

As well as the need for co-operation in court-oriented procedures, the Children Acts of 1989 and 2004 impose a duty to co-operate in providing services to children in need which applies to social services, education, housing and health authorities. Multi-disciplinary work is needed for day care, child protection and provision of services to children in need.

(5) **Working with the independent sector**

Social services departments work with voluntary and private organisations to provide a variety of services ranging from pre-school playgroups to registered children's homes. Local authorities have to monitor, coordinate and advise these services.

(6) **Policy formulation**

The Children Acts of 1989 and 2004 require local authorities to maintain policies and procedures in conjunction with other services. For example, a review of day care provision would involve the local education authority, the health authority and others, and a review of the preventative and leaving care services would involve housing departments, housing associations and voluntary organisations. Social workers are required by statute to coordinate the work that goes into producing each year a Children's Services Plan which describes the difficulties experienced by children and families in their local authority's area and the ways in which multi-disciplinary services to meet needs will be provided and coordinated.

(7) **Assessments**

In cases which go to court, the court has to be advised, amongst other things, of the likely effect on the child of a change in circumstances and on the capability of the child's parents to meet his or her needs. Assessments of a child's welfare and the likelihood of harm require assessments not only of the child but of the family system. These assessments need an understanding of developmental psychology, of attachment, separation and loss, and of the psychosocial transition from dependence to independence. An assessment framework must be followed.

(8) **Confidence in working with the law**

Social workers have to know the limits of their authority, how to use the authority which the law gives them and what duties and powers they have as employees of the local authority. They also have to keep to strict court-imposed timetables.

(9) **Organisational skills**

The Children Acts require skilled supervisors and highly developed information systems.

Independent Reviewing Officers

2.54 Every local authority must appoint an Independent Reviewing Officer (IRO) in connection with the review of each case of a child who is being looked after by it. An IRO must be an experienced social worker who has no involvement in the day-to-day or financial management of the case. 'Looked after children' include children who are the subject of full and interim care orders and who are accommodated under s 20 of the Children Act 1989, but not those who are being provided with accommodation because they are being provided with services under s 17.

The IRO's role is to monitor the local authority's performance in respect of the review, participate in the review and chair it. He must, as far as reasonably practicable, take steps to ensure that the child's views are understood and taken into account and that any matters of concern regarding the implementation of the decisions of the review are brought to the attention of persons of an appropriate level of seniority within the local authority.

As a result of new duties inserted into the Children Act 1989 by the Children and Young Persons Act 2008 and a prior commitment to revise the entire suite of Children Act 1989 Regulations and guidance, in 2009 the Government embarked on a programme of work to revise, strengthen, update and streamline regulations and guidance relating to IROs under the Children Act 1989. Late in 2009 the Department for Children, Schools and Families issued documents for consultation. For the outcome of those consultations go to www.dcsf.gov.uk.

CAFCASS

2.55 Cafcass stands for Children and Family Court Advisory Support Service and is a non-departmental public body accountable to the Secretary of State for Children, Schools and Families in the Department for Children, Schools and Families (DCSF). Cafcass is independent of the courts, social services, education and health authorities and all similar agencies. It operates within the law set by Parliament and under the rules and directions of the family courts. Its role is to:

- safeguard and promote the welfare of children;

- give advice to the family courts;
- make provision for children to be represented;
- provide information, advice and support to children and their families.

The main types of cases in which the courts ask Cafcass to help are when:

- parents or carers are separating or divorcing and have not reached agreement about arrangements for their children;
- social services have become involved and children may be removed from their parents' care for their safety;
- children could be adopted.

Cafcass has a role in relation to measures outlined in *Every Child Matters*, a Government programme for a national framework to support the 'joining up' of children's services, namely education, culture, health, social care, and justice. *Every Child Matters* sets out five key outcomes for children, young people and families:

- be healthy;
- stay safe;
- enjoy and achieve;
- make a positive contribution;
- experience economic well being.

The functions of Cafcass in Wales are devolved to the National Assembly of Wales where it is called Cafcass Cymru.

The roles of Cafcass officers

2.56   Cafcass champions the interests of children involved in family proceedings, advising the family courts in England on what it considers to be in the best interests of individual children. Cafcass' professionally qualified social work staff, called Family Court Advisers, work exclusively in the family courts. Cafcass has the responsibility in England of ensuring that children and young people's interests are represented to the court in family proceedings, to enable their voices to be heard, thus helping to ensure that the decisions made about them by courts are in their best interests and that they and their families are supported throughout the process. Cafcass officers have a number of roles in court proceedings, the main ones of which are listed below.

Children's guardian

2.57 When children are subject to an application for public law care or supervision proceedings by local authority children's services, Cafcass Family Court Advisers, some of whom are self-employed contractors, act as children's guardians. Children's guardians are experienced social workers who are now Cafcass officers appointed by the court. Their role is to be independent of the local authority and to safeguard and promote the welfare of the child in specified public law proceedings under the Children Act 1989. Under the 1989 Act there is a duty on the court to appoint a children's guardian on behalf of the child (unless satisfied that it is not necessary to do so). Specified proceedings include not only applications for a care or supervision order but also the discharge of such orders, applications for emergency protection orders and child assessment orders, and applications for secure accommodation orders in non-criminal proceedings.

Children and Family Reporter

2.58 When parents who are separating or divorcing cannot agree on future arrangements for their children and commence private law proceedings (usually under s 8 of the Children Act 1989), Cafcass Family Court Advisers act as Children and Family Reporters. A Children and Family Reporter can be requested by the court to prepare a welfare report under s 7 of the Children Act 1989. The Children and Family Reporter's role is to provide the court with advice and recommendations on matters relating to the welfare of the child.

Reporting Officer

2.59 In adoption applications Family Court Advisers can be asked to act as Reporting Officers. The role of the Cafcass officer in adoption proceedings depends on whether parents agree to the adoption. If, at the outset, the court believes the parents agree, the Cafcass officer is called a Reporting Officer. The process may then be quite straightforward. If a parent does not agree, or if there are special circumstances, the Cafcass officer is called a children's guardian and the proceedings are 'specified'. The matter will then need a more in-depth investigation. Cafcass is also involved where special guardianship (see **6.58**) is involved.

Guardian ad litem

2.60　Family Court Advisers act as guardians ad litem if separate representation of the rights and interests of the child is required in private law proceedings. These are called Rule 9.5 cases, see **4.22**).

Parental order reporter

2.61　Parental order reporters are appointed by the court in cases where an application for a parental order is made under s 30 of the Human Fertilisation and Embryology Act 1990.

Witnessing pre-court consent to adoption

2.62　With the implementation of s 22 of the Adoption and Children Act 2002, Cafcass officers have taken on a new role in witnessing pre-court consent to adoption and reporting back to the Adoption Agency prior to any court application.

Early intervention in private law cases

2.63　Most courts operate first hearing lists for considering new private law applications. The courts, supported by Cafcass court duty officers, seek to resolve suitable cases and to narrow the issues in others. Use may be made of mediation services or contact activities, such as parenting information programmes. While the detail of each scheme varies from court to court, all the schemes are designed to divert appropriate cases from the need for either contested hearings or the completion of welfare reports and many focus on the voice of the child as a driver for change. Such schemes are not subject to legal privilege (see **4.50** and **4.51**). Cafcass also offers a Family Group Conferencing (see **3.46**) service in many areas and commissions child contact services from voluntary bodies, in particular supported contact centres.

Cafcass officers

2.64　All Cafcass officers are social work qualified and have a minimum of 3 years' experience in working with children and families prior to appointment. During their work in children's proceedings, officers have to acquire enough knowledge from talking to those involved in the child's life to present the court with a view of the child's situation and the options available, and to make a clear recommendation about the appropriate action for the child.

All officers are required to register with the General Social Care Council (GSCC, see **2.52**) and are subject to enhanced Criminal Records Bureau (CRB) checks. Continuing professional development is a requirement of GSCC registration. Cafcass provides national and regional training for its officers and has developed toolkits, for example a *Safeguarding Framework* and a *Domestic Violence Toolkit*, both of which are available to the public on the Cafcass website.

The duties of Cafcass officers

2.65   The duties of children's guardians and reporting officers are prescribed by rules of court and their overall duty is to safeguard and promote the welfare of the child. The rules require guardians ad litem (in private law proceedings) and children's guardians (in public law proceedings under the Children Act 1989) to safeguard the child's interests by:

- meeting the child and ascertaining the child's wishes and feelings;
- ascertaining the range of possible options available to the court;
- giving the child appropriate advice;
- contacting or seeking to interview anyone whom he thinks appropriate or as the court directs;
- obtaining professional assistance where necessary;
- reporting to the court on all relevant matters;
- if the child is mature enough, telling the child what is in the documentation that has been filed at court and explaining to the child about decisions taken by the court; and
- attending all hearings unless excused from doing so by the judge.

The children's guardian in public law proceedings has the right to examine and take a copy of the local authority's records relating to the child; note that the guardian ad litem acting in private law proceedings does not have the right to do this.

Children's guardians will interview anyone whom they believe may be relevant in the proceedings, or who has

information which should be placed before the court.
The following people could be interviewed in any case:

- the child and family – parents, step-parents,
  cohabitants, other children of the family,
  grandparents, aunts, uncles and other family
  members;

- professional workers – foster parents (usually in
  public law proceedings), childminders and day
  nursery staff, school staff, residential home mother
  and baby home staff (again, usually in public law
  proceedings), hospital staff;

- professional agencies – social workers, health
  visitors, GPs, police, probation officers;

- other professionals – psychiatrists, paediatricians,
  psychologists, education welfare officers;

- any other Cafcass officer who was previously
  involved with the child or family.

In the report, the children's guardian must advise the
court about:

- the child's level of understanding including the
  child's ability to refuse a medical or other
  examination;

- the child's wishes;

- the level of court in which the case should be
  heard;

- the timetabling of proceedings;

- the options available to the court and what order
  he considers should be made;

- any other matter on which the court requires
  advice.

Since the introduction of the care proceedings Public
Law Outline (PLO) in April 2008, children's guardians
have to give written or verbal reports to the court at
each major hearing – the Case Management
Conference, the Issues Resolution Hearing and the
Final Hearing. These reports, with each one built
incrementally on those which have preceded it, are
intended to assist the court with an analysis of the case,
and bring to bear an independent scrutiny on the local
authority's position.

The duties of reporting officers and children's guardians in adoption proceedings

2.66 A reporting officer is appointed by the court when the natural parent(s) agree(s) to the proposed adoption of their child and also in step-parent adoptions when one of the applicants is the birth parent. The reporting officer has to make sure that the agreement of the birth parent(s) to the adoption is given freely and in full understanding. The reporting officer visits only the birth parent(s) and will not see the child or adoptive parents. If there are reasons why the child or adopters should be seen or if the birth parent has had a change of mind, the reporting officer will recommend to the court that a children's guardian should be appointed. If the court decides that a children's guardian is needed, it will usually appoint the reporting officer who has already begun work on the case. The reporting officer prepares a report which is solely for the court. Changes in the law arising from the implementation of s 22 of the Adoption and Children Act 2002 make a new provision for Cafcass officers to witness consent prior to the making of a court application. Their duties in this role mirror those of the reporting officer, but they will report to the Adoption Agency.

In adoption proceedings, a children's guardian is appointed by the court when the parent(s) do not agree to the adoption or if there are complicated issues involved or if it is an application to the High Court. Where parent(s) do not give consent the local authority must apply for a placement order, which usually arises in the context of care proceedings that are already under way. These are specified proceedings and a guardian must be appointed where a children's guardian is not already active in ongoing care proceedings. The guardian's main task is to safeguard the best interests of the child and make recommendations to the court which are independent of the parties.

The duties of child and family reporters in private law proceedings under the Children Act 1989

2.67 The duties, as set out in court rules, are to safeguard the welfare of the child by:

- meeting the child and ascertaining the child's wishes and feelings;

- considering the range of possible options available to the court;

- contacting or seeking to interview anyone whom he thinks appropriate or as the court directs;

- obtaining professional assistance where necessary;

- advising the court whether the child should be made party to the proceedings;

- attending court when directed to do so;

- reporting to the court on all relevant matters, and

- if the child is mature enough, explaining to the child what is in the report.

The duties of parental order reporters under the Human Fertilisation and Embryology Act 1990

2.68   Parental order reporters will comply with any of the duties of the children's guardian as are appropriate to the proceedings. In addition, the 1990 Act places a duty upon them to investigate various matters including the following:

- the conception, gestation and birth of the child;

- whether the child is living with the couple who are applying for the order;

- whether the woman who carried the child freely and unconditionally agrees to the order being made;

- any payment that may have been made.

The Safeguarding Framework

2.69   From 2007 Cafcass introduced a Safeguarding Framework that brought together a range of previously separate policies relating to safeguarding children into one single document. Safeguarding is the first of Cafcass' National Standards underlining its primary purpose to safeguard and promote the welfare of each child referred to it and to understand any specific safeguarding needs in each case. The framework outlines the joint roles and responsibilities of all Cafcass staff in safeguarding children and sets out the way in which it works with other agencies.

The Children and Adoption Act 2006, through inserting section 16A into the Children Act 1989, places a duty on Cafcass, where there are concerns about possible risk, to undertake an assessment and report to the appropriate family court. Cafcass now screens all cases for risk to the child or other family members. A continuous risk identification process is applied to all cases, using a three stage risk assessment tool. The three stages are:

- Screening: this process leads to a check of whether any factors that give rise for concern about the well-being or safety of the child or relevant adult family member are present.

- Risk identification: a structured approach, based on initial contact with the adult parties, to ascertain if any risk factors which are present, assessing the likelihood of harm and making an initial analysis about what needs to happen to reduce and/or manage the risk.

- Assessment: a more detailed process, over a lengthier period of time, during which there is an analysis of the factors causing concern; the current and potential involvement of various relevant agencies; and developing a long-term plan for the reduction and/or management of risk.

In most new private law cases, checks are made by Cafcass with local authority children's services and the police to see if information is already held about the child or the parties or any other adult who has or is likely to have substantial contact with the child. Allegations of sexual or physical abuse of children or of domestic violence arise in many cases, and in these circumstances, Cafcass officers will, following the first hearing, carry out further agency checks to assess the risk posed to a child. In cases where information is received which indicates that a child may be at current risk of significant harm, a Cafcass officer will make a child protection referral to the relevant local authority and will provide the necessary information to the court.

Cafcass acts as a core member of Local Safeguarding Children Boards (see **3.83**) and increasingly its staff participates in local Multi Agency Risk Assessment Conferences (MARACs; see **6.35**). An information-sharing protocol agreed with the Association of Chief Police Officers also enhances Cafcass' ability to screen for risk and carry out assessments where required.

Cafcass National Standards

2.70 New National Standards were introduced in 2007. They:

- promote early intervention and strengthen Cafcass' approach to safeguarding children;

- ensure that Cafcass actively works to understand each child's wishes and feelings and take these 'views into account;

- promote constructive agreements and work in a problem-solving way wherever possible;

- improves internal business processes;

- improves case management, case planning and our overall quality of service and customer care.

The full Cafcass National Standards can be viewed at: http://www.cafcass.gov.uk/about_cafcass/ national_standards.aspx

Children's guardians and solicitors

2.71 In public law proceedings under the Children Act 1989 and in private law proceedings where a guardian ad litem is appointed under r 9.5 of the Family Proceedings Rules 1991, the child is party to the proceedings and is therefore eligible for legal aid and has a solicitor. The children's guardian and guardian ad litem usually appoint the solicitor to act for the child unless the court has already done so or the child, if the child is sufficiently mature, has appointed his or her solicitor. A parent or social worker cannot instruct a solicitor for the child because of the potential clash of interests.

If there is a delay in the appointment of a children's guardian in public law proceedings, the Rules of Court allow the court to appoint a solicitor for the child in which case the solicitor will participate in the proceedings and undertake the following tasks in the absence of a children's guardian:

- to critically appraise the local authority's actions and test the evidence;

- to bring the need for a guardian to the attention of the court at every hearing;

- to request all relevant papers including copies of all case conference minutes and medical or other reports relating to the child, and attend relevant meetings;

- to attempt to see the child as soon as possible and ascertain any wishes and feelings of the child where it is possible to do so, and to ascertain whether the child's understanding is such that he is able to give his own instructions;

- to report to the court any wishes and feelings of the child which the solicitor has been able to ascertain.

A children's guardian would usually instruct a solicitor whose name is on the Children Panel. The solicitor's duty is to act on behalf of the child and to take instructions from the children's guardian unless the child is able, having regard to the child's level of understanding, to give instructions and these instructions conflict with those of the children's guardian. Good practice requires that the solicitor meets the child, whatever the child's age, and talks with the older child, explaining his role in the proceedings and getting a sense of the child as an individual and of his circumstances. The assessment of the child's ability to give separate instructions is something that the solicitor must discuss with the guardian, but ultimately the solicitor has to make up his own mind and act accordingly, informing the court if the child is to be represented separately.

There is an expectation that the solicitor and children's guardian meet or talk with one another early on in a case to sort out their mutual expectations and to decide which of them is to undertake the various tasks involved. The solicitor will want to complete the legal aid forms at the outset and is likely to be the person who will accept delivery of documents on behalf of the child. As the case progresses, he or she should discuss with the children's guardian what written information should be disclosed to the child and which one of them should disclose it.

Separate representation for the child and the children's guardian

2.72 In public law cases if the child is competent and forms a view which conflicts with that of the children's guardian, the child can give instructions to the solicitor direct. If this happens, the court can grant permission for the guardian to have separate legal representation. If the court does grant permission Cafcass can fund that legal representation, either by paying for a private practice solicitor to represent the guardian or by providing an in-house lawyer from Cafcass Legal to do so.

Cafcass and the new Private Law Programme

2.73   Early in 2008, the President of the Family
Division set up a working group to consider revising the
Private Law Programme (PLP) originally published in
January 2005. A new revised Private Law Programme
(PLP) was, at the time of writing, due to be introduced
in April 2010. For draft guidance and its implications
for Cafcass and CAFCASS CYMRU see **3.22**.

Alternative dispute resolution

2.74   The new Private Law Programme (see above) will
offer in-court mediation hopefully financially supported
by the LSC and designed to encourage the use of
mediation at any time during the family proceedings to
assist in resolving family disputes. It is part of a wider
Ministry of Justice programme to provide alternatives
to litigation so that courts are the last resort for people
involved in civil or family disputes. Under the new
programme, local family mediation providers work with
judges and Cafcass to identify cases where mediation
might be a suitable alternative to the court process.
Families are then offered the option of mediation over
the court process for resolving their family dispute.

Preparing reports for the Family Court

2.75   Section 7 of the Children Act 1989 states that a
court can ask either a local authority social worker or
Cafcass to report on matters relating to the welfare of
the child. The reporter is not a party to the proceedings,
is not legally represented and is independent. It is
unusual for local authority social workers to prepare
such reports except in those cases where they have a
recent or continuing involvement with the family
concerned and it is deemed appropriate for them to take
on the reporting role. On occasions, however, it may be
more appropriate for a Cafcass officer to be appointed
in cases where a local authority social worker is already
involved so that a fresh view can be obtained. Some
parties will request this if they consider that the local
authority is already committed to a particular course of
action. If the court feels that a care or supervision
order might have to be made, it may order a 'section 37
report' from the relevant local authority.

In preparing a section 7 welfare report, the reporting
officer assists the court by investigating the

circumstances of the child, talking to the important figures in the child's life, reporting back to the court, giving an assessment of the situation and, where appropriate, making a recommendation. The court is expected to make clear the matters that should be addressed within the report. The report might be limited to the issue of the child's wishes and feelings or another single issue. In more complex cases, there may be a number of issues requiring attention or Cafcass may provide, within the report, an assessment of risk in accordance with the section 16A risk assessment duty (see **2.69**). Children should always be seen unless there is a strong reason not to see them. According to their age and understanding, children must be given the opportunity to express their views but must not be forced to do so.

Skills

2.76 The skills of Cafcass officers may not be confined to those of enquiry and assessment but may include working with family dynamics, and dealing with feelings of loss, guilt and anger. Cafcass officers are dealing with people who may need to separate emotionally before they are able to concentrate on arrangements for their children. In this connection, the parenting information programmes, introduced as one of the types of contact activity by the Children and Adoption Act 2006, may offer assistance to parties by enabling them to learn more about the challenges of post-separation parenting.

Conflict management

2.77 Cafcass officers report to the court in parental disputes taken to court where arrangements regarding children cannot be agreed. It is likely that such cases will, by definition, involve high levels of parental conflict. Of great importance for a child affected by parental separation is the potential adverse effect of parental conflict (see further **6.7–6.12**). A key task for the Cafcass officer is to assist parents, at some level, to work together to meet the needs of their child. Continuing high levels of conflict will inevitably hinder or disrupt that process.

Domestic violence

2.78　Section 120 of the Adoption and Children Act 2002 clarified the definition of significant harm, as set out in the Children Act 1989, by making specific reference to the issue of children witnessing or otherwise experiencing domestic violence. In cases where such concerns are present, Cafcass' duty to undertake a risk assessment and provide it to the court is likely to be engaged. Similarly, the court may take the view that a finding of fact may be required, in accordance with the terms of the January 2008 Practice Direction 'Residence and Contact Orders; Domestic Violence and Harm'.

Cafcass Legal

2.79　Cafcass Legal is the in-house legal department of Cafcass consisting of lawyers who provide legal advice and assistance to Cafcass and its practitioners. The work of the in-house lawyers includes the following.

Duty lawyer

2.80　A lawyer is on duty every day during office hours from Monday to Friday to provide legal advice to employed and self-employed Cafcass practitioners and to other members of the legal profession or the judiciary.

Cafcass Legal also provides an out-of-hours service primarily for mainly medical treatment cases in the High Court. The lawyers take it in turns to carry a mobile phone so that they can be contacted during the night or in the early hours of the morning by the urgent business officer of the Royal Courts of Justice. Cafcass lawyers are supported by the availability of senior managers should it be necessary for a children's guardian to be appointed out of hours or social work advice is required.

See Practice Note
of 28 July 2006
[2006] 2 FLR 354

Official Solicitor, CAFCASS and the National Assembly for Wales: urgent and out of hours cases in the Family Division of the High Court

Legal representation for the Cafcass High Court Team

2.81　The Cafcass lawyers provide legal advice and representation for guardians in complex children's cases referred to the High Court team. The caseworkers in the High Court team can be authorised by Cafcass to conduct litigation and exercise a right of audience under s 15 of the Criminal Justice and Court Services Act 2000. When a caseworker takes on this role, he receives supervision on the legal aspects of the case from a Cafcass lawyer. Not all High Court team cases are dealt with in this way though, and if s 15 is not invoked, the case worker carries out a purely welfare, social work role in which case the in-house lawyers can provide traditional legal representation.

Separate legal representation

2.82 As indicated at **2.72**, the need for separate legal representation usually arises in public law proceedings where a child disagrees with the welfare recommendations of the guardian. In such cases, if the child is competent, the child can give instructions to the solicitor direct, leaving the guardian unrepresented. It is not always necessary for a children's guardian to have a solicitor in such cases, but if the court grants permission under r 4.11A(3)(iii) of the Family Proceedings Rules 1991, a lawyer from Cafcass Legal can act for the guardian. Alternatively, Cafcass can provide funding for a solicitor from private practice to do so.

Advocate to the Court

2.83 Cafcass Legal can be invited to act or instruct counsel as advocate to the High Court in family proceedings in which 'the welfare of children is or may be in question'. The role of advocate to the court is, quite simply, to offer such assistance to the court as it may require. The assistance can be in relation to a particular area of law, or may relate to the specific facts of a case, for instance if they are particularly difficult or extraordinary.

Young People's Board

www.cafcass.gov.uk

2.84 Cafcass has a Young People's Board which advises Cafcass on matters of policy and practice. Its website has a section dedicated to information for children.

Cafcass and Local Safeguarding Children Boards and Family Justice Councils

2.85   Cafcass is represented on all Local Safeguarding Children's Boards (LSCBs) and Local Family Justice Councils. Cafcass is defined as a core member of LSCBs by virtue of the Children Act 2004. Cafcass' membership of LSCBs enables it to take family justice issues into the safeguarding arena and issues relating to children's safeguards in the family justice system onto Family Justice Council's agendas.

Napo, Unison and NAGALRO

2.86   Napo (the National Association of Probation Officers) and UNISON are trade unions which together represent the majority of Cafcass staff. Both have an interest in professional issues affecting their members and the wider family justice system.

NAGALRO (the National Association of Guardians ad Litem and Reporting Officers) is the professional association for all family court advisors (children's guardians, guardians ad litem, children and family reporters and independent social workers). It aims to:

- promote good practice;
- provide support and advice to individual members;
- contribute to developments in the Guardian and Family Court Service;
- support communication between individual guardians and CAFCASS;
- encourage quality standards in independent social work with children and families;
- make links with child care solicitors and other professionals working with children;
- provide professional insurance cover;
- produce a quarterly journal;
- organise interdisciplinary conferences and training.

UNISON
Tel: 0845 355 0845
www.unison.org.uk

Contact Centres

2.87   The importance of comfortable contact for parents and children who are no longer living together is increasingly recognised. Social workers and Cafcass officers are all involved in reporting on contact, but in disputed cases or those where supervision is required to ensure the child's safety or to reassure the parent with residence, specialist skills are needed.

Facilitated contact is increasingly provided by specialist contact centres. In general these centres, known as 'supported contact centres' are run on a part-time basis by small voluntary organisations. Details of what happens in these contact centres sometimes have an element of privilege so that parents and children can relax and enjoy each other's company. Those writing reports often arrange to observe contact by agreement with the parents, older children and the centre workers.

In more complex cases, the skills of specialist contact workers, usually qualified social workers, are needed. Examples of centres where specialist contact workers are employed are The Meeting Place run by Thomas Coram in London, contact services provided by the Children's Society in the North West of England and The Contact Agency in the Midlands.

Public law contact work may be funded by children's services departments or, if used to facilitate the writing of a report to the court, by legal aid granted to the child or the parents. In private law cases, Cafcass has contracted with contact centres for them to provide supervised or supported contact in appropriate cases and Cafcass itself can be directed by the court to supervise contact. Cafcass works with the National Association of Child Contact Centres (NACCC) to strengthen monitoring and regulation through the development of specific professional standards for contact centres.

For further details see: www.naccc.org.uk

For more about contact centres and the National Association of Child Contact Centres see **3.110**.

MEDIATORS

2.88 Mediation is a process in which an impartial third person, the mediator, assists couples contemplating separation, divorce or dissolution to make arrangements, to communicate better, to reduce conflict between them and to reach their own agreed joint decisions. The issues to be decided may concern the divorce, the separation, the dissolution, the children, finance and property. Communications issues and emotional issues can also be addressed. In children cases the child, with the parents' consent, may also be directly consulted about his wishes and feelings. The mediator has no stake in the dispute, is not identified with any of the competing interests and has no power to impose a settlement on the participants, who retain authority for making their own decisions. Mediators do not prepare reports or make recommendations to the court. Couples voluntarily engage in mediation to work together on the results of family breakdown and to reach proposals for settlement, which may then be endorsed by their legal representatives and the courts, as appropriate.

Mediators prepare written summaries recording both the outcome of mediation (such summaries or 'Memoranda of Understanding' are without prejudice and subject to mediation privilege), and, in property and finance matters, the financial facts disclosed by the parties. Such Financial Summaries are open and available to the parties to use with their legal representatives and the court in order to secure endorsement of the decisions arrived at in mediation about financial matters.

Mediation often takes place 'in the shadow of the court' during private law proceedings, but also takes place well before and well after such proceedings. The aim is not to have to go to court at all, or to present the court with an agreement which can be turned into a court order. People can refer themselves to a mediator or mediation service at any stage in family breakdown. The only stipulation is that both parents or partners must eventually come to mediation meetings together and they must come voluntarily. Solo or joint introductory meetings are always offered.

Mediators do not act as arbitrators or adjudicators, make findings of fact or give opinions, give advice to either or both participants, impose solutions or outcomes nor condone or collude (or continue with the mediation process) where there are issues of harm against another person, most particularly a child or children. Some mediation services operate in more specialist fields, such as providing mediation between parents and adoptive or foster parents when it is in the child's interest for post-placement contact to be arranged and details are disputed, and in inter-generational disputes, such as grandparents seeking contact with grandchildren. Family mediators come from a range of different backgrounds such as lawyers, social workers, counsellors and psychologists as well as many other professional disciplines.

Organisation

2.89 There are a number of family mediation organisations in England and Wales including:

- National Family Mediation;
- Resolution;
- Family Mediators Association;
- College of Mediators;
- ADR Group;
- The Law Society.

Family Mediation Council www.familymediation council.org.uk

The Family Mediation Council was set up in 2007 with the aim of harmonising standards for family mediation. The Council's founder members (the organisations listed above) maintain registers of family mediator members who meet those standards. The Council is dedicated to working to promote best practice in family mediation and to ensuring the public can confidently access family mediation services offering such exacting professional and training standards. The Council's member organisations regulate their individual memberships.

Training

2.90 All Family Mediation Council membership organisations train and regulate their individual members, ensuring compliance with the Council's Professional and Training Standards.

Standards

2.91 The Family Mediation Council's membership organisations regulate their individual memberships to ensuring that family mediators:

- adhere to the Council's Code of Practice;
- have completed Council recognised family mediator foundation training;
- undertake Council accredited continuous professional development;
- receive Council recognised professional practice consultancy;
- adhere to a clear complaints procedure;
- hold relevant insurance;
- undertake additional specialist training where required;

- have effective equal opportunities policies.

The professional standards and quality of mediators are governed and regulated by the mediation organisations listed at **2.89**. There is also a quality assurance standard used primarily for publicly funded mediation in the form of a Mediation Quality Mark (MQM) and granted by the Legal Services Commission. Mediators are assessed as competent for the purposes of the MQM by the Family Mediation Council or (for solicitors and fellows of the Institute of Legal Executives only) by applying for practitioner membership of the Law Society's Family Mediation Accreditation Scheme.

Funding

2.92 Mediation can be either privately or publicly funded. National Family Mediation services may raise charitable or other funding to subsidise private paying clients or to subsidise children in mediation services. For those clients eligible for public funding the Legal Services Commission funds family mediation and currently contracts with around 200 family mediation services nationally in both the voluntary and independent sectors. Under the LSC Funding Code services can mediate on a 'family dispute', which is defined as a legal dispute arising out of a family relationship, including disputes concerning the welfare of children or which may give rise to family proceedings. Publicly funded clients are obliged to consider the use of mediation before they can make an application for Family Help (Higher) or Legal Representation but publicly funded mediation is available at any time, including after proceedings have been started. For further details on public funding see 'Paying for Legal Services', at **2.22–2.44** above.

Availability

2.93 Over 2000 mediators have been trained, but few are engaged in full time mediation work. The family justice system has been slow to give mediation a central role. Apart from the requirement that mediation must be considered before most applications for publicly funded Family Help (Higher) or Legal Representation, referrals are relatively few, particularly as regards property and finance. The government still resists making mediation assessments compulsory for all, not

Legal aid and mediation for people involved in family breakdown National Audit Office www.nao.org.uk

just for poor people, whereas a report from the National Audit Office in 2007 strongly recommended it should be. Opponents argue that compulsory mediation is a contradiction in terms (since the defining principle is empowering participants to reach their own decisions), will be less effective, more likely to disadvantage weaker parties, particularly women, and put victims of domestic violence and their children at risk. However, all mediators have screening processes whereby they can identify and respond appropriately to issues of domestic violence, so that one of the most potent arguments against mandatory mediation assessment should be weakened. Also, since 2008 the courts have been able to direct parents by means of a 'contact activity direction' to attend a mediation information meeting about their children. On the basis that it is never too late to mediate this is helpful, but much unhappiness and stress for parents and children might arguably be avoided if mediation assessments were compulsory before applications could be made to court. There already exists a power for the courts to direct persons to mediation on matters of finance and property but it is seldom used. For new initiatives on mediation in children cases see the practice direction at **2.73** above.

Family Mediation Helpline

2.94   The Family Mediation Helpline is government funded and is staffed by specially trained operators who provide:

- general information on family mediation;
- advice on whether your case may be suitable for mediation;
- information about eligibility for public funding; and
- contact details for mediation services in your local area.

Further information on:
Tel: 0845 6026 627
www.familymediation
helpline.co.uk

The telephone number is 0845 6026 627.

THE OFFICIAL SOLICITOR

2.95   The Official Solicitor to the Supreme Court acts for people who, because they lack mental capacity and cannot properly manage their own affairs, are unable to represent themselves and no other suitable person or agency is able and willing to act. He usually becomes formally involved when appointed by a court, and he may act as his own solicitor, or instruct a private firm of solicitors to act for him. The Official Solicitor works independently of the government and is answerable for his individual casework only to the judges.

In the Official Solicitor's Office there are around 190 staff, of whom 19 are lawyers. The staff are civil servants who specialise in particular areas of the work. About 115 of the staff are caseworkers, all of whom have access to in-house legal advice where appropriate, and some of whom have the conduct of cases under the direct supervision of the lawyers. His office and staff are shared with the Public Trustee who deals with the estates of deceased persons.

The Official Solicitor may act for children (other than those who are the subject of child welfare proceedings when Cafcass will be involved) or for parents who are themselves minors or who lack mental capacity in family or civil litigation in the High Court or county court. He acts as next friend or guardian ad litem in family proceedings and as litigation friend in civil proceedings. He is able to be appointed in magistrates' family proceedings courts in proceedings under the Children and Adoption Act 2002.

His family work covers a range of cases. The first are the public or private law Children Act 1989 cases in which he is acting (more usually) for a parent or (less frequently) child sibling. His duty is to convey to the court any wishes or views the party he represents has expressed and make recommendations and submissions to the court on their behalf in their best interests, bearing in mind that the welfare of the child who is the subject of the proceedings will be regarded as the paramount consideration. He performs the same role in representing a parent (or very occasionally child sibling) in proceedings under the Adoption and Children Act 2002 (where the child subject's welfare is the first consideration). A large amount of work comes from the divorce court where the Official Solicitor is usually called on to act for mentally incapable respondents to divorce petitions. The court has to be satisfied that their interests are properly protected, both in the divorce and in related disputes over financial provision and the care of children. He also acts for children in cases in which an adult is seeking a declaration of parentage.

Another increasing area of the Official Solicitor's work concerns cases concerning the exercise of the High Court's inherent jurisdiction relating to the welfare or healthcare of an adult who is unable by reason of mental disorder to make their own decision on the matter in question. Examples are: whether artificial nutrition or hydration should be withdrawn from a person who has entered a permanent vegetative state; whether a sterilisation, or an abortion, should be performed; and whether blood transfusions or other life saving or prolonging treatment should be given. In all these cases he provides independent assistance to the court on behalf of the patient to enable the court to reach a decision based upon that person's best interests. This work comes under the jurisdiction of the new Court of Protection.

Further information from:
Official Solicitor's Office
Tel: 020 7911 7127
www.officialsolicitor.gov.uk

The Official Solicitor may also be asked by any civil court to investigate and report on any matter arising in the course of litigation (a *Harbin v Masterman* enquiry) or (in the High Court) be or appoint an advocate to the court.

International Child Abduction

2.96 The Official Solicitor's International Child Abduction and Contact Unit (ICACU) is the Central Authority in England and Wales for the Hague Convention on the Civil Aspects of International Child Abduction (the Abduction Convention); the Council Regulation (EC) No 2201/2003 (Revised Brussels II); and the European Convention on Recognition and Enforcement of Decisions Concerning Custody of Children and on Restoration of Custody of Children (the European Convention).

Within each country which is a signatory to the Convention and to the Regulation there is an administrative body known as the Central Authority which is responsible for administering the operation of the Convention and the Regulation. In England and Wales the Central Authority is the Lord Chancellor who delegates the duties of the Central Authority to ICACU, based within the office of the Official Solicitor. ICACU provides advice to parents, solicitors and other interested parties on the steps they can take to recover abducted children.

Reciprocal enforcement of maintenance orders

2.97 The Official Solicitor's Office is the Central Authority in England and Wales for the reciprocal enforcement of maintenance orders (REMO). REMO is the process by which maintenance orders made by UK courts, on behalf of UK residents, can be registered and enforced by courts or other authorities in other countries against people resident there. This is a reciprocal arrangement governed by international conventions, which means that foreign maintenance orders in favour of individuals abroad can likewise be registered and enforced by UK courts against UK residents.

The Children's Commissioners

2.98   The role of the Children's Commissioners in England, Wales, Scotland and Northern Ireland is to promote awareness of the views, needs, rights and interests of children and young people, so as to raise their profile and improve their lives and well-being. This includes encouraging people working with children and with responsibility for children, in the public and private sectors, to take account of children and young people's views and interests. The Commissioners advise government on the views, needs and interests of children with regard to the United Nations Convention on the Rights of the Child when determining what constitutes the interests of children and young people.

The Commissioners can consider or research any matter relating to the interests of children, including the operation of complaints procedures. They also have a function to initiate and conduct inquiries into cases of individual children that raise issues of public policy of relevance to other children. The Commissioners must also take reasonable steps to involve children and young people in all work undertaken and, in particular, to pay regard to those children who may have no other adequate means of making their views known.

Children's Commissioners for:
England:
www.11million.org.uk
Northern Ireland:
www.niccy.org.
Scotland:
www.sccyp.org.uk
Wales:
www.childcom.org.uk

HEALTH CARE PERSONNEL

2.99   Members of primary health care teams (general practitioners, health visitors, midwives, school nurses, school doctors, community nurses and hospital consultants, paediatricians, nurses and other specialist staff) in the National Health Service have a key role in relation to the family justice system and not only in the area of child protection. They may be the first to learn about family breakdown – divorce, separation and partnership dissolution – not only when they are told by the parents but when they see the effects on the children. Decisions made in the family justice system may have profound impacts on children's health and particularly those with chronic physical or mental health problems. Paediatricians, child and adolescent psychiatrists, psychologists, therapists and specialist nurses have specialised professional skills and resources that may be critically important in the diagnosis, evaluation and meeting of children's physical, emotional and mental health needs. By having a working knowledge of local support agencies such as marriage counselling, mediation and legal advice, they can inform patients about alternative means of coping with not only stress but the practical difficulties of parental separation.

Health surveillance programmes are a well recognised part of the primary health service for children. Parents are encouraged to bring their children to child health clinics where the child's health and development are monitored. Children are brought for immunisation and other types of screening. Domiciliary visits are made in situations where these are judged to be helpful to the family, especially to those who do not readily take up the services offered. School nurses and doctors are involved in monitoring children's health and development in collaboration with parents and teachers. The Confidential Enquiry into Maternal and Child Health is an independent but government sponsored organisation which carries out national confidential enquiries into maternal and child health (the CEMACH programme) under contract to the National Patient Safety Agency (NPSA).

All health professionals who work with children and families should be able to:

- understand the risk factors and recognise children in need of support and/or safeguarding;
- recognise the needs of parents who may need extra help in bringing up their children, and know where to refer for help;
- recognise the risks of abuse to an unborn child;
- contribute to enquiries from other professionals about a child and their family or carers;
- liaise closely with other agencies including other health professionals;

- assess the needs of children and the capacity of parents/carers to meet their children's needs including the needs of children who display sexually harmful behaviours;

- plan and respond to the needs of children and their families, particularly those who are vulnerable;

- contribute to child protection conferences, family group conferences and strategy discussions;

- contribute to planning support for children at risk of significant harm, eg children living in households with domestic violence, parental substance misuse;

- help ensure that children who have been abused and parents under stress (eg who have mental health problems) have access to services to support them;

- play an active part, through the child protection plan, in safeguarding children from significant harm;

- as part of generally safeguarding children and young people, provide ongoing promotional and preventative support through proactive work with children, families and expectant parents; and

- contribute to serious case reviews and their implementation.

All health professionals and their teams should have access to advice and support from named and designated child safeguarding professionals and undertake regular safeguarding training and updating.

CEMACH
Tel: 020 7486 1191
www.cemach.org.uk

Designated and named professionals

2.100 The terms 'designated' and 'named professionals' denote professionals with specific roles and responsibilities for safeguarding children. All Primary Care Trusts (PCTs) should have a designated doctor and nurse to take a strategic, professional lead on all aspects of the health service contribution to safeguarding children across the PCT area, which includes all providers.

Designated professionals are a vital source of professional advice on safeguarding children matters to other professionals, the PCT, local authority children's services departments and the Local Safeguarding Children Boards.

General practitioners and other health professionals

2.101 General practitioners (GPs) and other health professionals have key roles to play both in the identification of children who may have been abused and those who are at risk of abuse and in subsequent intervention and protection. Surgery consultations, home visits, treatment room sessions, child health clinic attendance, drop-in centres and information from staff such as health visitors, midwives, and practice nurses can all help to build up a picture of the child's situation and can alert the team if there is some concern. It should be known when it is appropriate to refer a child to children's social care for help as a 'child in need', and how to act on concerns that a child may be at risk of significant harm through abuse or neglect.

GPs and members of primary health care teams are also well placed to recognise when a parent or other adult has problems which may affect their capacity as a parent or carer, or which may mean that they pose a risk of harm to a child. While GPs have responsibilities to all their patients, children may be particularly vulnerable and their welfare is paramount. If there are concerns that an adult's illness or behaviour may be causing, or putting a child at risk of, significant harm, there should be set procedures to follow.

Because of their knowledge of children and families, GPs and other health professionals have an important role in all stages of child protection processes such as: appropriate information sharing (subject to normal confidentiality requirements) with children's social care when enquiries are being made about a child; contributing to assessments; involvement in a child protection plan to protect a child from harm. Relevant information about a child and family should be made available to child protection conferences whether or not GPs or other primary health care team members are able to attend. All GPs have a duty to maintain their skills in the recognition of abuse, and to be familiar with the procedures to be followed if abuse is suspected.

Royal College of General Practitioners www.rcgp.org.uk

Health professionals should have a clear means of identifying in records those children (together with their parents and siblings) who are the subject of a child protection plan. This will enable them to be recognised by the partners of the practice and any other doctor, practice nurse or health visitor who may be involved in the care of those children. There should be good communication between GPs, health visitors, practice nurses and midwives in respect of all children and parents about whom there are concerns.

Hospital staff

2.102   Hospital staff need to be alert to indications of child abuse in the normal course of their duties, especially in accident and emergency departments. They have to be alert to the possibility that injuries or illness may be non-accidental and may have been caused by parents/carers. They should also be aware that carers may 'shop around' for medical services in order to conceal the repeated nature of a child's injuries. All hospital staff should be familiar with local procedures for checking child protection registers and should develop working relationships with social work departments. Arrangements should be in place for notifying other health professionals, including GPs, of all visits made by children up to the age of 16 to accident and emergency departments. Notification should also be sent to the GP.

Paediatric departments will normally take the lead once non – accidental injury, abuse or factitious symptoms are suspected and consultant paediatricians take responsibility for the conduct of investigation, diagnosis and management in the best interests of children.

Guidance

2.103   The Department of Health published in 2006 a children's services guidance *What to do if you're worried a child is being abused*. This document provides best practice guidance for those who work with children in order to safeguard their welfare. It also contains an appendix to help practitioners with the legal issues affecting the sharing of information. It provides general information for anyone whose work brings them into contact with children and families, focusing particularly on those who work in social care, health and education.

The guidance can be downloaded from www.dcsf.gov.uk/ everychildmatters/ resources-and-practice/IG00182/

Child and Adolescent Mental Health Services (CAMHS)

2.104   For a description of CAMHS see **2.49** above. In the course of their work, child and adolescent mental health professionals will inevitably identify or suspect instances where a child may have been abused and/or neglected. They may have a role in the initial assessment process in circumstances where their specific skills and knowledge are helpful. Examples include:

- children and young people with severe behavioural and emotional disturbance, such as self-harming behaviour;
- very young children, or where the abused child or adolescent abuser has severe communication problems;
- situations where parent or carer feigns the symptoms of or deliberately causes ill-health to a child; and
- where multiple victims are involved.

In addition, assessment and treatment services may need to be provided to young mentally disordered offenders. The assessment of children and adults with significant learning difficulties, a disability, or sensory and communication difficulties, may require the expertise of a specialist psychiatrist or clinical psychologist from a learning disability or child mental health service.

Child and adolescent mental health services also have a role in the provision of a range of psychiatric and psychological assessment and treatment services for children and families. Services that may be provided, in liaison with social services, include the provision of reports for court and direct work with children, parents and families. Services may be provided either within general or specialist multidisciplinary teams, depending upon the severity and complexity of the problem.

Adult mental health services

2.105   Adult mental health services, including those providing general adult and community, forensic, psychotherapy, alcohol and substance misuse and learning disability services, have a responsibility in safeguarding children when they become aware of or identify a child at risk of harm. This may be as a result of service's direct work with those who may be mentally ill, a parent, a parent-to-be, or a non-related abuser, or in response to a request for the assessment of an adult perceived to represent a potential or actual risk to a child or young person.

Close collaboration and liaison between the adult mental health services and children's welfare services are essential in the interests of children. This may require the sharing of information.

The Drug Strategy

2.106   Drug Action Teams (DATs) are local partnerships charged with responsibility for delivering the government's Drug Strategy at a local level, with representatives from local authorities (including education, social care, housing), health, police, probation, the prison service and the voluntary sector. DATs should ensure that the work of local agencies is brought together effectively and that cross-agency projects are coordinated successfully.

Adult services

2.107   Specialist drug agencies offer advice, treatment or support to people with drug problems. Nearly half the clients at drug agencies have children, a large proportion of whom continue to live with at least one parent with drug problems. These agencies are often the main ongoing contact with problem drug using parents and therefore have an important role in safeguarding and promoting the welfare of these children.

Drug agencies should always record whether the client has children; liaise with other agencies such as child health and social services and contribute to any assessment of the child's needs and ongoing support. This can include: aiming to reduce or stabilise the parent's drug misuse; discussing safety and stability of home life; supporting the client to access services and liaising with social services if there is a concern.

Young People's Substance Misuse Strategy

2.108   Guidance on young people and drugs is through the Every Child Matters – Young People and Drugs strategy. Drug Action Teams and children's services are involved as part of an overall strategy for meeting children and young people's needs. For more information see the Home Office website.

Specialist consultants

2.109   The normal route for patients wishing to see a specialist consultant is by referral through their GP, and

The Drug Strategy
http://drugs.homeoffice.gov.uk/dat/

Every Child Matters: Change for Children, Young People and Drugs
http://drugs.homeoffice.gov.uk/publication-search/young-people/every-child-matters.pdf

this applies equally to the private sector. The other route is by admission to hospital either as an accident or an emergency case.

Paediatricians

2.110 Paediatrics remains a specialty where most consultants remain generalists, though in most district hospitals, and in all regional centres, all will have a special interest and a few (most or all in regional centres) will be virtually full-time in a specialty. The largest specialties are community paediatrics and care of the newborn and practitioners in these may be full-time in these areas and not participate in general hospital acute paediatrics. Those in full-time community paediatrics may run a specialist on-call rota for the diagnosis and management of child abuse though many cases will first be seen in an acute hospital department.

Paediatricians, wherever they work, come into contact with child abuse in the course of their work. All paediatricians need to maintain their skills in the recognition of abuse, and be familiar with the procedures to be followed if abuse and neglect is suspected. Consultant paediatricians in particular may be involved in difficult diagnostic situations, differentiating those where abnormalities may have been caused by abuse from those which have a medical cause. In their contacts with children and families they should be sensitive to clues suggesting the need for additional support or inquiries.

Paediatricians will sometimes be required to provide reports for child protection investigations, civil and criminal proceedings and to appear as witnesses to give oral evidence. They act in accordance with guidance from the General Medical Council and professional bodies, ensuring their evidence is accurate. The core and case-dependent skills required are outlined in detail in Guidance on Paediatric Forensic Examinations in Relation to Possible Child Sexual Abuse (2007), produced by the Royal College of Paediatrics and Child Health and the Association of Forensic Physicians. Some paediatricians act as independent expert witnesses in legal proceedings. The Academy of Royal Colleges has issued guidance for those undertaking expert witness work.

General paediatrics

2.111   Most children requiring admission are treated
by general paediatricians in local hospitals and most
outpatient referrals for medical opinions on children are
seen in general paediatric outpatient clinics there. The
particular experience of the paediatrician allows
assessment and modification of management to take
note of the impact of an illness or disorder on the
child's life, particularly on his or her social,
psychological and emotional development.

Paediatric specialties

2.112   Some paediatricians concentrate entirely on a
narrower field. Paediatric specialists see referrals from
local hospitals. Because the number of such patients is
small, paediatric specialists cover a wide geographical
area and often are based in university teaching
hospitals.

Community child health

2.113   Prevention and surveillance of illnesses in
children is generally performed by GPs or by those
paediatricians working in community child health in
close collaboration with health visitors and practice
nurses. Essential areas of their work include health
education, immunisation, early detection of disabilities
such as deafness, developmental screening, school
health and complex special needs assessment. When a
second opinion or specialised assessment is needed in
these fields, the child is usually referred to a consultant
in paediatrics, or appropriate specialties such as ear,
nose and throat (ENT) or ophthalmology. The
specialised aspects of work in the community child
health service are now mostly provided by consultant
paediatricians.

Royal College of
Paediatrics and
Child Health
Tel: 020 7092 6000
www.rcph.ac.uk

Qualifications

2.114   The Medical Royal Colleges have an overall
responsibility for training doctors working in medical
specialties. For paediatricians, this responsibility has, for
many years, been held by the Royal Colleges of
Physicians, which have included paediatricians. All of
the Royal Colleges have worked closely with the British
Paediatric Association which was founded in 1928. In
1996, paediatricians were granted a Royal Charter for
the Royal College of Paediatrics and Child Health

(RCPCH), and this new Royal College has assumed the responsibilities previously held by the three Royal Colleges of Physicians for postgraduate training of paediatricians, the setting of standards and of examinations. Within the Royal College of Paediatrics and Child Health, there are a number of special interest groups concerned with particular aspects of paediatrics, the largest of which are the British Association for Community Child Health and the British Association for Perinatal Medicine.

The MRCPCH is a series of examinations which is required for entry into the senior training grades in paediatrics or general medicine. Fellowship of one of the Royal Colleges of Physicians is granted to between one-third and one-half of consultant paediatricians and physicians on the basis of peer recommendation and review. Fellowship of the RCPCH will be granted on attainment of an established NHS consultant post in this specialty. Both colleges also grant honorary membership and fellowship to small numbers of doctors of international standing, usually from outside the relevant specialty.

The MD and PhD are research degrees awarded by universities after successful presentation of research findings. In order to achieve specialist accreditation, paediatricians must have completed specialist registrar training in an approved post in the specialty.

In contrast to some professionals associated with the family justice system, doctors act as independent clinicians and may appear to be bound by few written rules. Guidance, however, assumes an ever increasing role in clinical practice and that promulgated by Royal Colleges, the BMA, the Department of Health and particularly the General Medical Council (GMC) carries such weight as to be equivalent to regulation.

The British Association of Community Child Health

2.115   The British Association of Community Child Health (BACCH) is a membership organisation that represents doctors and other professionals working in paediatrics and child health in the community. It is affiliated to the Royal College of Paediatrics and Child Health (RCPCH). Its Child Protection Special Interest Group (CPSIG) provides a forum for paediatricians working in the field of child maltreatment. The group aims to:

- perform peer reviews by the presentation of case histories and slides of injuries;

- reach a consensus as to the description of signs;

- form a platform upon which the interpretation of signs could be discussed;

- hold regular national meetings with formal lectures and time set aside for members to present cases;

- aid in the development of local peer group reviews which could then meet on a monthly basis.

The group runs in parallel with the RCPCH standing committee on child protection. The CPSIG forms the practical and educational side of this group complemented by the continued political activities of the child protection committee. CPSIG is open to BACCH and RCPCH members, and to all professionals working with children in need and in child protection.

Child Protection Special Interest Group
Tel: 020 7092 6083
www.cpsig.org.uk

Psychiatrists

2.116 Psychiatry is a medical specialty which aims to relieve the suffering of people with mental health problems. All psychiatrists will have spent 5 years at a medical school to qualify as a doctor. They will then spend one year in general medicine before starting their psychiatric training. It will take a further 7 years of training and working in a psychiatric service and they will need to pass two examinations run by the Royal College of Psychiatrists before they may become a consultant psychiatrist.

The majority of psychiatrists work for the National Health Service. Psychiatrists have a background in physical medicine and study those disorders of the mind which are caused by a physical illness, such as dementia. They will also talk to patients about their family, relationship or social problems. Because they are also doctors, they can prescribe medicines. They may work in the hospitals or in the community or both. They always work in teams with other professionals, including nurses, occupational therapists, social workers, psychologists and community psychiatric nurses. In order to see a psychiatrist, a person must usually be referred by his family doctor.

Psychiatrists often work in the following areas:

- psychotherapy (see **2.118**);

- child and adolescent psychiatry (see **2.117**);

- old age psychiatry, eg dealing with infirmity and dementia;
- learning disability (or mental handicap);
- general psychiatry, dealing with the mental health problems of adults, increasingly in the community;
- liaison psychiatry, working with physicians and surgeons on the psychiatric causes and consequences of physical illness;
- forensic psychiatry, working with people with mental disorders in the criminal justice system;
- substance misuse, helping people with alcohol and drug problems;
- military psychiatry, dealing with morale, stress and combat problems as well as the mental health of the armed forces.

Further information from:
Royal College of Psychiatrists
Tel: 020 7235 2351
www.rcpsych.ac.uk/

Since parents who have mental health problems, learning disabilities or addiction problems may experience difficulties which lead to the involvement of the family justice system, the work of the adult psychiatrist is particularly important. This work should be coordinated with that of the child psychiatrist and other child welfare services.

There is more to psychiatry than medication. There are different kinds of disorders which are not just medical problems but which have important psychological and social aspects. Psychiatry is concerned with all aspects of mental health and psychiatrists often call upon the expert knowledge and skills of clinical psychologists, occupational therapists and social workers. Some teams include psychotherapists. The professionals who make up the psychiatric team work together by collecting the facts and by bringing information together to obtain as complete a view as possible of the problems of each patient.

Child and adolescent psychiatrists

2.117   Child and adolescent psychiatrists are medically qualified doctors who specialise in understanding and working with the mental health problems of children and young people. Their training includes 3 years working in mental health services post-qualification and 4 years specialising in work with children, young people and their families. Specialist registrars are qualified doctors in higher specialist training towards becoming a consultant.

Within the National Health Service, child psychiatrists mainly work in CAMHS – child and family consultation services, out-patient clinics and hospitals. They work as part of a team with other child mental health professionals such as psychologists, psychotherapists, psychiatric nurses and social workers. Most of the work they do with children is carried out through outpatient contact – that is, the child continues to live at home. Child psychiatrists also work in units where children who need more help and care spend time as in-patients or attend each day over a period of time. They also often work in child development clinics, student health services, day nurseries and family centres. They are sometimes asked to provide expert opinion to the courts.

Child psychiatrists deal with a wide range of children's and young people's mental health problems. Typical problems are:

- In the under 5s
    - communication problems;
    - odd or unusual behaviour;
    - sleep problems;
    - difficult behaviour;
    - excessive clinging and fears;
    - delays in development.
- In school children
    - aggressive or disruptive behaviour;
    - hyperactive behaviour;
    - psychosomatic symptoms (stress-related aches and pains);
    - anxieties, phobias and compulsions;
    - school attendance difficulties;
    - soiling and wetting;
    - repeated stealing and lying;
    - excessive anti-social and aggressive behaviour;
    - emotional problems interfering with school work;
    - friend/relationship problems;
    - family problems.
- In teenagers
    - eating disorders;

- relationship problems with friends or family, e g withdrawing from social activities or always falling out with friends;

- sexual orientation problems;

- psychosomatic problems;

- depression;

- suicidal behaviour;

- substance abuse.

Post-traumatic stress disorders, obsessive compulsive disorders or anxiety states may occur in children of all ages.

Child psychiatrists also work with autistic spectrum disorders, (including Asperger's Syndrome), Attention Deficit Hyperactivity Disorder (ADHD) and, in older children, severe mental illness such as schizophrenia.

A large part of a child psychiatrist's work is to identify the child's problem, find out the causes and give advice about what may help. Child psychiatrists take into account a range of factors that may lead to these difficulties, including the child's family, school or the community, as well as the child's own innate difficulties. They carry out their assessments by interviewing the child and his or her family and by gathering information from the schools and other doctors or professionals who may have contact with the child, with the parent's and child's agreement.

On the basis of their assessments, the psychiatrists, together with their colleagues, provide different kinds of help for the child and the family. This may be individual, group or family therapy. It may include talking with children about the thoughts and feelings that are upsetting them and helping parents and others to understand and manage a child's difficult behaviour better. The child psychiatrist may also take a leading role in advising and assisting other professionals in planning how best to help the child and the family. Child psychiatrists may sometimes prescribe medication and only children with more serious conditions need admission to hospital.

Family doctors, school doctors where available, clinic doctors or paediatricians can arrange access to a child psychiatrist. Some child and family consultation services will accept referral from parents. Young Minds keeps a register of help across the country and can give the telephone number and address of local clinics or centres.

YoungMinds
Tel: 020 7336 8445
Youngminds.org.uk

Founded in 1949, the Mental Health Foundation is a leading UK charity that provides information, carries out research, campaigns and works to improve services for anyone affected by mental health problems, whatever their age.

Mental Health Foundation
Tel: 070 7803 1101
www.mentalhealth.
org.uk

Psychotherapists and psychologists

Psychotherapists

2.118   There are various types of psychotherapy, which may be practised in individual, couple, family or group contexts. They all aim to help people to overcome difficulties including those caused by emotional and relationship problems. The treatment involves talking to the therapist and sometimes doing things together. In the NHS, there are several different types of psychotherapy available:

British Association of Psychotherapists
Tel: 020 8452 9823
www.bap-psychotherapy.
org

- **Psychoanalytical, psychodynamic psychotherapy**

  This treatment involves exploring conscious and unconscious assumptions about relationship patterns. The understanding gained aims to free the individual from those patterns in order that he or she may make conscious choices about what happens in the future. This may involve brief therapy to help overcome circumstance-induced difficulties but where problems have a long-standing history, treatment might mean regular sessions over many months or even years. Early experiences are thought to be particularly relevant to problems which manifest themselves in social and work settings and sexual difficulties.

- **Behavioural psychotherapy**

  This approach tries to change patterns of behaviour directly, and focuses only on the present. It aims to help patients overcome fears by gradually spending more time in the situation(s) they fear or by learning ways of reducing their anxiety. This approach is particularly effective for anxiety, panic attacks and phobias.

- **Cognitive therapy**

  This approach encourages discussion of how the client thinks and aims to alter the negative perceptions of him or herself and the world. It has similarities to behaviour therapy, but rejects the conditioning used by the former. Focusing mostly on the present and the future, it is particularly successful with certain types of depression.

GPs can refer patients to qualified psychotherapists with a recognised qualification.

Psychotherapy for adults

United Kingdom
Council for
Psychotherapy
Tel: 020 7014 5955
www.psychotherapy.org.uk

2.119 Adult psychotherapy can be available under the National Health Service but most is done privately. It encompasses a range of approaches for treating behavioural and emotional problems. Some approaches focus on alleviating the symptoms suffered by the patient; others pay more attention to exploring dynamic factors that are instrumental in precipitating the symptom. Adult psychotherapists, in common with all psychotherapists who have qualified from a recognised and approved training course, will be registered with either the British Psychoanalytic Council (BPC), or the United Kingdom Council for Psychotherapy (UKCP).

Psychotherapy for children

2.120 Child psychotherapists aim for an understanding of the inner worlds of children and how early their childhood experience influence everyday life. They work with children, teenagers and their parents.

Child psychotherapists work in a variety of settings, frequently in CAMHS – child and family consultation services (child guidance clinics) and hospital outpatient clinics. They may also work in health centres and GPs' surgeries, hospital wards, student health services and walk-in centres for adolescents. They also practise privately. However, child psychotherapists are a rare resource and are more numerous in some parts of the country than others.

To be accepted for training as a child psychotherapist, an applicant must have an honours degree in a related field and experience of working with children. In addition, many have experience as qualified social workers, psychologists or teachers. The training takes a minimum of 4 years and is based on the study of psychoanalysis, child development, observation of babies and young children and supervised psychotherapy with children, adolescents and parents. An essential part of the training is for trainees themselves to undergo a personal analysis.

Problems can affect the feelings and behaviour of children of all ages. Child psychotherapists, sometimes working in conjunction with other mental health professionals, treat a wide variety of difficulties. Some children are very fearful and withdrawn. Some are very angry and hit out. Others feel overwhelmed and are sad. Children may be very anxious and tense and might not want to go to school. They may be afraid of being bullied or become regular truants. They may not be sleeping well, may be having nightmares or wetting the bed. They may find it difficult to accept authority at school, get into fights or be in trouble with the police. Children may be suffering the effects of a crisis or catastrophe in the family such as divorce or separation; they may be constantly moody, have no interest in making friends or in learning, or have learning difficulties.

Child psychotherapists work with children individually, although some may work with groups of children and families. They usually see a child once a week, but in some cases sessions may be more frequent. Some children will only need a few sessions, others may need to continue seeing the psychotherapist for several years. The psychotherapist observes and tries to understand the way a child behaves and relates to themselves and others, then returns this understanding to the child in a digestible form. This helps the child sort out the various feelings and thoughts they have about his life. Child psychotherapists are skilled in understanding a child's way of communicating and may use age-appropriate speech or play to communicate. The aim of the work is to help children through the maturational process when the conditions to do so have not been conducive to healthy emotional development.

Child psychotherapists who have completed an approved training course are eligible for membership of the Association of Child Psychotherapists (ACP). The function of this organisation is to maintain standards within the profession, and it is also the official regulating body of child psychotherapy. A list of qualified members is available from:

Association of Child Psychotherapists
Tel: 020 8458 1609
www.childpsychotherapy.org.uk

Psychotherapy for couples

2.121　The aim of couple psychotherapy is to provide for cohabiting or separating couples a setting in which both partners can be helped to explore their relationship, understand their difficulties and bring about changes.

Further information from:
Tavistock Centre for Couple Relationships (TCCR)
Tel: 020 7380 1975
www.tccr.org.uk

Psychotherapy for families

2.122   Family therapists are usually, but not always, professionally qualified as social workers, psychologists, psychiatrists and psychotherapists who have undergone additional specialist training. Family therapists work within the NHS in a variety of settings, for example:

- child and family consultation centres (child guidance clinics);
- adolescent units;
- drug abuse units;
- children's wards;
- psychiatric day and outpatient units;
- GP practices.

They also work in social services departments, voluntary agencies and private practice but it is possible to be referred to a family therapist via a GP which will be NHS funded.

Family therapy is a way of working with families so that they can understand and deal more effectively with problems that family members may be experiencing. The idea of family therapy is to draw upon the strength and commitment that exist within families to help tackle such problems. Family therapy can improve communication, help family members to understand one another better and overcome together the difficulties they are facing. When someone in the family has a problem it can affect all family members; pressures from outside can add to difficulties. For example, when parents are divorcing or separating, not only they themselves but children, grandparents, aunts and uncles may be put under a lot of pressure: tensions and disagreements may arise within the family circle. External events and misfortunes such as unemployment and financial difficulties can compound these problems. There may also be problems that remain unresolved from the past. In normal circumstances, most people cope well enough with these difficulties, but sometimes problems mount up and become destructive. Various family members may show signs of strain. A parent may become easily overtired, depressed or ill; a child may become withdrawn and lose interest in school or friends; a teenager may become delinquent and get into trouble in the community. Some may become violent or abusive.

Family therapists find it productive to meet with everyone in the family, or with as many family members concerned as possible, to address their problems. In certain circumstances they may see parents, including single parents, and the children by themselves or together, and may include cohabitees and step-parents, grandparents and other relatives when appropriate.

GPs can refer patients to qualified psychotherapists who must have a recognised qualification.

Institute of Family
Therapy
Tel: 020 7391 9150
www.ift.org.uk

Applied psychologists

2.123   Psychologists are trained to understand how people behave, think and learn. They use this understanding to help with a wide range of problems, from difficulties in learning and developing to problems with personal and social relationships. There are many types of applied psychologists: educational, clinical, forensic, health, counselling, occupational and research. Although there are differences with regards to the type of training they engage in to reach their particular specialism, all have an undergraduate degree in psychology. Their specialisms are developed via postgraduate training and qualification.

Most psychologists are members of the British Psychological Society (BPS), with the majority of psychologists 'Chartered' with the BPS. Chartered Psychologists earn their adjunct titles (ie Chartered Clinical, Chartered Educational, Chartered Forensic etc) via full membership of the relevant BPS Division (ie Division of Educational Psychology (DEP), Division of Clinical Psychology (DCP), Division of Forensic Psychology (DFP)). Full membership of a Division can only be obtained via postgraduate training.

Although there are many different types of psychologists, the focus here will be on three Divisions of the British Psychological Society most frequently utilised within family proceedings and matters: Educational, Clinical and Forensic.

Applied psychologists: educational and clinical psychologists

2.124   Both have similar backgrounds and training but educational psychologists deal with children and young people from an educational perspective while clinical psychologists work from the perspective of health and community care. Children of all ages, including pre-school children, can be helped by such psychologists.

The majority of educational psychologists are employed by local education authorities and undertake a lot of school-based work. Clinical psychologists usually work in the NHS in health centres and GPs' surgeries, hospitals and outpatient clinics. Clinical psychologists work with a range of different populations as part of their postgraduate training, and not just children, ie they also work with elderly individuals, adults with a learning difficulty and adults with mental health difficulties.

Both educational and clinical psychologists provide services in child and family consultation centres and work in close conjunction with other professionals concerned with children, including teachers, health visitors and social workers. Some educational and clinical psychologists work privately.

Educational and clinical psychologists complete a minimum of 6 years' training and usually obtain additional relevant practical experience before beginning to practise. Clinical psychologists undertake a 3-year professional training in clinical psychology. Educational psychologists obtain training and experience as teachers, plus one year's training in educational psychology, although this has recently changed with 3-year professional doctorate programmes for educational psychologists now available.

Educational and clinical psychologists work with individual children, families, groups of children and their parents. The specific type of work that they undertake will be dependent on their individual experience and developed expertise, but their work may include:

- assessing the ability and cognitive functioning of both adults and children;
- discussing in detail a child's problem behaviour, including what happens before and after an incident, and advising the child and parents about different ways of dealing with it;
- understanding how thoughts and feelings affect what people do and considering how other ways of thinking might change their behaviour;
- understanding how a child's behaviour fits in with what other people are doing in the family and

looking at possible ways of changing the whole
situation. Psychologists may want to meet with as
many members of the family as possible to help
most effectively;

- looking at how a child's educational development
  is affected by his feelings or behaviour.

Clinical and educational psychologists advise
organisations such as schools and hospitals on how best
to provide services to children and families with
difficulties. Educational psychologists have a special
knowledge of schools and, in most areas, are
responsible for writing the psychological advice which
contributes to a statement of children's special
educational needs (ie a professional opinion about a
child's abilities and educational difficulties which
informs those providing help and support for the child).

Applied psychologists: forensic psychologists

2.125   The Division of Forensic Psychology (DFP)
specialises in the application of psychology to civil and
criminal law dealing primarily with individuals who
come into contact with these systems, including victims,
perpetrators and witnesses. Forensic psychologists are
involved in both assessment and treatment with their
client group including adults, adolescents and children
who have come into contact with the legal system.

Chartered Forensic Psychologists have completed a
minimum of 6 years' training including an
undergraduate degree in psychology and postgraduate
qualifications, including supervised practice under the
supervision of a Chartered Forensic Psychologist.
Forensic psychologists are employed in a range of
settings including prisons, social services, probation,
universities, hospitals and the police. Some forensic
psychologists work privately.

With regards to the issues pertinent to family
proceedings (including private proceedings), depending
on the specific competency of the forensic psychologist
involved, examples of areas falling within the remit of a
forensic psychologist are as follows:

- Specialised assessments of risk for general and
  domestic violence that include an understanding of
  the circumstances under which risk is increased or
  decreased, and the treatment required to work
  towards an amelioration and/or effective
  management of risk. Such assessments treat risk as

a dynamic concept and incorporate up-to-date and defendable assessment guides and tools that assist with opinions on the contextual nature of the risks and the manageability of identified risks.

- Specialised assessments of risk for sexual violence. Such assessments have the same components as general and domestic violence assessments (see above) but require the administration of specific guides and tools to assess and manage risk. A number of forensic psychologists specialise in such assessments and are able to provide opinions on the nature of risk and the components of effective treatment.

- Risk assessments that include attention to the role of personality and cognitive functioning on parenting ability.

- The assessment of aggressive behaviour, including its function and impact on perpetrators, victims and/or witnesses. Aggression is defined here in its broadest sense to include physical, verbal and emotional abuse.

- Assessment of the content and conduct of interviews with vulnerable witnesses including children and the preparation of reports for the court.

- Assessment of the likelihood of sexual interest in children by one or other parties where sexual abuse is alleged.

- The ability of individuals to protect others (e g their children) from risk and/or victimisation.

- Assessment of the potential for reoccurrence of sexual or physical violence by one or other partner within the family setting.

- Assessments of conduct disorder in young age groups (e g juveniles).

- Methods of obtaining information from witnesses and the factors influencing the reliability and validity of evidence, including suggestibility and compliance.

- Assessment of child witnesses. There are a growing number of forensic psychologists who specialise in this area of work.

- Understanding and managing trauma reactions in victims.

- Treatment issues including the administration and utility of both individual and group based treatment programmes.

- The actual and/or potential impact of neglect on victims.

- Substance misuse and its impact.

- Forensic mental health.

- Assessments of complex behaviours and presentations such as personality disorder, psychopathy, arson, stalking, cognitive difficulties, and problems with regards to emotional functioning (eg anger management difficulties).

- The impact of problematic behaviour on an individual's functioning.

Contacting psychologists

2.126   Clinical, educational and forensic psychologists are, as mentioned earlier, chartered professions, which means that psychologists can register once they have qualified. For those who wish to consult a psychologist privately, the British Psychological Society (BPS) will provide a list of the chartered psychologists in a given area.

Further information from:
British Psychological Society
Tel: 0116 254 9568
www.bps.org.uk

Within the NHS, clinical psychological services are available in most areas: details are available from local district health authorities (telephone numbers in the phone book).

Young Minds has details of mental health services for children and young persons throughout the UK. Most GPs will refer patients to the local clinical psychology service if need be. Educational psychologists can be contacted through a child's school, through the local educational psychology service (listed by Young Minds) or the local education authority. Forensic psychologists can be contacted via local criminal justice agencies and contacts (eg prisons including young and juvenile offender units, secure psychiatric hospitals and probation). A good source for contacting forensic psychologists is the BPS.

Further information from:
Young Minds
Tel: 020 7336 8445
www.youngminds.org.uk

EXPERT WITNESSES

2.127   Experts from a wide variety of disciplines may be called upon in family proceedings. In any case, the court must give leave before a medical or psychiatric examination or other assessment of the child can take place. In private law cases under s 8 of the Children Act 1989 relating to residence and contact, courts tend to rely on a Cafcass report. However, in care and other public law proceedings, the use of expert witnesses has expanded, and the courts are now making concerted efforts to limit their use. It is also important to note that if a party to proceedings has, with the leave of the court, commissioned an expert's report, the contents of which are relevant to the future of the child in question, the court has power to override legal privilege and order that the report be disclosed to the other parties even if the party who has commissioned it is unwilling to disclose it voluntarily.

The most common experts in care cases are likely to be:

- paediatrician: to carry out or comment on development, causation and dating of injuries, long-term prognosis;
- paediatric haematologist: to advise on the causes of bleeding;
- paediatric neuroradiologist: for skull fractures and subdurals;
- paediatric neurosurgeon: to deal with subdural haematomas;
- paediatric ophthalmologist: for retinal haemorrhages;
- paediatric radiologist: to read the skeletal survey, MRI scan and/or CT scan;
- paediatric metabolic consultant: to test for any metabolic disorder;
- forensic pathologist: their exclusive experience is with death in suspicious circumstances; will conduct a post mortem and reach a decision as to the cause of death, and whether the explanation given is plausible;
- geneticist: may be able to provide an answer as to the possibility of a chromosomal abnormality, gene deficiency, or a rare syndrome.

There can be inconsistency in the way that psychiatrists and psychologists are used in care cases: in some parts of the country it is invariably a psychiatrist who is brought in as an expert, on parenting ability, attachment and contact issues; in others it is always a psychologist. However, they have some overlapping and some different skills:

- both have expertise in identification of personality disorders;
- a psychiatrist has expertise in terms of specialist knowledge of mental illness;
- a psychologist has expertise in general functioning and management of life's responsibilities.

Why experts?

2.128   Before the Children Act 1989 there was no widespread use of expert witnesses in child proceedings. How was the court to ensure that it had the benefit of professional opinion concerning the child's interests independently of the local authority and the parents? Independent social workers were frequently used by lawyers to consider service provision and plans for children. The experts had no right of access to local authority records, were frequently instructed for the parents and regarded as partial and there was no disclosure duty on the party obtaining the report.

The Children Act 1989 provided for a children's guardian to be appointed in public law cases to safeguard the children's interests. They would be regarded as experts in relation to general child care and development with a right of access to local authority records. Where care cases required specialist knowledge beyond the guardian's competence, it was hoped that a parent would accept an expert appointed by the guardian instead of seeking to instruct their own. Now it is usual for experts to be agreed by all the parties to proceedings and they are usually then jointly instructed. Their use can lead to delays and always further expense on the public purse and it is said that perhaps the reliance on experts has gone too far.

The expert's duty

2.129   An expert in family proceedings has an overriding duty to the court which takes precedence over any obligation to the person from whom he has received instructions or by whom he is paid. Among any other duties an expert may have, an expert shall have regard to the following duties:

- to assist the court in accordance with the overriding duty;

- to provide an opinion that is independent of the party or parties instructing the expert;

- to confine an opinion to matters material to the issues between the parties and in relation only to questions that are within the expert's expertise (skill and experience). If a question is put which falls outside that expertise the expert must state this at the earliest opportunity and to volunteer an opinion as to whether another expert is required to bring expertise not possessed by those already involved or, in the rare case, as to whether a second opinion is required on a key issue and, if possible, what questions should be asked of the second expert;

- in expressing an opinion, to take into consideration all of the material facts including any relevant factors arising from ethnic, cultural, religious or linguistic contexts at the time the opinion is expressed;

- inform those instructing the expert without delay of any change in the opinion and the reason for the change.

Instructing experts

2.130 Experts are a precious and expensive commodity to be called on sparingly and, wherever possible, instructed jointly. Too frequently, the expertise of social workers and children's guardians is underestimated. Accuracy, rather than a huge quantity, of information is essential when hard decisions need to be made. The Family Justice Council has addressed, in addition to the shortage of experts, the following.

- the standards, ie the skills and experience, that are required of experts;

- the purposes for which forensic and clinical practitioners are used by legal practitioners and the courts;

- the use of experts to advise the court at an early stage on case management decisions, in particular, the use and terms of instruction to experts;

- the development of improved letters of instruction (to ensure that the same material informs each of the experts in the case and to reduce the number of questions that are routinely asked or each expert);

- the purposes and funding of residential and non-residential assessments;
- the use of family group conferences and other inter-disciplinary and alternative dispute resolution environments.

The use of experts under the Public Law Outline

The Practice Direction

2.131 A Practice Direction relating to the use and instruction of Experts in Family Proceedings relating to Children came into force on 1 April 2008, together with the Public Law Outline itself. Family Proceedings include placement and adoption proceedings, and family proceedings held in private which:

- relate to the exercise of the inherent jurisdiction of the High Court with respect to children;
- are brought under the Children Act 1989 in any family court; or
- are brought in the High Court and county courts and 'otherwise relate wholly or mainly to the maintenance or upbringing of a minor'.

The guidance in the Practice Direction aims to provide the court in family proceedings relating to children with early information to determine whether an expert or expert evidence will assist the court to:

- identify, narrow and where possible agree the issues between the parties;
- provide an opinion about a question that is not within the skill and experience of the court;
- encourage the early identification of questions that need to be answered by an expert; and
- encourage disclosure of full and frank information between the parties, the court and any expert instructed.

The guidance reiterates that the court's permission is required to instruct an expert and to disclose information or documents to an expert – and, in Children Act 1989 proceedings, to have the child examined or assessed. Permission is to be asked of the court at the relevant hearing and as early as possible, which means in public law proceedings under the Children Act 1989, by or at the Case Management Conference, in private law proceedings under the

Children Act 1989, by or at the First Hearing Dispute Resolution Appointment, and in placement and adoption proceedings, by or at the First Directions Hearing.

Under the Practice Direction, the content of the expert's report is specified, as are the preliminary enquiries to be made of the expert by the potential instructing solicitor and the responses to be acquired from the expert before the relevant hearing. All matters in relation to the use and instruction of experts are strictly timetabled in order to avoid delay.

An annex to the Practice Direction sets out suggested questions in letters of instruction to (1) child mental health professionals or paediatricians, and (2) adult psychiatrists and applied psychologists, in Children Act 1989 proceedings.

Letters of instruction

2.132 The 2008 Practice Direction provides a summarised template letter of instruction to experts.

'Questions in letters of instruction to child mental health professional or paediatrician in Children Act 1989 proceedings

A. The Child(ren)

1. Please describe the child(ren)'s current health, development and functioning (according to your area of expertise), and identify the nature of any significant changes which have occurred

- Behavioural
- Emotional
- Attachment organisation
- Social/peer/sibling relationships
- Cognitive/educational
- Physical
    - Growth, eating, sleep
    - Non-organic physical problems (including wetting and soiling)
    - Injuries
    - Paediatric conditions

2. Please comment on the likely explanation for/aetiology of the child(ren)'s problems/difficulties/injuries

- History/experiences (including intrauterine influences, and abuse and neglect)
- Genetic/innate/developmental difficulties
- Paediatric/psychiatric disorders

3. Please provide a prognosis and risk if difficulties not addressed above.

4. Please describe the child(ren)'s needs in the light of the above

- Nature of care-giving
- Education
- Treatment
  in the short and long term (subject, where appropriate, to further assessment later).

B. The parents/primary care-givers

5. Please describe the factors and mechanisms which would explain the parents' (or primary care-givers') harmful or neglectful interactions with the child(ren) (if relevant)

6. What interventions have been tried and what has been the result?

7. Please assess the ability of the parents or primary care-givers to fulfil the child(ren)'s identified needs now.

8. What other assessments of the parents or primary care-givers are indicated

- Adult mental health assessment
- Forensic risk assessment
- Physical assessment
- Cognitive assessment

9. What, if anything, is needed to assist the parents or primary care-givers now, within the child(ren)'s time scales and what is the prognosis for change

- Parenting work
- Support
- Treatment/therapy

C. Alternatives

10. Please consider the alternative possibilities for the fulfilment of the child(ren)'s needs.

- What sort of placement
- Contact arrangements

Please consider the advantages, disadvantages and implications of each for the child(ren).

Questions in letters of instruction to adult psychiatrists and applied psychologists in Children Act 1989 proceedings

1. Does the parent/adult have – whether in his/her history or presentation – a mental illness/disorder (including substance abuse) or other psychological/emotional difficulty and, if so, what is the diagnosis?

2. How do any/all of the above (and their current treatment if applicable) affect his/her functioning, including interpersonal relationships?

3. If the answer to Q1 is yes, are there any features of either the mental illness or psychological/emotional difficulty or personality disorder which could be associated with risk to others, based on the available evidence base (whether published studies or evidence from clinical experience)?

4. What are the experiences/antecedents/aetiology which would explain his/her difficulties, if any, (taking into account any available evidence base or other clinical experience)?

5. What treatment is indicated, what is its nature and the likely duration?

6. What is his/her capacity to engage in/partake of the treatment/therapy?

7. Are you able to indicate the prognosis for, time scales for achieving, and likely durability of, change?

8. What other factors might indicate positive change?

(It is assumed that this opinion will be based on collateral information as well as interviewing the adult).'

Choosing an expert witness

The expert's qualifications

2.133 Care must be taken in the choice of any expert. It is prudent to find out:

- whether the CV indicates an expertise in the particular field which is relevant, for example:

  - a doctor qualified as a physician may have acquired knowledge as to the psychological aspects of the work, but would usually not be qualified to give a psychological or psychiatric opinion;

  - an adult psychiatrist will not usually be regarded as sufficiently expert to be called to give an opinion about his patient's capacity to parent their child;

  - a bio-chemist cannot give an opinion as a paediatrician;

- whether there has been any reported judicial criticism of the proposed expert;

- whether the expert has acknowledged a leaning towards a particular view;

- whether the expert usually gets the report in on time;

- how difficult it is to arrange for the expert to attend court hearings for a block period;

- whether the expert is suitable given case-sensitive issues such as allegations of sexual abuse, the gender of the child/ren, ethnicity, language and religion.

There is a move towards defining core competencies which an expert in a particular field should possess. Peer group review may also become a form of ensuring quality of expert work of those not working in a multidisciplinary team.

Court experience for experts

2.134   The Family Justice Council, through the Local Family Justice Councils, runs a mini-pupillage scheme for specialist registrars and consultants with the aim of introducing them to the work of the courts. See further Chapter 1.

Paying for experts

2.135   Following the consultation on the Chief Medical Officer's Report, *Bearing Good Witness:*

Proposals for reforming the delivery of medical expert evidence in family law cases, the LSC is piloting the key proposal.

The LSC is working with the Department of Health to develop and pilot arrangements to commission multi-disciplinary teams of health professionals from the NHS and other public, private or voluntary sector organisations to provide jointly instructed health expert witness services to family courts in public law childcare proceedings. These arrangements will enable the commissioning of both existing and prospective teams and are not intended to create a monopoly for NHS service providers. The purpose of the project is to extend the use of teams – particularly multi-disciplinary teams – and to develop, pilot and evaluate arrangements in which legal aid service providers are able to contract services from teams who undertake the work as part of their employment (rather than from individuals acting in their private capacity). The pilot started in Summer 2008. The pilot is to determine whether these arrangements will ensure:

- a sustainable supply of quality-assured, competent medical expert witnesses who can apply their work knowledgeably and responsively in the context of court processes;

- that medical expertise is tailored and prepared for the particular culture of the family court (public law) jurisdiction with its aim of using a largely inquisitorial system;

- an organisation framework within the NHS [and other organisations] with clear accountability for medical expert witnesses and which therefore moves away from the current reliance on medical expert witnesses who are acting in a private capacity;

- best value for money for the taxpayer.

It is anticipated that the use of multi-disciplinary teams of health expert witnesses commissioned directly from the NHS and other organisations will deliver the following benefits:

- easier for health professionals to secure engagement as health expert witnesses;

- sustainable increase in the supply of quality-assured expert witnesses;

- easier and quicker for solicitors and clients to access health expert witnesses;

- fewer delays in the provision of expert reports for the benefit of the child;
- improved quality-assurance through peer review and multi-disciplinary input;
- best use of public funds.

All teams have a core of psychiatrists and psychologists, and three include paediatricians. They also indicated that they could access other specialties if it was deemed necessary. The LSC is tendering for an organisation to evaluate the process, with the final evaluation report due in March 2011.

The Department of Health's *Bearing Good Witness* programme will undertake work that supports the LSC led project, including the provision of training for medical expert witness teams in court-related activities, the development of a National Knowledge Service to support them in their work and reviewing the process for effective resolution of vexatious complaints.

More generally, for public law family proceedings the LSC wants to work with the courts and others involved in the family justice system to find a way forward but where a case is subject to the Public Law Outline it will not take issue on the principle of instructing an expert nominated by the court for a particular task. Use of the pilot is not mandatory, and there will be no sanctions for not using a pilot team. Note, however, that this does not necessarily mean that the LSC will accept the amount of work proposed to be undertaken and/or the fees proposed to be charged. Also it will only accept a court directed apportionment of costs of assessment where that has been based on appropriate consideration by the court of all the issues. In addition, it should be noted that the limited Community Legal Service Fund cannot, legally, meet costs or expenses of or relating to the residential assessment of a child or costs or expenses of or relating to treatment, therapy, training or other interventions of an educative or rehabilitative nature. In this context 'residential assessment' means any assessment of a child, whether under s 38(6) of the Children Act 1989 or otherwise, in which the child, alone or with others, is assessed on a residential basis at any location other than his or her normal residence. It also includes an assessment or viability assessment, whether residential or not, preparatory to or with a view to the possibility of a residential assessment (LSC Funding Code paragraph 2.4). Solicitors contracted with the LSC to undertake publicly funded family work should be familiar with the legal position and the LSC's guidance in what has become a complex area.

For more information on public funding see **2.22–2.44**.

Finding an expert

2.136 It is not easy to find the right expert witness for a case. Asking other professionals in the same field of work about the experts they have instructed in similar situations can be productive. Qualifications are important, as are relevant experience, papers published and research projects. Those seeking further information should ask about the post-qualification training of the expert being considered. It is always useful to find out if a particular person has ever given evidence as a witness in court before, and if so, how many times.

Expert Witness Institute
Tel: 0870 366 6367
www.ewi.org.uk

Many organisations produce lists of experts. The problem with many lists is that those on the lists are self-referred and there is no guarantee of competence. It is wise, too, to beware of those private groups of experts who appear or claim to be able to cover all known cases and all known forensic science techniques. For more information on experts go to the Expert Witness Institute website at www.ewi.org.uk.

There is normally a shortage of experts in a number of fields which prevents the swift hearing of cases in some areas. A scheme to address this gap, proposed by the London Higher Specialist Training Schemes in Child and Adolescent Psychiatry for disciplines of child and adolescent psychiatry in Children Act work, organised by One Garden Court chambers and supported by the Family Justice Council, has been operating in the London area since September 2006. The scheme provides a formal mechanism for the recruitment and oversight of clinicians acting in the role of court reporter (referred to as 'Assessors' in the scheme). Such clinicians are experienced in their own field but new, or relatively new, to the role of court reporter. The objective of the scheme is to ensure that interested parties (the children concerned, the judiciary, child care lawyers and their clients and clinicians) are assured that forensic reporting work is undertaken to a high standard.

The scheme itself sets out a formal framework within which a court report will be accepted, prepared and presented. The roles of assessor and mentor are clearly defined. Whether an individual case is suitable for the scheme is a matter for the mentor and assessor to determine upon being invited to prepare a report subject to the scheme and is always subject to the direction of the court. Once a formal letter of instruction is received the mentor and assessor meet together to plan the assessment. The work necessary to complete the assessment is undertaken by the assessor.

In addition to the planning meeting between the mentor and assessor, the mentor meets the assessor at least once during the assessment in order to monitor the progress of the assessment. The mentor is available to offer telephone consultation throughout the assessment. The mentor meets the assessor at the conclusion of the assessment in order to consider its outcome. The report for court will be written by the assessor and he will attend court to give evidence.

Other organisations which may be able to provide information about expert witnesses include (but not exhaustively):

The Academy of Experts	www.academy-experts.org
Association for Child and Adolescent Mental Health	www.acamh.org.uk
Association of Clinical Pathologists	www.pathologists.org.uk
Association of Lawyers for Children	www.alc.org.uk
Faculty of Forensic and Legal Medicine	www.fflm.ac.uk/
British Academy of Forensic Sciences	www.bafs.org.uk
British Agencies for Adoption and Fostering	www.baaf.org.uk
British Association for Counselling	www.bacp.org.uk
British Association of Psychotherapists	www.bap-psychotherapy.org
British Association of Social Workers	www.basw.co.uk
British Psychological Society	www.bps.org.uk
CAMHS services	Local NHS
Family Rights Group	www.frg.org.uk
The Forensic Science Society	www.forensicsciencesociety.org.uk
Independent social workers	www.nagalro.org.uk
Local Law Societies	www.lawsociety.org.uk
Official Solicitor	www.officialsolicitor.gov.uk

Educational psychologists	www.aep.org.uk
Local education services	www.dfes.gov.uk
Royal College of Paediatrics and Child Health	www.rcpch.ac.uk
Royal College of Psychiatrists	www.rcpsych.ac.uk
United Kingdom Council for Psychotherapy (UKCP)	www.ukcp.org.uk
Lists, Registers and Directories	

Source	Title
UK Register of Expert Witnesses	www.jspubs.com/index.cfm
Expert Search	www.expertfamilylaw.co.uk/
Directory of Chartered Psychologists	www.bps.org.uk

The expert crisis

2.137   The contribution of forensic medical expertise in family court proceedings is unquestioned. The continuation of that contribution at the current level cannot be taken for granted. Multiple factors are deterring potential contributors from participating in family proceedings. In too many cases the expert evidence is being given by immensely experienced and respected child psychiatrists who have long since retired from their consultancies. An interdisciplinary search for solutions is essential and the responsibility for that lies as much with the users as with the providers of the expertise.

The introduction of the Public Law Outline highlighted the considerable delays caused by requesting experts' reports and new consultants' contracts constrained their participation. Altogether, specialists are much more wary of taking on expert work and some have withdrawn.

Media access

2.138   Concern across the family justice system in late 2009 regarding proposals to allow media access to court documents and reporting of the 'substance' of cases was unprecedented. The Children, Schools and Families Bill, published on 19 November 2009, outlined an automatic prohibition on reporting certain kinds of information allowing for the identification of children, parties or witnesses (but not experts instructed during proceedings) and contained a prohibition on publishing sensitive personal information, describing this as information regarding medical, psychological or psychiatric conditions, examination or evaluation of any person or information relating to health care, treatment or therapy (along with specification of purposes that would permit publication).

The Ministry of Justice indicated at that time a two-stage process for certain changes. A second stage, which might allow the lifting of restrictions on witness and sensitive information 'while still protecting the anonymity of children' would be put to a vote of both Houses of Parliament. This was to be revisited after a review of stage one and enabling clauses were contained in the Bill.

Media access and experts

2.139   The media are now being allowed into courts with the discretion of the judge or magistrates and are able to report on the proceedings. They are not permitted to divulge the identity of the child and family unless specifically directed by the judge so to do. As much of the evidence in family cases is in written form, including expert medical or other professional reports, listening to oral evidence alone will not enable the media to report fully and meaningfully. An anonymised transcript of the judgment provides the clearest summary of the evidence, the decision-making process and the reasons for the court's decisions. This process is now in the pilot stage.

It is now proposed that by 2012 the media will be allowed to read medical and other expert reports. This will pose serious difficulties for doctors and other professionals acting as expert witnesses, for a number of reasons. Experts are instructed on the basis that by using their clinical skills in meeting with family members they will be able to assist the court in its decision-making. The clinical professional is thus being utilised simultaneously as clinician and expert. The stock in trade of mental health professionals is their ability to converse with patients in a particular way so as to elicit information. To be of benefit to the patient and, in this case, also to the court, the context has to be one of trust – trust in the skill, expertise and integrity of the clinician, by both patient and court.

One of the fundamental assumptions underpinning clinical encounters is confidentiality. This is already being compromised by the knowledge that the clinician will be reporting to the court. In these circumstances, most patients/family members are able to extend the limits of confidentiality to include the court. There are issues which may be of importance and which a family member may not wish to discuss under these circumstances, compromising the quality of the expert report. That is an acceptable limitation.

However, for a clinician, it is inconceivable that one may now be put in a position of having to warn the patient that what is being discussed, almost invariably highly personal and often distressing, and already being necessarily included in one's report, will also be read by the media. It borders on insulting the family member and is thus unethical. It would also diminish significantly the quality of the clinical encounter and the information forthcoming. An assurance of anonymity is simply insufficient. Moreover, it is not currently even clear who, it is proposed, will carry out the anonymisation of the expert reports.

Source:
Danya Glaser
Consultant Child and
Adolescent Psychiatrist
Family Law,
October 2009

The GMC, the medical and other professional protection organisations and NHS-employing Trusts are yet to agree to this proposed clear breach of confidentiality. And the purpose? To appoint the media to interpret and judge the quality of expert evidence, until now assumed to be the task of the court.

THE POLICE

2.140   There are 45 police forces in England and Wales, each with their own practices, protocols, procedures and training as regards child protection and domestic violence. The main roles of the police are to uphold the law, prevent crime and disorder and protect the citizen. Children, like all citizens, have the right to the full protection offered by the criminal law. The police have a duty and responsibility to investigate all criminal offences and as Lord Laming pointed out in his report in 2003 into the circumstances leading to the death of Victoria Climbié whose suffering and death was attributed to gross failures in the child protection system:

> 'the investigation of crimes against children is as important as the investigation of any other serious crime and any suggestions that child protection policing is of lower status than any other form of policing should be eradicated'.

Offences committed against children can be particularly sensitive and will often require the police to work with other organisations, such as children's social care, in the conduct of any investigation. The police recognise the fundamental importance of inter-agency working in combating child abuse, as illustrated by well-established arrangements for joint training involving police and social work colleagues. All forces have child abuse investigation units (CAIUs), and despite variations in their structures and staffing levels, they will normally take primary responsibility for investigating child abuse cases. A guidance document, *Investigating Child Abuse and Safeguarding Children*, was published by the Association of Chief Police Officers (ACPO) in 2005, which sets out the suggested investigative doctrine, and terms of reference, for such units.

Safeguarding children is not solely the role of CAIU officers, it is a fundamental part of the duties of all police officers. Patrol officers attending domestic violence incidents, for example, are aware of the effect of such violence on any children normally resident within the household. The Children Act 2004 places a wider duty on the police to 'safeguard and promote the welfare of children'.

The police hold important information about children who may be at risk of harm as well as those who cause such harm. They share information and intelligence with other organisations where this is necessary to protect children. Similarly, they expect other organisations to share with them information and intelligence they hold to enable the police to carry out their duties.

The police are responsible for the gathering of evidence in criminal investigations. This task can be carried out in conjunction with other agencies but the police are ultimately accountable for the product of criminal enquiries. Evidence gathered may be of use to local authority solicitors who are preparing for civil proceedings to protect the victim. The Crown Prosecution Service (CPS) is usually consulted, but evidence will normally be shared if it is in the best interests of the child.

The police should be notified as soon as possible where a criminal offence has been committed, or is suspected of having been committed, against a child. This does not mean that in all such cases a full investigation will be required, or that there will necessarily be any further police involvement. It is important, however, that the police retain the opportunity to be informed and consulted, to ensure all relevant information can be taken into account before a final decision is made. Local Safeguarding Children Boards (see **3.83**) will have in place a protocol agreed between the local authority and the police, to guide both organisations in deciding how child protection enquiries should be conducted and, in particular, the circumstances in which joint enquiries are appropriate.

Source:
Working Together
to Safeguard Children
(2006)
www.dcsf.gov.uk/
everychildmatters

In addition to their duty to investigate criminal offences, the police have emergency powers to enter premises and ensure the immediate protection of children believed to be suffering from, or at risk of, significant harm. Such powers are used only when necessary, the principle being that wherever possible the decision to remove a child from a parent or carer should be made by a court.

Prosecuting domestic violence

2.141   The police service has a major part to play in responding to domestic violence as the foremost 24-hour emergency service. All forces have set up dedicated domestic violence units or appointed officers to deal specifically with domestic violence cases and to liaise with other agencies in the field. All forces now have policies which emphasise the overriding duty to protect victims and children from further attack and the need to treat domestic violence as seriously as other forms of violence. The police have taken a particularly active role in promoting and developing domestic violence forums throughout England and Wales and are the most widely represented of all agencies on local multi-disciplinary initiatives.

Where the police are called to an incident or threatened incident of violence in the home involving an adult or child, the officers attending will have to decide whether a criminal offence which justifies an arrest has been committed, such as assault, criminal damage or the use or threat of violence to gain entry to the home. If arrested, the alleged perpetrator will be charged if sufficient evidence is obtained from medical examination of the victim and the victim's statement. If the case continues through the criminal justice system it can be made a condition of bail that the defendant does not go near the victim or the victim's home. The Protection from Harassment Act 1997 is designed to assist in protecting victims of domestic violence through the criminal courts. Restraining orders can be made on conviction, prohibiting the defendant from doing anything described in the order, for the purpose of protecting the victim from further harassment or fear of violence. Compensation can also be ordered by the criminal courts.

Another way of protecting (usually) women and children is through the civil courts under the Family Law Act 1996. Non-molestation orders and occupation orders can:

- restrain the other party from using violence against the applicant;
- restrain the other party from using violence against a child living with the applicant; or
- exclude the other party from the matrimonial home or the area surrounding the home.

An order can include a power of arrest which empowers the police to arrest the perpetrator if he breaches the terms of the injunction. He will then be brought before the county court judge and be punished for contempt of court, inevitably by imprisonment.

The Domestic Violence Crime and Victims Act 2004 introduced additional remedies:

- restraining orders can be made on conviction or acquittal for any offence where the court considers it necessary;
- breaches of non-molestation orders under the Family Law Act 1996 (see below) are made a criminal offence;
- those who have never married or cohabited can seek protection under the Family Law Act 1996.

Police domestic violence units

2.142   There are a number of police domestic violence units, which have staff specially trained to help people experiencing domestic violence. They work closely with other organisations such as local solicitors and Women's Aid groups.

Inter-agency co-operation

2.143   The police are often the first point of contact with families in which domestic violence takes place. When responding to incidents of violence, the police should find out whether there are any children living in the household. They should see any children present in the house to assess their immediate safety. There should be arrangements in place between police and children's social care, to enable the police to find out whether any such children are the subject of a child protection plan. The police are already required to determine whether any court orders or injunctions are in force in respect of members of the household. It is good practice for the police to notify children's social care promptly when they have responded to an incident of domestic violence and it is known that a child is a member of the household. If the police have specific concerns about the safety or welfare of a child, they should make a referral to children's social care citing the basis for their concerns. It is also important that there is clarity about whether the family is aware that a referral is to be made. Any response by children's social care to such referrals should be discreet, in terms of making contact with women in ways that will not further endanger them or their children.

In some cases, a child may be in need of immediate protection. The amendment made in s 120 of the Adoption and Children Act 2002 to the Children Act 1989 clarifies the meaning of harm in order to make explicit that 'harm' includes, for example, impairment suffered from seeing or hearing the ill-treatment of another.

The guidance can be downloaded from http://www.everychild matters.gov.uk/resources-and-practice/IG00182/

The Department of Health published in 2006 a children's services guidance *What to do if you're worried a child is being abused*. This document provides best practice guidance for those who work with children in order to safeguard their welfare. It also contains an appendix to help practitioners with the legal issues affecting the sharing of information. It provides general information for anyone whose work brings them into contact with children and families, focusing particularly on those who work in social care, health, education and also the criminal justice system.

Domestic violence forums

2.144 Police forces are involved in local domestic violence initiatives. Domestic Violence Forums have been set up in most areas, to raise awareness of domestic violence, to promote coordination between agencies in preventing and responding to violence, and to encourage the development of services for those who are subjected to violence or suffer its effects. Each

Domestic Violence Forum and Local Safeguarding
Children Board (LSCB) has clearly defined links, which
should include cross-membership and identifying and
working together on areas of common interest. The
Domestic Violence Forum and LSCB should jointly
contribute, in the context of the Children and Young
Persons Plan (each local area's single, strategic,
overarching plan for all services affecting children and
young people), to an assessment of the incidence of
children caught up in domestic violence, their needs, the
adequacy of local arrangements to meet those needs,
and the implications for local services. Other work
might include developing joint protocols, safe
information sharing arrangements and training.

Police powers, child protection and criminal investigation

2.145   In child abuse cases, the police focus is to
determine whether a criminal offence has been
committed, to identify the person or persons
responsible and to secure the best possible evidence in
order that the Crown Prosecution Service (CPS) can
decide whether a criminal prosecution should be
brought. The decision whether or not to initiate a
prosecution is based on:

- whether there is enough evidence;
- whether it is in the public interest that a particular
  offender should be prosecuted;
- whether or not it is in the child victim's interests to
  prosecute.

A case has to be proved against the defendant in the
criminal courts 'beyond reasonable doubt'. The burden
of proof rests with the prosecution: that is, the
defendant does not have to prove that he is innocent. In
civil cases, such as private and public law proceedings
under the Children Act, the standard of proof is 'the
balance of probabilities'. The CPS may drop a case
against a defendant in the criminal courts because there
is not enough evidence to meet the higher standard of
proof but a case may still be made out in care
proceedings to protect the child from the same
individual because the standard of proof (ie the
balance of probabilities) is lower in the civil (family)
courts. The information which the police collect should,
where appropriate, be shared with other child protection
agencies, irrespective of the decision whether or not to
prosecute.

Child protection: joint investigation

2.146   There has to be a close working relationship between police, social services, medical practitioners, schools and others in the area of child protection both in terms of practice, planning and training. For example, as regards joint inter-agency investigations by police and social services, specialist staff should be selected for proper inter-agency training. Joint working should be established over and above the joint interviewing of child victims. There should be adequate planning and full consultation at all stages of an investigation. Those engaged in such investigations and their supervisors must understand the responsibilities of the two agencies, the powers available to them and the different standards of proof.

Police involvement in child abuse investigation stems from an overriding consideration of the welfare of the child and not only from their traditional responsibility to protect the community. They bring their own professional perspective which is concerned to marshal evidence and secure prosecution.

Different roles and responsibilities are adopted by social workers and police officers in child protection investigations despite the increasing emphasis on joint interviewing. Social workers are primarily concerned to predict the risk of child abuse while police officers concentrate on the likelihood of a crime having been committed. Social workers mainly focus their involvement on women and children while police officers concentrate on male perpetrators. Police are primarily concerned with gathering evidence, and research has shown that they express concern about social workers asking leading questions or discussing the alleged crime with the perpetrator, fearing contamination of the evidence which could affect subsequent legal proceedings.

Police protection

2.147   Local authorities and the police can apply under the Children Act 1989 for an emergency protection order (EPO) which gives them the power to remove a child from the child's home. If there is a fear that a person on the premises might be violent, the court can issue a warrant so that a police officer can assist in enforcing the EPO. An alleged perpetrator can be removed from the home instead of the child. The police have an emergency power under s 46 of the Children Act not available to other child protection agencies to detain a child in a place of protection without first applying to a court. The ground for action is that the police have reasonable cause to believe that the child would otherwise suffer significant harm. The police also have the power under s 46 to make sure that a child remains in suitable accommodation such as a hospital. Each police area must have a 'designated police officer' responsible for carrying out the duties imposed by the Children Act.

Assisting children's services departments

2.148 Warrants empowering police to enter premises and search for children can be obtained by children's services departments under s 102 of the Children Act 1989. In extreme cases, police officers can exercise their power under s 17 of the Police and Criminal Evidence Act 1984 to enter any premises and to search for and remove a child. Under this provision, no court order is required.

Police checks

2.149 Local authorities are under a duty to check with local police forces for the possible criminal background of those who apply to work with children including staff, volunteers, child-minders, those providing day care and foster parents.

Youth crime and youth justice

2.150 Major risk factors that increase the chances of young people committing crimes are:

- troubled home life;
- poor attainment at school, truancy and school exclusion;
- drug or alcohol misuse and mental illness;
- deprivation such as poor housing or homelessness;
- peer group pressure.

In 1998 and 1999 a number of new sentences and interventions were introduced designed to prevent offending and reoffending, some of which include:

- Referral Orders – The young person is required to agree a contract of behaviour with his parents/guardians and the victim (where appropriate), to repair the harm caused by the offence and address the causes of the offending behaviour.

- Action Plan Orders – 3-month, intensively supervised community service programmes focusing on education and involving the young person's parents/guardians.
- Reparation Orders – Court orders requiring a young person to repair the harm caused to an individual or the community, for example, through mediation or community service work.
- Parenting Orders – A requirement for parents to attend counselling and guidance sessions where they receive help in dealing with their children.
- Electronic Tagging, as part of an Intensive Supervision and Surveillance Programme (ISSP) – For the most persistent offenders aged 12–16 year olds, on bail or on remand in local authority accommodation.

Youth offending teams (YOTs) include representatives from the police, social services, health, education and housing. Their job is to identify the needs of each young offender and identify the problems that make the young person offend, as well as measuring the risk they pose to others. This enables the YOT to identify suitable programmes to address the needs of the young person, so they can be rehabilitated, through:

- education, training or employment;
- drug rehabilitation;
- mental health assessment and treatment;
- provision of accommodation.

For further information see: www.homeoffice. gov.uk/crime-victims/ reducing-crime/youth-crime

Private law

Search and recovery orders

2.151 Under the Family Law Act 1986, the court can make an order authorising a court officer or a police officer to take charge of a child and deliver him or her to a particular person. This may be as a result of a change of residence on a residence order or returning a child after a period of contact. With such an order, the police have the authority to enter and search premises for the child and to use necessary force to enforce the order.

Enforcing Section 8 (residence and contact) orders

2.152   Police officers can be called upon to provide a
police presence in order to prevent a breach of the
peace after a residence order or contact order has been
made when one of the parties was not in court. Courts
are entitled to expect that people who apply for ex parte
orders (ie orders made where only the applying party is
present in court) and their legal advisers will be
scrupulous in putting such orders into effect.

Child abduction

2.153   If child abduction takes place, the fact that a
criminal offence may have been committed will lead to
police involvement, which in turn may assist in the
recovery of the child. Where a police officer has
reasonable grounds for suspecting that a person is
attempting to commit, or is about to commit, an
offence under the Child Abduction Act 1984 he can
arrest the suspect and prevent the abduction. If the
abduction takes place and the child is still in the UK,
utilising police resources can be the most effective
means, if only in the short term, of tracing not only the
child but also the abductor who may well have
committed other offences such as criminal damage or
assault. The abductor might also be in contempt of a
court order with a power of arrest.

If the child is removed from the UK, extradition
proceedings can begin, but only if an extradition treaty
exists with the country where the abductor has gone,
and technically only the abductor has to be returned,
not the child. (For return of the child, if the country to
which the child has been taken is a part of the Hague
Convention and/or the European Convention those
procedures apply.) If the police are notified that an
attempt may be made to remove a child unlawfully from
the UK, they can, through their national computer
system, alert all other police forces and notify
immigration officers of the details of the child at risk.
This 'port alert' or 'port stop' system means that
immigration officers at all UK ports, including airports,
hold the child's name for 4 weeks. To set up a port
alert, an order such as an injunction under wardship or
a prohibited steps order under the Children Act 1989
must have been made.

*Further information
from:*
reunite
Advice Line: 0116 2556
234
Tel: 0116 2555 345
www.reunite.org

THE CROWN PROSECUTION SERVICE

2.154 The police collect evidence and charge offenders but it is the Crown Prosecution Service (CPS) which decides whether to prosecute, e g child and partner abusers. The CPS has a Domestic Violence Policy, a recent innovation being the introduction of domestic violence coordinators, supported by specialist prosecutors, who ensure effective preparation of domestic violence cases and have an important role to play in improving current practices and procedures. Advice is now available 24 hours a day to the police in most areas. The Domestic Violence Project is currently undertaking research into the work of specialist domestic violence courts. For some time, the problem of ensuring that perpetrators are punished if the victim retracts their statements have posed problems. The CPS is keen to ensure that retraction no longer prevents an effective prosecution. Polaroid and digital photos taken by the police, and the potential use of expert witnesses relying upon research findings are both options with which to support the prosecution case. A witness care programme now ensures that victims are kept informed and support is given by using lay advocates to advise them. Further consultations to revise current policy and to improve the position of victims are currently underway.

The CPS also supports the child's 'right' to give evidence. In contrast with family proceedings before the civil courts, the CPS suggests that a child should provide evidence in criminal proceedings if they wish to do so, even where the parent objects.

INTERDISCIPLINARY TRAINING

2.155 The Family Justice Council has put together a chart which highlights the elements of interdisciplinary training that the key professional groups in the family justice system undertake as part of basic training, post qualification training and continuing professional development. The chart can be viewed at http://www.family-justice-council.org.uk/docs/MappingExercise_Chart.pdf

INSPECTION OF THE FAMILY JUSTICE SYSTEM

2.156 Independent inspection is an important part of the family justice system. Not all the professionals in chapter 2 are subject to independent inspection but the following are.

Ofsted

2.157 Ofsted (the Office for Standards in Education, Children's Services and Skills) inspects or regulates the following services in England:

- Cafcass;
- adoption and fostering agencies;
- the quality of services and outcomes for children and young people in each local authority;
- residential schools, family centres and homes for children;
- childminders;
- childcare on domestic premises;
- childcare on non-domestic premises;
- all state maintained schools;
- some independent schools;
- pupil referral units;
- further education;
- initial teacher training;
- publicly funded adult skills and employment based training;
- learning in prisons, the secure estate and probation.

www.ofsted.gov.uk

Social workers

2.158 The Care Quality Commission is the independent regulator of health and social care in England. It regulates health and adult social care services, whether provided by the NHS, local authorities, private companies or voluntary organisations. It protects the rights of people detained under the Mental Health Act.

www.cqc.org.uk

Local authorities

2.159 Ofsted publishes its reports on all individual local authorities' children's and local services including Annual Performance Assessments, Joint Area Reviews, Youth Service Inspection Reports, Tellus2 Reports, adoption and fostering services, and other authority-wide reports. They can be viewed on: http://www.ofsted.gov.uk/oxcare_providers/list_by_la.

Health Service

2.160 See the Care Quality Commission at **2.158**.

Police

http://inspectorates. homeoffice. gov.uk/hmic/

2.161 Her Majesty's Inspectorate of Constabulary for England and Wales (HMIC) examines and improves the efficiency of the Police Service in England and Wales. Her Majesty's Inspectors of Constabulary are appointed by the Crown on the recommendation of the Home Secretary and report to Her Majesty's Chief Inspector of Constabulary (HMCIC), who is the Home Secretary's principal professional policing adviser. The HMCIC is independent both of the Home Office and of the Police Service.

Her Majesty's Courts Service

www.hmica.gov.uk

2.162 Her Majesty's Inspectorate of Court Administration (HMICA) has a duty, under the Courts Act 2003, to inspect the systems that support the Crown, county and magistrates' courts in England and Wales. HMICA's former responsibilities for the inspection of Cafcass have been transferred to Ofsted (see above). For more about Her Majesty's Courts Service (HMCS) see **3.2**.

CHAPTER THREE

THE SYSTEMS

THE LEGAL SYSTEM

3.1   Family law is primarily concerned with how families are to manage their day-to-day lives in the future and, in family life, disagreements and arguments are common even in contented and stable families. Although there is a useful place for lawyers and courts in family disputes, their role needs to be defined carefully to ensure that litigation is an extreme last resort and that the mere availability of the courts does not distort family life or lead to unreal expectations. Parents should be seen and treated as having the primary responsibility for securing their children's and family's welfare.

Family proceedings fall into the categories of either 'public law' or 'private law'. Public law cases involve the state intervening in the family to protect and promote the welfare and best interests of children. The state is usually represented by a local authority social services department, and examples of such cases would be care proceedings, applications for supervision orders, emergency protection orders and adoption. Private law cases involve disputes between individuals usually arising out of divorce, dissolution of a civil (same sex) partnership or separation after cohabitation. Inevitably, when the protection of children in private law disputes is at issue, the two categories can overlap.

The family justice system is not, of course, solely concerned with children. On divorce, all couples, whether parents or not, have to make decisions about dividing up their finances and property. It is beyond the scope of this book to explain the ins and outs of what is called 'ancillary relief', but people going through divorce or separation and who have children are aware that the process of dividing property and money and the welfare of their children are inextricably linked. Moreover, at least married people have the benefit of statute law to guide their decisions about money and property. Unmarried people have much more restricted legal protection and must depend on the limitations of the general law of property.

A further situation in which families can become involved in the court system is as a result of domestic violence. The government has acknowledged that it has a particular responsibility to make sure that the combined family and criminal justice systems provide an effective route to protection and that perpetrators of violence are brought to justice. Significant changes have been brought into play over the last 4 years to tighten up forms of protection for victims of domestic violence and the question of which court is most appropriate in which circumstance is no longer as straightforward as it might have been. Also, the different remedies available may well overlap. For example, any court granting an order resulting from domestic violence can at the same time make an order under s 8 of the Children Act 1989 as to the residence of the parents' children and the non-resident parent's contact with them. A wife or cohabitee can issue proceedings excluding her husband or partner from the family home, and her husband or partner can apply for a contact order in the same proceedings in order to keep in touch with his children (whether such an order would be in the children's best interests following violence perpetrated to the mother is another question). Lawyers, mediators and courts try to separate out the issues so that the welfare of children does not become a bargaining factor, for example regarding the division of property or money.

There is, as yet, no single comprehensive family court although the Children Act 1989 has done a lot to promote a unified approach (and see further at **3.14**). Family proceedings can take place in family proceedings courts, county courts and in the High Court, as well as coming into play in criminal courts. However, Her Majesty's Courts Service (HMCS) has been developing specialist family centres (SFCs) for some time now, the strategy being for county courts and family proceedings courts to work together as one regional unit to achieve greater flexibility in the use of resources and a seamless transfer of family work between Family Proceedings Courts, County Courts, and even the High Court in some circumstances. In SFCs, lay justices, District Judges, Circuit Judges and sometimes Circuit Judges 'sitting' as High Court judges now work together in their different courts but in the same building, hearing cases at all these various levels.

Families can, of course, come into contact with lawyers and the courts in many other contexts, for example:

- the making of wills;
- disputes about inheritance and succession;
- disputes about the validity of marriages;
- insolvency.

The Structure of the Courts

Royal Courts of
Justice
Tel: 020 7947 6000

3.2   Her Majesty's Courts Service (HMCS) brought together for the first time in 2005 the Magistrates' Courts Service and Court Service into one single organisation within the Ministry of Justice (MoJ). HMCS was launched on 1 April 2005, linking the administration of magistrates', Crown, county and High Courts together for the first time. HMCS is now responsible for the administration of more than 600 civil, family and criminal courts in England and Wales. HMCS works in partnership with 23 Courts Boards on which each has local representation. The Courts Boards scrutinise, review and make recommendations about how local courts are run, where they are located and how the level of service for court users can be improved. They are not involved in judicial decisions but fulfil an advisory role to identify and meet local needs. HMCS has 23 areas, each with an Area Director. These match the current criminal justice system areas and the areas in which the Local Family Justice Councils (see **1.15**) have been formed.

The Courts

Magistrates' (Family Proceedings) Courts

3.3   Magistrates who deal with family cases are drawn from a family panel of specially selected magistrates and will have received specific training. Based on guidance given by the Judicial Studies Board, family panel members are required:

- to develop skills in communicating with parties during the proceedings, in making decisions and in giving reasons for those decisions;
- to gain knowledge and understanding of the role of other bodies and persons involved in the proceedings and the support they can provide to children in need.

Like all magistrates, family panel justices cannot sit in court without a legally qualified legal advisor to give them legal advice.

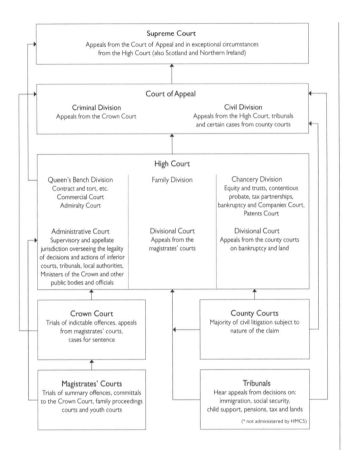

Family panel justices can hear contested section 8
Children Act applications (generally residence and
contact disputes) and can make those orders, but they
cannot deal with divorce-related matters. Justices deal
with emergency protection orders, care proceedings and
all other public law matters. Cases of complexity,
gravity, importance, or which would otherwise result in
unacceptable delay, can be transferred to a higher court,
but there is now a movement to keep as many cases as
possible in the family proceedings courts and to transfer
them down from the county court. Family justices have
powers in relation to matters concerning the occupation
of the family home and domestic violence but they
cannot deal with the transfer of tenancies.

Magistrates' Association
Tel: 020 7387 2353
www.magistratesassociation.
org.uk

Justices' Clerk and Legal Advisers

3.4   A justices' clerk is responsible for:

•   the legal advice tendered to the justices within the
        area;

- the performance of any of the functions set out below by any member of his staff acting as legal adviser;
- ensuring that competent advice is available to justices when the justices' clerk is not personally present in court;
- the effective delivery of case management and the reduction of unnecessary delay.

Justices' Clerks Society
Tel: 0151 255 0790
www.jc-society.co.uk

Justices' clerks rarely sit in court. However, they are available to give advice on matters of law, procedure and practice to both legal advisers and magistrates.

Legal advisers sit in court with magistrates, organise the day's proceedings and give magistrates legal advice on:

- questions of law (including European Court of Human Rights jurisprudence and the Human Rights Act 1998);
- questions of mixed law and fact;
- matters of practice and procedure;
- any relevant decisions of the superior courts or other guidelines;
- other issues relevant to the matter before the court;
- the appropriate decision-making structure to be applied in any given case.

Legal advisers assist magistrates with the formulation of their reasons for a decision and the recording of those reasons. They can also deal with certain directions, adjournments and other matters on their own using powers delegated by the Justices' Clerk in accordance with the Justices' Clerks Rules 2005. Legal advisers' case management role was viewed as vital by High Court judges during the review of the Public Law Protocol which came into operation in November 2003. It was said that legal advisers' unique combination of a delegated judicial jurisdiction and an administrative role was an example of best practice that could be shared with care centres in a unified family service.

District Judges (Magistrates' Courts)

3.5   District judges (magistrates' courts) sit permanently in magistrates' courts, mostly dealing with criminal matters. Some have the same jurisdiction as lay family panel members.

County Courts

3.6 There are four types of county court:

(1) Non-divorce county courts which cannot deal with children's matters but can deal with domestic violence.

(2) Divorce county courts where all private law proceedings can start but contested matters must be transferred to family hearing centres for trial.

(3) Family hearing centres which can deal with contested private law matters and make section 8 orders.

(4) Care centres which have full jurisdiction in all public law and private law matters.

All actions for divorce, judicial separation or nullity begin in a divorce county court, which has jurisdiction to deal with matrimonial cases. In London, the Principal Registry also acts as a divorce county court. Most work is carried out by district judges but appeals and defended matters are heard by circuit judges. The county courts make most of the injunctions in cases of domestic violence both in respect of married and unmarried partners.

In the county court, four grades of judge exercise differing levels of responsibility.

District judges can:

- pronounce a divorce decree nisi;

- consider arrangements for the children of divorcing parents;

- hear contested Children Act applications on issues relating to residence, contact and parental responsibility;

- grant domestic violence injunctions including power of arrest (but they cannot send a person to prison);

- make an ancillary relief order;

- make an anti-social behaviour order (ASBO);

- specialist district judges can deal with care proceedings.

Association of District Judges
Tel: 020 8333 4397
www.juduciary.gov.uk

In due course, mirror proceedings to divorce proceedings for dissolution or separation arising out of civil partnerships that have broken down and ancillary relief applications made as a result will come the way of district judges in specified county courts. There are currently 415 district judges authorised to hear family law in the county courts: the number of family law district judges changes according to the necessary business demand.

Circuit judges have full private law jurisdiction and deal mainly, by way of hearings, with applications that remain disputed.

Nominated recorders with family law tickets have the jurisdiction to try public law cases in the county court.

Care judges are also circuit judges and are based at care centres. They have full private and public law jurisdiction.

Source:
www.judiciary.gov.uk

Designated family judges are based at care centres and have full private and public law jurisdiction. They have a responsibility to chair the Local Family Justice Councils (see **1.15**). For fuller detail of which judge in which court for which proceedings see www.hmcourts-service.gov.uk – information about – judges.

Family Division of the High Court

Principal Registry
Tel: 020 7947 6000

3.7   The Family Division of the High Court has full jurisdiction to hear all cases regarding divorce and children, including private wardship proceedings. At present, there are about 15 judges in the Family Division who are headed by the President of the Family Division. Cases should be transferred up to the High Court from the lower courts in exceptional circumstances, for example where case-law could be made or where the case is a complex one or involves substantial assets.

Cases are only dealt with in the High Court if they are complex, difficult or serious. If, for example, a financial dispute involves substantial sums of money invested in complex assets and perhaps one party is not revealing his total wealth, the county court can decline jurisdiction and transfer the case to the High Court. The costs involved are prohibitive.

Administrative Court and Court of Protection

3.8   The jurisdiction on the Administrative Court is varied, consisting of the administrative law jurisdiction as well as a supervisory jurisdiction over inferior courts and tribunals. The supervisory jurisdiction, exercised in the main through the procedure of judicial review, covers persons or bodies exercising a public law function – a wide and still growing field. Examples of the types of decision which may fall within the range of judicial review include:

- decisions of local authorities in the exercise of their duties to provide various welfare benefits and special education for children in need of such education;
- certain decisions of the immigration authorities.

Since the January 2007 report, 'Justice Outside London', the Administrative Court has been regionalised so that its huge workload can be addressed more effectively. Administrative Court Centres have now operated in Cardiff, Birmingham, Leeds and Manchester since April 2009 and cases can be issued, administered and heard in each of these. High Court Judges regularly travel to these regions to sit there, together with locally based Deputy High Court Judges.

The Court of Protection is a specialist court created under the Mental Capacity Act 2005. It makes specific decisions, and also appoints other people (called deputies) to make decisions for people who lack the capacity to do this for themselves. These decisions are related to their property, financial affairs, health, and personal welfare. The Court of Protection replaced the former Office of the Supreme Court with the same name but which only dealt with property and financial affairs.

Court of Appeal

3.9   The Court of Appeal, which sits in London at the Royal Courts of Justice, consists of two divisions:

(1)   The Civil Division, which hears appeals from:

- the three divisions of the High Court (Chancery, Queen's Bench and Family Division);
- the county courts;
- certain tribunals such as the Asylum and Immigration Tribunal and the Social Security Commissioners.

(2)   The Criminal Division, which hears appeals from the Crown Court.

Court of Appeal
Civil Division
Tel: 020 7947 7882

The Supreme Court

The Supreme Court
Tel 020 7960 1500
Email
enquiries@supremecourt.
gsi.gov.uk
www.supremecourt.
gov.uk

3.10 The House of Lords was historically the highest court of appeal in the country until 30 July 2009. In October 2009, the Supreme Court took its place, having been created by the Constitutional Reform Act 2005 as part of a significant programme of constitutional change which sought as its culmination to transform the final court of appeal into a fully independent institution. The Supreme Court now acts as the final court on points of law for the whole of the United Kingdom in civil cases and for England, Wales and Northern Ireland in criminal cases. Its decisions bind all courts below. The Law Lords of the House of Lords have now been replaced by, or recreated as, Justices of the Supreme Court.

Local Court Activities

Local Family Justice Councils

3.11 Local Family Justice Councils (LFJCs) were set up under the auspices of the main Family Justice Council in 2005 (see further **1.15**).

Family Court Business Committees

3.12 An established network of Family Court Business Committees, Family Court Forums and Court User Groups handle operational aspects of the family courts at local level. They report to their LFJC and their work includes monitoring the performance of the courts in their area.

Professional Groups

Association of Lawyers
for Children
Tel: 020 8224 7071
www.alc.org.uk

3.13 In any particular area professional groups will be found which are encouraged to invite speakers from, and mix with, other disciplines. For example, family panels of justices will meet about four times a year, solicitors will form local groups under the auspices of Resolution (see **2.13**) or the Association of Lawyers for Children (see **2.18**), and barristers who practice in family law meet for discussions and hear expert speakers as part of the Family Law Bar Association (see **2.20**).

A Single Family Court

3.14 Work is progressing towards establishing a unified family court in each region in which judges of all these various levels will sit, with agreements being formulated to devise regional frameworks for each region's family courts and to improve the throughput and consistency of performance for those who use them. The recently built Manchester Civil Justice Centre, consisting of 47 courts and which opened in October 2007, is one such example of a large new court complex. In time, the Civil Division of the Court of Appeal would be incorporated into such court complexes, together with the Administrative Court and the Commercial Court. If a single Family Court were established within such complexes, it would occupy a family court centre located over several floors within the complex, where the various levels of judges would sit in their respective courts, including the lay magistrates and district judges (magistrates' courts) who currently sit in the family proceedings courts. Family panel justices can now also become more specialised and spend considerably less time adjudicating in the magistrates' (criminal) courts.

A Single Civil Court (DCA, 2005)

Types of Proceedings

(a) Children Cases

3.15 The Children Act 1989 established concurrent jurisdiction between family proceedings courts, county courts and the High Court in cases concerning children; cases can be transferred to the appropriate level for hearing. Public law cases (eg all care proceedings) usually start in the family proceedings court. Private law cases (eg residence and contact) usually now start in the county court. Where there are already proceedings for divorce which are pending (that is, no final order has been made) any private law applications under the Children Act 1989 must be made in the same proceedings, which will be in the divorce county court. An application to vary, extend or discharge an existing private law order must be made to the court which made the original order. Some cases will be transferred from the family proceedings court to the county court or the High Court. The court procedure will be the same but the case will be heard by a judge rather than a magistrate. Private and public law cases can be transferred down from the county court to family proceedings courts. If the magistrates refuse a request to transfer up then the parties can appeal to the county court.

Texts of Acts can be viewed on www.opsi.gov.uk

The court can make a different order from the one requested. Section 1 of the Children Act 1989 states that when reaching its decision the court must be sure that making the order would be better for the child than making no order at all.

(b) Family Homes and Domestic Violence

3.16 The Protection from Harassment Act 1997 is designed to assist in protecting victims of domestic violence through the criminal courts. Restraining orders can be made prohibiting the defendant from doing anything described in the order, for the purpose of protecting the victim from further harassment or fear of violence. Compensation can also be ordered by the criminal courts. Another way of protecting (usually) women and children is through the civil courts under the Family Law Act 1996 using non-molestation orders and occupation orders. An occupation order can include a power of arrest which empowers the police to arrest the perpetrator if he breaches the terms of the injunction. He will then be brought before the county court judge and be punished for contempt of court, inevitably by imprisonment. The new Domestic Violence Crime and Victims Act 2004 introduced additional remedies in the criminal and county courts and made it a criminal offence to breach a non-molestation order: perpetrators of breaches of these orders are now dealt with by the criminal courts even though the non-molestation order itself was originally made in a civil court.

This is all confusing and can lead to the same set of circumstances giving rise to proceedings in the criminal and county courts. If a perpetrator breaches both an occupation order which has a power of arrest attached to it and a non-molestation order then it is likely that only a family court could deal with the breaches as the criminal courts cannot deal with breaches of occupation orders. However, it is not common for both orders to be made concurrently in the same proceedings.

(c) Divorce and Finance

3.17 Divorce, nullity and judicial separation proceedings, including financial matters and arrangements for the children arising from them, are dealt with in the county courts and rarely the High

Court. Family proceedings courts do not have jurisdiction in these matters but they can enforce financial orders made in other courts. They enforce Child Support Agency arrears and they have jurisdiction under domestic violence legislation and matters relating to the occupation of the family home. They also deal with many domestic violence offences (eg common assault and causing actual/grievous bodily harm) in their criminal jurisdiction.

Procedures in Court

Divorce and Judicial Separation

3.18   Divorce is a legal process, which is carried out by the civil courts. The procedure begins with a petition and ends with a decree absolute, which dissolves the marriage. The timescale to complete the process differs from case to case. Separate but related issues arising from divorce that need to be resolved often include practical arrangements for the care of any children and future financial arrangements between the couple concerned. Those issues may in practice take precedence over the actual divorce itself.

A divorce petition cannot be issued unless the marriage has existed for more than one year. It does not matter where the marriage took place but it does matter where the couple are living at the time the petition is issued. The issue of where each person normally lives or connections they may have abroad may have to be considered by the courts, to determine whether a court has authority to deal with a particular divorce (known as 'the court's jurisdiction'). These matters, known as domicile and residence, can be complex but they can result in significant differences in the final financial arrangements granted to either party.

A divorce petition has to be accompanied by either the original or an official copy of the marriage certificate.

The only ground for divorce is that the marriage has irretrievably broken down. This is proved by establishing the existence of one of five factual circumstances. These are:

(a)   One spouse has committed adultery and the other finds it intolerable to continue to live with him/her. (This is the only ground which does not apply to a civil partnership.)

(b) One spouse has behaved in such a way that it would be unreasonable to expect the other to continue live with him/her.

(c) One spouse has deserted the other for a continuous period of 2 years or more.

(d) The couple has been living apart for 2 years or more and both parties agree to the divorce.

(e) One spouse has been living apart from the other for 5 years or more, whether or not both agree to the divorce.

It is no longer compulsory in a petition based on adultery to name the third person concerned.

The basis of the divorce does not have to be agreed but it is best to establish whether or not there is likely to be any opposition to the petition before it is issued at court. A divorce petition is a standard court form. It contains basic information about the names and addresses of the couple concerned, details of any children and a statement that the marriage has irretrievably broken down. It will also state the basis of the petition, such as adultery or behaviour. The contents of the petition must be true.

The petition concludes with a section known as the 'prayer' which sets out what is being sought. It therefore includes a request that the marriage be dissolved and may also include a request for the other spouse to pay some, or all, of the costs of the divorce. In addition, a request is usually made for an order for financial provision to be made by the court (known as 'ancillary relief').

A standard court form accompanies the divorce petition which outlines the current and proposed arrangements for any children of the family under the age of 16 or between 16 and 18 but still in secondary education. This includes details such as where and with whom the children live, which schools they attend, who looks after them and how often they see the other parent. This is known as a 'statement of arrangements'. The law encourages couples to reach an agreement over future arrangements for their children without the need for a court to become involved. As a matter of good practice the statement of arrangements should be sent to the other parent for agreement before the divorce petition is issued.

Parties only need to attend a hearing dealing with the divorce if the proceedings are contested. They may have to attend court if they are unable to agree arrangements for their children or for financial provision. Court proceedings in family law are usually held in private although from 27 April 2009, accredited media have been allowed to attend all levels of family courts. The court is still able to restrict attendance if, for example the welfare of a child requires it, or for the safety and protection of parties or witnesses. Media representatives who attend family courts must be holders of the UK Press Card.

Negotiations in relation to financial arrangements for the future can take place at any time before, during or after the divorce. It is usually not necessary for negotiations to have been completed before the divorce can be finalised. Particular issues, such as maintenance, may need to be resolved in advance of an overall settlement being reached. Neither party to the marriage is free to remarry until the final decree of divorce has been made (known as the 'decree absolute').

Source:
Resolution
www.resolution.org.uk

A decree of judicial separation is not a divorce and the parties remain married but, in effect, all the normal marital obligations come to an end. A decree of judicial separation can be granted for any of the grounds which would justify a divorce – unreasonable behaviour, adultery etc – but it is not necessary to prove that the marriage has irretrievably broken down. Also, there are not two decrees as there are in divorce – decree nisi and decree absolute – but simply one decree pronouncing the judicial separation once the court is satisfied that the requirements are met. A decree of judicial separation has three main effects:

- the parties are no longer obliged to live together;
- the court can exercise all the powers which it has to divide the matrimonial property etc just as it can in the case of a divorce; and
- the decree operates just like a divorce in terms of its effect on any will – the spouse no longer takes any benefit unless a new will is made specifically stating that is to be the case.

The number of decrees of judicial separation which are awarded every year is tiny in comparison to the number of divorces (and decrees of judicial separation are almost exclusively granted at the request of wives rather than husbands). There seem to be three main reasons why the parties to a marriage may seek a decree of judicial separation rather than a divorce:

- at least one of the parties to the marriage is opposed to divorce for some reason – typically for religious reasons;

- one of the parties requires certainty as to the arrangements of the matrimonial property – perhaps if one spouse is having difficulties with the financial arrangements of the marriage – but divorce itself is not wanted by either spouse;

- there is an absolute bar to divorce within the first year of a marriage and so judicial separation may be all that is available if the parties are determined to formalise the break by court proceedings within that first year;

- for some reason it may be difficult to prove the irretrievable breakdown of the marriage necessary for a divorce.

Source: www.terry.co.uk

The other ways to end a marriage are by petitioning for nullity or presumption of death.

Separation after Cohabitation

3.19 For cohabitants there is no need to take any legal action to formalise the separation. However, there may be issues concerning children, property and money to manage. This can be done either by informal agreement or by a written separation agreement. If partners cannot agree, a court can order who should stay in the home in the short-term and can also transfer a tenancy. Where there are children, a court can make orders about where the children should live and have contact with and the sale of any jointly owned property. The Child Maintenance and Enforcement Commission can deal with maintenance for any children of the relationship if agreement cannot be reached. For the 2007 Law Commission proposals on cohabitation see **5.4**.

Dissolution of Civil Partnership

3.20 'Dissolution' is the term used to describe the termination of a civil partnership – a procedure similar to divorce – and a dissolution can be obtained after one year of civil partnership. The main difference is that adultery is not one of the five factual circumstances which evidence a 'ground'. A 'petition' is applied for by one partner which states why the civil partnership has 'irretrievably broken down'. Just as in divorce, if there are children of the family a court has to approve a 'statement of arrangements' concerning plans made for the children once the dissolution is final. See above **3.18**.

Children Cases

3.21   Good case management can minimise expense and delay. In private children cases procedures are dictated by the Private Law Programme. In public law cases, management procedures have, since 1 April 2008, been dictated by the Public Law Outline (the PLO). Under the PLO, the overriding objective of all children's proceedings is to enable the court to deal with every (children) case justly, having regard to the welfare issues involved. Dealing with a case justly includes, so far as is practicable:

(a)   ensuring that it is dealt with expeditiously and fairly;

(b)   dealing with the case in ways which are proportionate to the nature, importance and complexity of the issues;

(c)   ensuring that the parties are on an equal footing;

(d)   saving expense; and

(e)   allotting to it an appropriate share of the court's resources, while taking into account the need to allot resources to other cases.

Private Cases: the new Private Law Programme

Draft Guidance Note for Implementation of the Revised Private Law Programme

3.22   Early in 2008, the President of the Family Division set up a working group to consider revising the Private Law Programme (PLP) first published in January 2005. The working group was chaired by Mrs Justice Hogg. His Honour Judge Altman was the vice-chairman and members of the group included circuit and district judges, a family panel magistrate, a justices' clerk and senior representatives from the Ministry of Justice, Department for Children, Schools and Families and Cafcass. (All references to Cafcass include CAFCASS CYMRU.) Members worked in close liaison with others including Her Majesty's Courts Service (HMCS) and the Legal Services Commission.

In November 2008 the group asked court users and agencies across the family justice system to send them comments on a draft of the revised PLP. They received nearly 40 responses which they considered at four meetings and which helped them to formulate the revised PLP which was trialled in six county courts (Birmingham, Newcastle, Milton Keynes, Plymouth, Reading and Sheffield) and their associated family proceedings courts over the summer of 2009.

Those courts collected agreed data to assist the group to evaluate the practicability of national implementation of the revised PLP. Evaluation of the data showed that the revised PLP had had a positive impact on the progress of private law cases. Therefore, the President of the Family Division was, at the time of writing, due to issue the revised PLP in the form of a Practice Direction (PD) in April 2010.

While the PD would provide a framework within which local arrangements should be made to ensure the most effective operation of the revised PLP, the key elements of the revised PLP would be set out in the PD and were to be followed across the jurisdiction.

It is fundamental to the purposes, as well as the provisions, of the PLP for the timescales set out to be observed rigidly at all courts throughout England and Wales. It is for this reason that the Practice Direction provides that, after it comes into effect, there will be a substantial period of time for the implementation of its provisions in local courts.

In the trial courts, all concerned agreed the need to change their practices in order to implement the new Programme as a whole in order to achieve the maximum benefits for the children whose cases are considered under the new regime, which aims to achieve a speedy resolution of cases. Therefore, Designated Family Judges (DFJs) might wish to consider putting in place a local team representing Cafcass, HMCS and the judiciary/magistracy to implement and keep under review the new arrangements.

'Summary of Key Elements of the Revised PLP

Before First Hearing:

1. Application made on form C100 accompanied by C100A in due course. It is recognised that the ability of Cafcass to contact the parties and to ask other agencies to carry out safeguarding checks is dependent upon properly completed forms. Court staff may be encouraged to assist applicants in

person to fill out forms and, where possible, to draw attention to missing information. However, where there is sufficient information to issue proceedings, staff should not be instructed to return, or refuse to accept, incomplete application forms.

2.   The court issues the application and sends it with the notice of hearing to the applicant for service with copies to Cafcass. This must be done within 24 hours of receipt of application (48 hours in those county courts that allocate to the family proceedings courts (FPCs) in the district judges' boxwork). It will be clear from the terms of the revised PLP that its success rests to a large extent on Cafcass being able to complete checks in advance of the first hearing. It is essential, therefore, that the court sets up with Cafcass an efficient system for ensuring the forms from all court offices where they are issued reach Cafcass within this timeframe.

3.   The court will continue to send guidance leaflets to the applicant.

4.   Save in urgent cases, the first hearing should be listed within 4 weeks from the date of the application unless it is not practicable to do so, in which case it should be no later than six weeks from the date of application. Those courts which determine at the time of introduction of the revised PLP that it is not then practicable to list the first hearing within the 4 week period should, with Cafcass, formulate a timetable to review the position in order to achieve this listing pattern and advise their court users and the President's Office of this timetable.

5.   Cafcass will make safeguarding checks in advance of the first hearing. These checks include the traditional police and local authority checks. As part of this initial checking process, Cafcass will also make telephone calls to the parties to ask them about any domestic violence or other safeguarding issues and, where such calls indicate the need for further clarification of allegations of violence or allied safety issues, Cafcass may arrange a meeting with

either/both of the parties to take place in advance of the first hearing.

6.   Any work in this connection by Cafcass will be confined to safeguarding investigations; the general and welfare issues in the case will not be discussed and will be postponed to the First Hearing. Parties will be informed that the opportunity to discuss welfare issues will be at the First Hearing and Cafcass will not initiate any contact with the children before that hearing. The practice for children being asked to attend the First Hearing, which exists in some courts, will no doubt continue.

7.   Prior to the First Hearing Cafcass will send a standard form note to the court outlining any safety issues that have emerged. Cafcass will also send the note to the parties unless Cafcass thinks it would be inappropriate to do so. The court will be advised if this is the case and will address this issue at the First Hearing.

At the First Hearing:

8.   The successful operation of the revised PLP is dependent upon attendance of a Cafcass officer at this hearing. (All references to Cafcass officer include a Welsh family proceedings officer.) Local listing arrangements for these First Hearings should be made after full discussion between the Designated Family Judge, Justices' Clerk, HMCS and Cafcass.

9.   Before going into court, the Cafcass officer will, unless there is good reason not to do so, speak to each party alone. This discussion is intended to alleviate any apprehensions about proceedings and to make any final safeguarding checks.

10. At the first hearing the court will conduct a conciliation process with the assistance of the Cafcass officer and may refer the matter to a mediator at court where available. Discussions at court will not be legally privileged and may be disclosed subsequently or referred to in the course of proceedings, where relevant. Pre-existing local guidance or practice

directions which provide for privilege, such as at the PRFD, are amended accordingly by this Practice Direction.

11. Where the parties reach agreement, the court will scrutinise and approve or refuse to approve the agreement, taking account of any safety issues in accordance with the *Practice Direction: Residence and Contact Orders: Domestic Violence and Harm (DVPD)* of 14 January 2009 reported at [2009] 2 FLR 1400.

12. Where safety checks have not been completed, and this should be rare, the PLP makes provision for the court to adjourn proceedings and to make a consent order in the absence of the parties following receipt from Cafcass of satisfactory safeguarding information.

13. Where agreement is not reached, the court should remind itself of the advantages of mediation and parenting information programmes and in appropriate cases, adjourn for the parties to go to mediation, consider whether it has sufficient information to order attendance at contact activities or whether to adjourn for Cafcass to provide a report regarding suitability for contact activities.

14. Other suggested methods of moving towards resolution where appropriate may include a short period of observed contact (possibly by the Cafcass officer), use of a supervised contact centre, contact monitoring orders, adjournment for interim arrangements or discussions between the parties.

15. Where agreement is not reached, the court will conduct a case management discussion with the assistance of Cafcass to identify those issues that are agreed, and those issues that remain and, if a further hearing is required in relation to any outstanding issues, directions will be given for timetabling of evidence and the listing of the hearing. The parties will be advised of the next date of hearing before they leave court.

16. Where there are unresolved safety issues that may affect determination of the welfare issues in accordance with the DVPD the court will

consider the need for a fact finding hearing and, if so, provide for it by listing in accordance with the DVPD.

17. In accordance with the Allocation and Transfer of Proceedings Order 2008, at all First Hearings in the county court, consideration will be given to transferring the case for further hearings to take place in the family proceedings court. In the absence of any good reason to the contrary, an order for such transfer will be made.

18. In those cases where a report from a Cafcass officer is required to address particular determinative issues the court and the parties, with the assistance of the Cafcass officer, will identify such issue or issues as narrowly as practicable to enable Cafcass to prepare a short focused report without delay.

19. Where, in the view of the court, a review hearing is desirable, a report for that hearing will only be ordered where the court considers this necessary, if possible taking into account the views of Cafcass on this point and, again, such order will be accompanied by an identification of the narrow issue upon which the report is to focus.

20. Where reports under s 7 or s 37 are sought from the local authority, arrangements should be agreed to ensure that requests are properly communicated in accordance with the Practice Direction governing the PLP.

21. The order of the court will set out, by way of preamble, a detailed recital of the positive steps and arrangements so far made, the issues that are agreed and the issues that remain to be resolved. A form of standard template order will be available to assist in this regard if helpful. The form of order will not be prescribed.'

Source:
Family Law -
March 2010

This is a draft of the guidance note that was intended for publication together with the Practice Direction in April 2010.

Public Law Cases: the Public Law Outline

3.23 A new Protocol for Judicial Case Management in Public Law Children Act Cases, the Public Law Outline('the PLO') came into operation in April 2008. It applies to all courts, including family proceedings courts, hearing applications issued by local authorities under Part IV (Care and Supervision) of the Children Act 1989 ('care cases'). The aim of the PLO is to reduce delay and improve the quality of justice for children and families by the following means:

- judicial continuity: having not more than two case management judges throughout;

- firmer, active court control of proceedings;

- introducing new case management tools for use throughout all cases;

- the consistent application of best practice by all courts.

Time limits are set as 'target times' for each stage of care proceedings. The overall 'target time' for the completion of a care case is 40 weeks from the issue of the application. The PLO requires the 'target times' to be treated as maximum permissible times for the taking of the steps concerned and requires the forms in the Annexes to the PLO to be used.

The PLO is constructed in the style of a step-by-step guide through a care case.

The new Protocol ('PLO') can be downloaded from www.hmcourtsservice.gov.uk/docs/protocolcomplete.pdf

---

PRE-PROCEEDINGS
PRE-PROCEEDINGS CHECKLIST

The Checklist Documents:

Documents to be disclosed from the LA's files:

- Previous court orders & judgments/reasons
- Any relevant Assessment Materials
  - Initial and core assessments
  - Section 7 & 37 reports
  - Relatives & friends materials (for example, a genogram)
- Other relevant Reports & Records
  - Single, joint or inter-agency materials (e g health & education/Home Office & Immigration documents)
  - records of discussions with the family
  - Key LA minutes & records for the child (including Strategy Discussion Record)

- Pre-existing care plans (for example, child in need plan, looked after child plan & child protection plan)
- Social Work Chronology
- Letters Before Proceedings

Documents to be prepared for the proceedings:

- Schedule of Proposed Findings
- Initial Social Work Statement
- Care Plan

Allocation Record & Timetable for the Child

STAGE ONE	
ISSUE	FIRST APPOINTMENT
On DAY 1 and by DAY 3	By DAY 6
Objectives: To ensure compliance with pre-proceedings checklist; to allocate proceedings; to obtain the information necessary for initial case management at the FA	Objectives: To confirm allocation; to give initial case management directions
On Day 1:	

• The LA files:
 	
  – Application Form
 	
  – Supplementary Form PLO 1
  – Checklist documents
	• Parties notify LA & court of need for a contested hearing
	
	• Court makes arrangements for a contested hearing
	
	• Initial case management by Court including:
	  – Confirm Timetable for the Child

• court officer issues application	– Confirm allocation /transfer
• Court nominates case manager(s)	– Identify additional parties & representation (including allocation of children's guardian)

• Court gives standard directions on issue including:
  – Pre-proceedings checklist compliance
	– Identify "early Final Hearing" cases
	
	  – Scrutinise Care Plan

– Allocate and/or transfer	• Court gives standard directions on FA including:

– Appoint children's guardian	– Case Analysis and Recommendations for Stages 2 & 3
– Appoint solicitor for the child	– LA Case Summary
– Case Analysis for FA	– Other Parties' Case Summaries
– Invite OS to act for protected persons (non subject children & incapacitated adults)	– Parties' initial witness statements
– List FA by Day 6	– For the Advocates' Meeting
– Make arrangements for contested hearing (if necessary)	– List CMC or (if appropriate) an Early Final Hearing
	– Upon transfer

By Day 3	
• Allocation of a children's guardian expected	• LA serves the Application Form, Supplementary Form PLO 1 and the Checklist Documents on parties

STAGE TWO	
ADVOCATES' MEETING	**CMC**
No later than 2 days before CMC	No later than day 45
Objectives: To prepare the draft Case Management Order; to identify experts and draft questions for them	Objectives: To identify issue(s); to give full case management directions
• Consider all Other Parties' Case Summaries and Case Analysis and Recommendations	• Detailed case management by the court
• Identify proposed experts and draft questions in accordance with Experts Practice Direction	– Scrutinise compliance with directions
• Draft Case Management Order	– Confirm Timetable for the Child
• Notify court of need for a contested hearing	– Identify key issue(s)

• File Draft Case Management Order with the case manager/case management judge by 11am one working day before the CMC	– Confirm allocation or transfer
	– Consider case management directions in the Draft Case Management Order
	– Scrutinise care plan
	– Check compliance with Experts Practice Direction
	• Court issues Case Management Order
	• Court lists IRH and, where necessary, a warned period for Final Hearing

STAGE THREE	
ADVOCATES' MEETING FOR THE IRH	IRH
Between 2 & 7 days before the IRH	Between 16 & 25 weeks
Objective: To prepare or update the draft Case Management Order	Objectives: To resolve and narrow issue(s); to identify any remaining key issues
• Consider all Other Parties' Case Summaries and Case Analysis and Recommendations	• Identification by the court of the key issue(s) (if any) to be determined
• Draft Case Management Order	• Final case management by the court:
• Notify court of need for a contested hearing/time for oral evidence to be given	– Scrutinise compliance with directions
• File Draft Case Management Order with the case manager/case management judge by 11am one working day before the CMC	– Consider case management directions in the Draft Case Management Order

	– Scrutinise Care Plan
	– Give directions for Hearing documents:
	– Threshold agreement or facts/issues remaining to be determined
	– Final Evidence & Care Plan
	– Case Analysis and Recommendations
	– Witness templates
	– Skeleton arguments
	– Judicial reading list/reading time/judgment writing time
	– Time estimate
	– Bundles Practice Direction compliance
	– List or confirm Hearing
	• Court issues Case Management Order

STAGE 4
FINAL HEARING
In accordance with the Timetable for the Child
Objective: To determine remaining issues
• All file & serve updated case management documents & bundle
• Draft final order(s) in approved form
• Judgment/Reasons
• Disclose documents as required after hearing

A feature of the PLO has been the focus on the pre-proceedings checklist which should in most cases (other than where proceedings are issued on an emergency basis) be completed by the local authority before issuing proceedings, to enable as much information as possible to be available to the court and the other parties at the earliest possible stage. Stages one, two and three are split into two parts each, to enable better case management of the case. Stage four, the final hearing, will only take place if there are issues still outstanding after the Issues Resolution Hearing. The final hearing could itself also be split into two parts if a fact-finding hearing proves necessary (see **3.37**).

The Ministry of Justice published a best practice guide, *Preparing for Care and Supervision Proceedings*, in 2009.

It is designed to complement the Statutory Guidance and the Public Law Outline and is for use by all professionals involved with children and families pre-proceedings and in preparation for applications made under s 31 of the Children Act 1989. It is available to download from http://www.justice.gov.uk/guidance/docs/preparing-care-supervision-proceedings.pdf.

'Ex Parte' and 'Inter Partes' Applications

3.24 In emergencies, applications under s 8 of the Children Act and some other applications, for example concerning domestic violence and child abduction, can be made 'ex parte' or without giving notice to the other party to the proceedings. Financial orders such as the freezing of assets can also be made without notice. This means that one person can get a temporary order from the court, in an emergency, without the other party knowing. That other person must be sent a copy of the order within a very short time and a hearing with both parties present (an 'inter partes' hearing) must follow.

Directions at the First Hearing

3.25 Because of the great emphasis nowadays on good case management, in order to minimise expense and delay, attempts are made to clarify and specify issues at first (directions) hearings. In public law proceedings, this first hearing is called the First Appointment. Parties come before the judge, magistrate or justices' clerk at an initial hearing or First Appointment many weeks before the date set down for the actual (or final) hearing. Issues which can be agreed are agreed at this early stage, leaving the court to give directions about how the proceedings will be conducted thereafter. This might cover the timetabling of the proceedings; deciding at which court level the proceedings should be heard, setting or varying the times within which certain acts have to be completed, such as the obtaining of a medical assessment or report on children; stating when documents should be served on the parties and stating when and what evidence should be given to the court; giving the permission of the court (called 'leave') for medical examination of the child or for papers to be disclosed, and listing for a contested hearing if that is possible at this stage.

In cases concerning the local authority, an assessment can be ordered to look at, for example, the potential of possible carers for the child concerned. At a directions hearing or First Appointment, the court should specifically deal with:

- the setting of a timetable for the filing and service of witness statements and documents;
- the setting of dates for subsequent directions and hearings;
- persons to be joined as parties;
- whether the child should attend court;
- the submission of evidence including experts' reports;
- the preparation of court reports on children;
- transfer to another court or consolidation with other proceedings concerning the family;
- applications for interim orders;
- other matters which the court considers appropriate.

All the parties should attend first directions hearings or 'FA's', preferably with their legal representatives but not the children unless they wish to speak for themselves and are old enough to do so.

In private law cases, since the private law programme (see **3.22**) and the new emphases on mediation and conciliation, the first hearing is known as a first dispute resolution appointment. Courts and the individual local jurisdictions currently have their own local policies about the utilisation of Cafcass in their local areas (see Chapter 5).

Transfer

3.26 Justices' clerks, legal advisers (if their justices' clerk delegates that authority), a district judge or the magistrates in the family proceedings court can all decide that a case should be allocated to a higher court in public law cases on the grounds of consolidation with other cases, or exceptional complexity, gravity or importance of the proceedings, or where perhaps a parent may be a protected party and require specialised representation. Alternatively, a case may be heard in a higher court initially or for a specific hearing and then be transferred downwards again. Under the Public Law Outline, there is flexibility of transfer built in to utilise as best possible the courts' resources.

In private law cases, the criterion for transfer is the interests of the child.

Timetabling

3.27   In general, a child's welfare is likely to suffer as a consequence of a delay in proceedings. In all Children Act 1989 cases, a timetable must be set and it is important that this is adhered to so that the proceedings do not take an excessive amount of time to complete. For example, although sometimes delay can be purposeful, the absolute maximum a court would normally allow for filing any one statement is 28 days but statements should be filed much more quickly to allow subsequent statements to comment on those filed earlier. For public law cases, see the Public Law Outline at **3.23**, which introduced the concept of the 'Timetable for the Child', the meaning of which is that the timetable set by the court for the conduct of public law cases should be appropriate for the child/ren concerned.

Listing of Cases

3.28   Cases are set down for hearing when there is space in the court diary. Often they are set down ('listed') many weeks or months ahead. This can result in the court diary system becoming blocked up by hearings which are set down for a few days but which in fact on the day 'go short', that is, they are settled just before the hearing takes place, often on the day itself, and do not take the time originally allowed for them. This can result in the court being empty on days when there are many other cases urgently waiting for hearing time. Court officials are responsible for the best use of the court time available but robust judges, magistrates and legal advisers can also contribute to the best use of court time.

Under the Public Law Outline the parties' advocates are required to meet to discuss the issues and conduct effective case management several days before both the Case Management Conference (Stage Two) and the Issues Resolution Hearing (Stage Three). Also, there is an emphasis on not listing further hearings until directions are made at a preceding hearing, by which time a more realistic timeframe for the next hearing should be achievable. Local jurisdictions have developed their own policies about this.

Case Management Conference

3.29 The Case Management Conference in public law cases is intended to consider all the judicial management issues that will be relevant for the conduct of the case. This includes the scheduling of all expert evidence, disclosure of papers to the necessary resources, listing for any contested hearings (if these have not already been listed at the First Appointment), and the filing of evidence. Before the Case Management Conference, the parties' advocates will have held a meeting to discuss the key issues at that stage of the proceedings and to draft a Case Management Order which, under the Public Law Outline, serves as an aide memoire to everyone concerned with the proceedings as to the progress of the case timetable, and the issues and decisions which need addressing by the court at the Case Management Conference itself. This draft Case Management Order is then sent to the judge having conduct of the proceedings in time for him/her to read and consider it before the hearing.

The Issues Resolution Hearing

3.30 In public law cases the Issues Resolution Hearing should take place between 16 and 25 weeks after commencement of the proceedings. As with the Case Management Conference, an advocates' meeting will have taken place prior to the 'IRH' in order to discuss the issues which are by then outstanding and again to draft a Case Management Order specific to the IRH which will be sent to the judge before the hearing for his/her consideration. At the advocates' meeting, the parties' advocates will discuss all the evidence which came in since the Case Management Conference and will try to resolve as many outstanding issues as possible. The intention, under the Public Law Outline, is to try to finish the proceedings at the IRH itself and the judge who has conduct of the IRH will manage the case robustly to try to enable the parties to settle the case on that occasion. Under the Public Law Outline, if the case cannot settle at the IRH then only at that stage is a final hearing to be listed, although in some cases waiting until this late stage in the proceedings is still not practical.

In private law proceedings, the IRH is replaced by a pre-hearing review (as it also used to be in public law cases) if the issues in the case are complex or the case is listed for final hearing of a day or more.

Witness Statements and Reports

3.31   The parties to an application for a care or supervision order must file with (ie send to) the court and serve on (ie send to) the other parties a written statement of the party's oral evidence which they intend to rely on in court and copies of any documents, including experts' reports, which they will also use as evidence. 'Evidence' is any material placed before the court to persuade it of the truth or probability of some fact. A witness statement provided for proceedings constitutes evidence. Apart from statements, the other forms of documentary evidence for the court to consider are usually reports, which may be from the guardian, Cafcass officer and/or other experts. When a report is submitted, the facts contained in the report may be treated as evidence and the person who wrote the report can be cross-examined on them. All parties should see the witness statements and reports in advance of the hearing so that they can consider everything that the court will see. The Children Act 1989 places an emphasis on the disclosure of written statements before a case is heard. All parties are required to file witness statements from persons whose evidence they intend to call.

Applicants for a section 8 order cannot file or serve any documents other than those required or authorised by the rules without the permission ('leave') of the court. Once a direction has been made for the filing of evidence, written statements and reports must be served on the other parties, including any Cafcass officer who might also be involved.

The emphasis in the family courts is on transparency of all the evidence, so that all parties in proceedings should be able to see and read all the evidence before each of the hearings. This way, no party should be taken by surprise by any documentary evidence put before the court, so that they each have time to consider the evidence fully, to take advice about it, and to give instructions to their representatives in the light of it.

Assessments and Medical Examinations

3.32   In cases involving the local authority, once an application for an order has been made the child cannot be medically or psychiatrically examined without permission ('leave') of the court. If the child is of sufficient understanding, he is entitled to refuse to be examined. If the local authority wants to refer the child and/or family for an assessment, the court must be told:

- the issues to be addressed in the assessment;
- why allowing time for the assessment or examination is in the best interests of the child;
- the category of expert evidence in question;
- its relevance to the welfare of the child and the issues to be decided;
- the name and qualifications of the individual expert or organisation involved;
- the time needed to carry out the assessment;
- dates to avoid for the expert in scheduling;
- the views of the other parties.

Under the Public Law Outline, all parties are to give consideration to whichever expert assessment/s will be needed in the proceedings right at the outset, or as early into the proceedings as possible. A Practice Direction about the use of experts in family proceedings relating to children came into force on 1 April 2008, the same day on which the PLO came into force. This sets out the guiding principles to be adhered to when experts are to be instructed. The letter instructing the expert must specify the issues to be addressed in the report. Ideally, all the parties should agree one expert and the court should be advised by the children's guardian. The 2008 Practice Direction relating to the use and instruction of experts includes a list of questions to be asked of experts on instruction (see **2.132**).

Statutory guidance published by the Government at the same time as the Public Law Outline states that local authorities should provide information from a core assessment as part of their information to support the application. That would be available in all the non-urgent applications before the court. Those core assessments would comprise input from the range of professionals working with the child and family. In addition, where the core assessment had indicated the need for a further assessment in relation to a specific need, that information would also have been obtained by the local authority in advance of the application. However, shortage of resources has to date limited the scope of further assessments which local authorities are able to obtain prior to commencement of proceedings.

Once the case is before the court, there might be a need for evidence in relation to the threshold criteria (see **3.37** below). There might also be a need for further assessment – 'welfare assessments' – to assist the court in ascertaining what final outcome ('disposal') would be in the best interests of the child. Specifically, the court would need to know in all cases how the parents had responded to the challenge of the court process and how able they were to make the necessary changes in order to parent successfully in light of the individual needs and characteristics of the child. Overall, the court needed to hear advice on what timescale might be required to enable the parents to meet those changes and how those balanced with the timescale of the child's needs. Under the PLO, independent experts mostly provide the necessary welfare assessments, and multi-disciplinary assessments are still in their early stages in most areas, but more and more agencies are now working towards being able to provide them.

In cases where the threshold criteria need to be proved, based on contested medical evidence, the court usually takes steps to ask for preliminary advice from medical experts as to the key issues and whether further medical information would be required in order to help the court reach a decision about the threshold criteria.

For further information on expert witnesses see **2.127**.

The Care Plan

3.33 In cases involving the local authority, once a local authority assessment is complete, a care plan can be prepared and provided to the court and to the parties setting out what the local authority intends to do if a care order is made. The care plan should get careful scrutiny by the court when it is considering whether or not to make a care order. Once an order is made the court has no control over the local authority's care plan (except on matters of contact), so if the court does not like the plan its only sanction is not to make the order. The care plan should identify the child's best interests, look at the least detrimental alternatives for the care and assessment of the child and be realistic about the resources available. It should tell the court about:

- the child's identified needs;
- how those needs are to be met;
- the aim of the plan and timescale;

- whether a placement is proposed, and if it is with whom and its duration;
- other services to be provided for the child and/or family;
- arrangements for contact and rehabilitation;
- plans for adoption;
- the role of the parents;
- arrangements for review.

At all hearings up until the final hearing (or the IRH, if that is the final hearing) the local authority will have submitted an 'interim' care plan. This will be changed to a final care plan for the final hearing. If, during the course of proceedings, there is a significant change of the child's circumstances, the local authority is then obliged to submit a revised interim care plan taking the change into consideration in its planning.

Presentation of Evidence in Court

3.34   At many hearings in family proceedings, only the advocates talk to the judge in court, having received their instructions from their lay client beforehand. At some hearings however, the need will arise for the judge to hear oral evidence from one or more parties in order for a decision on a controversial fact to be made. Final hearings may be contested on all, some or none of the issues. At these hearings, the court is likely to need full evidence from all the parties including oral cross-examination, but it can accept agreed statements and limit the examination of one or more of the parties. Unless the court directs otherwise, evidence and final submissions from the advocates should be given in the following order:

- by the applicant;
- by the person/s with parental responsibility for the child;
- by other respondents;
- by the guardian;
- by the child, if he is not a party and there is no guardian.

The Court of Appeal has described a 'spectrum of procedure' for family cases ranging from a hearing on 'minimal evidence' to a 'detailed investigation on oral evidence which may be prolonged'. How a case is to be determined on this spectrum is determined by the court.

If the evidence which has been filed (sent to court beforehand) is controversial, the party who challenges that evidence should have the chance to cross-examine the witness. If no evidence is called, the court is unlikely to be able to decide issues of fact 'on paper' (ie just by reading the documents in the court bundle). Only in very exceptional circumstances would a party's legal representative not be heard. Not allowing an advocate to address the court would be a basis for challenging the decision.

Oral evidence should be given by each party, as a statement in itself does not become evidence that the court can consider until the maker of the statement attests to or affirms the truth of it. This attestation or affirmation ('swearing in') is done by the party concerned when he/she is about to give oral evidence. Advocates' submissions (speeches made by lawyers at the end of a hearing summing up their case) are also not 'evidence', but of course they are taken into consideration by the judge. In cases involving the local authority, each party may cross-examine the evidence in turn, and all of this is followed by the local authority's, the parents' and the child's advocates' closing submissions. In these cases, the guardian usually talks on behalf of the child/ren. The guardian himself is represented by a solicitor whilst the proceedings are ongoing, and either by a solicitor or barrister as advocate in court. However, if the guardian's solicitor is taking separate instruction from the child in the proceedings because the child has a different view from that of the guardian, the guardian is then likely to be unrepresented, but he or she still has the right to be heard and to cross-examine witnesses, usually doing so between the advocate/s for the parents and the advocate for the child. None of these rules need be rigidly applied and the parties may agree with the court to a different order of presentation, perhaps to accommodate an expert witness or to assist the court in understanding the issues at stake. All parties can and should now see the witness statements and reports in advance of the hearing.

Length of Hearing

3.35 Courts should exercise strict control over the advocates, the witnesses and the evidence. They should ensure that there is full disclosure, that there is sensible use of expert witnesses and that the evidence is relevant

to the issues to be decided. Cases must be well prepared
and presented. Failure by practitioners to conduct cases
in an economically efficient way could result in orders
for costs and wasted costs being made against them;
that means that the party which suffered increased costs
because of the other side's profligacy could recover his
costs from the other side. Costs orders of any kind are
very rare in children's cases.

In private financial cases after divorce, wasted costs
orders can be made at any stage in the proceedings
when the court thinks that the conduct of a party in the
proceedings means that this would be appropriate.
Usually however, in these cases each party bears their
own costs, the principle being that there are no
'winners' or 'losers' in such cases.

Interim Orders

3.36   Courts can order interim orders, that is, orders
pending a final decision by the court. As regards care
and supervision orders in public law cases, the court
must bear in mind that an interim order is only a
holding order. All relevant risks must be considered
when making any interim order and the following
principles apply:

- the final hearing should take place as soon as
  possible;
- the case could be transferred laterally to another
  available court in order to avoid delay;
- findings of fact should not be made on disputed
  facts;
- a child's residence should not normally be changed
  as the disruption caused could be to his detriment;
- the court should have advice from the guardian at
  all appropriate stages, preferably in writing;
- documents should be read and evidence recorded;
- reasons must be given for any order made.

As to private law (section 8) interim orders, the court
should again be mindful of delay, but an interim order
made whilst perhaps a monitored programme to restart
contact is put into action can be sensible and realistic.
The courts have said that an interim contact order may
be made where:

- it is part of the adjudication process, usually on
  the advice of a Cafcass officer or a child
  psychiatrist;

- there is sufficient information to order contact despite the possibility of a different order at the final hearing: this is usually after the court has heard evidence and had advice from a Cafcass officer;

- the issue is the nature or quantum (frequency) of contact.

Threshold Criteria and Fact Finding

3.37 Care or supervision orders can only be made if the court decides that the 'threshold criteria' have been reached, meaning that:

- the child has been significantly harmed or is at risk of being significantly harmed in the future; and

- the harm is due to the care given to the child falling below what would be reasonable to expect a parent to give the child, or because the child is beyond parental control.

(Harm includes not just the child being ill-treated him/herself, but also a child seeing or hearing the ill-treatment of another, such as in cases of domestic violence.)

Often the parties will be able to agree in the early stages of proceedings that the threshold criteria have been reached on the background facts as they stand but it is sometimes difficult for local authorities to decide on a care plan for the child where certain facts about what has happened in the past are not agreed and need to be determined. For example, was the child sexually abused or perhaps non-accidentally injured and, if so, by whom? There may be no history of inadequate parenting or of children's services' involvement with the family until the occurrence of an injury or alleged abuse, and until questions about what exactly happened and who the perpetrator was are answered a sensible care plan cannot be made. For these purposes, the courts have approved the use of split trials. Here, an initial 'fact finding' hearing determines the relevant background facts and decides whether the threshold criteria have been met. If relevant facts are able to be determined and the threshold criteria are found to have been met, the local authority will then be able to revise or decide its care plan for the child. There will then be a subsequent hearing to decide what, if any, order should be made in the light of this care plan.

Final Hearings and Final Orders

3.38 The golden rule of the Children Act 1989 is that
when a court is considering whether or not to make an
order under the Act, it must not make an order unless it
considers that doing so would be better for the child
than making no order at all. That said, the 1989 Act
gives a court great flexibility in its powers to make
orders – in its simplest terms, a court need not be
constrained by the applications before it. The
paramount consideration is the child's welfare and most
of the orders under the Children Act can be made on
the application of a party or on the court's own
instigation at any time in the proceedings.

For example, when making a section 8 order for
residence or contact, the court can make a parental
responsibility order, appoint a guardian, make an order
for financial provision for the child or make a
supervision order. It can even make a prohibited steps
order against a person who is not a party to the
proceedings or who is not present in court if that is
absolutely necessary to protect the child.

When making an order or refusing an application, a
court (including family justices) must state any findings
of fact and the reasons for the court's decision. The
court must deliver its judgment as soon as is practicable
and the reasons must be read out at the same time as
the order made. A copy of the order must be served on
(given to) the parties and anybody with whom the child
is living.

When making a care or supervision order the court is
not allowed to dictate to the local authority how its
care plan should be carried out nor to attach any
conditions to it. Once a care order is made, the only
other order which can be made under the Children Act
is one (under s 34) concerning contact with the child in
care.

Alternative Dispute Resolution

3.39 The Children Act 1989 supports the belief that
children, as far as possible, are best looked after within
the family, with both parents playing a full part and
with legal proceedings being a last resort to protect a
child's welfare. The 1989 Act supports the principle that
disputes are best settled out of court, for instance by
alternative methods of dispute resolution such as
mediation. The same philosophy can be applied to the

For further
information about
the conduct of
proceedings and the
range of orders, see
the Judicial Studies
Board Family Bench
Books on
www.jsboard.co.uk/
family_law/index.htm

division of money and property on divorce. Many couples now use Alternative Dispute Resolution (ADR) to share their finance and property, as well as to make decisions about their children on divorce or separation.

ADR is a collective title given to a range of procedures for resolving disputes. Although often 'free standing', these procedures can be used as an adjunct to litigation or adjudication and can be complementary to the judicial process, not a replacement of it. The procedures can include:

- Negotiation – which can take place directly between the people in dispute, or with an adviser negotiating on behalf of one or both sides. Most disputes begin with an attempt to resolve the issues through negotiation.

- Where negotiation fails, there are a range of options available for attempting to reach solution, namely:

  - in court conciliation (see **3.22**);
  - collaboration (see **2.16**);
  - mediation.

Family Mediation

3.40   The principle that decision-making authority rests with the participants is fundamental to family mediation. Mediators respect the participants' authority to make decisions even in circumstances of stress and upheaval. Consequently, the participants' perceptions and values are taken into full consideration. It is this principle which distinguishes family mediation from other dispute resolution processes such as lawyer negotiation, litigation and adjudication. Family mediation is a process which provides an impartial third person (or persons) to facilitate the participants' negotiations together. The mediator:

- provides the forum for the negotiations to take place in a safe, balanced and managed way;

- works at the pace of and with the content brought by the participants, assisting them to consider all issues and concerns;

- encourages the development of the widest range of options appropriate to the needs of each family and assisting the careful exploration of appropriate outcomes;

- undertakes 'reality tests' with the participants to ensure their informed and realistic decision making;
- recognises when mediation is not the appropriate or preferred procedure and acts accordingly.

The Principles of Mediation

3.41 The fundamental principles of family mediation, practised by all independent family mediators, are that mediation is voluntary, impartial and confidential, and that decision making rests with the participants. The process is divided into five major stages:

(1) establishing the arena;

(2) clarifying the issues;

(3) exploring the issues;

(4) developing options; and

(5) securing agreement.

What Mediation Does

3.42 Mediation can assist couples at the point of breakdown of their relationship to consider their options and make arrangements they can live with. It can help parents to make and, when necessary or appropriate, to review arrangements for their children, reflecting the changing needs of both parents and children. 'All issues mediation' (AIM) helps couples to look at financial arrangements including decisions about property in an informed environment. Couples are advised to take their proposals to their personal lawyers and mediation services should provide summaries of proposals or memoranda of understanding to individuals and their respective lawyers – with the agreement of both participants.

Compulsory Assessment for Mediation

3.43 It has been suggested that it would be beneficial if new Family Proceedings Rules (due to come into force in 2011) could allow the introduction of compulsory information concerning the nature and availability of the mediation process as a form of dispute resolution. Parties could be ordered by the court to attend an assessment meeting with a mediator so that they can receive information concerning the process, its principles and working, and its cost so that they could decide from an informed basis whether or

'Family Mediation: the Future'
Jane Robey,
Chief Executive,
National Family Mediation
Family Law,
August 2009

not they wish to participate in mediation. At such a meeting the mediator could also assess whether or not mediation would be suitable given the issues and/or the parties themselves. Such an assessment would include screening for domestic violence. Given the voluntary nature of participation in the mediation itself, such information meetings would not prejudice in any way the fundamental principle of a party's right to access to justice. It is to be hoped that the Family Justice Review, announced in January 2010, will bring in compulsory assessment for all.

Mediation and Domestic Violence

3.44   Greater numbers of couples are likely to use mediation in the light of the increasing recognition of all forms of alternative dispute resolution. The UK College of Family Mediators have long had a policy aimed at avoiding:

(1)   people being pressured into mediation;

(2)   cases which are inappropriate for mediation such as those involving domestic violence being referred to mediation. Research indicates that domestic violence may be a feature in one in three cases of separation and divorce.

Good practice requires that each participant makes a fully informed and voluntary decision to enter mediation. Family mediators are trained to establish that parties are not coerced into 'agreements' for fear of reprisals, whether physical or emotional. See further **5.11**.

In-court Conciliation

3.45   The government intends to promote and extend in-court conciliation nationwide and look at different models around the country and their outcomes, see the new Private Law Programme at **3.22**.

Family group conferencing

3.46   In public law child care cases, a family group conference (FGC) is a decision-making meeting in which a child's family network takes a decision and makes a plan about the future arrangements for the child. The term 'family' includes both blood relatives and non-related significant family friends and neighbours. The plan arrived at should be accepted by the referring agency (usually a local authority) subject to the plan being safe for the child. The process is designed to give the wider family and the child a clear voice. They are an inclusive and effective way of decisions being made.

An FGC can be offered to a family in any situation in which a decision about the future of children has to be made. The decision may be about, for example, where children should live, how they can be protected from harm and made safe, who they should have contact with and what support a family needs in order to care for them. When the future of a child is being considered by a court, it is preferable, though not always essential, that an FGC be offered early in the proceedings. Since the Public Law Outline their use has begun to increase. Usually there are four steps to the process of a Family Group Process.

Step one: The Referral. This is when the family agrees the need for a FGC and an independent coordinator is then appointed. This person should reflect the race and culture of the family and share the same first language. Where necessary, the professionals who come to the FGC can use interpreters.

Step two: Preparation for the Meeting. The co-ordinator, in conjunction with the child, young person and their immediate carers, identifies the family network which can include close friends.

Family groups should be facilitated to attend an FGC through financial and practical assistance with travel, the choice of the venue, the availability of interpreters etc.

When inviting family members, a date, time and venue for the meeting, convenient to the family, is agreed. Preparing family members to participate is a key responsibility for the coordinator at this stage.

The coordinator meets the child or young person to discuss who will be their support person or advocate in the meeting. It is important that a child or young person has someone who is there for both expected and unexpected events. Thought needs to be given to who should fulfil this role, particularly given the family's private time. There may be other people in the family group who will need someone in the conference to support them, and it is the coordinator's job to ensure this happens.

The coordinator also makes contact with the professional network to organise their attendance at the meeting and to clarify that they have prepared clear, comprehensive and straightforward information about the strengths of the family, their concerns, their legal mandate and about resources available. This information should be provided in an accessible way for the family, and take account of their needs.

Step Three: Information Giving. At the start of the meeting, staff from agencies give the family the information they have about the child or young person and about services, resources and support that may be available. It is important that families are given full information in order that they can make decisions that take account of the agencies' concerns. The family can then give information themselves, and seek clarification and/or ask questions. The coordinator will chair this part of the meeting.

The family will then be given private family time. This is when the coordinator and the professionals all withdraw and leave the family to discuss matters between themselves, to agree a plan and contingency plans, and how to review and monitor the plan. The coordinator will still be available during this time to provide any necessary clarification and further information.

The family will then agree a plan and once they have done so, the coordinator, the referrer and the key professionals meet the family again to hear the plan and negotiate resources. It is generally the referrer's task to agree the plan. Good practice suggests that, where the professionals are happy with the plan, it should be agreed in principle, even if there is the need for further agreement or negotiation of resources outside of the meeting. The only reason for not agreeing the plan is if it puts the child at risk of significant harm. This needs to be outlined to the family immediately and an opportunity to address concerns given immediately.

It is important that at this point the timescales and the names of those responsible for any tasks are clarified. Contingency plans and reviewing arrangements should also be agreed.

Step 4: Reviewing the Plan. The level of monitoring will depend on the reason for the referral. The family will have their own monitoring arrangements, and will need to know about the professional responsibilities for monitoring. The success of the plan will depend on the family and professionals working together, and informing each other about the progress of the plan.

The way in which the plan is reviewed will depend very much on the needs of the child, young person and family and the statutory responsibilities of any agencies involved. A review family group conference is often recommended and if no date is set, agreeing how family members can initiate the FGC process is important.

Source:
Family Rights Group
Tel: 020 7923 2628
www.frg.org.uk

Local Authorities

Children Act 2004

3.47   The Children Act 2004 provided a legislative spine for improving the life chances of all children. The overall purpose of the 2004 Act was to encourage integrated planning, commissioning and delivery of children's services as well as improve multi-disciplinary working, remove duplication, increase accountability and improve the coordination of individual and joint inspections in local authorities.

Texts of Acts
can be viewed on
www.opsi.gov.uk

Details about the implementation of the 2004 Act and the wider reform programme are available in *Every Child Matters: Change for Children*, which is a revised and comprehensive approach to securing the well-being of children and young people from birth to age 19. The programme places better outcomes for children firmly at the centre of all policies and approaches involving children's services. The outcomes are:

- be healthy;
- stay safe;
- enjoy and achieve through learning;
- make a positive contribution to society;
- achieve economic well-being.

The programme requires that all organisations that provide services to children work together in more integrated and effective ways and was brought in after the tragic death of Victoria Climbié, and the subsequent report by Lord Laming, which highlighted a need for improved integration and accountability across children's services (see further **4.40**).

The government published in 2006 a revised version of *Working Together to Safeguard Children* which incorporated the changes brought about by the 2004 Act.

Working Together to
Safeguard Children
(DfES, 2006)
www.dcsf.gov.uk/
everychildmatters/

Every Child Matters

3.48   A range of guidance documents has been produced to assist local partners in delivering the Every

See further:
www.dcsf.gov.uk/
everychildmatters/

Child Matters programme, including statutory guidance under the Children Act 2004. They are available on www.dcsf.gov.uk/everychildmatters/. The government believes that improved outcomes for children can only be achieved and sustained when agencies work together to design and deliver integrated services around the needs of children and young people.

Children's Trusts and Children's Services' Authorities

3.49 Children's trusts bring together all services for children and young people in an area, underpinned by the Children Act 2004 duty to co-operate, in order to focus on improving outcomes for all children and young people. Children's trusts are intended to support those who work every day with children, young people and their families to deliver better outcomes – with children and young people experiencing more integrated and responsive services, and specialist support embedded in and accessed through universal services. People working in multi-disciplinary teams, will be trained jointly to tackle cultural and professional divides, using a lead professional model where many disciplines are involved, and be co-located, often in extended schools or children's centres.

Children's Trusts are the government's preferred model for achieving local integration of social care and some health services for children and young people. The Trusts are expected to help to deliver better services and outcomes for children, young people and their families In addition to the NHS Primary Care Trusts (PCTs – see **3.79**), Children's Trust partners also include Connexions, Youth Offending Teams and Sure Start local programmes. Other local partners may include housing, leisure services, the police, youth justice, independent sector organisations such as voluntary organisations, and community sector organisations such as churches.

The new duties under the Children Act 2004 require local authorities and their 'relevant partners' to co-operate to improve children's wellbeing. A set of effective local arrangements, operating at every level, will be a children's trust in action. The Children Act 2004 required every top-tier or unitary local authority in England to appoint a director of children's services (DCS) and to designate a lead member for children's services (LM) to provide local leadership and drive forward change.

The relevant partners include:

- district councils: services provided which impact upon children's well-being include housing, leisure and recreation and are to be considered within the context of children's trusts;
- the police authority and the chief officer of police for a police area any part of which falls within the area of the local authority;
- a local probation board for an area, any part of which falls within the area of the local authority;
- the youth offending team (YOT);
- the Strategic Health Authority (SHA) and Primary Care Trust (PCT) for the area.

As the universal service provider that maintains contact with most children 5 days a week throughout most of the year, schools are central to the drive to improve all five outcomes for children and young people. They should therefore be appropriately involved in the local children's trust co-operation arrangements. (Local Education Authorities are no longer so called. They now come under the umbrella of local authority children's services departments.)

> The Children Act 2006 extends local authorities' statutory duties as regards childcare. See the Act and Explanatory Note on www.opsi.gov.uk

The Education and Inspections Act 2006: In autumn 2005 the Government published Higher Standards, Better Schools for All, White Paper. This was a major step towards the Government's aim of ensuring that every child gets the education they need to fulfil their full potential.

The Local Government White Paper, *Strong and Prosperous Communities*, published in 2006 attempted to achieve a reform of the relationship between central government and local government and its partners through a new, more streamlined, local performance framework. Its framework consisted of five key elements:

- A National Indicator Set (NIS) of 198 outcome focused indicators for local government to deliver (alone or in partnership), replacing all existing indicator sets.
- Statutory Local Area Agreements (LAAs) to set out how local and national priorities will be delivered. Each LAA should contain 'up to 35' targets agreed with government, drawn from the NIS.

- A risk-based monitoring system, Comprehensive Area Assessment (CAA), to replace the existing inspection regime from 2009–10.

- Support and challenge for LAs and partners, established by the National Improvement and Efficiency Strategy (NIES).

- More funding freedoms, many grants paid on a non-ring fenced basis through Formula Grant or the new Area Based Grant. There was to be a strong presumption against ring fenced grants.

Children's Trusts, fulfilling the new leadership role outlined for them in the Children's Plan, are expected to work within this framework. They will have an important job to do in coordinating the work of local partnerships and, drawing on the local Children and Young People's Plan, in driving forward the process of identifying children, young people and families' improvement priorities for new LAAs.

The Childcare Act, passed into law on 11 July 2006, was aimed at being pioneering legislation and is the first ever legislation exclusively concerned with Early Years and childcare. The Act aimed to transform childcare and Early Years services in England, taking forward some of the key commitments from the Ten Year Childcare Strategy published in December 2004.

Measures in the Act formalised the important strategic role Local Authorities play through a set of duties requiring authorities to improve the five Every Child Matters (ECM) outcomes for all pre-school children and reduce inequalities in these outcomes; secure sufficient childcare for working parents; and provide a better parental information service. The Act also reformed and simplified Early Years regulation and inspection arrangements providing for a new integrated education and care quality framework (for pre-school children) and the new Ofsted Childcare Register. The sufficiency, information and outcomes duties came into effect from 1 April 2008 and the remaining provisions from September 2008.

Statutory guidance was also published by DCSF in July 2007 to assist Local Authorities in completing their duties to secure sufficient childcare to enable parents to work and undertake training. This duty came into force from April 2008.

Other duties to secure information, advice and training for childcare providers came into force from October 2007.

These duties were introduced under ss 6–10 and s 13 of the Childcare Act 2006.

The Childcare Act has four parts: duties on local authorities in England (Part 1); duties on local authorities in Wales (Part 2); regulation and inspection arrangements for childcare providers in England (Part 3); and general provisions (Part 4).

The Children's Plan

3.50 The Department of Children, Schools and Families was created in June 2007 to lead the whole network of people who work with or for children and young people. The DCSF then drew up a Children's Plan, focusing on:

- securing the well-being and health of children and young people;
- safeguarding the young and vulnerable;
- ensuring an excellent education for all our children and young people;
- keeping them on the path to success;
- providing more places for children to play safely.

In December 2007 the Government published the Children's Plan, setting out ambitious goals to improve the lives of families, children and young people by 2020. Local authorities will play a key role in delivering these reforms.

The Children's Plan sets out the Government's intention to further strengthen Children's Trusts so that by 2010 there are in place consistent high quality arrangements to identify and help all children with additional needs. The Government is also taking forward further legislation to:

- extend the number of Children's Trust partners;
- make the Children's Trust Board a statutory body, so that it can have specific functions;
- give the Board legal responsibility for producing and securing delivery of the Children and Young People's Plan (CYPP).

2020 Children and Young People's Workforce Strategy

3.51 Following the case of 'Baby Peter', the news of which shocked the nation in 2008, in December 2008 the Government published the 2020 Children and Young People's Workforce Strategy. This set out the Government's vision that everyone who works with children and young people should be:

- ambitious for every child and young person;
- excellent in their practice;
- committed to partnership and integrated working;
- respected and valued as professionals.

Whatever the person's role in working with children and young people, the aim is to ensure that members of the workforce have the skills and knowledge to do the best job they possibly can to help children and young people develop and succeed across all the outcomes which underpin Every Child Matters.

The development of the strategy was supported by an expert group of professionals and leaders from different parts of the children and young people's workforce, which had a major influence on both the overall direction and detail of the strategy. The strategy is also a result of collaboration with key government departments with responsibility for improving services for children and young people, including the Department of Health, the Department of Culture, Media and Sport, the Home Office and the Ministry of Justice.

Proposals in the strategy include:

- Investment of £73 million over the next three years to improve social-work training, induction, practice and recruitment.
- Establishing a Social Work Taskforce to support this programme of reform.
- Setting up a development programme for senior leaders which will offer structured training and support to every director of children's services.
- Setting out the ambitions for every part of the children and young people's workforce.

ADULT AND CHILDREN'S SERVICES

3.52   Central government is responsible for all matters concerning health care, community care and personal social services, including child care and adoption. The statutory basis for the organisation of personal social services in England and Wales is the Local Authority Social Services Act 1970 which gives the Secretary of State for Health the power to issue guidance to local authorities as amended by subsequent legislation, such as the Children Act 2004. Due to the complexity of the duties imposed by the Children Act 1989, 11 volumes of guidance were published at the time it came into force. Subsequent guidance and standards have been published, for example, on fostering and adoption work. Following the Review of the Child Care Proceedings System in England and Wales, published in May 2006, and further public consultation between June and September 2007, the guidance issued in 1991 was replaced by revised Guidance and Regulations which came into effect simultaneously with the Public Law Outline, on 1 April 2008.

Circulars can be mandatory or advisory and are used to explain aspects of health and social care policy and regulation more fully. Many circulars are quasi-legislative and include a direction or requirement to take specific action.

Current guidance, circulars and letters can be viewed on www.dcsf.gov.uk/everychildmatters/

Overall responsibility at central government level for children and families moved from the Department of Health (DOH) to the Department for Education and Skills in 2002. The DCSF was created in 2007 (see the 'Children's Plan' at **3.50** above). The DCSF publishes statistics, makes an annual report to parliament, funds research, disseminates findings and undertakes inquiries. DCSF and DOH support the work of some voluntary organisations and pay for specific training initiatives. The Care Quality Commission is the single, independent inspectorate for social care in England.

Social workers are employed by local authorities. Local authorities at county level or unitary authorities are now called children's services authorities and have specific duties in respect of children under the Children Acts 1989 and 2004. They have a general duty to safeguard and promote the welfare of children in need in their area, and, provided that this is consistent with the child's safety and welfare, to promote the upbringing of such children by their families, by providing services appropriate to the child's needs. They do this in partnership with parents and in a way which is sensitive to the child's race, religion, culture and language, and where practicable, taking account of the child's wishes and feelings. Services might include day care for young children, after school care for school children, counselling, respite care, family centres or practical help in the home.

Children Act 2004

Children's social care staff act as the principal point of contact for children about whom there are welfare concerns. They may be contacted directly by children, parents, or family members seeking help, concerned friends and neighbours, or by professionals and others from statutory and voluntary organisations. The need for support needs to be considered at the first sign of difficulties as early support can prevent more serious problems developing. Contact details are on local authority websites and in telephone directories.

Structure

General Social Care
Council (GSCC)
Tel: 020 7397 5100
www.gscc.org.uk

3.53 The structures that support the delivery of child and family social care are very varied. Some social workers work in-house in teams with a management hierarchy, others work as independent practitioners either for agencies or in independent social work organisations. All registered social workers are accountable for their conduct and for the provision of a competent service to the General Social Care Council, working to the GSCC's code of conduct, although the GSCC also issues a code of requirements for agencies employing social workers and other social care workers. Agencies are inspected by the Commission for Social Care Inspection (CSCI).

Social work is not a 9-to-5 job. Clients may have to be visited outside normal working hours and problems can arise at any time. Most agencies and local authorities provide a 24/7 emergency service.

The Children's Services Director is accountable to local councillors, one of whom fulfils the role of Cabinet (or Lead) Member responsible for policy with respect to Children's Services.

Family Support Services for Children in Need

3.54 Local authorities are under a general duty under s 17 of the Children Act 1989 to safeguard and promote the welfare of children within their area 'who are in need'. This is achieved through their children's services departments. As far as is consistent with that duty, local authorities must promote the upbringing of such children by their families. They have to fulfil their duties by providing, or arranging for others to provide, a range and level of services appropriate to those children's needs.

There is a related duty under Schedule 2 to the Children Act 1989 for local authorities to take reasonable steps to identify the extent to which there are children in need within their area and to take reasonable steps, through the provision of services, to prevent children in their area suffering ill-treatment or neglect. Local authorities must take reasonable steps designed to reduce the need to bring proceedings for care or supervision orders or criminal proceedings against children in their area. It is fundamental that a local authority's services cannot be imposed on anyone without an appropriate court order.

Children in Need

3.55   Section 17 of the Children Act states that a child is in need if:

- that child is unlikely to achieve or maintain, or have the opportunity of achieving or maintaining, a reasonable standard of health or development without services provided by the local authority;
- the child's health or development is likely to be significantly impaired or further impaired without the provision of those services;
- the child is disabled, ie is blind, deaf and/or dumb, suffers from a mental disorder or is handicapped by illness, injury or a medical disorder.

The aim of the provision of services to support families is to avoid the breakdown of family relationships and help parents fulfil their parental responsibilities. For example, the accommodation of a child or the provision of day care by the local authority is a service which may provide positive support to a child and his or her family. Children are now 'looked after' by the local authority in partnership with parents in times of family crisis. Although some 'looked-after' children may be the subject of care orders, their parents must be involved in planning for their care to the extent that this can be achieved without detriment to the child.

Local authorities must keep a register of children with disabilities, preferably in conjunction with health authorities, and they must also take positive steps to identify the extent to which there are needy children in their area. They must provide for those children:

- day care services for children under the age of 5 and not yet attending school;
- care or supervised activities outside school hours or during school holidays;
- accommodation.

They must also provide, as considered appropriate:

- advice, guidance and counselling;
- occupational, social, cultural and recreational activities;
- home help (including laundry facilities);
- assistance with travelling to services;
- assistance with holidays.

Local authorities must also facilitate the provision of services by others, for example, by contracting with a voluntary agency to provide a family centre. They may also call on other agencies, for example, the housing department of a local NHS Trust, to facilitate the provision of services to families under s 27 of the Children Act 1989. Where children cannot be looked after by parents or family, social services have a duty to accommodate them and safeguard their welfare. They do this by funding and supporting foster carers, providing residential homes or placing children in residential homes run by voluntary agencies.

The adequacy and extent of services for children has to be reviewed periodically by the local authority in co-operation with the local education authority.

Looked After Children

3.56   Under the Children Act 1989, local authorities must if necessary provide accommodation for children in need when they are lost, abandoned or without carers who can provide accommodation (s 20). It is also possible for a child to be looked after by the local authority (s 22). This phrase describes a child who is either in care or has been provided with accommodation for more than 24 hours. It is the duty of the local authority looking after any child:

- to safeguard and promote the child's welfare;
- to make such services available for children cared for by their own parents as appears to the local authority reasonable in the child's case.

Children who are accommodated by the local authority under s 20 of the Act are not 'in care'. They are receiving help under a voluntary agreement with their parents or, if they are over the age of 16, at their own request. Children in care are looked after by the local authority as a result of a court order with which their parents may not have agreed. In exceptional circumstances, where children or young people may be a danger to themselves or others, they may be subject to a secure accommodation order (s 25). Where children are accommodated, the local authority must draw up a plan for each child, involving both parents and child, and agreed in writing. When children are in care, they and their parents should be consulted but the formal agreement with the parents is not a statutory requirement. Written agreements will set out details of how, why and where a child is to be looked after and for how long.

Child Protection

3.57   The local authority has a duty to make enquiries if it has reasonable cause to suspect that a child is suffering or is likely to suffer significant harm. The police have a duty to investigate where a crime is suspected. In practice, investigations in the most serious cases involving allegations of physical or sexual assault are conducted jointly. The local authority can call upon other county or district councils and health authorities to assist, in particular by providing relevant information and advice. Those other bodies must assist in the enquiries unless it would be unreasonable to do so. The main court orders used in the care and protection of children are: care orders, supervision orders, emergency protection orders, child assessment orders and family assistance orders. In an emergency, where the police have reasonable cause to believe a child would otherwise be likely to suffer significant harm, then the police can remove a child from where he/she is and accommodate him/her in police protection for a limited period under a police protection order.

In any family proceedings before the court in which a question arises with respect to the welfare of any child, and where the court thinks it may be appropriate for a care or supervision order to be made but there is no such application before the court, the court may direct the local authority to make an investigation of the child's circumstances (a 'section 37 investigation'). If the local authority decides not to apply for a care or supervision order, it must report to the court the reasons why not, and any services or action they intend to give or take.

Foster Placements

3.58 Under the Children Act 1989, local authorities must make arrangements which enable children to live with a member of their family unless it would be inconsistent with the child's welfare. Many children remain with or are returned to their families after a care order is made, and even more families receive local authority preventative and support services where there are no orders made at all. It may, however, be more appropriate to place a child with an alternative family for a period of time. Arrangements for placements are generally made by the local authority or an approved voluntary organisation with approved foster parents, but parents can make their own arrangements with private foster carers where there is no court order. Local authority foster carers have to be approved by the relevant panel within their area, and they can be approved for different purposes: as short or long-term carers, to offer respite care for the parents, to offer care for certain categories of children (ie for young people on remand, or disabled children, or for mother and baby placements).

Local authority foster care is governed by regulations (the Fostering Services Regulations 2002, SI 2002/57) and guidance (Fostering Services: National Minimum Standards) which ensure that both the foster carer and his or her household are suitable for the placement of children. Prospective foster carers are subject to a demanding assessment and approval process, which includes training and thorough checks. Once approved, the foster carers will be allocated a supervising social worker and other support and training from their local authority. They will initially be approved for one year and then they will be subject to annual reviews. The regulations also require local authorities to keep a register of foster carers in their area, to keep records of foster carers and to keep records of children placed with them.

The local authority exercises a lesser degree of statutory control over private foster carers, but still sufficient to safeguard children's welfare. It must assess the suitability of private fostering arrangements under separate Regulations and in some areas, these assessment reports are referred to the local authority's fostering panel.

Community Homes

3.59   Community homes are provided and managed by the local authorities or by voluntary organisations under designated arrangements and are covered by the Children Act 1989 guidance and regulations. Registered children's homes are run by private organisations and must be registered with the local authority if they care for more than four children. They are then covered by the same regulations as local authority homes. Voluntary children's homes are run by non-profit making organisations and must be registered and regulated as above. Residential schools are also registered with and regulated by the local authority, but independent boarding schools are subject to inspection only.

Other Local Authority Services

Leaving Care

3.60   When a young person aged 16 or over ceases to be looked after by a local authority, the young person is entitled to after-care services up to the age of 21 years (or longer, if the child's programme of education extends beyond that age). The Children (Leaving Care) Act 2000 amended and extended the duties already contained in the Children Act 1989 and social workers' guidance is set out in the Children (Leaving Care) Act 2000: Regulations and Guidance. The main purpose of the 2000 Act is to improve the life chances of young people living in and leaving local authority care. Fulfilling these duties may range from preparing the young person with practical life skills while the young person is still being accommodated by the local authority to providing advice and assistance on further education or accommodation at a later stage. The general duty is to advise and befriend the young person but assistance can also be provided in kind or in cash. Most local authorities provide 'leaving care' grants for young people who cease to be 'looked after'. The underlying principles are that the young person's views should be taken into account, they should be consulted and kept informed, due consideration should be given to their race, culture, religion and linguistic background, the importance of their families and parents should be recognised, their welfare should be safeguarded and promoted, and there should be a recognition of interagency responsibility. Preparation for the child leaving accommodation or care should start well in advance and will focus on three main aspects:

(1) enabling the young person to build and maintain relationships with others (both general and sexual relationships);

(2) enabling the young person to develop their self-esteem;

(3) teaching practical and financial skills and knowledge.

Assistance to the Courts

3.61 Under s 16 of the Children Act 1989 in any family proceedings the court can make a family assistance order where there are exceptional circumstances and the people named in the order agree. The officer named in the order can advise, assist and, where appropriate, befriend the person named in the order who would be the child, the parent, the guardian, the special guardian or the person with whom the child is living and who is named in the order. A family assistance order can last for a maximum of 12 months. They are in practice rarely used.

Youth Justice

3.62 The youth court deals with all offenders between the ages of 10 and 17. Many children who commit offences would probably meet the criteria for intervention as children in need under the Children Act. It is important for those involved with civil proceedings to be aware of the 'section 17' family support service to which families under stress may be entitled. However, the principal aim of the youth justice system as described by the Crime and Disorder Act 1998 is to prevent offending by children and young persons and that Act revives a direct criminal route into care. Local authorities can also apply for anti-social behaviour orders (ASBOs) which conflicts with its safeguarding duty.

Source:
Elizabeth Isaacs and
Carmel Shepherd
*Social Work
Decision-Making
– A Guide for Childcare
Lawyers*
(Family Law, 2008)

Local authorities must establish youth offending teams (YOTs) comprising a probation officer, social worker, police officer and representatives from health and education authorities.

See further:
Goldthorpe and Munro,
Child Law Handbook
(Law Society, 2005)

Contact Centres

3.63   Local authorities can directly provide or fund centres where children, separated from parents, can have comfortable contact with them if this is not possible in the family home. These facilities are usually for public law cases but may also be used in private law cases. Some are provided jointly with the court welfare service or voluntary agencies. See further **3.110**.

Further information from:
National Association of
Child Contact Centres
(NACCC)
Tel: 0845 4500 280
www.naccc.org.uk

Adoption

3.64   The Adoption and Children Act 2002 came into force in 2005 and the current adoption regime is based on this Act. It was the most significant reform in children law since the 1989 Children Act. The 2002 Act was brought in to meet several important needs: the system of adoption needed overhauling and modernising; the number of adoption orders in the UK had fallen to a low of 4,387 in 1998; and increasingly children were being adopted from abroad. The Act set new national adoption standards with prescribed timescales, created an Adoption Register for matching, increased the scope of people who are now able to adopt children, and placed a duty on local authorities to maintain an adoption service, including arrangements for the provision of adoption support services and an inter-country adoption service. In addition to local authorities, there are also a number of voluntary adoption agencies which provide an adoption service.

The Commission for Social Care Inspection (CSCI) is responsible for the inspection of local authority adoption services and the inspection and registration of voluntary adoption agencies in England. In Wales this function is the responsibility of the National Assembly for Wales. National minimum standards cover both voluntary adoption agencies and local authority adoption services in England and Wales.

See National Minimum
Standards for Voluntary
Adoption Agencies
in England and
Wales and Local
Authority Adoption
Service in England
(2003, DoH) and
www.DCFS.gov.uk/
adoption/lawandguidance.

Inter-country Adoption

3.65   The Adoption (Intercountry Aspects) Act 1999 was passed to give effect to the 1993 Hague Convention on Protection of Children, which itself had been

See further:
Department for
Education and Skills
www.dcsf.gov.uk/
intercountryadoption.

created because of increasing concerns about intercountry adoptions and the general inadequacy at that time of domestic legislation to control them. Both the Act and the Convention had as their objectives the safeguarding of children of intercountry adoptions and the creation of a coherent framework of legally binding standards and supervision. The 2002 Act subsequently incorporated most of the provisions of the 1999 Act, providing for people to be convicted of criminal offences if the statutory framework is circumvented.

The Children and Adoption Act 2006 brought in suspension of intercountry adoption from specified countries where there are concerns about practices in connection with the adoption of children. It also amends s 83 of the Adoption and Children Act 2002 to make it even harder for intercountry adopters to circumvent restrictions on bringing children into the UK.

In England and Wales, only registered voluntary adoption agencies (VAAs), and local authorities are permitted to make arrangements for adoption. This includes assessing and approving individuals as eligible and suitable to adopt. The government encourages intercountry adoption in circumstances where:

- the child cannot be cared for in any suitable manner in their own country;

- the adoption would be in the best interests of the child and with respect to the child's fundamental rights as recognised in international law;

- the adopter has been assessed as eligible and suitable to adopt from overseas by an adoption agency.

Source:
www.dcsf.gov.uk;
www.jsboard.co.uk/
family_law/

Applicants who intend to adopt from abroad will be approved to adopt from a specific country. If they wish to adopt from elsewhere they must demonstrate that they fully understand the cultural and other needs of a child from that country and obtain a new approval from the agency. There is no single process for finding a suitable child. Applicants may use the services of an overseas agency or an intermediary and in some countries it remains possible to identify a child directly through an orphanage. The 1993 Hague Convention applies where both child and prospective adopters are habitually resident in Convention countries. Where a child is adopted overseas in a country listed in the Adoption (Designation of Overseas Adoptions) Order 1973, SI 1973/19, the adoption is an 'overseas adoption'. Designated countries include many but not all Commonwealth countries, members of the EU and some other European countries, the USA and China. Where a child has not been adopted in either a Convention or Designated country, an adoption order must be obtained from a court in the UK. Certain courts are now designated as intercountry adoption centres. All intercountry adoption proceedings should be listed before a High Court judge or an authorised adoption judge. A copy of the Court Service Guide on Intercountry Adoption and the 1993 Hague Convention (Form A21) can be obtained from www.courtservice.gov.uk.

The Adoption Register

3.66 The 2002 Act consolidated three adoption registers into one. The Adoption Register has been in operation since 1 December 2004. From that date until 31 August 2009, it had assisted in matching 925 children with families. It operates as follows:

(1) The Adoption Register for England and Wales links children needing new families with people waiting to adopt. The Register holds information on children and adoptive families on a computer database, and electronic links are made between them. The Register is free to use by local authorities and VAAs. The Register's website can be found at www.adoptionregister.org.uk. The British Association for Adoption and Fostering (BAAF) operates the Register on behalf of the Department for Education and Skills and the National Assembly for Wales.

British Association for Adoption and Fostering (BAAF)
Tel: 020 7421 2600
www.baaf.org.uk

(2) The Adoption Contact Register is kept by the Registrar General whereby birth parents and other relations can assure an adopted person that they want to be contacted. The adopted person can register his wish to contact relatives.

(3) The Adopted Children Register is kept by the Registrar General so that it is possible to trace the original birth registration of an adopted child. Since 1976, adopted adults can obtain a copy of their original birth certificate. Anyone adopted before 1976 is required to attend a counselling session before being given information from birth records. Anyone adopted since 1976 may have voluntary counselling. Local authorities are required to provide a counselling service.

Children

3.67 Agencies refer to the Register those children who have a plan for adoption but where there is not already a link identified locally which is being actively pursued. The children will be referred at the latest by 3 months after the agency has formally decided that adoption is in the child's best interest and either:

- a full care order with a plan for adoption has been made; or

- there is an interim care order and all required consents, including that of the Court, have been obtained; or

- the child is accommodated and the consent of those with parental responsibility has been obtained.

Once a child's details have been recorded on the Adoption Register database, a search will be undertaken to identify potential adopters for him/her. Brief details of the families identified and of their adoption agency will be sent to the child's social worker who will consider the proposed link further.

Families

3.68 Agencies can refer adopters to the Adoption Register as soon as they have been 'approved' by the agency and will usually do this if it seems unlikely that the adopters will be matched quickly with a suitable child in their own region. Agencies must refer adopters to the Adoption Register 3 months after they have been approved if there is not a match with an identified child being actively pursued.

Agencies who are referring families to the Adoption Register must certify that they have the families' consent to referral. Adopters can, of course, decide that they do not wish to be referred to the Adoption Register, but this will reduce the opportunity for them to be matched with an appropriate child.

Adopters who have not been referred to the Register 3 months after their approval can fill in a form to refer themselves to the Register.

Once the details of a family have been recorded on the Register database, a search will be undertaken to identify a child who matches the family's approval profile. Relevant details of the family, including a written description (profile), and details of the approving agency will be sent to the child's social worker who will consider the proposed link further.

Information about the family can initially be sent out up to five times to different social workers for consideration with children. At this point the family's Register entry will be put 'on hold' whilst the social workers are given time to pursue possible links with any of the children. If none of the suggested links is pursued, the family's details on the Adoption Register database will again be made available to enable further searches and links to be made with other children.

For further information on adoption see **5.77**.

Source:
http://www.adoption
register.org.uk

Secure Children's Homes or Secure Accommodation

3.69   Local authority secure children's homes provide care and accommodation for young people placed under a secure welfare order for the protection of themselves or others, and for those placed under criminal justice legislation by the Youth Justice Board. For juveniles remanded to local authority accommodation the maximum period a court may authorise such restriction of liberty is the period of the remand, up to 28 days, after which a further application must be made, enabling a further review of the situation. For non-remand cases (see below), the maximum periods a court may authorise a child to be kept in secure accommodation are 3 months on first application, and 6 months for further applications.

Section 25 of the Children Act 1989 provides that a looked after child (whether in care or accommodated) cannot be placed or kept in 'accommodation provided for the purpose of restricting liberty' except if it appears:

'(a)   that—

(i)   he has a history of absconding and is likely to abscond from any other description of accommodation;

(ii)   if he absconds, he is likely to suffer significant harm; or

(b)   that if he is kept in any other description of accommodation he is likely to injure himself or other persons.'

Whether the grounds are met for up to 72 hours' detention in any 28–day period is a matter for the local authority (Children (Secure Accommodation) Regulations 1991, SI 1991/1505). If the secure placement lasts no longer than that, no court authority is required. If, however, the authority wants the placement to continue beyond 72 hours, it must apply for court authority. The court determines whether the grounds set out in s 25 are made out on the evidence, but this is the limit of its role. The child's welfare is not the court's paramount consideration; it is a question of whether the grounds are made out or not. If they are, the order is made authorising the local authority to place the child in a secure unit. It is up to the authority then to decide whether exercising this power is the right way to proceed. If an order is made authorising a child to be placed in secure accommodation, the local authority must review this placement within 1 month of the initial placement and then not more than every 3 months thereafter.

The Children Act 1989 Guidance and Regulations - Volume 1

Under the revised Guidance and Regulations to local authorities which came into force in April 2008, there has been a shift in outlook regarding the use of secure accommodation. Placements in secure accommodation are now to be regarded as a placement of choice rather than as a last resort. However, in any applications to court for an order under s 25, the child must be legally represented at court, except where the child has been offered the opportunity to obtain legal representation but has refused or failed to obtain it.

Housing Authorities and Registered Social Landlords

3.70 Housing and homelessness staff in local authorities can play an important role in safeguarding and promoting the welfare of children as part of their day-to-day work, recognising child welfare issues, sharing information, making referrals and subsequently managing or reducing risks.

Sport, Culture and Leisure Services

3.71 Sport and cultural services designed for children and families such as libraries, play schemes and play facilities, parks and gardens, sport and leisure centres, events and attractions, museums and arts centres are directly provided, purchased or grant aided by local authorities, the commercial sector, and by community and voluntary organisations. Many such activities take place in premises managed by authorities or their agents who should be aware of causes for concern.

Youth Services

3.72   Youth and Community Workers (YCWs) have
close contact with children and young people and
should be alert to signs of abuse, neglect and possibly
child trafficking, and how to act upon concerns about a
child's welfare.

Complaints against Local Authorities

3.73   Local authorities must ensure that parents and
children, including those looked after by them, have
access to a complaints procedure with an independent
element. Details of the procedure must be published.

HEALTH CARE

Department of Health

3.74   The Department of Health (DOH) is responsible
for:

- setting the overall direction and leading
  transformation of the NHS and social care for
  adults;
- setting national standards to improve quality of
  services;
- securing resources and making investment
  decisions to ensure that the NHS and social care
  are able to deliver services;
- working with key partners to ensure quality of
  services, such as:
  - Strategic Health Authorities, the local
    headquarters of the NHS;
  - the Healthcare Commission and the
    Commission for Social Care Inspection
    (CSCI);
  - the National Institute for Clinical Excellence
    (NICE), the Social Care Institute for
    Excellence (SCIE) and a range of health
    professional bodies and voluntary
    organisations to identify and spread best
    practice locally.

The National Health Service

Organisation of the NHS

3.75   The NHS was set up in 1948 and is the largest organisation in Europe.

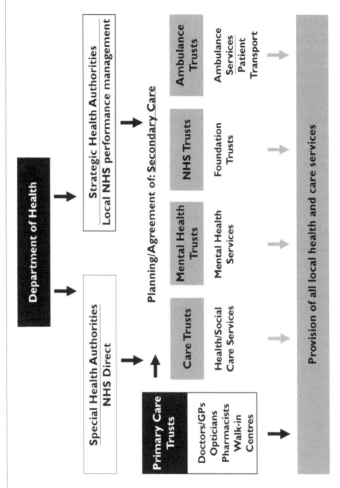

The Key National Health Service Bodies

Further information and contact details of individual NHS organisations can be found on www.nhs.uk/nhsengland/Pages/NHSEngland.aspx .

3.76   The following section describes the key NHS bodies and their responsibilities. The requirement of s 10 of the Children Act 2004 for local authorities and their relevant partners to co-operate to improve children's well-being applies to strategic health authorities and primary care trusts.

Special Health Authorities

3.77   Special Health Authorities (SPHAs) provide a health service to the whole of England, not just to a local community. They are as follows.

- Health Protection Agency
- Mental Health Act Commission
- National Institute for Health and Clinical Excellence
- National Treatment Agency
- National Patient Safety Agency
- National Treatment Agency
- NHS Blood and Transplant
- NHS Business Services Authority
- NHS Professionals Special Health Authority
- Health and Social Care Information Centre
- NHS Institute for Innovation and Improvement

Special health authorities are health authorities that provide a health service to the whole of England, not just to a local community – for example, the National Blood Authority. They have been set up to provide a national service to the NHS or the public, under s 11 of the NHS Act 1977. They are independent, but can be subject to ministerial direction like other NHS bodies.

Strategic Health Authorities

3.78   Created by the government in 2002 to manage the local NHS on behalf of the secretary of state, there were originally 28 strategic health authorities (SHAs). On 1 July 2006, this number was reduced to 10. Fewer, more strategic organisations will deliver stronger commissioning functions, leading to improved services for patients and better value for money for the taxpayer. Strategic health authorities are responsible for:

- developing plans for improving health services in their local area;
- making sure local health services are of a high quality and are performing well;
- increasing the capacity of local health services – so they can provide more services; and
- making sure national priorities – for example, programmes for improving cancer services – are integrated into local health service plans.

NHS Northern
Ireland
www.healthandcareni.co.uk

Strategic health authorities manage the NHS locally and are a key link between the Department of Health and the NHS.

SHAs form a key link between the Department of Health and the NHS. SHAs manage the NHS locally, developing strategies for the NHS, and monitoring local NHS performance. Their plans should include a clear indication of what services are needed by children, young people and, where appropriate, their families. SHAs should also ensure that the approach to managing children's services across local partner organisations is consistent and that this is reflected in organisational and joint plans.

Primary Care Trusts

3.79   Primary Care Trusts (PCTs) are local health organisations responsible for commissioning and some provision of health services in a geographical local area. Primary care is the care provided by people that individuals normally see when they first have a health problem, be it with their teeth, their general health, their vision, or just needing some medication from a pharmacist. NHS walk-in centres and the NHS Direct phone line service are also part of primary care. All of these services are managed by local primary care trusts (PCTs). There are currently 152 PCTs in England.

PCTs are now at the centre of the NHS and control 80% of the NHS budget. As they are local organisations, the intention being that they are best positioned to understand the needs of their community, they can make sure that the organisations providing health and social care services are working effectively.

PCTs work with local authorities and other agencies to make sure the community's needs are being met and provided. Thus, through commissioning they fund the provision of services by hospitals, primary care (general practitioners, dentists, community nurses and health visitors, opticians, NHS walk-in centres) and mental health services.

Care Trusts

3.80   Care Trusts are organisations that work in both health and social care. Normally they carry out a range of services, including social care, mental health and primary care services. Care Trusts are set up when the

NHS and local authorities agree to work closely together, usually where it is felt that a closer relationship between health and social care is needed or would benefit local care services. At the moment there are only a small number of Care Trusts, though more should be set up in the future.

Mental Health Trusts

3.81   There are currently 60 community mental health trusts covering England (CMHTs), which provide health and social care services for people with mental health problems. Mental health services can be provided through a GP, other primary care services or through more specialist care. This might include counselling and other psychological therapies, community and family support or general health screening. For example, people suffering bereavement, depression, stress or anxiety can get help from primary care or informal community support. If they need more involved support they can be referred to secondary care for specialist care.

More specialist care is normally provided by community mental health trusts or local council social services departments. Services range from psychological therapy, through to very specialist medical and training services for people with severe mental health problems. About two in every 1,000 people need specialist care for conditions such as severe anxiety problems or psychotic illness.

CMHTs also deliver some aspects of Child and Adolescent Mental Health services (CAMHS). It is estimated that among 5–10 year olds, 10% of boys and 6% of girls have a mental disorder. In the older age group, 11–15 year olds, the proportion of children with any mental disorder were 13% for boys and 10% for girls (source: Mental Health of Children and Adolescents in Great Britain, ONS 1999). There is a wide range of CAMHS, from counselling sessions to treatment in specialist inpatient units. CAMHS is unusual in that it spans health and social care boundaries. Local authorities have an important role to play in both the commissioning and delivery of CAMHS (see **3.85**).

For further information see www.camhscares. nhs.uk/

Only a very small proportion of mental health practice is covered by statute law. The Care Programme Approach (CPA) is guidance only but it is routinely followed, provided by the Department of Health. Adults requiring a mental health assessment will follow the process below:

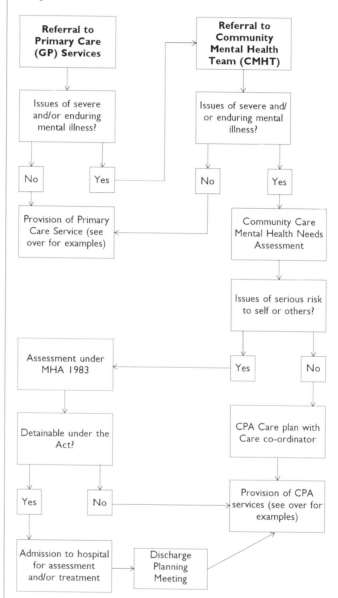

NHS Acute Trusts and Foundation Trusts – Hospitals

3.82 Primary Care Trusts are responsible for planning and funding hospital care for the resident population based on health needs of the local community, improvement plans and priorities set locally. Hospitals are managed by NHS Trusts (also known as Acute

Trusts) or by Foundation Trusts. They employ most of the NHS workforce, including nurses, doctors, dentists, pharmacists, midwives and health visitors as well as people doing jobs related to medicine – physiotherapists, radiographers, podiatrists, speech and language therapists, counsellors, occupational therapists and psychologists. Some NHS Trusts are regional or national centres for more specialised care, for example Great Ormond Street or other dedicated children's hospitals.

Foundation Trusts are a new type of NHS hospital run by local managers, staff and members of the public. They have been given much more financial and operational freedom than other NHS Trusts and have come to represent the government's commitment to de-centralising the control of public services. Foundation Trusts remain within the independent inspection system but financial probity is managed by Monitor – the independent regulator of NHS foundation trusts. There are currently 115 NHS Foundation Trusts. Government policy supports the eventual establishment of all hospitals within foundation trust management.

Independent Sector

3.83 Primary Care Trusts (PCTs) should ensure, through their contracting arrangements, that independent sector providers deliver services that are in line with PCTs' obligations with respect to safeguarding and promoting the welfare of children. PCTs will need to work with those independent providers to ensure suitable links are made to Local Safeguarding Children Boards (LSCBs) and that the provider is aware of LSCB policies and procedures.

Children's National Service Framework

3.84 The National Service Framework (NSF) for Children aims to improve the lives and health of children, young people and those needing maternity care. The NSF sets quality standards for local health organisations and council social services, as well as some education services. Full implementation of the standards will take up to 10 years. The standards are intended to bring about real improvements for children, young people and families. They are key components of delivering the government's 'Every Child Matters'. The agenda aims to improve every child's ability to:

- be healthy;
- stay safe;
- enjoy and achieve;
- make a positive contribution; and
- achieve economic well-being.

The NSF specifically aims to ensure that the care that children receive:

- is quicker and easier to access;
- more closely matches the needs of individual children and young people;
- is better coordinated so the child does not have to see too many professionals;
- is better at involving the child in decisions about his/her care;
- is better at achieving good results and outcomes for children and young people; and
- more closely reflects what children and young people and pregnant women say they want.

Child and Adolescent Mental Health Services (CAMHS)

3.85 Child and Adolescent Mental Health Services (CAMHS) are a comprehensive range of services available within local communities, towns or cities, which provide help and treatment to children and young people who are experiencing emotional or behavioural difficulties, or mental health problems, disorders and illnesses. Some of these services are based in National Health Service (NHS) settings such as Child and Family Consultation Services, in-patient and outpatient departments of hospitals, in GP surgeries and health centres and in private health care. Others are based in educational settings such as schools, colleges and universities or in youth centres, walk-in centres for young people and counselling services.

In recent years, CAMHS have generally been conceptualised around a four-tier strategic model of service provision, although there is some variation in the way in which the four-tier model has been developed and applied. Tier 1 covers universal services that are provided at primary care level by GPs, health visitors and social workers, for example; Tier 2 refers to services traditionally provided by uni-professional groups, who usually relate to each other through a network rather than a team; Tier 3 covers specialised multi-professional services for children with more complex mental health problems; and Tier 4 comprises specialist mental health services, such as in-patient units, day units and highly specialised out-patient teams.

For those with concerns about a child or a young person's mental health it might be helpful to speak to any of the following: a GP, a teacher, head teacher or head of year, school nurse, health visitor, social worker or youth counselling service for advice and referral for specialist help within these services.

For further information see Young Minds on www.youngminds.org.uk/camhs

Child and Family Consultation Services

3.86 Child and Family Consultation Services (child guidance clinics) are part of CAMHS and are places where parents can discuss worries about their children and where professionals can help children, young people and families to understand and deal with their problems. They are free and open to all. The service is confidential except where a child is at serious risk. Sometimes the family is seen together, especially to start with. Sometimes it is necessary to contact teachers, GPs, psychiatrists and social workers. This is done only with the full agreement and understanding of the parents or carers and the child concerned. The ways of making contact with the service are:

- self-referral – in some areas parents or young people can telephone or walk in for information and/or an appointment without a formal referral;
- health visitors, GPs and social workers can all refer. At some services, a young person under the age of 16 will be advised to seek help in his own right. However, almost everywhere the service will expect to contact the parents or carers should further help be required.

FORMAL LINKS BETWEEN AGENCIES

Local Children's Safeguarding Boards

3.87 The Children Act 2004 provides the legal underpinning for the transformation of children's services as set out in the *Every Child Matters: Change for Children* programme. Section 10 of the Act provides the statutory basis for Children's Trusts (the duty to co-operate). The Children Act 2004 sets out new duties to ensure that child welfare is highlighted in the work of all relevant agencies and in the way that they work together. It places a duty on key statutory agencies to discharge their normal functions with an emphasis on the need to safeguard and promote the welfare of children. Revised Children's Trust (CT) guidance on the 'duty to co-operate' was published on 18 November 2008. The relevant agencies must also ensure that the same approach is followed by any other bodies that provide services on their behalf, for example, GPs providing services on behalf of Primary Care Trusts (PCTs.) This parallels the duty that the Education Act 2002, s 175 placed on local authorities and on school and college governing bodies (the government is currently consulting on guidance, prior to implementation of this duty).

The 2004 Act requires each local authority to replace the non-statutory area child protection committee with a statutory Local Safeguarding Children Board. The purpose of the LCSBs is to coordinate and ensure the effectiveness of local arrangements and services to safeguard children, including services provided by individual agencies. This means:

- analysing current arrangements;
- identifying any improvements needed;
- agreeing how agencies will work together to achieve these – including commissioning services through the children's trust and identifying training needs.

The core LCSB partners are:

- local authorities including district councils;
- NHS bodies;
- police;
- local probation boards;

- Connexions (Connexions Direct – web information for children and young people
-www.connexions-direct.com);
- local prisons;
- young offender institutions;
- Children and Family Court Advisory and Support Services (Cafcass);
- the Learning and Skills Council (LSC).

The relevant partners are placed under a 'duty to co-operate in the making of arrangements to improve well-being' and have a power to pool budgets and share other resources.

The Government is intending to add to this list of relevant partners other bodies including maintained schools, Academies, further education and sixth form colleges and Job Centre Plus, to bring key delivery partners into the strategic planning role of the CT. Other agencies, including local voluntary and community sector agencies, should be represented on LCSBs. Regulations will enable the Secretary of State to set out the functions of LCSBs, such as the review or investigation of cases, and set out the means by which the functions will be delivered, for example, to ensure that LCSB partners can be represented in a manageable way rather than all partners needing to attend all meetings.

From 1 April 2008, all Local Safeguarding Children Boards (LSCBs) have had a statutory responsibility to review the deaths of all children from birth (excluding still-born babies) up to 18 years. The purpose of reviewing child deaths is to reduce the number of preventable child deaths in line with indicator 4 in PSA 13: *Improve children and young people's safety*. A serious case review (SCR), where abuse or neglect is known or suspected, may be triggered by a child death review. When a child dies, and abuse or neglect is known or suspected to be a factor in the death, the Area Child Protection Committee, in future the Local Safeguarding Children Board, has a responsibility to convene a case review (also commonly known as a Part 8 review or serious case review) into the involvement of all agencies and practitioners with the child and family. In addition, a SCR should always be carried out when a child dies in custody, either in police custody, on remand or following sentence, or where the child was detained under the Mental Health Act 2005.

All the documents are accessible on www.dcsf.gov.uk/ everychildmatters/ strategy/guidance

Case reviews are not enquiries into how a child died or who is culpable (which are matters for the coroner, police and courts); the purpose of the case review is to establish whether there are any lessons to be learned about the way in which agencies work together to safeguard children and to implement any necessary changes.

In March 2009 the Department for Children, Schools and Families (DCSF) published The Protection of Children in England: A Progress Report in which Lord Laming made a number of recommendations to strengthen and clarify the serious case review (SCR) process. His recommendations were accepted in full by the Government with an undertaking to update statutory guidance set out in Chapter 8 of Working Together to Safeguard Children. The revised guidance aims to improve the quality, consistency and impact of serious case reviews and is directed in particular at Local Safeguarding Children Boards (LSCBs) who by law undertake a serious case review whenever a child dies or is seriously injured and abuse or neglect is known or suspected to be a factor. Changes proposed to the guidance include:

- clearly setting out that the prime purpose of an SCR is to learn lessons both at an individual and inter-agency level;

- emphasising the importance of undertaking SCRs in a way that promotes learning; and

- extending the timescale for completing most SCRs from 4 to 6 months, given the inter-relationship between SCRs and other processes, such as criminal prosecutions or coroners inquests.

All these documents are accessible on www.dcsf.gov.uk/everychildmatters/ strategy/guidance.

The Child Protection Conference

Working Together to Safeguard Children (DfES, 2006) www.dcsf.gov.uk/ everychildmatters

3.88   The Child Protection Conference is a key part of the arrangements for inter-agency co-operation for the protection of children. Guidance on the role of and procedures for Child Protection Conferences is contained in Chapter 5 of *Working Together to Safeguard Children* (2006). There are two types of child protection conference. An initial child protection conference is a formal inter-agency meeting convened following a Section 47 enquiry. It brings together family members (including the child, where appropriate) and professionals involved with the child and the family, in order to make a judgment about whether the child is at continuing risk of significant harm and subject to a child protection plan, in which case a child protection plan will be drawn up.

A child protection review conference is also a formal inter-agency meeting (the practitioners invited will usually be the same as for the initial conference) to ensure that the child continues to be adequately safeguarded, and to consider whether any changes are required to the child protection plan. Responsibility for drawing up child protection procedures (which include those governing investigation of allegations of child abuse and the Child Protection Conference itself) is charged to the Local Safeguarding Children Boards/Area Child Protection Committees. Agencies represented on each committee will include social services, the police, health authorities, the local education authority, the probation service, the NSPCC and other agencies having a role in the child protection process.

The Initial Child Protection Conference

3.89   The initial child protection conference brings together family members, the child where appropriate, and those professionals most involved with the child and family, following Children Act 1989, s 47 enquiries. Its purpose is:

•   to bring together and analyse in an inter-agency setting the information which has been obtained about the child's developmental needs, and the parents' or carers' capacity to respond to these needs to ensure the child's safety and promote the child's health and development within the context of their wider family and environment;

•   to consider the evidence presented to the conference, make judgments about the likelihood of a child suffering significant harm in future and decide whether the child is at continuing risk of significant harm; and

•   to decide what future action is required to safeguard and promote the welfare of the child, how that action will be taken forward, and with what intended outcomes.

The Child Protection Plan

3.90 This is a detailed inter-agency plan for a child who is considered to be at a continuing risk of significant harm. The plan is based on current findings from any relevant assessment and information held from any previous involvement with the child and family. It sets out what needs to change in order to safeguard the child from harm. A key worker from social services is appointed, the core group members are identified, and decisions are made about what further assessments are required to inform the outline plan. An outline of the child protection plan is drawn up at the initial child protection conference, and is further developed by the core group members; it is reviewed at each subsequent child protection review conference.

The Child Protection Review Conference

3.91 The first child protection review conference should be held within 3 months of the initial child protection conference, and further reviews should be held at intervals of not more than 6 months for as long as the child remains the subject of a child protection plan. A decision to remove a child's name from a child protection plan will be taken at a child protection review conference.

Working Together to Safeguard Children can be downloaded from www.dcsf.gov.uk.

Children Looked After by the Local Authority

3.92 Each responsible authority is required to appoint an independent reviewing officer (IRO). The IROs are responsible for monitoring the local authority's review of the care plan for a child, with the aim of ensuring that actions required to implement the care plan are carried out and outcomes monitored. The Regulations give IROs power to refer a case to Cafcass to take legal action as a last resort where a child's human rights are considered to be in breach through failure to implement the care plan.

The Children and Young Persons Act 2008 introduced significant changes to the independent reviewing officers (IRO) role and function. Changes to the statutory framework enable the IRO to have a more effective independent oversight of the child's case. The IRO Handbook provides statutory guidance addressed to each IRO about how they should discharge their distinct responsibilities to looked after children. The IRO handbook is available on www.dcsf.gov.uk.

See further **2.54**.

THE BENEFITS SYSTEM

3.93   The benefits system provides practical help and financial support for people who are unemployed and looking for work. It also provides additional income to people when earnings are low, who are bringing up children, are retired, care for someone, are ill or have a disability.

Further information from:
www.direct.gov.uk
www.citizensadvice.org.uk
www.adviceguide.org.uk

The Department for Work and Pensions (DWP) manages most benefits through Jobcentre Plus offices. Benefits and entitlements for pensioners are dealt with through a network of pension centres which provide a face-to-face service for those who need additional help and support. Other agencies or government departments are also involved, such as local council or HM Revenue and Customs (HMRC).

People of Working Age

3.94   Benefits and services for people of working age, for example Jobseeker's Allowance and income support, are managed by Jobcentre Plus offices. Jobcentre Plus deals with:

- finding work;
- starting a business;
- managing on a low income;
- illness or accidents caused by work.

Pensioners and People Planning for their Retirement

3.95   The Pension Service, which is part of the DWP, provides services to:

- people planning for their retirement;
- people approaching retirement;
- people who have already retired;
- employers;
- pensions providers and advisers.

The Pension Service deals with benefits and entitlements such as the State Pension, Pension Credit and Winter Fuel Payments.

Families and Children

3.96 Jobcentre Plus deals with benefits and services for families, including those:

- bringing up children, including children with special needs;
- managing on a low income, including help with health costs.

Further information from: www.cmoptions.org/ www.hmrc.gov.uk

The Child Support Agency (CSA) works with the Child Maintenance and Enforcement Commission (C-MEC, see further **3.100**). The tax system (HMRC) deals with Child Benefit, Guardian's Allowance and tax credits. Tax credits are for people who start work and are on a low income. If people are responsible for at least one child or young person who normally lives with them, they may qualify for Child Tax Credit to help with the cost of looking after them.

Disabled People and Carers

3.97 The Disability and Carers Service, which is part of the DWP, is responsible for benefits and services for people who are sick or have a disability, for example, Disability Living Allowance and Attendance Allowance. A Jobcentre Plus office is the first point of contact for accessing these benefits and services.

Housing Benefit and Council Tax Benefit

Further information from: www.direct.gov.uk www.citizensadvice.org.uk www.adviceguide.org.uk

3.98 Local authorities deal with Housing Benefit and Council Tax Benefit.

Child Trust Funds

3.99 Child trust fund accounts are a new type of universal long-term investment account for children. In principle, all children born after 31 August 2002 will qualify for an account; each account will be credited with an initial Treasury endowment of £250. If the child is part of a household getting Child Tax Credit, with a household income at or below the threshold (which is £16,040 for tax year 2009-10), the child will get an additional £250 which will be paid directly into the Child Trust Fund account. Once the child reaches 7 years of age, the child will get a further payment of £250 (£500 if the family is on a low income).

A government voucher is issued which is to be used to open a special account that each child will be able to access when they reach 18. Parents, family and friends can add up to £1,200 to the account each year. There is no tax to pay on the CTF income or any gains (profits) it makes until the child reaches age 18. A child will be eligible if he:

- was born on or after 1 September 2002;
- qualifies for Child Benefit;
- is living in the UK;
- is not subject to any immigration restriction.

A child will not be eligible for a Child Trust Fund if his/her parent is an asylum seeker waiting for an asylum claim to be processed.

There are special arrangements for children looked after by local authorities, or health trusts in Northern Ireland, to make sure they do not miss out. Since April 2007, for every continuous year a child is looked after in the care of a local authority (health trust in Northern Ireland) they should receive £100 – these payments are made by the local authority/health trust.

Also, since April 2009, if a parent receives Disability Living Allowance for the child, the child will receive an annual payment of £100, with severely disabled children receiving £200 – these payments will be paid directly into the Child Trust Fund account starting from April 2010.

CHILD SUPPORT AGENCY AND C-MEC

3.100   There are currently two main options that parents can choose from for arranging a child maintenance agreement:

- making a private arrangement with the other parent;
- using the Child Support Agency (CSA) as the statutory maintenance service to calculate and collect maintenance.

The Child Maintenance Options service is a free service providing impartial information to help both parents make an informed choice about maintenance.

Child Maintenance and Enforcement Commission (C-MEC) www.childmaintenance.org

If the parents with care or their current partners who you live with are claiming Income Support, income-based Jobseeker's Allowance or income-related Employment and Support Allowance, the first £20 per week of any maintenance they receive will not affect those benefits. This arrangement has been extended across the CSA's old and new schemes and it also applies if maintenance is arranged through a private agreement.

The CSA's role is to:

- trace parents who no longer live with their children (the non-resident parent) in cases where the parent residing with the children (the parent with care) wants support in seeking maintenance;

- work out how much child maintenance should be paid by the non-resident parent, to help meet their child's everyday living costs;

- (in some cases) handle the payments from the non-resident parent to the parent with care;

- monitor these payments and taking appropriate enforcement action where payments are late or missed.

There are two broad categories of maintenance applicants under the Act: (i) parents with care who claim income support, family credit and disability working allowance who must have their child maintenance assessed by the CSA and (ii) others who can choose to do so. In 2000 the government passed legislation setting out a new method for calculating child support. This system began in 2003 and operates broadly as follows:

- The non residential parent (NRP) pays a percentage of net income to the parent with care (PWC/residential parent). This is set at 15% for one child, 20% for two children and 25% for three or more children. Net income is income minus tax, NI contributions and full pension contributions.

- The income of the PWC is not to be taken into account under any circumstances.

- There is a one-seventh reduction in liability for shared care of more than 52 nights per year,

increasing to one-half plus £7 for each child the
NRP has shared care of for 175 nights or more a
year.

- There will be a reduction for second and step
  families.

- A minimum payment of £5 per week will apply for
  NRPs on benefits (those who have shared care are
  exempted from this).

- Those with an income of less than £200 per week
  will pay reduced rates.

- Those with an income of less than £100 per week
  will pay a flat rate of £5 per week.

Due to difficulties with the CSA system a new Child
Maintenance and Enforcement Commission (C-MEC)
is gradually being established. The Child Maintenance
and Other Payments Act 2008 (CMOPA 2008) Act
establishes the framework for the redesign of the child
support system.

C-MEC represents a new approach (see
www.cmoptions.org) and is expected to take over the
CSA's functions shortly, although the transition process
is likely to extend until at least 2014. The main incentive
is the increased maintenance disregard for PWCs who
are on means–tested benefits. There will also be a new
range of weapons to be added to the Commission's
collection and enforcement armoury.

C–MEC may be allowed to charge fees for its services
(s 6) although the Government has announced that fees
will not be introduced until 2010 at the earliest.
C–MEC may make agency arrangements for the
provisions of services (s 7) and can also contract out
certain services (s 8). C–MEC must make an annual
report to the Secretary of State (s 9), which has to be
published and must consider the Secretary of State's
guidance and comply with ministerial directions (s 10).

Some provisions of CMOPA 2008 are already in force
(see CMOPA 2008 (Commencement) Order 2008,
SI 2008/1476). Crucially, until the law changed, if the
parent with the main day-to-day care was on benefits,
he/she had to arrange child maintenance using the
Child Support Agency (CSA), and was not able to opt
out and make a private agreement with the other
parent. Since 27 October 2008, all parents have had the
choice of setting up a child maintenance arrangement
using the CSA or making a private agreement about
child maintenance with the other parent. The

requirement that parents with care (PWCs) on income support (or income–based jobseeker's allowance) must apply for child maintenance was abolished with effect from 14 July 2008 (s 15 of the CMOPA 2008, repealing s 6 of the Child Support Act 1991). The benefit penalty under s 46 of the 1991 Act for those PWCs who fail to comply was also abolished. So new claimants cannot be required to apply for child support and equally cannot be penalised for failing to do so. So far as existing benefits cases are concerned, those PWCs are still formally subject to the s 6 compulsion but any benefit sanction for non–compliance must be lifted from these cases.

The CSA can be accessed through www.csa.gov.uk or a telephone helpline on 08457 133 133 or through Jobcentre Plus offices. See also www.cmoptions.org.

HOUSING

3.101   Under the Housing Act 1996, local councils allocate accommodation when they provide a secure tenancy in their own stock or nominate someone to be an assured tenant of a housing association. A council must have an allocations scheme which sets out the priorities and procedures for allocating housing. A council will:

- provide an application form to anyone who wishes to apply for housing;

- assess whether someone who has made an application is eligible to be allocated social housing;

- assess the housing needs of the applicant and their household;

- prioritise each application according to the criteria set out in the allocation scheme;

- tell each applicant what priority he has for housing.

The fact that a person is eligible does not guarantee that he will be allocated accommodation. As regards priorities, an allocation scheme must give reasonable preference to certain categories of persons. These are:

- people who are homeless;

- people living in insanitary, overcrowded or unsatisfactory housing;

- people who need to move on medical or welfare grounds;
- people who need to move to a particular locality in the district of the authority, where failure to meet that need would cause hardship to themselves or to others.

The scheme may give additional preference to people in the above categories who are considered to have more urgent housing needs. Many councils have developed complex points-based systems to determine the level of an applicant's housing need, and will normally allocate available housing to the person on the register who has the highest number of points. However, some councils use simplified 'banding' schemes. Under such a system applicants are grouped into 'bands' reflecting different levels of housing need, with prioritisation of applicants within these groups usually being determined by waiting time. As a general rule, the number of bands in the system will depend on the demand for housing in the area and the allocation schemes system of prioritising applicants.

Some councils are now operating choice-based lettings (CBL) schemes. CBL schemes allow people to apply for available council/registered social landlord accommodation which is openly advertised (eg in local press or via a website). Applicants can see the full range of available properties and apply for any home to which they are matched. The successful bidder is the one with the highest priority under the scheme. Councils provide feedback which helps applicants assess their chances of success in future. The Department for Communities and Local Government (DCLG) has set a target for all councils to adopt a CBL scheme by 2010.

Further information from:
www.direct.gov.uk.

EDUCATION AND SCHOOLS

3.102 The Department for Children, Schools and Families is the central authority responsible for national policy on education and for raising standards. It is the duty of the local authorities (which were called local education authorities) and, where there are sufficient grant-maintained schools in the area, the Training and Development Agency for Schools to ensure that education is available to meet the needs of the population in their areas. They must work within the framework established by the Education Act 1993 (now consolidated in the Education Act 1996). Local authorities are empowered to bring legal proceedings against parents who fail to ensure that their children of compulsory school age receive sufficient full-time education. Parents can meet their obligations by sending them to non-state schools or, more rarely, by showing that other suitable arrangements have been made for the education of their children, for example at home. When a child is absent from school, the parent is normally required to give a legally acceptable reason such as:

- sickness or unavoidable emergency;
- a day of religious observance for the child and her family;
- participation in an entertainment;
- a family holiday with leave granted by the school.

For more information see
www.dcfs.gov.uk

Special educational needs (SEN) and disability

3.103   Children must be educated in accordance with their age, ability and aptitude and in accordance with any special educational needs that they may have. Under the Education Act 1996, governing bodies of all maintained schools are under a duty to use their best endeavours to secure that appropriate provision is made to meet a child's special educational needs. Local authorities have a duty to identify those children in their area whose special needs cannot be met within the facilities and resources normally available to mainstream schools in the area, and to conduct a multi-professional assessment of the child, taking medical, educational, psychological and other relevant factors into account. The local authority has a duty to prepare a 'statement' in respect of the child if, after the assessment, it considers that it is necessary to determine the special educational provision which is required. If the parents and the local authority do not agree about the proposed educational provision, the parents have the right to appeal to an independent Special Educational Needs Tribunal.

Sure Start works with parents and children to promote the physical, intellectual and social development of pre-school children to ensure they are ready to learn on entry to school. Sure Start providers help identify children at risk of developing learning disabilities and provide or arrange to provide appropriate early intervention and support.

The Government's strategy for SEN was launched in February 2004. It sets out the Government's vision for enabling children with SEN to realise their potential and a programme of sustained action and review over a number of years to support early years settings, schools and local authorities in improving provision for children with SEN in four key areas. It builds on the proposals for integrating children's services in the *Every Child Matters* Green Paper and includes a strategy for improving childcare for families of children with SEN and disabilities.

The strategy sets out the Government's objectives and priorities for future action in the short and longer-term, embedding SEN and disability in mainstream policy and practice, and focusing on improving outcomes for children and young people.

Special educational needs coordinators (SENCOs)

3.104   The role of the SENCO is crucial for early years settings in supporting early identification and intervention for children with special educational needs. The SENCO is responsible for maintaining a setting's recording and documentation process with respect to special educational needs, liaising and working with the parents, securing training for workers and liaising with outside agencies with respect to a child's SEN.

Area special educational needs coordinators (Area SENCOs)

3.105   Area SENCOs are employed by local authorities and are responsible for supporting approximately 20 non-maintained settings within their district. The aim of the area SENCO is to support the work of the setting based SENCO and promote inclusion in early years settings, reduce the underachievement gap and enable all children to reach their full potential.

The Sure Start, Extended Schools and Childcare Group has produced guidance for local authorities and Early Years Development and Childcare Partnerships on the role of area SENCOs.

Welfare

The Children's Plan – Promoting Children's Well-being

3.106   The Education and Inspections Act 2006 laid a duty on the governing bodies of maintained schools, primary, secondary, special and Pupil Referral Units, in discharging their functions relating to the conduct of the school, to promote the well-being of pupils at the school. The duty came into effect in September 2007. Since that date, an equivalent requirement has been placed on new academies through their funding agreements. Well-being is defined in law in terms of the five Every Child Matters (ECM) outcomes:

- be healthy;
- stay safe;
- enjoy and achieve;
- make a positive contribution; and
- achieve economic well-being.

Schools are already inspected against these outcomes by Ofsted. In promoting well-being schools must have regard to the Children and Young People's Plan for their area and to the views of parents. The Children's Plan is commitment to develop school level indicators of a school's contribution to pupil well-being to be reflected in the Ofsted cycle of inspections beginning in September 2009. The purpose is to provide additional benchmarked data to inform schools' evaluation of their contribution to well-being and their consideration of priorities, and to inform Ofsted judgments of schools' performance. Ofsted will not, however, judge schools on the indicators alone which will be evidence, not inspection judgments.

Schools also contribute through the curriculum by developing children's understanding, awareness and resilience.

Creating a safe learning environment means having effective arrangements in place to address a range of issues. Some are subject to statutory requirements, including child protection arrangements, pupil health and safety, and bullying. Others include arrangements for meeting the health needs of children with medical conditions, providing first aid, school security, tackling drugs and substance misuse, and having arrangements in place to safeguard and promote the welfare of children on extended vocational placements.

Education staff have a crucial role to play in helping identify welfare concerns, and indicators of possible abuse or neglect, at an early stage: referring those concerns to the appropriate organisation, normally social services colleagues, contributing to the assessment of a child's needs and where appropriate to ongoing action to meet those needs. When a child has special educational needs, or is disabled, the school will have important information about the child's level of understanding and the most effective means of communicating with the child. They will also be well placed to give a view on the impact of treatment or intervention on the child's care or behaviour.

Childcare

3.107   Childcare services – family and children's centres, day nurseries, childminders, pre-schools, playgroups, and holiday and out of school schemes – play an important part in the lives of large numbers of children. Many childcare providers have considerable experience of working with families where a child needs to be safeguarded from harm, and many local authorities provide, commission or sponsor specific services, including childminders, to work with children in need and their families.

Childminders and everyone working in day care services should know how to recognise and respond to the possible abuse or neglect of a child. Private, voluntary and local authority day care providers caring for children under the age of 8 must be registered by Ofsted under the Children Act 1989, and should have a written statement, based on the procedures laid out in the booklet *What To Do If You're Worried A Child Is Being Abused – Summary*. This statement should clearly set out staff responsibilities for reporting suspected child abuse or neglect in accordance with Local Safeguarding Children Boards procedures and should include contact and telephone numbers for the local police and children's social care.

The Childcare Act, passed into law on 11 July 2006, was aimed at being pioneering legislation and is the first ever legislation exclusively concerned with Early Years and childcare. The Act aimed to transform childcare and Early Years services in England, taking forward some of the key commitments from the Ten Year Childcare Strategy published in December 2004.

Measures in the Act formalised the important strategic role local authorities play through a set of duties requiring authorities to improve the five Every Child Matters (ECM) outcomes for all pre-school children and reduce inequalities in these outcomes; secure sufficient childcare for working parents; and provide a better parental information service. The Act also reformed and simplified Early Years regulation and inspection arrangements providing for a new integrated education and care quality framework (for pre-school children) and the new Ofsted Childcare Register. The sufficiency, information and outcomes duties came into effect from 1 April 2008 and the remaining provisions from September 2008.

Statutory guidance was also published by DCSF in July 2007 to assist local authorities in completing their duties to secure sufficient childcare to enable parents to work and undertake training. This duty came into force from April 2008.

Other duties to secure information, advice and training for childcare providers came into force from October 2007.

These duties were introduced under ss 6–10 and s 13 of the Childcare Act 2006.

The Childcare Act has four parts: duties on local authorities in England (Part 1); duties on local authorities in Wales (Part 2); regulation and inspection arrangements for childcare providers in England (Part 3); and general provisions (Part 4). Key provisions are as follows.

Sections 1-5 require local authorities and their NHS and Jobcentre Plus partners to work together to improve the outcomes of all children up to age 5 and reduce inequalities between them, by ensuring early childhood services are integrated to maximise access and benefits to families – underpinning a Sure Start Children's Centre for every community.

Sections 6, 8-11 and 13 require local authorities to assess the local childcare market and to secure sufficient childcare for working parents. Childcare will only be deemed sufficient if it meets the needs of the community in general and in particular those families on lower incomes and those with disabled children. Local authorities take the strategic lead in their local childcare market, planning, supporting and commissioning childcare. Local authorities are not expected to provide childcare direct but are expected to work with local private, voluntary and independent sector providers to meet local need.

Section 7 re-enacts the duty for local authorities to secure a free minimum amount of early learning and care for all 3- and 4-year-olds whose parents want it.

Section 12 extends the existing duty to provide information to parents, to ensure parents and prospective parents can access the full range of information they may need for their children right through to their twentieth birthday. Local authorities are required to ensure that this service is available to all parents and that it is pro-active in reaching those parents who might otherwise have difficulty accessing the information service.

Sections 39–48 introduced the Early Years Foundation Stage (EYFS) which builds on and brings together the existing Birth to Three Matters, Foundation Stage and national standards for under-8's day care and childminding. The EYFS supports providers in delivering high quality integrated early education and care for children from birth to age 5.

Sections 31–98 reform and simplify the framework for the regulation of childcare and early education to reduce bureaucracy and focus on raising quality and standards. All providers caring for children from birth to the 31 August following their fifth birthday are required to register on the Early Years register and deliver the Early Years Foundation Stage (unless exceptionally exempted). Childcare settings providing for children from the 1 September following their fifth birthday up to the age of 8 must register on the compulsory part of the Ofsted Childcare Register (unless they are exempt). The Act introduced certain requirements that all providers who are registering on the Ofsted Childcare Register need to meet, some of which are provided for in the Act but most of which are laid down in associated Regulations made under the Act. Those childcare providers who are not obliged to register on the compulsory part of the Ofsted Childcare Register can choose to join the voluntary part of the Register. These providers also need to meet certain requirements, which are laid down in Regulations made under the Act.

Sections 99–101 allow for the collection of information about young children to inform funding and support the local authority duties under the Act.

Educational Psychologists

3.108   See **2.124**.

Interpreters

3.109   The National Register of Public Service Interpreters (NRPSI Ltd) is a facility for the use of public service organisations and agencies which they work through to obtain professional, qualified and quality assured interpreters. Like other professional registers, it comprises individuals who have satisfied selection criteria in terms of qualifications and experience, agreed to abide by a Code of Conduct and are subject to disciplinary procedures where there are allegations that the code has been breached.

Public Service Interpreters, as the name implies, are interpreters who work in the context of public services, such as the legal profession, health services and local government related services, which include housing, education, welfare, environmental health and social services. Public service organisations and agencies that they work through can obtain access to the National Register via a subscription service which is available through a website via a secure Online Register.

The Register is administered by NRPSI Ltd, a wholly owned and not-for-profit subsidiary of the Chartered Institute of Linguists. The Chartered Institute of Linguists is the UK's largest language professional body and was established in 1910.

Further information from www.nrpsi.co.uk 0845 4500 280 and Fax 0845 4500 420, Minerva House, Spaniel Row, Nottingham, NG1 6EP

Particular care should be taken in choosing an interpreter, having regard to their language skills, their understanding of the issues under discussion, their commitment to confidentiality, and their position in the wider community. There can be difficulties in using family members or friends as interpreters and this should be avoided. Children should not be used as interpreters.

Contact Centres

3.110   The National Association of Child Contact Centres (NACCC) is a national charity supporting more than 300 member centres in England, Wales and Northern Ireland. Centres ensure that the interests of the child always receive priority and comply with a comprehensive code of practice. Referrals to centres can be made by: solicitors, CAFCASS officers, children's services, Citizens Advice Bureaux, family mediators and Relate. The contact centre will make its own assessment as to whether contact is suitable at its premises. It cannot be ordered to provide a contact facility.

The work of contact centres is usually regarded by the courts as privileged and has similarities with mediation. All NACCC Child Contact Centres are expected to achieve Accreditation. They must also subsequently maintain these standards. In December 2008 the Legal Services Commission amended its decision-making guidance to reflect the Children and Adoption Act 2006 and in relation to the funding of contact centres/assessments.

As a result, the costs of an assessment of supervised contact or other professional assessment of contact will no longer be treated as a solicitor's disbursement and cannot be reimbursed out of the Community Legal Service Fund on behalf of funded clients. This extends to contact re-introduction and to any report based, in whole or in part, on an observation or observations of contact with a child/children.

For further details contact:
NACCC,
Minerva House,
Spaniel Row,
Nottingham,
NG1 6EP.
Tel: 0845 4500 280
www.naccc.org.uk

VOLUNTARY AGENCIES

3.111 The voluntary sector is made up of thousands of varied organisations which complement, support, extend and influence the informal and statutory systems. Voluntary services may receive grants from either central or local government to maintain their administrative and organisational structure, for particular short-term projects or in payment for specific services. Voluntary and non-statutory bodies act as pressure groups for social reform, co-operate with local authorities in formulating policies and plans, provide support services and fill some of the gaps in statutory provision. They vary in size and objectives and provide between them a very wide range of services, including the care of children and parents. Councils for Voluntary Service (CVS) have been set up in a large proportion of district council areas. They are independent charities whose role is to support and develop other voluntary services and create links and liaison between the statutory and voluntary sectors. Over the years, many voluntary organisations have developed considerable knowledge about services for young children and their families and how these support parents. They involve the community in a variety of ways in their activities and services, and their presence in an area can help to

Every Child Matters
www.dcsf.gov.uk/
everychildmatters/

improve the quality of provision. Local authorities have a detailed knowledge of local voluntary organisations so that they can work in partnership with them. Children England (which used to be called The National Council for Voluntary Child Care Organisations: the name was changed in December 2008) acts as a coordinating group.

Major Agencies Concerned with Children and Families

3.112 Services for children and families were pioneered by voluntary organisations in the nineteenth century. They may be grant-aided by central or local government, but most rely considerably on voluntary income as well. They vary in size and objectives and provide between them a very wide range of child care services. A full list is available in Appendix B below.

McKenzie Friends

3.113 A McKenzie Friend (MF) is someone who assists a litigant in person in court. An MF does not represent the litigant and does not have rights of audience. MFs have no official legal status but a litigant in person wishing to have the help of an MF should be allowed to do so unless the judge is satisfied that fairness and the interests of justice do not so require, in which case the judge should give reasons for refusing to allow a litigant in person to have a MF. The presumption in favour of permitting an MF is a strong one. An MF is allowed to:

- provide moral support for the litigant;
- take notes;
- help with case papers;
- quietly give advice on:
  - points of law or procedure;
  - issues that the litigant may wish to raise in court;
  - questions the litigant may wish to ask witnesses.

An MF:
- has no right to act on behalf of a litigant in person. It is the right of the litigant to use the assistance of an MF if he so requires;

- is not entitled to address the court, nor examine any witnesses. If he does so he becomes an advocate and requires the grant of a right of audience;
- may not attend a closed court unless the litigant has received permission from the court for the MF to do so at the start of a hearing;
- may not act as the agent of the litigant in relation to the proceedings nor manage the litigant's case outside of court, for example, by signing court documents.

The following are not good reasons for refusing a MF:

- the litigant in person appears to be sufficiently intelligent to be able to conduct the case on his/her own;
- the litigant in person appears to have sufficient grasp of the facts and documentation;
- it is a directions or case management hearing;
- the proceedings are confidential.

In the light of the growth of litigants in person in all levels of family court, the President of the Family Division issued guidance on the subject on 14 April 2008 ([2008] 2 FLR 110) which provides helpful detail as to this issue.

Litigants in person should also be aware of the services provided by local Personal Support Units (PSU) and Citizens Advice Bureaux (CAB).

Citizens' Advice Bureaux (CAB) at the Royal Courts of Justice tel: 020 7947 6564

Volunteers

3.114   The voluntary sector has an important role in the family justice system. For example, contact centres are staffed by volunteers and the government has made clear that the voluntary and community sector has a vital role to play in the *Every Child Matters: Change for Children* programme. Voluntary sector organisations are key partners for local authorities in the development of children's trusts. The DCFS has developed an overarching strategy for working with the voluntary and community sector to deliver change for children and young people and children's trusts are the new way of working at local level so harnessing the contribution of all agencies working with children, young people and families in the planning, commissioning and delivery of services. Local authorities are expected to involve

www.dcsf.gov.uk/ everychildmatters/

voluntary and community organisations at all levels of children's trusts – from governance to integrated service delivery.

The Third Sector

3.115   The Third Sector is a diverse, active and passionate sector of organisations which share common characteristics of being non-governmental, value-driven and which principally reinvest any financial surpluses to further social, environmental or cultural objectives.

The term encompasses voluntary and community organisations, charities, social enterprises, co-operatives and mutuals, both large and small.

As part of the Cabinet Office, the Office of the Third Sector (OTS) leads work across government to support the environment for a thriving third sector, enabling the sector to campaign for change, deliver public services, promote social enterprise and strengthen communities. The OTS was created at the centre of government in May 2006 in recognition of the increasingly important role the third sector plays in both society and the economy.

The aim of the OTS is to develop and support an environment which enables the third sector to thrive, growing in its contribution to Britain's society, economy and environment. It works in partnership with central and local government and the third sector to enable campaigning and empowerment, particularly for those at risk of social exclusion. It also aims to strengthen communities, drawing together people from different sections of society, to transform public services, through delivery, design, innovation and campaigning, and to enable social enterprise growth and development, combining business and social goals.

Further information from:
www.cabinetoffice.gov.uk

On 11 September 2009, Angela Smith, Minister for the Third Sector, announced the launch of the 12 week consultation on the draft Charities Consolidation Bill. The draft Bill would bring together provisions of the Recreational Charities Act 1958, the Charities Act 1993 and most of the Charities Act 2006 into a single piece of legislation.

The Consumers

The Family and Parenting Institute

3.116   The Family and Parenting Institute is the leading centre of expertise on families and parenting in the UK. Its mission is to support parents in bringing up children, and its aim is the well-being of children and families. To achieve this, it carries out research and policy work to find out what matters to families and parents, and develops ideas to improve the services families use and to improve the environment in which children grow up. The FPI works to inform policymakers and public debate and to develop practical resources for people working with families.

The FPI produces a wide range of publications for professionals concerned with families and for families themselves, and also offers free downloads from its website. The types of publications offered are:

- Consultation responses
- Information for families
- Policy discussion papers
- Speeches and presentations
- Case Studies
- Fact Sheets
- Information for practitioners
- Research publications
- Surveys

The FPI holds events throughout the year; Meet the Parents and Parents' Week are two of the major events held throughout the year.

The FPI is funded by a mixture of grants from government departments, charitable trusts and foundations, fees for research and consultancy work that it undertakes and sponsorship and donations from corporate partners. It also maintains a continuous programme of fundraising.

Further information from:
www.familyandparenting.org
Tel: 020 7424 3460

THE ROLE OF CENTRAL GOVERNMENT

3.117   Central government's role in the family justice system is shared between several government departments, listed below. This will inevitably lead to certain tensions, not particularly between the departments themselves but between each of them and the Treasury.

Government Departments

The Ministry of Justice

Further information from:
www.justice.gov.uk

3.118   The Ministry of Justice is one of the largest government departments. Every year around nine million people use its services in 900 locations across the United Kingdom, including 650 courts and tribunals and 139 prisons in England and Wales. Its work spans criminal, civil and family justice, democracy, rights and the constitution.

Department for Children Schools and Families

3.119   The Department for Children, Schools and Families (DCSF) is responsible for issues affecting people in England up to the age of 19, including child protection and education including:

- family policy – supporting families – private and public law;
- relationship breakdown and resolution;
- Cafcass;

See further.
www.dcsf.gov.uk

- domestic violence;

Department of Health

See further.
www.dh.gov.uk

3.120   The Department of Health (DoH) has responsibility for standards of health care in the country, including the NHS. It sets the strategic framework for adult social care and influences local authority spend on social care.

Home Office

See further
www.homeoffice.gov.uk

3.121   The Home Office is the lead government department for immigration and passports, drugs policy, counter-terrorism, crime and police.

Department of Work and Pensions

3.122   The Department for Work and Pensions has two operational organisations:

- Jobcentre Plus, a service dedicated to helping people back into work and administering related and other, Social Security benefits (Jobseeker's

Allowance, Incapacity Benefit, Income Support, Employment and Support Allowance, Bereavement Benefits, Maternity Allowance, Industrial Injuries Benefits, Social Fund).

- The Pension, Disability and Carers Service containing two sub-organisations, the Pension Service and the Disability and Carers Service. The former facilitates the state pension and Pension Credit systems and provides information on other related issues and the latter provides financial and practical support to disabled people and their carers.

See further:
www.dwp.gov.uk

Foreign and Commonwealth Office

3.123   The Foreign and Commonwealth Office, commonly called the Foreign Office or the FCO, is the British government department responsible for promoting the interests of the United Kingdom overseas, created in 1968 by merging the Foreign Office and the Commonwealth Office. The Forced Marriage Unit (FMU) is dedicated to preventing British nationals being forced into marriage overseas. Contact the FMU on: tel 020 7008 0151.

See www.fco.gov.uk

CHAPTER FOUR

CORE PRINCIPLES OF LAW

THE WELFARE OF CHILDREN

4.1   Tens of thousands of children are involved in family proceedings each year. Most have little or no formal say in arrangements about their future, such as where they will live or with whom they will have contact. This may be particularly so where parents are separating or divorcing without serious dispute. For a minority of children, there is provision for their voices to be heard indirectly as part of the court process. The courts and Cafcass deal with more than 80,000 children each year where future plans for them have to be carefully scrutinised. Such children include those whose separating parents are unable to agree about their future care or their contact with the non-resident parent, or whose parents cannot offer adequate care without formal local authority involvement underpinned by a care or supervision order or who are placed for adoption or elsewhere outside the close family unit, or even those children whose property or income arising from such property requires administration. Although these children have diverse needs, they all require that their welfare is safeguarded.

The Children Act 1989 addresses child welfare across the full spectrum, making no distinction between children in private law proceedings, children in public law proceedings and children in need. It sets out the central principles that must be applied by any court in relation to all children's cases, namely decisions about who should be allowed to exercise parental responsibility for the child, reduction of delay in reaching decisions about children's welfare and minimum intervention in children's lives. All principles of the law are related to and subsumed by an overarching principle, that the child's welfare must be the court's paramount consideration.

The general principles of the 1989 Act are that:

(1)   the child's welfare is the court's paramount consideration for any court deciding any question with respect to the upbringing of a child (s 1(1));

(2) any delay in deciding the issues involved is likely to prejudice the welfare of the child and should be avoided if possible (s 1(2));

(3) a court cannot make any order in respect of a child unless it is satisfied that making the order would be better for the child than making no order at all (s 1(5) – the 'no order' principle).

Welfare is a concept easy to recognise but hard to define. In framing the Children Act 1989, the Law Commission used the following definition:

> 'Welfare is an all encompassing word. It includes material welfare in the sense of adequacy of resources to provide a pleasant home and a comfortable standard of living and in the sense of adequacy of care to ensure that good health and due personal pride are maintained. However, while material considerations have their place, they are secondary matters. More important are the stability and security, the warm and compassionate relationships, that are essential for the full development of the child's own character, personality and talents.'

The Welfare Checklist (section 1(3))

4.2 The 1989 Act made definition easier as well as more consistent by laying down a checklist, each item of which a court has to address before coming to a decision:

- the ascertainable wishes and feelings of the child concerned (considered in the light of the child's age and understanding);
- the child's physical, emotional and educational needs;
- the likely effect on the child of any change in the child's circumstances;
- the child's age, sex, background and any individual characteristics which the court considers relevant;
- any harm which the child has suffered or is at risk of suffering;
- how capable each of the parents, and any other person in relation to whom the court considers the question to be relevant, is of meeting the child's needs;
- the range of powers available to the court.

No one factor has priority over another, nor is the list exhaustive.

Paramount Consideration

4.3   This means that the child's welfare is to be treated as the top item in a list of items relevant to the matter in question. When all the relevant facts, relationships, claims and wishes of parents, risks, choices and other circumstances are taken into account, the course to be followed is that which is most in the interests of the child's welfare. The question is not what the justice of the case requires, but what the best interest of the child requires. The paramountcy principle applies in Children Act 1989 proceedings and not in other matters concerning children such as criminal proceedings, child support, immigration, income support or housing legislation.

The paramountcy principle is now also applied in adoption proceedings, since the coming into force of the Adoption and Children Act 2002, in which the considerations to be considered regarding the child's welfare vary slightly. Here, the check list is as follows (s 1(4)):

- the child's ascertainable wishes and feelings regarding the decision (considered in the light of the child's age and understanding);

- the child's particular needs;

- the likely effect on the child (throughout his life) of having ceased to be a member of the original family and become an adopted person;

- the child's age, sex, background and any of the child's characteristics which the court or agency considers relevant;

- any harm (within the meaning of the Children Act 1989) which the child has suffered or is at risk of suffering;

- the relationship which the child has with relatives, and with any other person in relation to whom the court or agency considers the relationship to be relevant, including:

  - the likelihood of any such relationship continuing and the value to the child of its doing so;

- the ability and willingness of any of the child's relatives, or of any such person, to provide the child with a secure environment in which the child can develop, and otherwise to meet the child's needs;
- the wishes and feelings of any of the child's relatives, or of any such person, regarding the child.

Under the 2002 Act, the principles to be applied are similar to those under the 1989 Act, including the reduction of delay and the 'no order' principle. The 2002 Act however, also requires an adoption agency, in placing a child for adoption, to give due consideration to the child's religious persuasion, racial origin and cultural and linguistic background (s 1(5)).

Delay

4.4   The avoidance of delay in making decisions about a child's welfare is a basic tenet of both the 1989 and the 2002 Acts. The laying down of the original principle was tempting fate as years later persistent delay is still a major cause of concern. Unnecessary delay is seen as inimical to a child's well-being. Three months' separation from a caring parent will seem interminable to a young child who has no sense that that period of time will end, and on matters of residence and contact it can be difficult for the 'non-resident' parent to re-establish a relationship with his/her child after a period of time:

> 'Each and every child who comes before the court is an individual with a unique past, present and future. Unfortunately the children are not often in a position to tell the story for themselves or indeed to have reached a sufficient level of understanding to be able to tell it at all. It may have to be pieced together from the evidence of many individuals, and will often remain incomplete. The court's task is to weigh up all the factors and, on balance, to select the course of action which is likely to do least harm. To see it as a balancing act rather than a straightforward and obvious course of action is probably the first step towards effective decision making in this very difficult area.'

Source:
The Welfare of the Child: Assessing Evidence in Children Cases (Magistrates' Association, 2000)

The delay principle can, in certain circumstances, be tempered by the necessity, for example, for a proper assessment of a child's needs to be made by the local authority, for an interim contact order to be tested or for mediation to take place. There is no excuse, however, for children to remain for long periods in unplanned foster care or in a children's home while decisions are made about their future. There is no court control over what happens to children once a care order is made, although many members of the judiciary have not been content with the situation. Section 118 of the Adoption and Children Act 2002 inserted into s 26 of the Children Act 1989 provides a requirement for local authorities to appoint Independent Reviewing Officers (IROs) to review cases and their care plans as necessary. See further **6.55**.

The No Order Principle

4.5 While the 'no order' principle applies to all 1989 Act cases and adoption cases under the 2002 Act, it is also a cornerstone of private law section 8 orders. Where divorcing parents agree on where their children will live and when they will see the other parent (the majority of cases) there is no need for these arrangements to be rubber-stamped by an order. There may be tactical and psychological reasons for asking for an order where there is consent, but the principle of 'private ordering' – allowing people to come to their own arrangements – is now firmly established. This does create problems for practitioners who may be concerned about some of these private arrangements, but professionals are, by their codes of practice, obliged to intervene if a child is likely to be harmed by parents' agreements.

Child Development

4.6 The following table gives basic information about:
- what can reasonably be expected from children at different ages;
- the likely effects of disruption on a child's development;
- the kind of behaviour which might result from disruption.

Age	Normal development involves . . .	Impaired development may result in . . .	Resulting behaviour may include . . .
Birth–1 year	• rapid physical growth	• failure to thrive both physically and emotionally	• passivity
	• beginnings of language development	• poor language development	• unresponsiveness
	• gaining of muscular control	• insecurity	• poor muscle control
	• the beginning of trust	• mistrust	• little movement or speech
	• the formation of attachments to key people		• persistent crying
Toddler years, 1–3	• standing, walking, picking up small objects – 'into everything'	• poor physical development and co-ordination	• regression to baby behaviour – for example rocking, sucking, baby language
	• use of primary caretaker as base from which to explore the world	• lack of trust in caretaking adult	• very clingy and dependent, following adults around all the time
	• attempts to gain some control over their world – anger and frustration when attempts fail	• inability to control anger and frustration	• stubborn, resistant to control, trying to 'parent' themselves
	• rapid language development	• delayed language development	• temper tantrums

Age	Normal development involves . . .	Impaired development may result in . . .	Resulting behaviour may include . . .
3–6	• curiosity and eagerness for information	• lack of curiosity	• withdrawn or 'frozen' behaviour
	• enjoyment of physical activity	• poor physical co-ordination – fear of physical activity	• nightmare terrors
	• use of imaginative and dramatic play	• excessive fears	• feelings of being a 'bad' child
	• beginnings of sharing with others	• feelings of being out of control	• extreme clinginess
	• enjoyment of company of other children and adults	• lack of control over own bodily functions	• restless energy – e g hurtling around the room
	• increasing self-reliance: is toilet trained, can dress self		• aggression towards self, other children, animals, objects
6–10	• development of reasoning skills	• poor performance at school	• truanting
	• new physical skills	• inability to make friends	• aggressive or withdrawn behaviour
	• ability to discern a sense of order in the world – a sense of time and space	• lack of confidence	• being disruptive in classroom or at home
	• development of a conscience	• poor concentration	
		• lack of curiosity	
		• lack of control	

Age	Normal development involves . . .	Impaired development may result in . . .	Resulting behaviour may include . . .
10–16	• the onset of puberty and a number of important physical changes	• insecurity	• violence/aggression
	• a need to assert independence from the family	• poor self-esteem	• 'shutting-off' from adults
	• coming to terms with strong emotional feelings, especially sexual feelings	• great intensity of emotions	• constant challenges to authority
	• a questioning of adult values and changing views about the world	• inability to make lasting friendships/relationships	• inappropriate attention seeking – for example, stealing, sexual provocation
	• the consolidation of a sense of identity	• identity confusion	• truanting
			• running away, both literally and emotionally, through excessive drinking or drugs

Attachment, Separation and Loss

4.7   Children have the following needs:

•   There are particular needs at particular times with sensitive times for forming basic relationships.

•   There is the need for warmth and approval and the development of positive self-esteem.

•   There is the need increasingly to explore and develop independence from a secure base.

•   There is the need for a sense of security, stability, continuity and 'belongingness'.

Source:
The Welfare of the Child: Assessing Evidence in Children Cases (The Magistrates' Association)

Cognitive development affects children's ability to remember and to hold people in their minds; it affects their ability to understand situations.

Those working in the family justice system should have, or have access to, some knowledge of:

- attachment theory;

- relationships and interactions with carers, parents, siblings and the extended family;

- effects of loss when families are disrupted;

- effects of adverse care;

- the child's interaction with the environment; questions of resilience and vulnerability;

- significance of cultural factors.

Source:
'Contact and Domestic
Violence – The Experts'
Court Report' [2000]
Fam Law 615

All of the above hold different relevance for different children at different ages. A young child experiencing loss through separation or trauma through exposure to violence will express his feelings through behaviour such as agitation, sleep disturbance and 'naughtiness' rather than any coherent account of what the child is feeling and why. Older children and adolescents may also act out their distress and confusion through their behaviour rather than expressing this directly. The more emotionally mature and well adjusted the child is, the more able (but not necessarily willing) the child will be to put their feelings and wishes into words. There are also innate factors brought into the situation by virtue of the child's own unique genetic make-up and temperamental factors, including the sex of the child.

Stability and Identity

4.8   Children need to know who they are and where they belong. These factors are precisely what they are likely to have lost if their lives have been particularly troubled and it must be the goal of those working with them to regain a sense of stability and identity for them. Children should, in accordance with their age and understanding, be partners in the decisions about how they are to be helped and where they should be placed. There should be an agreed protection plan for all children at risk, and for those whose long-term needs are not being adequately met, there must be a clear plan for their future. Research has shown that the well-being of such children depends not only on the meeting of their basic physical and psychological needs, which they share with all children, but in the provision of a sense of stability and also a sense of their own identity. These two must be kept in balance if the child is to develop the sense of self-worth which is essential for satisfying relationships in the future. Whatever their circumstances, children need to be given a sense of continuity and belonging.

Transition

4.9 A transition involves moving away from the familiar to the unfamiliar – from people and places a child knows. Sometimes the transition is voluntarily undertaken and can therefore be planned and prepared for, such as marriage and, sometimes, divorce. Sometimes it comes upon people suddenly and with no warning, such as bereavement. The voluntary, predictable transition is obviously the easiest to cope with. Even an involuntary but predictable transition, such as starting school, can be made easier by showing children around beforehand. The sudden unexplained transition remains the hardest and that is the kind of transition that children coming into care have to cope with. The trend in social work practice is, in keeping with the 1989 Act principle of working in partnership with families, to make clear plans for children and to keep them and their parents fully informed.

For further information on the effect of relationship breakdown on children, see **5.7–5.19**.

THE NATURE OF RIGHTS

Children's Rights

4.10 Lawyers use the term 'right' to indicate something which others have a duty to allow or assist. For example, if a person has a right to make an application for a court order, the court cannot refuse that person. A duty is different from a power. A person with a duty *must* do something, whereas someone with a power *may* do something.

The Children Act 1989, the UN Convention on the Rights of the Child 1989, the European Convention on Human Rights 1950 and the Human Rights Act 1998 all provide a framework for children's rights. In 1989, the United Nations adopted the UN Convention which has been ratified by over 193 countries including the UK (see below). However, the UN Convention is not incorporated into English law and individual children cannot rely on its provisions directly in the English courts. The 1989 Act gives children rights in that it states that the wishes and feelings of the child must be taken into account (but children's wishes and feelings

UN Convention on the Rights of the Child www.unicef.org/crc/

are subordinate to parental agreement in private law proceedings). For example, if the child is of sufficient understanding to make an informed decision, that child may refuse to submit to medical examination in public law proceedings, although the court may override such a refusal. The child is also able to initiate some applications to court on his own behalf, although obtaining the permission ('leave') of the High Court is the first step. In most public law cases the court will appoint a children's guardian to represent the child's interests, although the child generally does not have the benefit of a representative in private law cases (but see rule 9.5 at **4.21**) and never in a divorce, where the rights of children in reality become subsumed to the interests of their parents or their views about what constitutes the child's best interests.

Children have the same rights as adults, for example a right to life, a right to family life and a right to a fair trial. Other rights are specific to children, for example the right to education. As regards family life, parents have the power and responsibility to make decisions about their children as reflected in the concept of parental responsibility (see **4.32**). Once a child has acquired sufficient maturity to make decisions about an area of his life, the law has accepted (in *Gillick*, see **4.14**) that, generally, the child obtains and the parent loses the right to make the decision. This basic principle may be overridden by statute (for example, no child under the age of 16 has the right to marry). Whether the child has sufficient maturity to make a particular decision is a question of fact, usually to be determined by the professional (eg doctor, social worker or solicitor) working with the child. However, the courts have held that the decision as to whether a child has the maturity to bring private law family proceedings is a matter for the judges.

Children's Rights to Make Applications to Court

4.11   If given leave by the High Court or county court and if the court thinks that this would be appropriate, children of sufficient understanding can make their own applications for section 8 orders. The court has until now taken a paternalistic approach to this power given by the Children Act 1989. The general view of the court, as expressed in case-law, has been that it is not normally in a child's best interests to be personally caught up in litigation and that the child's interests can be adequately looked after by parents and Cafcass officers. That view may now be changing. The decision as to whether a child is of sufficient understanding is initially taken by the child's solicitor but ultimately by the court.

In public law care proceedings, children's wishes and feelings are relayed to the court through the children's guardian who appoints a solicitor for the child. If the child disagrees with the guardian and is of sufficient understanding, the child may instruct the solicitor. The guardian then has to continue unrepresented or appoint another solicitor.

Children's Rights and Medical Treatment

4.12 In an emergency, a doctor can undertake medical treatment if the well-being of the child would suffer by delay, but it is normal practice to obtain the consent of a person with parental responsibility. There may be circumstances, however, in which the child will decide whether to grant consent.

Young People aged 16 or 17

4.13 A person reaching the age of 16 has the right to give informed consent to surgical, medical or dental treatment, and the consent is as effective as if the person were 18. Where consent is given under this section, it is not necessary also to get the consent of the patient's parent or guardian. So, if a patient is aged 16 or 17 either the patient or the patient's parent can give a valid consent to medical treatment and neither can override the other's consent and exercise a veto.

Children and Young People aged under 16

4.14 A patient under the age of 16 can give valid consent to or refusal of medical treatment if the doctor judges the patient to be 'Gillick competent' in relation to the particular treatment proposed. 'Gillick competent' means that a child is deemed to have sufficient understanding and intelligence to be capable of making up his/her own mind on the matter requiring decision. The House of Lords decided in *Gillick v West Norfolk and Wisbech Area Health Authority* in 1985 that a doctor who prescribed contraceptives to a girl under the age of 16 without the consent of her parent(s) did not commit a criminal offence, provided that the doctor acted in a bona fide exercise of his clinical judgment as to the patient's interests.

In most cases, the consent of someone with parental authority, either a parent or local authority (if it has a care order) will override a child's refusal. A decision by a parent to consent or refuse to consent to an operation on a minor can be overridden by the High Court which will be guided by its decision as to what is in the child's best interests. See also the General Medical Council (GMC) guidance at **4.17**.

The Right to Accept or Refuse Medical or Psychiatric Examination or Assessment

4.15 The Children Act 1989 gives courts the power to order such examinations when one of the following orders is in force:

• an interim care order;

• an interim supervision order;

• an emergency protection order;

• an child assessment order.

A child of sufficient understanding can, however, still refuse to be examined. In extreme cases where such refusal puts the child in danger, the High Court can overrule the refusal.

Mentally Disordered Children

4.16 Where a young person aged under 18 is mentally ill and unable to make a legally valid decision for himself, the High Court can give consent on that person's behalf under its inherent jurisdiction. Parents can arrange for the informal admission of children under 16 to hospital for treatment and those over 16 if they are incapable of making their own decisions. Although children may be sectioned, it is more common to treat them under a care order or by relying on their parents' consent.

Confidentiality

4.17 A child under 16 has no right to choose his own GP and must be registered by a parent. A child under 16 is entitled to a confidential consultation with a doctor, provided that the child makes it clear that the parents must not be informed. However, a doctor can refuse to discuss the matter if he is unwilling to accept the request for confidentiality. A person aged 16 or above can register with a doctor and is entitled to confidential advice and treatment. The guidance on confidentiality for children under 18 from the General Medical Council states:

> 'The same duties of confidentiality apply when using, sharing or disclosing information about children and young people as about adults. You should:
>
> a.   disclose information that identifies the patient only if this is necessary to achieve the purpose of the disclosure – in all other cases you should anonymise the information before disclosing it
>
> b.   inform the patient about the possible uses of their information, including how it could be used to provide their care and for clinical audit
>
> c.   ask for the patient's consent before disclosing information that could identify them, if the information is needed for any other purpose, other than in the exceptional circumstances described in this guidance
>
> d.   keep disclosures to the minimum necessary.'

Source:
http://www.gmc-uk.org/

Children's Rights and the UN Convention

4.18   Under the UN Convention on the Rights of the Child, all children have rights to:

- *Civil liberties.* Participation in decision-making, freedom of expression, thought, conscience and religion, freedom of association, freedom from discrimination, physical and personal integrity and freedom from all forms of violence.

- *Social provision.* Education, health care, opportunities for play, a clean and safe environment and an adequate standard of living.

- *Protection.* From sexual, economic or any other form of exploitation, from harmful drugs, abduction and armed conflict.

These rights are enshrined in the UN Convention which the UK government ratified in December 1991. In doing so, it agreed to respect these rights for all children in this country. The Convention is not incorporated into

English law, and English children cannot rely on its provisions in the English courts. However, international standards are becoming increasingly important and the Convention has been endorsed both by the European and domestic Courts.

The Convention identifies three key principles:

(1) all rights guaranteed by the Convention must be available to all children without discrimination of any kind (Article 2);

(2) the best interests of the child must be a primary consideration in all actions concerning children (Article 3);

(3) children's views must be considered and taken into account in all matters affecting them in accordance with the age and maturity of the child (Article 12).

The UN Convention furthers the recognition of children as individuals with needs and rights of their own rather than as the property of their parents.

In ratifying the Convention, the UK accepts an obligation to respect, protect, promote and fulfil the enumerated rights—including by adopting or changing laws and policies that implement the provisions of the Convention or its Protocols.

The Convention places equal emphasis on all of the rights for children. There is no such thing as a 'small' right and no hierarchy of human rights. These rights are indivisible and interrelated, with a focus on the child as a whole. Governmental decisions with regard to any one right must be made in the light of all the other rights in the Convention.

Source:
http://www.unicef.org/crc/

Governments that ratify the Convention or one of its Optional Protocols must report to the Committee on the Rights of the Child, the body of experts charged with monitoring States' implementation of the Convention and Optional Protocols. These reports outline the situation of children in the country and explain the measures taken by the State to realise their rights. In its reviews of States' reports, the Committee urges all levels of government to use the Convention as a guide in policymaking and implementation.

Human Rights Act 1998

The Human Rights Act 1998 can be viewed on www.opsi.gov.uk

4.19 The principal effect of the Human Rights Act 1998 is to allow allegations of a breach of the European Convention on Human Rights to be raised in the UK's domestic courts. The most used parts of the

convention are Article 6 (right to fair trial) and
Article 8 (right to respect for private and family life).
Article 6 guarantees a fair and public hearing of both
civil and criminal cases. Judgment must be pronounced
publicly. Those who cannot understand English are
entitled to the free services of an interpreter. Legal aid
is guaranteed in criminal cases for those of insufficient
means and when the interests of justice require.
Article 8 relates to the right to respect private and
family life. It states that everyone has the right to
respect for his private and family life, his home and his
correspondence. There can be no interference by a
public authority with the exercise of this right except in
accordance with the law and as is necessary in a
democratic society in the interests of national security,
public safety or the economic well-being of the country
for the prevention of disorder or crime, for the
protection of healthy morals or for the protection of
the rights and freedoms of others.

Court proceedings must be conducted with due regard
to such rights, for example in relation to delay, time for
preparation, equality of arms, access to documentation
and rehabilitation, and courts must ensure that any
order sought regarding a child is 'legal and
proportionate'. So saying, the effects of the Human
Rights Act 1998 are not confined to the court process.

The 1998 Act has been successfully used to challenge
certain decisions made by local authorities in
connection with Articles 6 and 8.

The Right to be Heard

4.20   There is apparently no conclusive research
evidence either favouring or warning against greater
child involvement in family proceedings, including child
attendance at court hearings. Some research suggests
that children often wish to be more involved. There is at
present a wide range of activities which constitute
involvement of children in family proceedings:

- giving children party status;
- talking to children, listening to them and
  answering their questions;
- ascertaining children's wishes and feelings;
- examining children as an expert;
- explaining the contents of written reports;
- interpreting to children where there are language
  or other special needs;

- giving children age-appropriate written information;
- drawing to children's attention other sources of appropriate information;
- facilitating children's attendance at court for appropriate parts of the proceedings;
- supporting children where they give direct evidence as a witness;
- ascertaining children's views as service users about the quality of services received;
- supporting children wishing to make a complaint; and
- assuring children that Cafcass and court staff are carefully recruited and trained.

Where the involvement of children is being considered, agencies also need to keep in mind other factors, including:

- children have a right to know what is happening at court in relation to key decisions about their lives;
- children also have the right to opt out of being involved in aspects of family proceedings;
- involvement in family proceedings does not imply that children should be responsible for court decisions or feel under pressure to choose between options that may be available;
- age and maturity are key determinants in assessing how and to what extent any child should be involved in family proceedings; and
- children are individuals and their needs and wishes about any involvement in family proceedings should be assessed individually; they cannot be assumed.

Source:
http://www.unicef.org/crc/

Current research opinion is in favour of reversing, in appropriate situations, the current presumption against child attendance. The argument is that a child is a citizen, no less so because he is a minor. Article 12 of the United Nations Convention on the Rights of the Child provides that a child should be heard in any judicial proceedings affecting him, either directly or through a representative. Similarly Article 12 requires that the child who is capable of forming his own views has the right to express those views freely in all matters affecting him. Article 13 accords to a child the right to freedom of expression. In Every Child Matters the government stressed the importance of involving children and young people and listening to their views.

In 2005 the Court of Appeal reviewed and referred to the benefits of the 'tandem model' (ie the possibility of a child having both a solicitor and a guardian) of representation of children in the English courts. The court said it was simply unthinkable to exclude young persons aged 17, 15 and 13 from knowledge of and participation in legal proceedings that affected them so fundamentally.

The 2006 Care Proceedings Review emphasised that local authorities must inform and involve children and young people to a greater extent. Local authorities should, for example:

- give a simple language document drafted before issue of proceedings to explain local authority concerns to families, especially to older children;

- provide better information for parents and children. Children of sufficient age and understanding who are subject to care proceedings should routinely be given detailed information by their social worker about what to expect in language they understand.

The Review also suggested that through judicial training and best practice guidance, the judiciary should be encouraged to address parents directly, listen sympathetically and show an interest in all the participants (including children, when they are present in court), and to avoid legal jargon.

Current judicial guidance states that as a general rule, attendance of a child in court during the hearing is discouraged as not being in the interests of the child. However, a request by an older child (perhaps a teenager) may have to be looked at more closely. The judge will consider why the child wants to be there, the likely effect on the child of being present or of being refused permission to be present, if present, for how much of the proceedings that should be, and that it would generally be very unwise for any child to be present whilst any family member was giving evidence. The test is, of course, the welfare of the child, and before reaching any decision, the judge will take into account the views of all parties in the case.

Source:
www.jsboard.co.uk

Separate Representation for Children

4.21 Rule 9.5 of the Family Proceedings Rules 1991 allows for a children's guardian to be appointed in private law proceedings in certain circumstances. The child therefore gets party status and the ability to take a pro-active stance in the court forum, through representation by the guardian and a solicitor. Judicial guidance has said that only a circuit judge should appoint a guardian in private law cases apart from exceptional circumstances when a district judge may appoint. An appointment is usually made in the following circumstances:

(1) Cafcass officer recommendation;

(2) child's standpoint or interest inconsistent with or incapable of being represented by any adult parties;

(3) intractable dispute over residence or contact, irrational but implacable hostility to contact, or child suffering associated with the contact dispute;

(4) the views or wishes of child cannot be adequately met by report to the court;

(5) an older child is opposing proposed course of action;

(6) complex medical or mental health issues;

(7) international complications;

(8) serious allegation of abuse, or domestic violence, not capable of being resolved with the help of Cafcass officer;

(9) proceedings concern more than one child and welfare of the children is in conflict, or one child disadvantaged;

(10) contested issue about blood testing.

There is currently a debate about whether rule 9.5 is under or over used.

Appointment of Children's Guardians in Private Law Proceedings

4.22 In 2006 Cafcass and the National Assembly for Wales issued a new Practice Note on the appointment of guardians in private law proceedings to replace the April 2004 Practice Note. It is issued with the approval of the President of the Family Division. The Practice Note should be read together with the President's Practice Direction *Representation of children in family proceedings pursuant to Family Proceedings Rules 1991, Rule 9.5* [2004] 1 FLR 1188 which remains in force.

The 2004 Practice Direction provides guidance as to the circumstances that may require the child to be made a party to non specified proceedings and a guardian appointed to act for that child party (r 9.5 of the

Family Proceedings Rules 1991). The accompanying 2006 Practice Note sets out practical guidance to the judiciary on such matters as:

- the wording of an order appointing a guardian;
- the appropriate office of Cafcass/Cafcass Cymru to which the order and court papers should be sent;
- timescales for notification; and
- the assistance that can be provided by the lawyers in Cafcass Legal and the Welsh Assembly.

The main aim of the Practice Note is to ensure that court requests to Cafcass/Cafcass Cymru to appoint a guardian in private law matters are dealt with in a consistent and timely manner and are referred to the appropriate office to avoid delays in allocation.

The April 2004 Practice Note required updating for a number of reasons, including the devolving of functions to the Welsh Assembly in April 2005 and changes within Cafcass. The 2004 Note made provision for some cases to be referred to 'Cafcass Legal', which has since been restructured. The 2006 Practice Note also sets out a clearer set of criteria as to which cases should be referred to the Cafcass High Court Team or Assembly Lawyers rather than to the local Cafcass/Cafcass Cymru offices.

Emergency measures

4.23   During 2009 Cafcass was struggling with a backlog of work due to a recent increase in public law applications and its own shortage of financial resources. For that reason, the President issued Interim Guidance for England in July 2009 setting out short-term measures to enable Cafcass to deliver their services to children, families and the courts during the current time of increased pressure in their services. The Guidance was intended to cease to have effect in March 2010. Amongst other points, the Guidance stated that Cafcass and Her Majesty's Courts Services (HMCS) must nominate a person with authority to make agreements about local arrangements: this is to be a Designated Family Judge (DFJ). It remains to be seen (at the time of writing, at the beginning of 2010) whether the guidance is a temporary solution to help in an emergency situation and whether the backlog will have been substantially reduced.

Rule 9.5 and the National Youth Advocacy Service

4.24   The National Youth Advocacy Service (NYAS) represents children in family proceedings under r 9.5 of the Family Proceedings Rules 1991. NYAS is unique: it offers information, advice, advocacy and legal representation to children and young people through a network of advocates throughout England and Wales, and it is the only children's charity which is also a Community Legal Services help point, with its own family law practice. It has developed and delivered a range of socio-legal services of information, consultation, social work support, casework and legal advice and representation to children and young people resident in the UK from birth to 25 years of age. The majority of NYAS's legal work is concerned with the representation of children involved in private law proceedings and, in particular, long-running disputes about residence and contact arrangements. In relation to these disputes, NYAS has developed a model in which its caseworkers work alongside a team of in-house family lawyers, in very much the same way as children's guardians work with children's panel solicitors in public law proceedings.

Further information from NYAS on:
www.nyas.net
Tel: 0151 649 8700
Email: main@nyas.net

Almost all of NYAS's cases involve an intractable dispute over contact where children are found to be caught between two warring parents who overtly attempt to influence them. About half of such children are extremely reluctant to express their opinions because they are not consistent with their parent's views. NYAS caseworkers are frequently instrumental in achieving resumed contact in cases in which contact had previously completely broken down. Supervised contact is a significant part of this work and can also involve a wide range of other relevant people or bodies such as schools, relatives or other professionals. NYAS has advocates and solicitors who are trained and experienced in working with children and young people and will only take their instructions from the child or young person with a problem. The service is confidential and nothing will be done or said without the young person's consent (unless of course, that young person is in serious danger, and even then the policy is that no action is taken without them knowing). In 2006 a protocol was agreed between Cafcass and NYAS with respect to children made parties in private law proceedings under r 9.5 in order to clarify which of them should do the work in a particular case (see Cafcass and NYAS Protocol [2006] Fam Law 243).

Involving Children in Public Law Cases

4.25 Children of sufficient age and understanding often have a clear perception of what needs to happen to ensure their safety and welfare. Listening to children and hearing their messages requires training and special skills, including the ability to win their trust and promote a sense of safety. Most children feel loyalty towards those who care for them, and have difficulty saying anything against them. Many do not wish to share confidences, or may not have the language or concepts to describe what has happened to them. Some may fear reprisals or their removal from home.

Children and young people need to understand how they will be involved in decision-making and planning processes. They should be helped to understand what the key processes are, how they work and that they can contribute to decisions about their future in accordance with their age and understanding. However, they should understand that whilst their wishes and feelings will be taken into account, ultimately decisions will be taken in the light of all the available information contributed by themselves, professionals, their parents and other family members, and other significant adults. See also **4.20**.

Family Group Conferences

4.26 Family Group Conferences (FGCs) may be appropriate in a number of contexts where there is a plan or decision to be made. FGCs do not replace or remove the need for child protection conferences, which should always be held when the relevant criteria are met. They may be valuable, for example:

- for children in need, in a range of circumstances where a plan is required for the child's future welfare;

- where Children Act 1989, section 47 enquiries do not substantiate concerns about significant harm but where support and services are required;

- where section 47 enquiries progress to a child protection conference, the conference may agree that an FGC is an appropriate vehicle for the core group to use to develop the outline child protection plan into a fully worked-up plan.

See further **3.46** and **5.30**.

Support, Advice and Advocacy to Children and Families

Family Rights Group
Second Floor
The Print House
18 Ashwin Street
London E8 3DL
Tel: 020 7923 2628
Email: office@frg.org.uk

4.27 However sensitively enquiries are handled, many families perceive unasked-for professional involvement in their lives as painful and intrusive, particularly if they feel that their care of their children is being called into question. Children and families can be supported by advice and advocacy services and they should always be informed of those services which exist locally and nationally, such as those provided by the Family Rights Group. The Family Rights Group is the charity in England and Wales that advises, advocates and campaigns for families whose children are involved with, or require, social care services. It provides confidential telephone advice and support for parents and family members, including grandparents who are raising grandchildren who cannot live at home. Independent advocates can play a vital role in ensuring children have appropriate information and support to communicate their views in formal settings such as child protection conferences and court proceedings.

For children and young people whose parents are separating, a school counsellor might be helpful. Some mediation and other services provide counselling. The 'It's not your fault' website is written for children by NCH (National Children's Homes) to help them understand more about divorce/separation and their feelings – see www.itsnotyourfault.org.uk.

Criminal Injuries
Compensation
Authority
Tel: 0800 358 3601
www.cica.gov.uk

Where children and families are involved as witnesses in criminal proceedings, the police, witness support services and other services such as those provided by Victim Support can do a great deal to explain the process, make it feel less daunting and ensure that children are prepared for and supported in the court process. The best interests of a child are paramount when deciding whether, and in what form, therapeutic help is given to child witnesses. Information about the Criminal Injuries Compensation Scheme should also be provided in relevant cases.

Communicating with and Information for Children

For court addresses see
www.hmcourtsservice.
gov.uk

4.28 A variety of materials are available to assist children and young people who are the subject of care proceedings to understand the court process and the different roles of the professionals involved. Many might appreciate the Power Pack, published in two versions by the NSPCC in conjunction with Cafcass, one for older and one for younger children, if there is to be delay in the allocation of a children's guardian. The Power Pack is designed to assist children and young people to understand the court process and the different roles of the professionals. Local courts and CAFCASS regional offices may have available stocks. Otherwise the packs can be downloaded or ordered at a postage and packing charge from www.nspcc.org.uk/inform (click on 'Publications').

The local authority has a responsibility to make sure that children and adults have all the information they require to help them understand the processes that will be followed when there are concerns about a child's welfare. Information should be clear and accessible and available in the family's preferred language. If a child and/or family member has specific communication needs, because of language or disability, it may be necessary to use the services of an interpreter or specialist worker, or to make use of other aids to communication.

Mediation and Listening to the Views of Children

4.29   Disputes between family members can be extremely distressing for everyone involved and can have a long term and widespread impact throughout the whole family. Mediation can help family members sort out the problems that have lead to the dispute, clear up misunderstandings and help them to find a practical way forward. Family mediators can help resolve a range of disputes including:

- contact arrangements for children;
- property and finance arrangements when couples separate and/or divorce;
- parent/grandparents disputes;
- disputes between parents and their grown (or growing up) children;
- arguments between sisters and brothers;
- family business disputes.

Sorting a family dispute through mediation means that those directly involved decide how things are resolved. This avoids the need to resort to legal action or asking a court to make a decision to resolve a dispute.

The Family Mediation Council and the College of Mediators (formerly the UK College of Family Mediators) have a positive policy that family mediators should actively encourage parents and/or other participants in mediation:

- to talk with and listen to their children so that the decisions parents make about arrangements for their children are reached in the light of an understanding of each child's perspective;
- to consider the different ways in which children may be involved or consulted, including, when appropriate, offering opportunities for them to take part directly in discussions with the mediator(s).

See:
www.familymediation
council.org.uk/
www.collegeofmediators.
co.uk/
Tel: 01179 047 223

Mediators can also consult children directly. Direct consultation enables the views of the child to be heard as part of the mediation process. Direct consultation can be of great assistance when the perspective of the child may be missing from parental discussions. Whether children should be consulted directly, how, by whom, and at what stage, are matters agreed jointly by the mediator and the parents.

Children's Rights Officer

See also
www.Rights4me.org.uk
- Children's Rights

4.30   Many local authorities run a Children's Rights Service. A children's rights officer is employed to make sure that children and young people in care know their rights and are treated fairly. The officer offers information, help and advice over the telephone, by letter and by visiting young people. The officer can also attend meetings, help young people get legal advice and support them in making complaints about social services. The service is available to children and young people being looked after by social services; to young people who have been looked after in the past; and also to parents if their child agrees. The children's rights officer is not a social worker and offers confidentiality unless he suspects harm to a child. See also the Children's Commissioner at **2.98**.

Information about
The Children in Care
Councils Consortium
can be accessed
via the National
Childrens Bureau
www.ncb.org.uk/

The National Centre for Excellence in Residential Child Care and CROA (Children's Rights Officers and Advocates) envisaged the need for local, regional and national support and coordination. The Children In Care Councils Consortium was recently set up with the aim of supporting and coordinating the development of councils in each local authority and across the country. The idea of Children In Care councils was first announced as part of Care Matters. It is anticipated that the Consortium will grow as other children's organisations are included.

Further Information on Children's Rights

4.31   The **Children's Legal Centre** runs a helpline on
01206 873820, see www.childrenslegalcentre.com. Other
helplines are:

- **Childline**

    Freephone Helpline: 0800 1111

    www.childline.org.uk

- **NSPCC**

    Tel: 0808 800 5000

    www.nspcc.org.uk

- **The Children's Society**

    Tel: 0845 300 1128

    www.childrenssociety.org.uk/

Parental Responsibility

4.32   Parental responsibility is defined by the Children
Act 1989 as 'the rights, duties, powers, responsibilities
and authority which by law a parent of a child has in
relation to the child and his property'. This concept
shifts the emphasis from parents having rights over
children to having responsibilities towards them.

The idea of parental responsibility is that it is intended
to be a reflection of everyday life – the everyday reality
of being a parent and all that that entails – as well as
emphasising that parenthood is a responsibility which
begins at the child's birth and which cannot be
surrendered. There is deliberately no statutory list of
the matters which parental responsibility includes, but
some of its aspects have been acknowledged by the
courts as follows:

- determining the child's religion;
- determining the child's education;
- naming the child;
- appointing a guardian for the child;
- consenting (or not) to the child's medical
  treatment;
- consenting to the taking of blood for testing;
- consenting (or not) to marriage;
- representing the child in legal proceedings;
- consenting (or not) to adoption;
- lawfully correcting the child;

- arranging the child's emigration;
- consenting to the temporary removal of the child from the jurisdiction for holidays or extended stays;
- protecting and maintaining the child;
- administering the child's property;
- having physical possession of the child;
- having contact with the child;
- providing for the burial or cremation of the deceased child;
- allowing the child to be interviewed;
- allowing confidential information relating to the child to be published.

The courts have also given guidance on how parents could share out these responsibilities when living apart:

(1) Decisions that could be taken independently and without any consultation or notification to the other parent:

- how the children are to spend their time during contact;
- personal care for the children;
- activities undertaken;
- religious and spiritual pursuits;
- continuance of medicine prescribed by GP.

(2) Decisions where one parent would always need to inform the other parent of the decision, but did not need to consult or take the other parent's views into account:

- medical treatment in an emergency;
- booking holidays or to take the children abroad in contact time;
- planned visits to the GP and the reasons for this.

(3) Decisions that you would need to both inform and consult the other parent prior to making the decision:

- schools the children are to attend, including admissions applications. With reference to which senior school the child should attend, this is to be decided taking into account the child's own views and in consultation and with advice from the child's teachers;
- contact rotas in school holidays;

- planned medical and dental treatment;
- stopping medication prescribed for the children;
- attendance at school functions so they can be planned to avoid meetings wherever possible;
- age that children should be able to watch videos, ie videos recommended for children over 12 and 18.

Who has Parental Responsibility?

4.33   An unmarried father can acquire parental responsibility by making an agreement with the mother which must be properly witnessed and registered with the court and/or by having his name registered on the child's birth certificate. Unmarried fathers can now also acquire parental responsibility under s 111 of the Adoption and Children Act 2002 by being registered as the father of the child under the Births and Deaths Registration Act 1953. In cases where the parents are unable to reach agreement, the father can apply for a parental responsibility order. Courts should almost always grant such orders. Courts have to consider:

Family Administration Branch Children Section Principal Registry of the Family Division Tel: 020 7947 6000 (switchboard) Tel: 020 7947 7930 (public children matters) Tel: 020 7947 6980 (private children matters)

- the degree of commitment which the father has shown to the child;
- the degree of attachment between father and child;
- the reasons for the father applying for the order.

Parental responsibility for fathers is increasingly the norm. A parental responsibility order can be granted even if contact is refused. There would have to be a powerful case against an order if a court were to refuse it. Parental responsibility is not a welfare issue, it is the means by which a father gains status. It does not mean that he can interfere with the day-to-day management of the child's life.

A child's mother always has parental responsibility for her child. This cannot be removed, suspended, or altered in any way at any time, whatever other orders are made. Even when a local authority has obtained a care order or a placement order, and thereby acquired parental responsibility, the mother still has parental responsibility. The only exception to this rule is when an adoption order is made in respect of the child, which has the effect of vesting adopters with parental responsibility for the child and extinguishing all other persons' parental responsibility, or when a parental order is made. As well as mothers and fathers, parental responsibility can be granted to other persons such as:

- a step-parent;

- a local authority that has a care order or an interim care order;

- a person who obtains an emergency protection order (only during the continuance of the order);

- a guardian appointed in accordance with CA 1989;

- a person who obtains a residence order;

- adopters and adoption agencies and, in certain circumstances, applicants for adoption;

- a person with a pre-existing custody, or care and control order;

- a commissioning parent in a surrogacy arrangement who obtains a parental order.

When parental responsibility is acquired by a person, it may be acquired in addition to those who previously had parental responsibility, or it may cause those who previously had parental responsibility to lose that responsibility, depending on their status and the circumstances. So several people can have parental responsibility, as shown in the following table.

Order/ Status	Who has parental responsibility ?

No Order in force	1. Mother.
	
	2. Father if he:
	
	  a. was married to the mother when the child was born; or
	
	  b. married the mother after the child was born; or
	
	  c. appears as father on the birth certificate and the birth was registered after 1 December 2003; or
	
	  d. has signed a parental responsibility agreement (PRA) with the mother; or
	
	  e. has obtained a parental responsibility order (PRO); or
	
	  f. has obtained a residence order.
	
	3. Step-parent if they have signed a PRA or obtained a PRO.

Care Order	1. Local authority. 2. Mother. 3. Father if he has PR under the 'no order' rules above.
Supervision Order	As under 'no order' above, unless there is also another order in force.
Residence Order	1. The person(s) named in the Residence Order (RO); plus 2. as under 'no order' above.
Placement Order	1. Local authority (adoption agency); 2. birth parent(s); and 3. prospective adopters (where the child is placed for adoption). NB, if the child is subject of a placement order, but not placed for adoption, the foster carers do not have PR.
Special Guardianship Order	1. The special guardian(s). 2. Anyone holding a RO. 3. Others as per 'no order' above.
Freeing Order- (where these still exist)	The local authority (adoption agency) only.
Adoption Order	The adopter(s) only, unless additional orders are made after the adoption order.

Who has parental responsibility can also be important when a child is to be taken abroad.

No order in force	Any removal requires either the consent of every person with PR or the leave of the court. Removal of a child under 16 without consent is an offence of child abduction.
Residence Order	• Holder of a residence order may remove for up to one calendar month. • Longer removal requires written consent of everyone with PR or leave of the court.
Care Order	• Local authority may remove from UK for up to one calendar month. • Longer removal requires written consent of everyone with PR or leave of the court. • Living outside England and Wales requires leave of the court.

Source: George Eddon, 'Parental Responsibility: A Quick Reference', [2006] Fam Law 223 www.familylaw.co.uk

Supervision Order	As for 'no order', unless there is a residence requirement under the Children Act in force.
Placement Order	• Adoption agency/prospective adopter may remove from the UK for up to one calendar month. • Longer removal requires written consent of each parent/guardian with PR or leave of the court. • Removal for the purpose of adoption requires an order under the Adoption of Children Act 2004.
Special Guardian-ship	• Special guardian can remove from the UK for up to 3 months. • Longer removal requires written consent of everyone with PR or leave of the court.

Loss of Parental Responsibility

4.34   Parental responsibility is ended if the order granting it is revoked by the court. Fathers who have parental responsibility by virtue of an order or agreement (but not by marriage) can lose it in this way, as can anyone who has parental responsibility by virtue of a residence order or appointment as a guardian. Parents lose parental responsibility if their child is adopted. They have the status of former parents when the adoption takes place. They can also lose their parental responsibility when a parental order is made under s 30 of the Human Fertilisation and Embryology Act 1990: s 30 allows a married couple (as commissioning parents) to apply for an order that they be treated in law as the parents of a child born to a woman by partial or total surrogacy. The effect of a parental order is very similar to adoption and results in the transfer of parenthood and parental responsibility to the commissioning parents, with the consequence that the child is for all purposes treated in law as a child of their marriage and not the child of any other person.

INTERVENTION/NON-INTERVENTION

4.35   The Children Act is premised on the belief that children are generally best looked after within the family with both parents playing a full part and without resort to legal proceedings. When a court is considering making an order under the 1989 Act it must not do so unless it considers that doing so would be better for the child than making no order at all. See further **4.5**.

This principle has had a profound effect upon matrimonial proceedings where there are children. Formerly, orders for custody and access were routinely made in a procedure called 'section 41 children's appointments'. Nowadays, orders in relation to children within matrimonial proceedings are the exception, rather than the rule. Indeed, dropping the word 'custody' and replacing it with 'residence' took the question of where a child should live away from the notion of 'possessing' a child and restated it in the simple and practical terms of where the child would spend most of the time.

The same principles apply to the disputes of non-married parents about children. In addition, the Children Act 1989 allows those parents to make a parental responsibility agreement which requires some formalities, including lodging the agreement with a court in London called the Principal Registry, but does not require a court order. Both parents then have full parental responsibility for the child (see **4.32–4.34**).

There are, however, circumstances where a court order is beneficial even though the parents are in agreement:

- where 'door of the court agreements' have been reached, in order to confer some form of security (although whether such 'agreements' last is another issue);

- residence orders confer status – parental responsibility – on carers who are not parents;

- a residence order would be useful where there is a risk of child abduction.

Finance Cases

4.36   The practice of avoiding resort to legal proceedings is also being applied to ancillary relief (ie sorting out finance and property issues) in divorce proceedings. Couples have always been able to come to their own agreements about finance and property on divorce. They are well advised to have their agreement checked out by their own independent legal advisers and to have the agreement made into a court order ('consent order') but there is now a greater emphasis on mediation and collaboration for couples who cannot agree. Enlightened matrimonial solicitors and all those who are members of Resolution subscribe to the view that a negotiated agreement is better than a court-imposed order. All professionals, and especially the Legal Services Commission, encourage people to come to agreements through either mediation, collaboration or negotiation through solicitors. If couples go to court they have to have a 'financial dispute resolution' (FDR) meeting with the judge to explore whether agreement is possible.

Pre-marital Contracts

Resolution
Tel: 01689 820272
www.resolution.org.uk

4.37 The solicitors' organisation, Resolution, believes that it is an anomalous position that husbands and wives (and registered same-sex partners) are unable to bind themselves with a contractual pre-marital/partnership agreement, whereas cohabitants may do so. Instead, divorcing couples and separating registered partners face financial outcomes which may be seen to represent a judicial lottery based on the exercise of statutory discretion. Resolution thinks that the increased demand for pre-marital agreements reflects the higher number of second and subsequent marriages; the wider multicultural and multinational community in which we now live; and the general public being more attuned to the idea of self-ordering. With the media following high-profile marriages and divorces, there is possibly now a greater desire towards self-ordering and the concept of preventative 'medicine' to mitigate the cost of litigation.

Pre-marital agreements are not currently enforceable in England and Wales. This is because they are seen to be contrary to public policy because they may undermine the institution of marriage and the ability of the courts to tailor-make financial solutions for families upon marriage breakdown. However, since House of Lords judgments in some recent high profile cases, the movement towards pre-marital contracts has grown. (See further **5.3**.)

Children – Private Law

4.38 The 'no order principle' in private law means that if a case comes to court, the court should hold back from interfering and thereby encourage parents to exercise their powers of parental responsibility in decision-making and the resolution of disputes. The simple question is, 'will it be better for the child to make the order than not?'. The courts have recently confirmed that s 1(5) of the Children Act 1989 does not create a 'no order' principle or presumption, but that an order can provide security to the parent in knowing that he/she can rely upon it in the event of any future doubt as to his/her legal position and that if the parties regard an order as of value to their management of their children's lives, the court should be slow to reject their opinion. This is not intended to encourage parties to seek a 'package' of orders even where there is no dispute between them. The courts have been influenced by histories of bitter and difficult litigation over children litigation where there was a need for the certainty and predictability an order would bring. The Women's Aid Federation has been particularly critical of the no order principle where there has been domestic violence and would say that, in such times of turmoil and often hostility, mothers and children need the stability and security that a court order can offer.

Agreements between parties are nonetheless encouraged by the courts and, while the courts should not rubber stamp what parents agree, circumstances would have to be truly exceptional to justify them in discarding arrangements already negotiated. The thinking is that the welfare of children is generally better served by the development of harmonious communication between parents and the institution of arrangements mutually agreed rather than arrangements imposed on one or both parents by judicial authority.

Non-intervention in Child Protection

4.39   The government stated clearly in Every Child Matters that all children deserve the opportunity to achieve their full potential. There are five outcomes that are key to children and young people's well-being (A revised *Every Child Matters Outcomes Framework* was launched at the Children's Plan Implementation Conference on 3 April 2008):

- stay safe;
- be healthy;
- enjoy and achieve;
- make a positive contribution;
- achieve economic well-being.

To achieve this, children need to feel loved and valued, and be supported by a network of reliable and affectionate relationships. If they are denied the opportunity and support they need to achieve these outcomes, children are at increased risk not only of an impoverished childhood, but of disadvantage and social exclusion in adulthood. Abuse and neglect pose particular problems. Patterns of family life vary and there is no one, perfect way to bring up children. Good parenting involves caring for children's basic needs, keeping them safe, showing them warmth and love and providing the stimulation needed for their development and to help them achieve their potential, within a stable environment where they experience consistent guidance and boundaries. Parenting can be challenging. Parents themselves require and deserve support. Asking for help should be seen as a sign of responsibility rather than as a parenting failure.

A wide range of services and professionals provide support to families in bringing up children. In the great majority of cases, it should be the decision of parents when to ask for help and advice on their children's care and upbringing. However, professionals do also need to engage parents early when to do so may prevent problems or difficulties becoming worse. Only in exceptional cases should there be compulsory intervention in family life: for example, where this is necessary to safeguard a child from significant harm. Such intervention should – provided this is consistent with the safety and welfare of the child – support families in making their own plans for the welfare and protection of their children.

Local authorities have a duty under s 17 of the Children Act 1989 to safeguard and promote the welfare of children in their area who are in need and, so far as is consistent with that duty, to promote the upbringing of children by their families. Local authorities have to provide a range and level of services appropriate to those children's needs. This includes provision of accommodation for children who live away from home with foster carers or in local authority residential care. Families cannot, however, be compelled to accept services from the local authority unless a care or supervision order has been made.

If the local authority's help and assistance is not accepted or the local authority is not able to ensure adequate care and it does not look as though there will be an improvement before the child suffers actual harm, care proceedings can be initiated and in cases of emergency an emergency protection order can be sought. The local authority can also apply for a child assessment order under s 43 which requires production of the child for assessment, and also the person in a position to produce the child must comply with the terms of the order.

However, the philosophy of the 1989 Act is that these stages should be reached only after other methods have failed or where evidence can be produced that, if tried, they would be likely to fail and the child might be harmed in the interim. Parents should be advised always to co-operate with the local authority in these circumstances. Where parents are co-operating, it can forcefully be argued that an order is not necessary because the local authority has the same power to provide services whether or not an order is granted. However, it may also be argued that lack of an order may result in harm to the child, for example if the child is removed from foster care precipitately without a proper assessment of the impact. There may also be concerns that parental co-operation will not last.

Local Authority Approaches to Intervention

4.40   The Children Act 2004 places a renewed emphasis on safeguarding and promoting children's welfare. The Department of Health had commissioned a number of research programmes and individual studies which showed, together with Social Services Inspectorate inspection reports and a joint Chief Inspectors' report that:

The Children Act 2004 can be viewed on www.opsi.gov.uk

- The identification of children in need was frequently restricted to children at risk of suffering significant harm. The refocusing debate in the late 1990s helped shift away from section 47 enquiries as the primary route to provision of services, but more matching of children's needs to family support services was required.

- Difficulties in recruiting and retaining staff had, in many authorities, continued the emphasis on identifying acts of abuse rather than on understanding its effect on the child's welfare.

- Too often assessments and section 47 enquiries were restricted to discovering whether abuse or neglect had occurred, without considering the wider needs and circumstances of the child and family. There was an urgent requirement for staff to have a common understanding that safeguarding and promoting the welfare of children had a wider focus than child maltreatment, and that they went hand in hand rather than being separate entities.

- There was inconsistent use made of the (then) child protection register which was not consulted for 60% of children for whom there were child protection concerns.

- Practitioners experienced difficulties in analysing the information gathered during the assessment, consequently plans and services did not always relate to the child's developmental needs.

- Discussions at child protection conferences tended to focus too heavily on decisions about registration and removal rather than on future plans to safeguard and promote the welfare of the child and support the family in the months after the conference.

- Enquiries into suspicions of child abuse or neglect could have traumatic effects on families. Good professional practice could ease parents' anxiety and lead to co-operation that helped to safeguard the child.

Shortcomings were brought into the spotlight most clearly with the death of Victoria Climbié and the subsequent government inquiry in 2003 (see **3.47**). The inquiry revealed themes identified by past inquiries which resulted in a failure to intervene early enough. These included:

- poor co-ordination;

- a failure to share information;

- the absence of anyone with a strong sense of accountability; and

- frontline workers trying to cope with staff vacancies, poor management and a lack of effective training.

The Victoria Climbié Inquiry www.publications. parliament.uk/ www.victoria-climbie-inquiry.org.uk/ finreport/ finreport.htm

The examination of the legislative framework set out in the Children Act 1989 was found to be basically sound: the difficulties lay not in relation to the law but in its interpretation, resources and implementation. The recommendations from the inquiry upheld the principles of the Children Act 1989 and made it clear that support services for children and families could not be separated from services designed to make enquiries and protect children from harm. These research and inspection findings gave rise to some important lessons for policy and practice enshrined in the Children Act 2004 and the new edition of *Working Together to Safeguard Children* published in April 2006.

ACCESS TO INFORMATION

4.41 For successful interdisciplinary co-operation, the ground rules have to be set for the exchange of information, with the caveat that collaboration must not become collusion. All persons involved in the family justice system, including parents, require information from others. That has to be balanced against other interests, especially children's. For example, arrangements for the protection of children from abuse, and in particular child protection conferences, can only be successful if the professional staff concerned do all they can to work in partnership and share and exchange relevant information such as medical proof, in particular with social services departments or the police. Those in receipt of information from professional colleagues in this context must treat it as having been given in confidence. They must not disclose such information for any other purpose without consulting the person who provided it.

Ethical and statutory codes concerned with confidentiality and data protection are not intended to prevent the exchange of information between different professional staff who have a responsibility for ensuring the protection of children, but a basic knowledge is required of the duty of confidentiality, the Data Protection Act 1998 and the Human Rights Act 1998. In addition, professionals might need to seek clarification from their professional bodies in particular cases.

The government originally published cross-government information-sharing guidance in April 2006, and this has been brought up-to-date to reflect current policy and extended to cover practitioners working with adults and families as well as those working with children and young people. The revised guidance and supporting materials were published in late 2008. It seeks to provide clarity on the legal framework for practitioners sharing information and give practitioners confidence in making decisions.

This guidance includes:

- *Information sharing: Guidance for practitioners and managers* – giving practitioners clear practical guidance, drawing on experience and the public consultation.

- *Information sharing: Pocket guide* – a summary of the key decision-making considerations (see below for printing instructions).

- *Information sharing: Case examples* – a set of case examples which illustrate information sharing situations

- *Information sharing: Further guidance on legal issues* – a summary of the laws affecting information sharing in respect of children and young people, updated to reflect the 2008 version of the guidance.

- *Information sharing: Posters* – the seven golden rules and the flowchart of key questions for information sharing from Information Sharing: Guidance for practitioners and managers.

- *Information sharing: Quick reference guide* – a credit card sized tool containing the seven golden rules and the flowchart of key questions for information sharing from Information Sharing: Guidance for practitioners and managers.

- *Information Sharing: Endorsements and statements* – details of organisations who have formally endorsed the guidance and what they have said.

- *Information sharing: Introductory training course* – published on CD-ROM and designed to be run from the CD or copied onto PCs for local use. It can be used by practitioners as self-study or by trainers as part of a classroom based course.

www.dcsf.gov.uk/everychildmatters.gov.uk
Tel: 087 0000 2288
Email:
info@dcsf.gsi.gov.uk

All of this guidance can be downloaded from www.dcsf.gov.uk/everychildmatters/. Hard copies of some of these publications can be obtained from DCSF Publications. All publications are available free of charge.

Professionals generally owe a common law duty of confidentiality to those who rely upon them, including children, but confidentiality can be breached to prevent serious crime, eg where there has been or there is a likelihood of serious harm to the client or others, particularly children. Sometimes legislation imposes specific obligations of confidence (eg the Abortion Act 1967), and sometimes disclosure is required (eg the

Child Support Regulations). Even so, whether to disclose or not may involve a balancing act between the obligation to maintain confidentiality and the need to disclose. The starting point is still the common law duty of confidentiality which provides that where there is a confidential relationship, the person receiving the confidential information is under a duty not to pass on the information to a third party. But the duty is not absolute and information can be shared without breaching the common law duty if:

- the information is not confidential in nature; or
- the person to whom the duty is owed has given explicit consent; or
- there is an overriding public interest in disclosure; or
- sharing is required by a court order or other legal obligation.

The common law duty of confidentiality is explained in sections 3.12 to 3.16 of the cross-Government guidance *Information Sharing: Guidance for practitioners and managers.*

Data Protection Act 1998

4.42   The provisions for access to information or files held by local authorities and others is contained in the Data Protection Act 1998 (DPA 1998). The DPA 1998 deals with the processing of personal (both sensitive and non-sensitive) data. Personal data is data which relates to a living person, including the expression of any opinion or indication about the intentions in respect of the individual. Sensitive personal data is personal data relating to racial or ethnic origin, religious or other similar beliefs, physical or mental health condition, sexual life, political opinions, membership of a trade union, the commission or alleged commission of any offence, any proceedings for an offence committed or alleged to have been committed, the disposal of proceedings or the sentence of any court in proceedings. Information about an individual will often contain information from several sources, for example from schools, doctors or the police and may contain their names and business addresses. It may also include information about other people, for example the individual's family members. These people are usually referred to in the DPA 1998 as 'third parties'. Information about third parties is personal information and should be treated accordingly. If an individual is no longer alive their personal information is not covered by the DPA 1998 although a duty of confidence may require some or all of their personal information to be kept confidential.

Subject to a limited number of exemptions, a person who is the subject of personal information held and processed by a social care authority has a right of access to that data. A person does not have the right to know what is recorded about someone else (eg a family member) without that person's consent, but there may be cases where it is reasonable in all the circumstances to comply without that other person's consent. Where a child or young person under the age of 18 makes a request for access to records, the authority will need to decide whether or not he has sufficient understanding to do so. If the child or young person does not have sufficient understanding to make a request, a person with parental responsibility can do so.

The exemptions are:

- prevention or detection of crime;
- where disclosure to the applicant would be likely to prejudice the carrying out of social work by causing serious harm to the physical or mental health or condition, of the applicant or another person;
- the local authority must not disclose information about physical or mental health or condition without first consulting an appropriate health professional, eg GP or psychiatrist;
- where other enactments themselves prevent disclosure, then an applicant cannot rely on the Data Protection Act to seek access to records, eg adoption records and reports.

The authority can disclose information with the consent of the relevant individual, but it is necessary to ensure that the processing is fair and lawful. Where disclosure of data is necessary to comply with a legal obligation imposed on an authority, then the consent of the individual is not necessary but he should be informed that such an obligation exists. An authority can disclose personal information to social care staff directly involved in a case and their line managers. They may also disclose personal information to anyone else who cares for one of their clients, eg a voluntary body or foster carers or any independent providers.

Volunteers and informal carers may also need to be given some personal information about an individual. Other organisations may also require personal information to discharge their statutory functions, eg health, education, inspection/audit, legal advisors, local authority finance staff and police. The local authority may be required to disclose information to other bodies. Examples are disclosure of information to the police, courts, tribunals, statutory inquiries, Secretary of State for Health, children's guardians and health and safety executive. Where disclosure is ordered by the courts, social care services are advised by the Department of Health to take professional and legal advice and that any information disclosed should be the minimum necessary to meet the requirements of the situation. The authority should record its reasons for disclosure.

In any proceedings under the Children Act 1989, the children's guardian has the right to examine and take copies of relevant children's services files. The information obtained is admissible in the proceedings as evidence, notwithstanding any rule of law which would make it otherwise inadmissible.

Further information is available in a publication from the Information Commissioners Office entitled Data Protection Act 1998 Legal Guidance, available on the ICO website.

Human Rights Act 1998

4.43   Regard must be had to the European Convention on Human Rights (see **4.19**) at all times. Article 8 of the European Convention on Human Rights was incorporated into UK law by the Human Rights Act 1998 and recognises a right to respect private and family life. Article 8 ECHR states, 'Everyone has the right to respect for his private and family life, his home and his correspondence'. However, specifically in this context there is a distinction between privacy and confidentiality. There is no right to privacy in English law as distinct from the legal protection given to confidentiality.

Sharing confidential information may be a breach of an individual's Article 8 rights: the question is whether sharing information would be justified under Article 8 and proportionate. The right to a private life can be legitimately interfered with where it is in accordance with the law and is necessary, for example, for the prevention of crime or disorder, for public safety, for the protection of health or morals, or for the protection of the rights and freedoms of others. There is a need to consider the pressing social need and whether sharing the information is a proportionate response to this need and whether these considerations can override the individual's right to privacy. If a child or young person is at risk of significant harm, or an adult is at risk of serious harm, or sharing is necessary to prevent crime or disorder, interference with the individual's right may be justified under Article 8.

Specific legislation contains express powers or provisions which imply powers to share information:

Freedom of Information Act 2000

For further information see:
The Information Commissioner's Office
www.ico.gov.uk

4.44 The Freedom of Information Act 2000 gives the right to access information held by a public authority including central government, local authorities, the NHS, schools and the police. To obtain personal information, the DPA 1998 will apply. If the information is not personal but in relation to a public authority, the Freedom of Information Act 2000 will apply. It gives a general right of access to 'recorded' information held by public authorities.

Children Act 1989

4.45 Section 47 of the Children Act 1989 places a duty on local authorities to make enquiries where they have reasonable cause to suspect that a child in their area may be at risk of suffering significant harm. Section 47 states that unless in all the circumstances it would be unreasonable for them to do so, the following authorities must assist a local authority with these enquiries if requested, in particular by providing relevant information:

- any local authority;
- any local education authority;
- any housing authority;
- any health authority;
- any person authorised by the Secretary of State.

Children Act 2004

4.46 Section 10 of the Act places a duty on each children's services authority to make arrangements to promote co-operation between itself and relevant partner agencies to improve the well-being of children in their area in relation to:

- physical and mental health, and emotional well-being;
- protection from harm and neglect;
- education, training and recreation;
- making a positive contribution to society;
- social and economic well-being.

The relevant partners must co-operate with the local authority to make arrangements to improve the well-being of children. The relevant partners are:

- district councils;
- the police;
- the Probation Service;
- youth offending teams (YOTs);
- strategic health authorities and primary care trusts;
- Connexions;
- the Learning and Skills Council.

Education Act 2002

4.47 The duty laid out in s 11 of the Children Act 2004 mirrors the duty imposed by s 175 of the Education Act 2002 on LEAs and the governing bodies of both maintained schools and further education institutions. This duty is to make arrangements to carry out their functions with a view to safeguarding and promoting the welfare of children and follow the guidance in Safeguarding Children in Education (DfES 2004). The guidance applies to proprietors of independent schools.

Education Act 1996

4.48 Section 408 and the Education (Pupil Information) (England) Regulations 2005 (SI 2005/1437) require the transfer of the pupil's common transfer file and educational record when a pupil changes school. Section 434(4) of the Act requires LEAs to request schools to provide details of children registered at a school.

Learning and Skills Act 2000

4.49 Section 117 of the Learning and Skills Act 2000 provides for help to a young person to enable them to take part in further education and training. Section 119 enables Connexions Services to share information with Jobcentre Plus to support young people to obtain appropriate benefits under the Social Security Contributions and Benefits Act 1992 and Social Security Administration Act 1992.

Education (SEN) Regulations 2001

4.50 Regulation 6 of the Education (Special Educational Needs) Regulations 2001 (SI 2001/2216) provides that when the LEA is considering making an assessment of a child's special educational needs, it is obliged to send copies of the notice to social services, health authorities and the head teacher of the school (if any) asking for relevant information.

Regulation 18 provides that all schools must provide Connexions Services with information regarding all Year 10 children who have a statement of special educational needs.

Children (Leaving Care) Act 2000

4.51 Sharing information with other agencies will enable the local authority to fulfil its statutory duty to provide after care services to young people leaving public care.

Mental Capacity Act 2005

4.52 The Mental Capacity Act 2005 and the associated Code of Practice contain guidance that is applicable to considerations of a person's capacity or lack of capacity to give consent to information sharing. (See also the Mental Capacity Act 2005 Code of Practice).

Local Government Act 2000

4.53 Part 1 of the Local Government Act 2000 gives local authorities powers to take any steps which they consider are likely to promote the well-being of their area or the inhabitants of it. Section 3 is clear that local authorities are unable to do anything (including sharing information) for the purposes of the well-being of people – including children and young people – where they are restricted or prevented from doing so on the face of any relevant legislation, for example, the Human Rights Act, the Data Protection Act or by the common law duty of confidentiality.

Criminal Justice Act 2003

4.54 Section 325 of this Act details the arrangements for assessing risk posed by different offenders. The following agencies have a duty to co-operate with these arrangements:

(a) every youth offending team established for an area;

(b) the Ministers of the Crown, exercising functions in relation to social security, child support, war pensions, employment and training;

(c) every local education authority;

(d) every local housing authority or social services authority;

(e) every registered social landlord who provides or manages residential accommodation;

(f) every health authority or strategic health authority;

(g) every primary care trust or local health board;

(h) every NHS trust;

(i) every person who is designated by the Secretary of State as a provider of electronic monitoring services.

Crime and Disorder Act 1998

4.55 Section 17 applies to a local authority (as defined by the Local Government Act 1972); a joint authority; a police authority; a national park authority; and the Broads Authority. As amended by the Greater London Authority Act 1999 it applies to the London Fire and Emergency Planning Authority from July 2000 and to all fire and rescue authorities with effect from April 2003, by virtue of an amendment in the Police Reform Act 2002. It recognises that these key authorities have responsibility for the provision of a wide and varied range of services to and within the community. In carrying out these functions, s 17 places a duty on them to do all they can to reasonably prevent crime and disorder in their area.

National Health Service Act 1977

4.56 Section 2 of the Act provides for sharing information with other NHS professionals and practitioners from other agencies carrying out health service functions that would otherwise be carried out by the NHS.

National Health Service Act 2006

4.57 Section 82 of the National Health Service Act 2006 places a duty on NHS bodies and local authorities to co-operate with one another in order to secure and advance the health and welfare of the people of England and Wales.

Adoption and Children Act 2002

4.58 The Adoption and Children Act 2002 and the associated Regulations make provision for obtaining, recording and keeping confidential information about adopted children and/or their relatives. The Act and Regulations, give limited express power to share information, in prescribed circumstances as laid out in the legislation. Information about pre-2002 Act adoptions remains governed by the provisions of the Adoption Agencies Regulations 1983. Legal advice should be sought before any disclosure from adoption records.

Public Interest Immunity

4.59 The exception to disclosure by any party, but especially by a local authority, is public interest immunity, which means: is the public interest in the withholding of confidential documents from a party greater than the public interest in the open administration of justice? It is always a matter for the judge's discretion as to whether a document is held to be privileged from disclosure. Guidance for a local authority seeking protection of documents on the grounds of public interest immunity is as follows:

- a local authority should disclose to parents all relevant information to help parents rebut their case, save where public interest immunity is claimed;

- if public interest immunity is claimed it is for the party seeking disclosure of the document to say why it should be disclosed;

- if a document appears to be covered by public interest immunity, the local authority should indicate the document's existence and prepare a précis for the court. The précis alone could be disclosed if so ordered;

- the local authority should draw the guardian's attention to public interest immunity documents and where the guardian sees relevant documents he or she should invite disclosure by the local authority. A guardian may not disclose documents covered by public interest immunity.

Most of the reported cases upon public interest immunity are concerned with the protection of some vital interest of the State, or some aspect of the functioning of central government. In cases involving children, public interest immunity is more likely to arise when disclosure of medical records or local authority or NSPCC records is sought.

Information Sharing

4.60   The balancing exercise about whether or not confidentiality can be breached is at its starkest when it comes to child protection. It is difficult to protect children from abuse if information is not available to the full range of professionals concerned with their welfare. Often, it is only when the information from a number of sources has been shared and is then put together that it becomes clear that a child is at risk or suffering harm.

The Court of Appeal said in 2002 that there is not, as a matter of law, a presumption in favour of disclosure and each case had to be decided on its own merits. However, the court emphasised the advantages of disclosure as a matter of good practice in modern interdisciplinary child protection. For example, information recorded as part of the investigation but not filed at court can be disclosed to police without the permission of the court. Information which has been filed at court requires the permission of the court to be disclosed to anyone not a party. However, the Court of Appeal in 2002 said that the relationship between the children's guardian and the judge was a collaborative one and in urgent cases he must be free to report concerns direct to social services and then inform the judge.

Sharing Information Safely: MARAC

4.61 All too often in cases of domestic abuse, a victim, their children and the abuser will be involved with a wide range of agencies including, for example, both the family and criminal courts, the health service, substance misuse services and the housing department. There are frequently significant gaps in the information held by different agencies. Thus, for example, the police will know that they have been called on numerous occasions to a particular house to respond to a domestic abuse incident. Often these incidents are recorded as 'non-crime domestics' or so called 'verbal' incidents. What the police may not usually know is the involvement the victim has had at the same time with the health service. Without knowing the victim's history of Accident and Emergency (A & E) attendances, the police may not be in a position to offer the appropriate response.

This fragmented picture in relation to information about victims is now being changed thanks to the introduction of Multi Agency Risk Assessment Conferences, or MARACs. A MARAC is a regular monthly or fortnightly meeting attended by 10–15 different agencies from both the statutory and voluntary sectors. It is designed to facilitate information sharing between these agencies about the highest risk victims in an area and then to create and implement a safety plan for each one. Links should be made with the safeguarding boards in relation to children and vulnerable adults, and to Multi Agency Public Protection Arrangements (MAPPAs) in relation to offenders. The agencies represented are those who would normally come into contact with domestic violence victims namely the police, the primary care trust, the acute trust, children's services, housing, substance misuse services, the local refuge and crucially the independent domestic violence advisors (IDVAs) whose role it is to offer specialist support to these high risk victims. MARAC is a volume process, quite unlike child protection case conference for example, with between 15–20 cases being reviewed briefly at a typical meeting. The boundaries of the MARAC are usually consistent with a local police division.

Use of the common risk identification tool is important for a sound MARAC, as are clear protocols about information sharing. The focus of the MARAC is on safety, whether this is addressed within or outside the court system. This is highlighted in the volume of referrals to the meeting from agencies outside the criminal justice system, namely the specialist domestic violence services, and health services.

There are now over 200 MARACs running across England and Wales which have almost all been established within the past 3 years. Co-ordinated Action Against Domestic Abuse (CAADA) has been responsible for training and implementing these MARACs with support from the Home Office. Indeed the national roll out of MARACs by 2011 now forms part of the Home Office plan for tackling violent crime. The rapid take up of MARACs without any significant funding to support their development reflects the desire of many practitioners to offer a more coordinated response to victims of domestic abuse and to address the risks that they face more effectively.

At a typical MARAC meeting information from police, IDVAs, health practitioners and others will be shared. For instance, the police may believe that someone who is banned from his ex-partner's home is adhering to his bail conditions, while a midwife visiting a home may find the offender there. At the time of the visit, she may have no idea about the bail conditions. At the MARAC these two bits of information would be linked and the police could arrest for breach of bail, while the midwife might coordinate a visit with an IDVA to offer additional support to the woman. The education welfare officer could inform the school of the domestic abuse, which could in turn support the children in a more appropriate way, for example by being made aware of who can be allowed to collect the children.

In December 2008 Cafcass (no longer CAFCASS) launched its new website, developed with the help of the

Source:
Fam Law -
May 2009

Cafcass Young People's Board and designed to make it easier for children and families to find out more about Cafcass and the family court system. The new site has a number of new features, including animations for children explaining what the organisation does and a forum where children can get support from young peer mentors.

CAADA (London Office)
Tel: 0207 922 7891
www.caada.org.uk/

Cafcass has also finalised a joint protocol with the Association of Chief Police Officers (ACPO) on disclosure of information from the police. The protocol sets out the principles of information sharing between Cafcass and all local police forces in England and Wales. It includes a standard request form which Cafcass practitioners will use to highlight the areas of risk (as set out in the Safeguarding Framework) that they have already identified. The guiding principle is that evidence of one risk or from one incident will act as a key to allowing the police to provide information about all risks and all incidents.

Disclosure in Court Proceedings

Children Act Proceedings

4.62 Where an application is made for disclosure of documents filed in family proceedings for use in criminal proceedings, there is a distinction between those cases where the two sets of proceedings are factually connected, and those where they are not. A balance has to be struck in each case between the importance of maintaining confidentiality in the family case, the interests of the child (which are not paramount in criminal proceedings) and the public interest in making relevant information available for other proceedings. Directions from the court should be sought on difficult issues of disclosure, if necessary at the case management conference.

Since 1996, there has been clear authority that the matters for the judge to consider in deciding whether to order disclosure are:

(i)   the welfare and the interest of the child concerned and of other children generally;

(ii) the maintenance of confidentiality in children cases and the importance of encouraging frankness;

(iii) the public interest in the administration of justice and the prosecution of serious crime;

(iv) the gravity of the alleged offence and the relevance of the evidence to it;

(v) the desirability of co-operation between the various agencies concerned with the welfare of children;

(vi) in cases where section 98(2) of the Children Act applied, fairness to the person who had incriminated himself and any others affected by the incriminating statement;

(vii) any other material disclosure which had already taken place.

More recent authority states that disclosure is the norm and non-disclosure should be permitted only where the case for doing so is compelling (see *A Local Authority v M* [2009] EWHC 1574). The Article 8 ECHR rights of adults may also justify non-disclosure where the risk is of harm to them rather than a child.

The principles to apply to a Children Act case are therefore as follows:

'(1) It is a fundamental principle of fairness that a party is entitled to the disclosure of all materials which may be taken into account by the court when reaching a decision adverse to that party ...

(2) ... the court should first consider whether disclosure of the material would involve a real possibility of significant harm to the child.

(3) If it would, the court should next consider whether the overall interests of the child would benefit from non-disclosure, weighing on the one hand the interest of the child in having the material properly tested, and on the other both the magnitude of the risk that harm will occur and the gravity of the harm if it does occur.

(4) If the court is satisfied that the interests of the child point towards non-disclosure, the next and final step is for the court to weigh that consideration, and its strength in the circumstances of the case, against the interest of the parent or other party in having an opportunity to see and respond to the material. In the latter regard the court should take into account the importance of the material to the issues in the case.

(5)   Non-disclosure should be the exception not the rule. The court should be rigorous in its examination of the risk and gravity of the feared harm to the child, and should order non-disclosure only when the case for doing so is compelling.'

Documents and information in Children Act 1989 proceedings can be shared with:

- a legal representative or other professional legal adviser;

- any other parties;

- a Children and Family Court Advisory and Support Service (Cafcass) officer, Welsh family proceedings officer or a welfare officer;

- the Legal Services Commission;

- an expert authorised by the court;

- a professional, including the police and the NSPCC, whose job it is to protect children; and/or

- an independent reviewing officer appointed in respect of a child who is, or has been, subject to proceedings to which this rule applies.

Source:
Family Proceedings
Rules 1991,
Part XI, r 11.2

If a party so authorises, the same rules allow, in addition, the sharing of information connected with Children Act proceedings to any person where necessary to enable that party:

(i)   by confidential discussion, to obtain support, advice or assistance in the conduct of the proceedings;

(ii)   to engage in mediation or other forms of alternative dispute resolution;

(iii) to make or pursue a complaint against a person or body concerned in the proceedings; or

(iv)   to make or pursue a complaint regarding to the law, policy or procedure relating to family proceedings;

Where information is communicated to any person in accordance with (i) above, no further communication by that person is allowed.

When information relating to the proceedings is communicated to any person in accordance with (ii), (iii), or (iv) above –

(a) the recipient may communicate that information to a further recipient, provided that –

(i) the party who initially communicated the information consents to the further communication; and

(ii) the further communication is made only for the purpose or purposes for which the party made the initial communication; and

(b) the information may be successively communicated to and by further recipients on as many occasions as may be necessary to fulfil the purpose for which the information was initially communicated, provided that on each such occasion the conditions in paragraph (a) above are met.

Source:
Family Proceedings Rules 1991, Part XI, r 11.4

The rules also make specific provision for communication of information by Cafcass officers or officers of CAFCASS CYMRU (r 11.6) and specific provision for the communication of information to and by ministers of the Crown and Welsh ministers for the purposes of proceedings before the European Court of Human Rights and for consideration of policy issues (r 11.7).

For other purposes, a person specified in the first column of the following may communicate to a person listed in the second column such information as is specified in the third column for the purpose or purposes specified in the fourth column:

A party	A lay adviser, a McKenzie Friend, or a person arranging or providing pro bono legal services	Any information relating to the proceedings	To enable the party to obtain advice or assistance in relation to the proceeding
A party	A health care professional or a person or body providing counselling services for children or families		To enable the party or any child of the party to obtain health care or counselling

A party	The Secretary of State, a McKenzie Friend, a lay adviser or the First-tier Tribunal dealing with an appeal made under section 20 of the Child Support Act 1991	For the purposes of making or responding to an appeal under section 20 of the Child Support Act 1991 or the determination of such an appeal
A party	An adoption panel	To enable the adoption panel to discharge its functions as appropriate
A party	The European Court of Human Rights	For the purpose of making an application to the European Court of Human Rights
A party or any person lawfully in receipt of information	The Children's Commissioner or the Children's Commissioner for Wales	To refer an issue affecting the interests of children to the Children's Commissioner or the Children's Commissioner for Wales
A party, any person lawfully in receipt of information or a proper officer	A person or body conducting an approved research project	For the purpose of an approved research project
A legal representative or a professional legal adviser	A person or body responsible for investigating or determining complaints in relation to legal representatives or professional legal advisers	For the purposes of the investigation or determination of a complaint in relation to a legal representative or a professional legal adviser

A legal representative or a professional legal adviser	A person or body assessing quality assurance systems		To enable the legal representative or professional legal adviser to obtain a quality assurance assessment
A legal representative or a professional legal adviser	An accreditation body	Any information relating to the proceedings providing that it does not, or is not likely to, identify any person involved in the proceedings	To enable the legal representative or professional legal adviser to obtain accreditation
A party	A police officer	The text or summary of the whole or part of a judgment given in the proceedings	For the purpose of a criminal investigation
A party or any person lawfully in receipt of information	A member of the Crown Prosecution Service		To enable the Crown Prosecution Service to discharge its functions under any enactment

The new rules do not apply to court orders, nor to disclosure in adoption proceedings where different rules apply.

Local authorities should disclose all relevant material affecting the child who is in their possession, but not documents protected by public interest immunity (see above) which might be of assistance to the natural parent(s) in rebutting charges that one or both of them was in any way ill-treating the child. Social workers should disclose all the information on which they base their case, both negative and positive, and their judgment has to be based on objectively reviewed and disclosed material. Proceedings involving children are supposed to be investigative, not adversarial, so special rules as to disclosure apply.

Guardian's Report and Investigations

4.63   The children's guardian's report for the court is confidential, as is the information he collects when preparing a report.

Source:
Family Proceedings
Rules
1991, Part XI,
rules 11.1–11.9

Adoption

4.64 In adoption cases, the rules relating to disclosure are different from those relating to Children Act 1989 cases in which all reports should be openly available to all parties unless the court orders otherwise. In adoption proceedings, reports are filed initially on a confidential basis.

Disclosure of Police Evidence

4.65 Where the local authority wishes to see documents from the Crown Prosecution Service relating to forthcoming criminal proceedings, disclosure can be ordered where the reason is to enable the local authority to make a more informed decision about the future of children in its interim care. Disclosure to all parties in the case would not necessarily be ordered by the court. Police and hospitals can release video evidence to solicitors, the solicitors undertaking not to copy them, save to expert witnesses. If the police/hospitals refuse, application could be made to the court which, in appropriate cases, might award costs against the police/hospital.

See also Victor Smith, 'In Defence of the Prosecution Disclosure Protocol', [2006] Fam Law 457 www.familylaw.co.uk

A national protocol for exchange of information between local authorities and the police relating to child abuse cases has been drawn up by the Home Office and others. The principal aim of the protocol is to provide an agreed, non-legally binding framework between the parties for the sharing and exchange of relevant material in child protection investigations. It is intended to serve as a model and chief crown prosecutors, chief officers of the police and chief executives of local authorities are encouraged to adopt it as necessary to suit local needs. It further aims to ensure that these parties employ a consistent approach to information sharing locally.

In the absence of pending court proceedings, communication and sharing of information between social services and police must depend upon working relationships established between professionals, in the spirit of the published guidance.

In private law CA 1989 proceedings, as a matter of strict law, discovery of documents cannot be ordered against persons who are not parties, for example the police or a local authority. But the court has the jurisdiction to compel such discovery by order provided suitable undertakings as to confidentiality and the use of the material are given.

Privilege

4.66 Some information may be privileged, that is, a claim can validly be made that certain documents need not be disclosed and so used in court proceedings. The main bases for claiming privilege are as follows.

Legal Professional Privilege

4.67 Communications between a client and his legal representative (whether or not proceedings are pending) cannot be disclosed, even by order of the court. For Law Society guidance to solicitors as to when the privilege does not apply with respect to children, see **6.23**.

Communications between a solicitor and third parties where proceedings are pending are privileged. There is an exception when communications and reports come into existence after the court has given leave in children cases for the release of confidential documents, for example to an expert on behalf of the party given leave. Once leave is granted, the report must be filed at court and served on the other parties. Experts need to know that their reports may be disclosed to third parties even if the party wanting it later chooses not to use it.

A party in care proceedings who is also involved in criminal proceedings is entitled to claim legal professional privilege in the care proceedings in respect of his direct or indirect communications with experts instructed solely for the purposes of the criminal proceedings. So long as he does not waive the privilege, he has an absolute right to refuse to disclose those reports and communications. He is also entitled to refuse to disclose the names of the expert witnesses that he has instructed in those criminal proceedings.

A local authority cannot rely on legal professional privilege to prevent the disclosure of all relevant documents and experts' reports in wardship or Children Act 1989 proceedings.

Information received by a social worker acting as 'an appropriate adult', or by an interpreter, by their attendance at an interview between a child and his solicitor is covered by legal professional privilege and it is not open to the social worker/interpreter or the solicitor to waive that privilege by disclosing what was said in the interview to any other person.

Disclosure Injurious to Public Interest

4.68 Mediated agreements are always marked 'without prejudice' and so are many solicitors' letters. This means that the agreements or offers are not legally binding. This is because it is public policy to encourage people to settle cases and so it is public policy to exempt from disclosure any letter or other document – whether or not marked 'without prejudice' – which is an attempt to settle a case. The principle also applies to discussions with a Cafcass officer when he is acting as a mediator (but not when he is acting as an in-court conciliator, see **2.74**). The privilege is overridden where there is a likelihood of serious harm to a child. The privilege belongs to the parties themselves and can be waived if they so choose.

Documents Tending to Incriminate

4.69 As a general rule, a person is not bound to answer any question if it might expose him to criminal proceedings. This principle is overridden in public law children proceedings where no person is excused from giving evidence on any matter, or answering any question put to him during the course of his evidence, on the ground that to do so might incriminate him or his spouse in an offence. Thus, the privilege against self-incrimination does not apply, but the witness has a partial indemnity in that a statement or admission made in such proceedings cannot be admissible in evidence against the person making it, or his spouse, in proceedings for an offence other than perjury. However, the court can order documents arising as a result, and which tend to incriminate, to be disclosed to the police on the basis of balancing the need for maintaining confidentiality in family cases against the public interest in making possible a criminal trial of a serious offence.

Confidentiality, Privilege and Mediation

4.70 All communications (except the disclosure of finances) to which mediators are party are made solely for the purpose of attempting to reach a settlement and are made on the basis that such communications are confidential and will not be referred to in evidence in any court proceedings about the same issues (ie they are privileged). Financial disclosures are made on the basis that they can be disclosed to the parties' solicitors and can be used in evidence in court (ie they are not privileged).

Privilege in Relation to Children

4.71 Statements made by either of the parties in the course of mediation cannot be disclosed in proceedings under the Children Act 1989 except in the exceptional case where such a statement indicated that the maker had in the past caused or was likely to cause serious harm to the well-being of a child. When a Cafcass officer is acting as a mediator the information given by parties is privileged: where he is acting as an in-court conciliator it is not (see **2.63**) and can be reported to the court.

Privilege in Relation to Finance and Property

4.72 The privilege of 'without prejudice' negotiation belongs to the parties and not to the mediator or to the process. It can be waived by the parties. It attaches to negotiations for settling disputes but not to the binding agreements that result from such negotiations. Although no privilege exists as a matter of law to protect confidential communications (other than between a lawyer and client) the court is likely in practice to protect such disclosures because public policy has always favoured the settlement of disputes.

Publicity

4.73 Parents have a right to information about their children. Access to confidential information relating to their child is an aspect of parental responsibility. However, parents have a duty to respect the confidentiality which is entrusted to them and not to seek publicity.

It was previously the rule that in proceedings in the magistrates' (family proceedings) court, nobody may be present in court other than the officers of the court, the parties, their solicitors and counsel, witnesses and other people directly concerned in the case, journalists and other people if given permission by the court. If the court thought that it was in the child's best interests, it could hear applications in private. In the county court and High Court, proceedings were generally heard in private ('in chambers').

The issues of access to family proceedings (in the sense of the public being permitted to be present in court) and the reporting of family proceedings (in the media) were reviewed by the government in 2006. The judiciary were generally in favour of more openness as they believed that criticisms of the family justice system stem mainly from the 'secrecy' of proceedings. They felt that while wholesale publicity and access would be inappropriate in cases concerning children, more information would be helpful to the public if suitably anonymised.

In April 2009, the government introduced greater media attendance into the family courts. There are now two clear categories of what may not be published. In cases involving the welfare of children, nothing can be published which may tend to identify the child or its school. The media is well aware of these restrictions already, and they have not changed: that leaves a great deal of scope nevertheless. The terminology which the legislation relies upon for exclusion is 'necessary in the interests of any child concerned in, or connected with, the proceedings'. Unless the media can be excluded on that basis, they have no greater restriction on publication save the anonymity provisions. A child will be concerned in proceedings if they are the subject of Children Act proceedings, including possibly Schedule 1 proceedings for their maintenance.

The media cannot have access to the court file, nor quote from it. Because a great deal of family court litigation rests on the documentation, this is a perhaps significant restriction on balanced reporting. The difficulty of course is that balanced reporting is in the interests of justice, so as matters stand, the restriction may be said to do more harm than good. There is express approval for identification of parties and witnesses. There is express approval for publication of the particulars, and for the judgment.

The move to allow greater reporting of family court matters by the media has caused great concern in some quarters. Whether or not this concern is justified remains to be seen:

> 'The ostensible reason for this move is to increase transparency about court proceedings in order to better inform the public and disabuse them of wrong perceptions, such as the belief that the courts freely and unnecessarily remove children

For the Government consultation paper see further Introduction, p 10

Source:
Fam Law -
August 2009

from their parents' care. There is an added agenda, namely to scrutinise specifically the opinion and evidence of expert witnesses.

The media are now being allowed into courts with the discretion of the judge or magistrates and are able to report on the proceedings. They are not permitted to divulge the identity of the child and family unless specifically directed by the judge so to do. As much of the evidence in family cases is in written form, including expert medical or other professional reports, listening to oral evidence alone will not enable the media to report fully and meaningfully.

As has been extensively argued elsewhere, an anonymised transcript of the judgement provides the clearest summary of the evidence, the decision-making process and the reasons for the court's decisions. This process, although agreed upon, has not yet materialised.

Meanwhile, it is now proposed to allow the media to read medical and other expert reports. This will pose serious difficulties for doctors and other professionals acting as expert witnesses for a number of reasons. Experts are instructed on the basis that by using their clinical skills in meeting with family members they will be able to assist the court in its decision-making. The clinical professional is thus being utilised simultaneously as clinician and expert. The stock in trade of mental health professionals is their ability to converse with patients in a particular way so as to elicit information. To be of benefit to the patient and, in this case, also to the court, the context has to be one of trust – trust in the skill, expertise and integrity of the clinician, by both patient and court.

One of the fundamental assumptions underpinning clinical encounters is confidentiality. This is already being compromised by the knowledge that the clinician will be reporting to the court. In these circumstances, most patients/family members are able to extend the limits of confidentiality to include the court. However, there are issues which may be of importance and which a family member may not wish to discuss under these circumstances, compromising the quality of the expert report. That is an acceptable limitation.

However, for a clinician, it is inconceivable that one may now be put in a position of having to warn the patient that what is being discussed, almost invariably highly personal and often distressing, and already being necessarily included in one's report, will also be read by the media. It borders on insulting the family member and is thus unethical. It would also diminish significantly the quality of the clinical encounter and the information forthcoming. An assurance of anonymity is simply insufficient. Moreover, it is not currently even clear who, it is proposed, will carry out the anonymisation of the expert reports; funding for the anonymisation of judgements, already agreed, has thus far not been forthcoming.

The General Medical Council (GMC), the medical and other professional protection organisations and NHS-employing Trusts are yet to agree to this proposed clear breach of confidentiality. And the purpose? To appoint the media to interpret and judge the quality of expert evidence, until now assumed to be the task of the court.'

Source:
Danya Glaser,
Consultant Child and
Adolescent Psychiatrist,
Department of Child
and
Adolescent Mental
Health,
Great Ormond Street
Hospital for Children,
Member of the Family
Justice Council

EVIDENCE

4.74 Proceedings under the Children Act are essentially inquisitorial because the focus of the proceedings is the welfare of the child. This means that the court should be taking control of the proceedings and ensuring that all relevant information is available. Special rules of evidence apply to family proceedings which make the exchange and disclosure of information possible. Essentially, the thrust of the legislation and subsequent case-law is to allow the court to have:

- access to and use of information from the outside world. This is an evidence issue relating to the identifying and subpoenaing of witnesses;

- access to and use of its own determined and acquired information from the outside world. Once information is put before the court, the court will decide who has access to it and, for example, the court will allow experts' reports to be available to other doctors. This is dealt with by directions in the proceedings.

The general law of evidence applies to all family cases. All evidence which is sufficiently relevant to an issue is admissible. The standard of proof is the same as in all civil cases, that is, the balance of probabilities. This means that if, in a child abuse case, the court can say 'we think it more probable than not' that the child was hurt non-accidentally, then the burden of proof is discharged. It is up to the party alleging the abuse to prove it on the balance of probabilities. This is different to the criminal standard of proof which is 'beyond reasonable doubt'. In a child abuse case, a parent may be prosecuted by the police but acquitted by the criminal court because the prosecution does not have enough evidence to prove the abuse beyond reasonable doubt. However, the same evidence might be enough in care proceedings to establish, on the balance of probabilities, that the child was, more likely than not, abused.

Hearsay Evidence

4.75 The normal rule is that one person cannot give evidence to the court about what another person said. However, the Children Act 1989 allows hearsay evidence in family proceedings in the magistrates' courts, the county court and the High Court in cases relating to the upbringing of a child. The purpose is to provide a way for the evidence of children to be placed before the family court without the need for children to attend. A child who is the subject of care proceedings might already have had to repeat his story to perhaps an initial confidante such as a teacher, then maybe a duty social worker, a doctor and a police officer. The child has a solicitor and guardian who know the content of the statement and that if there is anything the child wants to discuss further about it the child is able to do so. By the time of the court proceedings, a child is likely to need help with the consequences of his disclosure rather than the original events themselves. It is now accepted that most children do tell the truth, whether about sexual abuse or anything else, and the presumption is to believe them in the absence of any contradictory evidence.

The Children Act 1989 in addition allows the court to take into account any statement made in the guardian's report. The report can include copies of local authority records and the court can treat the record not only as evidence that the local authority has the information contained in it but that what is described in the records is true. The court can take account of any statement made in a court welfare officer's report and any evidence given in respect of the matters referred to in it.

Witnesses

4.76   In cases concerning children, the parties must give evidence orally. They will already have sent written, signed statements to the court. Normally, the court will take the contents of these statements 'as read' so there is no need for the witness to repeat in the witness box what is said in the statement apart from updating or correction. Any person can be required by subpoena or witness summons to produce documents at court notwithstanding that they might contain confidential information about, for example, a patient. In order to ensure that this is available before the trial it might be required by pre-trial order. See also **4.69**.

Evidence of Children

4.77   The general rule in civil proceedings is that a child can give sworn evidence. The evidence of a child witness who does not understand the nature of the oath can be heard by a court if, in its opinion, the child understands that it is his duty to speak the truth and that he has sufficient understanding to justify the evidence being heard. However, courts are reluctant to involve young children in proceedings and their views can be ascertained through the Cafcass officer, mediation, the guardian ad litem and the child's solicitor. Whether the child attends is a matter for the court. Some judges very occasionally see children in chambers but until now magistrates have been positively discouraged from seeing children at all. The court should be very cautious before it requires the attendance of a child complainant to give oral evidence in abuse cases. The risk of harm to the child arising from the process of giving evidence must be considered. The correct starting point is that it is undesirable that a child should have to give evidence in care proceedings and that particular justification will be required before that course is taken. There will be some cases in which it will be right to require oral evidence, but they will be rare. The forensic need for the evidence to be given orally has to be balanced against the risk of harm to the child.

Older children might want more input. A child who is able to give instructions may want to give evidence. The solicitor will need to advise the child client about the advantages and disadvantages of such a course of action. Another option is for the child to write a letter to the judge. The Care Proceedings Review recommended that the judiciary learn to communicate better with children.

Expert Evidence

4.78 Expert evidence is often used to prove basic factual premises and not just to provide expert opinion. An expert witness should describe his experience and qualifications and it is up to the court to decide whether the witness has the expertise necessary for giving an opinion. Experts must only express opinions which they genuinely hold and which are not biased in favour of one party. It is preferable for all the parties to instruct one expert. An expert witness can be called by any party to the proceedings, even if he was not instructed by them. For guidance on instructing and using an expert, see **2.117–2.129**.

CHAPTER FIVE

CORE INFORMATION

RELATIONSHIP BREAKDOWN

5.1 It is easy to fall into the trap of calling on our own experience when making decisions about families and it is important to remember that our personal view of reality is different from others. There is abundant evidence that, even in the present day where family breakdown is common, as a rule, families provide the best environment for growing and developing children.

However, too much emphasis can be placed on 'the family' as the bulwark against all ills. The family can be both a source of support and a place of oppression. A family is only as strong as its members, and rather than relying on the family unit, society has a duty to individuals and families to provide a network of support and understanding. The network may consist of friends, relatives, neighbours, work colleagues, school friends, etc, as well as paid professionals such as teachers, doctors and nurses. It might well be for lack of such support that the nuclear family of today is far more likely to self-destruct than the extended and geographically close family of preceding generations.

Before the industrial revolutions of the eighteenth and nineteenth centuries, 'the family' was a wide unit, with constantly changing boundaries, and children of unknown paternal origin could be easily absorbed, as additional labour was an economic asset. What are the general recognised forms of relationship in the twenty-first century? Other forms continue to emerge – such as the growing number of partners who are 'committed' to each other but continue to live in separate households (the 'living apart togethers' or LATs) – and many households now comprise single parents and especially single mothers, who might never have had a settled relationship at all.

Marriage

5.2 A hundred years ago the basis of the family was a
marriage that was Christian (or if not Christian, then
its secular equivalent) and, at least in theory, lifelong.
The family of today is very different for, although there
is no lack of interest in family life (or at least in
intimate relationships), the figures demonstrate a
striking decline in marriage. In our present multicultural
and pluralistic society, the family takes many forms.
Many marry according to the rites of non-Christian
faiths. People live together as couples, married or not,
and with partners who may not always be of the
opposite sex. Children live in households where their
parents may be married or unmarried. They may be
brought up by a single parent. Their parents may or
may not be their natural parents. Their siblings may be
only half-siblings or step-siblings. Some children are
brought up by two parents of the same sex. The fact is
that many adults and children, whether through choice
or circumstance, live in families more or less removed
from what, until comparatively recently, would have
been recognised as the typical nuclear family.

Source:
Cretney, *Family Law
in the Twentieth
Century:
A History*
(Oxford University
Press, 2003)

Everyone can recite the statistic that one in three
marriages ends in divorce. The facts are a little more
complicated. The Office for National Statistics figures
show that since the early 1980s, the divorce rate has
stabilised, largely due to the decline in marriage and the
increasing proportion of couples cohabiting,
particularly since 1990. The number of divorces in the
UK fell by 2.6% in 2007 to 144,220, compared with
148,141 divorces in 2006. The downward trend largely
reflects the fall in the number of first marriages.
According to the Office for National Statistics there
were only 231,000 marriages in England and Wales in
2007, the lowest total in 112 years. Four out of 10 are
likely to end in divorce; 143,000 were first marriages,
the others second or further remarriages. Remarriages
are statistically more likely to break down than first
marriages. We have the highest divorce rate in Western
Europe, at 6.68 per 1,000 married people compared
with, say, Germany at 4.57 and France at 2.01.

Office for National
Statistics
Tel: 0845 601 3034
www.statistics.gov.uk

The related costs of a high rate of divorce are high.
Mediation has not worked as well as had been hoped
either, even though the conciliation and mediation
professions have grown greatly. Mediation is not to be
confused with reconciliation, which latter is an attempt
to bring the parties together again. Mediation and
conciliation are designed to help a single person or
couple reach the appropriate decisions concerning the
breakdown of the marriage. They are not designed to

promote or assist reconciliation. As such, mediation is useful but is unlikely to hold down the rate of divorce.

Source: Family Law, November 2009

It has been proposed that marriage education might be coupled with existing sex education programmes, each reinforcing the other. A marriage education programme could perhaps focus on the factors that are known to make for a happy or unhappy marriage, the financial costs of splitting up, the dangers to children of broken marriages, the paternal role, and the career prospects and post-divorce situation of women. Another remedy might be to tighten divorce procedures by insisting on a delay before freedom to remarry in divorces based on the adultery or unreasonable behaviour grounds, which can be processed relatively quickly at the moment. It is also arguable that none of this matters because of the tendency to cohabit rather than divorce, thereby avoiding the courts.

Pre-marital Agreements

5.3 On marriage breakdown a great deal of time, energy, money and emotion are spent on dividing the family's assets. The tensions which inevitably arise can often spill over into couples' arrangements about children and the bitterness over money can last for years. Apart from mediation and collaboration (which deal with financial and children matters at the same time – unlike the courts which impose separate proceedings for each), is there another way of minimising this hardship? Pre-marital agreements (or contracts) are not currently enforceable in England and Wales as they are deemed contrary to public policy because they may undermine the institution of marriage and the ability of the courts to tailor-make financial solutions for families upon marriage breakdown. Spouses and registered same-sex partners are therefore, at least at the end of 2009, unable to bind themselves with a contractual pre-marital/partnership agreement.

Nevertheless, the courts are increasingly coming to recognise the increasing importance of pre-nuptial agreements and cohabitants are encouraged to make 'living together' agreements. Although pre-marital and pre-registration property agreements made between spouses and civil partners (or those contemplating marriage or civil partnership) are not currently enforceable in the event of the spouses' divorce or the dissolution of the civil partnership, agreements are a material consideration under s 25 of the Matrimonial

Causes Act 1973 (MCA 1973) and recent court machinations on the subject of marital property agreements has led the Court of Appeal to suggest that there is a 'lack of clarity in the treatment of pre-nuptial contracts under our present law'.

The government's position in the consultation document *Supporting Families* (1999) addressed measures to strengthen the family and bolster marriage as the best basis for raising children and for building strong communities. It considered whether making pre-marital agreements binding on divorce would provide parties with more choice, encourage them to take responsibility in their own lives or, by addressing financial issues before marriage, provide a solid foundation for the marriage. While not suggesting that such agreements become mandatory, the government felt that they should be allowed subject to certain safeguards.

These days, current data suggests that the most frequent 'type of client' seeking pre-nuptial agreements is a client who has the additional matter of third party involvement in the pre-nuptial agreement, such as a family who are anxious to protect business or other assets, or wealthy parents wanting to protect the inheritances or trust funds of their children. The second most frequent type of client seeking these arrangements is a client with an international background, followed by the client who wishes to protect family wealth.

Post-nuptial agreements might now be sought from mid-marriage clients for a range of tax and property reasons and parties upon the reconciliation of their relationship. In this latter situation, a post-nuptial agreement is used to cement the relationship after a rift between the parties. A solid proportion of post-nuptial agreements are really pre-nuptial negotiations that have run out of time where the client who wants a post-nuptial agreement is generally the client who has run out of time to sign the (originally intended) pre-nuptial agreement. This is because they either went to see the practitioner too late and/or the case was complex due to the assets/jurisdictional issues involved.

Source: Family Law November 2009

The Law Commission's recent project on marital property agreements commenced on 1 October 2009 and it is anticipated that a report and draft Bill will be published in late 2012. Many lawyers think that reform would address the lack of clarity and certainty of outcome for parties on divorce and meet a general desire to self-order. It would also protect children and inherited wealth, and allow a consistency of approach with treatment of other social groups. It might reduce the cost of litigation, produce fairness of outcome and give greater choice at the outset of married relationships or registered civil partnerships. It might even encourage more to choose marriage as an option for family life. Since the decisions of the Supreme Court in several high profile (and millionaire-oriented) cases, particularly *Radmacher v Granatino* in 2010, pre-marital contracts could be recognised more often by the courts.

Cohabitation

5.4 There is no legal definition of cohabitation: it generally means to live together as a couple without being married or in a civil partnership. Recognising it is a question of fact. Heterosexual cohabitation has increased from the 1960s onwards and 'living together' is now accepted as normal (there are in the twenty-first century over 2 million opposite sex unmarried couples living together in England and Wales) but 90% of cohabitants and former cohabitants appear to take no legal steps before or after starting to cohabit. Although cohabitants are now given legal protection in several areas, they and their families have significantly fewer rights and responsibilities than their married counterparts. Six out of ten cohabiting couples think that there is such a thing as 'common law marriage', but in fact when a relationship ends, a lone parent who lived with a partner for 10 years and contributed to household bills:

- has no right to a share of the family home;
- has no right to maintenance payments;
- may be deemed to have made himself intentionally homeless; and
- may lose his right to council housing.

The exception is where the state – without using the term – takes cohabitees' means into account for state benefits, legal aid or council tax or some other exceptional situations, in particular the right to inherit a tenancy.

On the breakdown of their relationship, cohabiting couples have none of the guidance or protection of matrimonial divorce law. As far as property is concerned, they have to rely on normal property law principles and one cohabitee cannot apply for maintenance from the other as a spouse can. Where there are children, however, there is less of a distinction between married and unmarried parents but a focus on children (after separation the home can be kept on trust for the children) does nothing for the childless cohabitee. The difficulty in legislating for cohabiting couples is the need to recognise and respond to the increasing diversity in people's living arrangements.

The Law Commission published proposals for reform in 2007 in *Cohabitation: The Financial Consequences of Relationship Breakdown*. These were that property rights for cohabitants will depend on whether they come within certain eligibility criteria. The criteria include cohabitants who have had a child together or who lived together for a specified number of years. The latter was referred to as a 'minimum duration' requirement the period suggested being a period of between 2 and 5 years. The report also makes a recommendation for a scheme where couples can disapply the statute by means of an opt-out agreement, leaving them free to make their own financial arrangements but subject to some statutory protection to prevent couples opting out without fully understanding the legal implications of the opt-out. Claimants will have to demonstrate that they have made 'qualifying contributions to the parties' relationship which have given rise to certain enduring consequences at the point of separation. These proposals are limited and are a long way from becoming law. Even if they were adopted there are still serious omissions such as the way the courts would calculate financial settlements.

Cohabitation: The Financial Consequences of Relationship Breakdown, Law Com No 307 (TSO, 2007)

The present government shows no appetite for reform and recent attempts by Lord Lester to introduce legislation in 2009 have also met with no immediate success and neither the government nor the opposition has given support. So the apparent inequity remains and the cohabitant who wishes to claim a share of property after the relationship has broken down must continue to rely on property rules for such rights. The rules are notoriously complex and have long been criticised for failing to reflect a couples' true understanding of their property rights. The property rules for both resulting and constructive trusts have strict requirements which do not come close to reflecting the reality of family life today and the way couples treat the sharing of their assets and the family home.

Source: Family Law December 2009

Civil Partnership

5.5 The Civil Partnership Act 2004 came into force on 5 December 2005. It enables same-sex couples to obtain legal recognition of their relationship. Couples who form a civil partnership have a new legal status, that of 'civil partner' and have equal treatment in a wide range of legal matters with married couples, including:

- tax, including inheritance tax;
- employment benefits;
- most state and occupational pension benefits;
- income-related benefits, tax credits and child support;
- duty to provide reasonable maintenance for civil partners and any children of the family;
- ability to apply for parental responsibility for the civil partner's child;
- inheritance of a tenancy agreement;
- recognition under intestacy rules;
- access to fatal accidents compensation;
- protection from domestic violence;
- recognition from immigration and nationality purposes.

There were introduced at the same time changes affecting same-sex couples who claim income-related benefits, regardless of whether the couple decides to form a civil partnership.

More information on:
www.direct.gov.uk

For dissolution of civil partnerships see **3.20**.

The Effect of Relationship Breakdown on Couples

5.6 Marital and couple problems may be communicated to doctors through illness, to lawyers through litigation, to probation officers through delinquency, to social workers and health visitors through problems with children, to teachers through learning difficulties, to the clergy through spiritual unease, to work managers through under-performance as well as directly to couple counsellors and therapists. Knowledge about the causes of marital, couple and family stress, awareness of emotional transactions in relationships and understanding of interactive processes are relevant to all these professions at practitioner and management levels.

Couple relationships are at the centre of personal and social life for most adults and at the centre of family life when adults become parents. The extent of unhappiness in marriage and couple relationships is unquantifiable: the divorce statistics represent only the tip of the iceberg. The breakdown of marriage is ranked second only to bereavement among the most stressful experiences of life. In many ways, it is worse, as the person who is 'lost' is still present, as a constant reminder of the anguished feelings associated with parting and the couple are linked forever if there are shared children. The actual separation is remembered by many as the worst experience of their lives, although in one study of court users many commented that the humiliation they experienced in court was an even worse feature of the experience. Just as a couple's relationship can enrich the contribution they make in other areas of life, so the impact of a broken marriage or couple relationship often extends beyond the couple to affect their children and other aspects of their lives, including health and work performance.

A good recovery from divorce can be characterised, as can bereavement, by a painful period of mourning, after which good memories of being happy and in love are able to rise to the surface again. Some 'second' families show the signs of full recovery and some single-parent households live contentedly, but some divorced parents never quite achieve this. Single-parent households are still represented too prominently in the poverty statistics and researchers describe how in many instances conflict and feelings as strong as rage or as persistent as guilt can carry on for many years. Research shows that a critical factor in children's long-term well-being after separation or divorce is the well-being of the parent with whom they live and the capacity of parents to protect their children from being involved in the conflict between them.

The Effect of Relationship Breakdown on Children

5.7   For children, their parents' separation has been described as a 'psychological emergency'. Some researchers show that the life-chances of some children are affected for many years. Instead of setting up a competition over who should have residence and who should have contact, the Children Act 1989 states that each parent continues to hold parental responsibility even after divorce or separation (if the father has parental responsibility). The 1989 Act removed the old fighting terminology and replaced it with a law which encourages parents to reach agreement, seeking court orders only if they cannot agree. The court will make an order only if it thinks it is in the child's best interests and that to make an order is preferable to making no order at all.

Gingerbread – for single parent families

5.8 Gingerbread is a charity which works nationally and locally, for and with single parent families, to improve their lives through providing support services, free advice and information. Membership of Gingerbread is free and open to all single parent families in England and Wales. Benefits offered include:

- Meeting other single parents families for mutual support through self help groups.

- Information, news and competitions through Gingerbread's exclusive members' monthly e-newsletters.

- Discounts and days out: regular information about discounts on services, goods and days out.

- Making your voice heard: the opportunity to get involved in campaigns and research to change government policy.

- Training: help getting back to work or setting up your own community group.

Gingerbread has advisers, support workers, policy makers and researchers working with them to assist single parents. The charity also provides information for advisers and support workers, and policy makers and researchers who work with single parents.

The Gingerbread Single Parent Helpline
Tel: 0808 802 0925
www.gingerbread.org.uk

In an effort to engage more constructively with those involved in family law (and move forward in areas where Gingerbread already has well-established relationships), in 2009 a new membership initiative was launched, 'Legal Friends of Gingerbread'. Apart from regular updates about the work of Gingerbread and priority access to newly published policy research, members of this initiative are offered free attendance to an annual seminar and can enjoy networking and professional development opportunities.

What Children Need

5.9   While all children are distressed by their parents'
separation or divorce, given appropriate explanation
and support, many, if not most, can get past the crisis.
They all need:

- to continue loving relationships with each parent;
- to make their own sense of why their parents
  divorced. They need to rethink this as their
  cognitive abilities grow and develop;
- help to acknowledge the ending of the marriage or
  partnership;
- to regain a sense of direction and freedom to
  pursue their own social agenda of friends, school
  activities and day-to-day individual lives;
- to deal with the loss of their family as they knew it
  and to give up the longing for it to be restored;
- to deal with feelings of rejection;
- to accept the permanence of divorce;
- to come to feel comfortable and confident in
  relationships;
- to develop unique relationships and separate lives
  with each parent.

Children's Understanding

5.10   Children's understanding of parental conflict
depends on many factors including such characteristics
as their temperament and pre-divorce adjustment.
Pre-school children are the most vulnerable:

- they have little understanding of the nature of
  family relationships;
- they tend to regress to earlier levels of behaviour,
  ie develop sleep and toilet problems;
- they become frightened and confused;
- they blame themselves or fear they will be sent
  away;
- they return to solitary play;
- they become more dependent and anxiously
  demanding.

School age children:

- express feelings of sadness and fear abandonment;
- find it difficult to express anger;
- continue to hope for their parents' reconciliation;

- blame others;
- become unable to concentrate and focus on school work;
- feel lonely and rejected;
- become unable to cope with divided loyalties between their parents.

Adolescents are the second most vulnerable group:

- they are often surprised, upset, angry or have mixed feelings which frequently change;
- they may deliberately withdraw from the adults;
- they may feel pressured to become more independent;
- they become more dependent on the functioning of the residential parent;
- they will benefit if parents do not seek them as a source for meeting their own needs.

Young adults:

- have strong views about the divorce of their parents. They expect them to remain the same so that they are able to begin their adult lives and come and go to suit themselves;
- become anxious that their journey into adulthood will be interrupted by the need to look after one or other parent.

Differences between sexes:

- boys are more likely to be aggressive and act out their difficulties externally;
- girls are more likely to internalise their difficulties and blame themselves.

Telling the Children

5.11 It is continuing parental conflict which is the most damaging to children. The best people to tell children about parental divorce and separation are the parents, together if possible. If this is too difficult or painful then they should agree what the children should be told so that the other parent can talk with them later. If children are told different 'stories' or if one or other parent is 'blamed' for the break-up then, subsequently, children may find it difficult to trust one or both parents. If one parent in pain or anger has said things that the parent regrets and which may have distressed the children, the other parent and the children should be told.

Friends and relations may take sides, so they might not be the best people to support the children.
Grandparents are especially important as a source of family continuity, but they need to be able to manage their own feelings and not take sides.

The ability of children to cope is enhanced by being told the truth about what is happening in ways which they can understand. They do not have to be told everything at once. It must always be the parents who decide with whom the children will live. Children should never be asked to choose. They can be consulted as to their ideas about how they share their time with each parent or how often they would like to see the other parent, but parents should make the actual decisions.

If court proceedings become inevitable because parents cannot agree, it should be explained to the children so that they know who makes the decisions relating to them. Children need the implicit and explicit permission of both parents to ask questions as they arise for them. If they cannot do so, according to their age and stage of development, they may worry secretly. They need to be told that both parents love them and that the separation is not their fault.

RESIDENCE AND CONTACT

5.12 On divorce and separation, parents should be encouraged to plan their children's lives co-operatively so that the children can see as much of both parents as possible with as little conflict as the parents can manage. Conflict can be a damaging condition for children. Parents should respond to their children's needs for clear explanations of what is happening, for reassurance about their continued security and for an assurance of contact with whichever parent leaves home. The most important contribution a parent can make to a child's mental health, in the event of divorce, is 'loving permission' for them to see the other parent. If parents cannot come to their own arrangements either on their own or with the help of mediation, then recourse must be had to the residence and contact orders in s 8 of the Children Act 1989.

The Ministry of Justice announced in November 2007 a number of developments in the *Relationship Breakdown Programme*, including a range of measures to help more separating parents reach agreement themselves about the future parenting arrangements for their children. A free self help guide *Parenting Plans – Putting your children first: A guide for separating parents* was published to help separating parents work out for themselves the best contact and residence arrangements for their children. The guide is available on www.cafcass.org.uk

Sections 6 and 7 of the Children and Adoption Act 2006 came into force on 1 October 2007. Section 6 (in section 16 of the Children Act 1989) extends the maximum period of a family assistance order from 6 to 12 months, and removes the requirement for there to be exceptional circumstances. Section 7 (in section 16A of the Children Act 1989) places a statutory duty on the Children and Family Court Advisory and Support Service (Cafcass) to complete risk assessments in Children Act private law cases where there is cause to suspect that a child is at risk of harm. However, Cafcass' resources were, at the beginning of 2010, very much overstretched (see **6.15**).

Stepfamilies

5.13 Family relationships are dynamic and subject to change over time. Divorce and separation are simply extreme examples of such change. The formation of stepfamilies poses problems of residence and contact for which there are rarely once-and-for-all solutions. A family in which there has been a divorce not only has to negotiate the usual traumas of parental responsibility but must do so within entirely new parameters. The result is a sustained and enervating negotiation process around issues of contact, possessions, discipline and relationships, at best conducted face-to-face and at worst conducted through the child. Assistance and support in dealing with such issues is in short supply. Lawyers might achieve certain successes on behalf of clients, but these successes are often of little value. In general, the complexities of emotional and family life after divorce and separation render the law a blunt instrument: a last resort which is all too often the very first resort for parents.

See further: www.parentlineplus. org.uk

In the majority of cases, whether the parents have been married or not, the courts take the view that a child should not be brought up to believe that a step-parent is a natural parent – a child needs to know the truth.

However, expert professionals should be called upon, if necessary, to help a child learn of the child's true parentage.

Residence

5.14 Most parents come to their own arrangements about where their children should live. It is important for children to have a secure base and sense of belonging, but there is a need for flexibility depending on the circumstances of each child and each family. For the most part, parents know what is best for their children and court orders are not necessary. Professionals should be aware of the effect of the Child Support Agency/Child Maintenance and Enforcement Commission (C-MEC) on parents' decisions about residence. A non-resident parent's maintenance assessment will be reduced pro rata with the number of overnight stays the children have with that parent.

Residence Orders

5.15 A residence order determines where and with whom a child should live. The law makes no presumption about which parent a child of any age should live with, the only legal principle being that the welfare of the child is paramount. As a general rule, courts do not alter the status quo (ie the existing residential situation) unless there is a very good reason to do so. Nor is there any legal presumption that young children should reside with their mother, although, in practice, if the father is in full-time work it is far more likely that young children will stay with their mother, whether or not she works.

Shared parenting is what most people do for themselves. The courts have in the past been unwilling to make shared (ie joint) residence orders, as it was thought that it required a high degree of parental co-operation to work and if there were that level of co-operation there would be no need to come to court at all. Recently, however, courts are becoming more amenable because shared residence orders give each parent equal status – particularly in the eyes of their children. Parental co-operation is not now a pre-condition for a shared residence order. Shared residence orders might instead be appropriate where they reflect the reality of the arrangements for the child's care, although this does not mean that shared residence orders imposed by the courts or conceded under pressure from the other party have any power to produce better outcomes for children.

A residence order can be made in favour of any person and need not be limited to parents or relatives of the child or to the parties to proceedings before the court. Once a residence order is made, no one can take the child out of the UK without the agreement of the parents or the leave of the court. The exception is where the child is being taken abroad for less than one month, say for a holiday, by the parent with the residence order.

It is thought undesirable to split siblings. The myth that children brought up in same sex homes will show signs of dysfunction has been well and truly laid to rest.

See:
www.BeGrand.net

A new, publicly-funded resource was launched in January 2010 on www.BeGrand.net offering online advice and services on a range of topics to grandparents, including offering legal advice to grandparents who are caring for children after parental separation, and about keeping children safe.

Contact

5.16 A consensus has emerged about the importance of maintaining the link between the non-resident parent (usually the father) and children after divorce or separation. This pro-contact ideology now permeates the legal and welfare systems, but is beginning to be questioned, especially where the mother has been subjected to abuse. It is seen as the right of the child to have contact and the assumption is that it will be of benefit to the child, not only immediately but in the long term. As children grow up they will make their own decisions about contact and will also come to their own conclusions about how their parents dealt with the matter in the past. Dr Danya Glaser and Dr Claire Sturge have outlined what contact is for, namely:

- warmth, approval, feeling unique and special to a parent;
- extending experiences and developing (or maintaining) meaningful relationships;
- information and knowledge;
- reparation of distorted relationships or perceptions.

They make clear, however, that when contact taking place results in heightened parental tensions, that might well serve to undermine the child's stability and sense of emotional well-being, resulting in tugs of loyalty and a sense of responsibility for the conflict; it might affect the child's relationship with both parents. They talk of the child attempting to reduce the conflict by polarising relationships, often by way of enmeshment with the resident parent and rejection of the non-resident parent. Whilst continuing parental conflict is seen by the experts as the major contextual risk factor, Sturge and Glaser note some direct risks associated with contact:

- abuse – physical, sexual or emotional: emotional abuse could include denigration of the child or resident parent and using contact as a means of continuing or escalating the war with the resident parent;

- continuation of an unhealthy parent–child relationship, for example controlling, domineering or manipulative characteristics;

- undermining the child's stability – by deliberately setting different standards of morality or behaviour (beyond the reasonable differences between two households). Separated parents need broadly to agree child rearing and related practices with one another;

- lack of endorsement of the child as a valued and individual person by showing little interest, unstimulating activities or unreliable contact attendance.

Risks are identified around the dangers of placing a child in an unresolved adult scenario, where conflict is unremitting, where each parent criticises the other and where parents show no sign of working towards change or accepting their share of responsibility for the past and/or present troubles. Such scenarios are likely to stress, depress and alienate the child. Often a child's refusal to attend contact is the only means he has to demonstrate a sense of distress and hopelessness about the entrenched parental conflict. While courts often see indirect contact as the bare acceptable minimum in very high conflict cases, Sturge and Glaser warn of the risks to a child when the non-resident parent is able to convey undermining and distorting messages through whatever indirect contact medium is agreed. There is greatest scope for harm in telephone contact and least in vetted contact such as letters.

Source:
Sturge and Glaser
'Contact and Domestic
Violence – the Experts'
Report' [2000] Fam
Law 615

Contact Orders

5.17 The purpose of a child having contact with a parent is to:

- sustain an already established relationship;
- establish a relationship which has not yet developed;
- provide a child with knowledge and understanding of the child's roots and to affirm the child's identity.

The Children Act 1989 enables the court to make an order requiring the person with care to allow contact. It is judicially accepted that children should ideally know the identity of both parents. Courts encourage contact wherever possible unless there are convincing reasons why contact should be denied and it is not necessary for a parent to show positive advantage to the child in order for a contact order to be granted. However, the court has to decide whether the fundamental emotional need of every child to have an enduring relationship with both parents is outweighed by the harm the child would be at risk of suffering by virtue of a contact order.

The introduction or re-introduction of contact can cause short-term upset to the child but the long-term benefits are considered generally to outweigh this. If direct contact is impossible then contact can be maintained indirectly through letters, photographs and school reports. Contact can also be supervised either by friends or relatives or at a contact centre. Contact centres provide supported contact where the parents have been unable to agree on venue or pick-up arrangements.

A child contact centre is a safe, friendly and neutral place where children of separated families can spend time with one or both parents and sometimes other family members. They are child-centred environments that provide toys, games and facilities that reflect the diverse needs of children affected by family breakdown. Contact centres do not, however, usually supply supervised contact and cannot usually provide assessments of the quality of contact, nor can they guarantee the safety of any user if there is a history of domestic violence in the family.

Child contact centres are run by fully trained volunteers or staff. They are impartial, so they do not take sides. They work to a strict confidentiality policy and have all

National
Association of Child
Contact Centres
Tel: 0845 4500 280
www.naccc.org.uk

make arrangements. Even before proceedings start, they (and their children) are highly distressed. Court users have more severe parenting problems than separated parents generally. Domestic abuse and violence is a major problem for many mothers (more usually than fathers). Given this distress and distrust, it is unsurprising that contact disputes are not easily resolved in court. About one in six court applications involve breach of orders and some parents become locked in contact litigation for years.

The Children and Adoption Act 2006 came into force at the end of 2008 and brought with it enforcement measures for parents who default on contact arrangements for their children. Now the courts are able to encourage and support contact by making 'contact activity directions and conditions', requiring an individual who is a party to court proceedings to take part in an activity that promotes contact with the child concerned. The courts may also request a Cafcass officer to monitor the compliance of person in relation to contact. Warning notices are also now attached to contact orders, warning a party of the consequences of failing to comply with a contact order. On non-compliance, an enforcement order may be made, imposing unpaid work on the defaulting person, and again a Cafcass officer is to be asked to monitor or arrange for the monitoring of the compliance with the unpaid work order and to report back to the court. Another new aspect of the new provisions is that a person in breach of a contact order may now be asked to pay financial compensation for financial loss caused by his/her breach, and such compensation is recoverable as a civil debt.

The Children and Adoption Act 2006 can be viewed at www.opsi.co.uk

There are other steps that the court can take to make contact arrangements work. It can appoint a guardian to represent the child, or seek assistance from or an assessment by a suitably qualified expert. It can also involve the local authority by making a direction under s 37 of the Children Act 1989 that the child's circumstances are to be investigated by the local authority which should consider whether or not it ought to apply for a care order or a supervision order, or provide services or assistance for the child or his/her family, or take any other appropriate action. The court may even transfer residence of the child to the other parent.

Contact with Children in Care

5.19 Where a child is in care, the local authority must, unless it is inconsistent with the child's welfare, endeavour to promote reasonable contact with the child's parents and other relatives. This applies whether the child is accommodated by voluntary arrangements or as a result of a court order. Financial support for contact can be provided. Other than on a very short-term basis, contact can only be stopped if a court order has been obtained to end it. For the majority of children, their welfare and interests are best served by efforts to sustain or create links with their natural families. For instance, not all foster arrangements will be long-term arrangements and, if there is a prospect of rehabilitation with the child's parents, contact should be maintained. There may be no question of a child or young person returning to his family yet contact, however occasional, might continue to be valuable.

Particular difficulties can arise when, in the child's interests, contact should ideally occur in the foster home because that is where the child feels relaxed and secure. However, not every foster parent can cope with such an arrangement and not every natural family can be relied upon to respect it. Such matters should be considered prior to placement and foster parents prepared and encouraged to facilitate contact within their home, but there will always be cases where the child's needs for placement will outweigh the need for contact to be in the foster home and some other venue must suffice. A court should not make an order for contact in a foster home without satisfying itself that the foster parents have given an informed consent to the specific order sought.

The British Agencies for Adoption and Fostering (BAAF) has produced guidance which identifies a number of the functions of contact generally, namely:

- enabling a child to develop a realistic understanding of the circumstances leading to separation;
- enabling a child to grieve the loss;
- enabling a child to move on and develop an attachment to new carers with the blessing of his parents;
- reassuring the child that the birth parents or other relatives continue to care about the child, which may enhance the child's self-esteem;

- promoting stability in a new or existing placement by providing continuity and enabling connections to be made;
- reassuring the child about the well-being of birth relatives;
- providing an understanding of personal and family history, cultural background and socio-geneological connectedness (the guidance emphasises that this factor may be critical, say, in the case where the child has one black and one white parent);
- maintaining a flow of communication which could facilitate future contact.

The BAAF guidance also identifies the following factors which should be taken into account when considering contact:

- the child's wishes and feelings, emotional and developmental functioning, psychological resilience and ability to form and extend attachments;
- a general assessment of the birth relatives' functioning, including their relationship with the child;
- the views, attitudes and experience of the current carers;
- a clear sense of purpose – specifying whose needs are being met by contact;
- any conflict inherent in the proposed plan and how this is to be addressed;
- what support supervision or mediation is required to facilitate any planned contact;
- what review arrangements are in place.

The emphasis placed on the need to recognise and address issues of contact, as part of the contact plan, is a crucial factor if children's needs are to be satisfactorily met. BAAF produces a good practice guide for local authorities, *Contact in Permanent Placement: Guidance for Local Authorities in England, Wales and Scotland* as well as a number of advice notes for birth families on contact for children who are either fostered or adopted, which are all available for a small charge via its website.

BAAF can be contacted at:
Tel: 020 7421 2600
www.baaf.org.uk

ALTERNATIVE DISPUTE RESOLUTION

Private Law

5.20　These days only the most determined private clients will get their day in court, and that might well be because one or both sides is legally aided. The divorce procedure is a paper exercise and most issues concerning finance, property and children are settled by the parties' agreement, by negotiation between lawyers or by mediation. The trend is inevitably towards less court intervention. Court proceedings are time-consuming and expensive and a blunt instrument with which to deal with family change. On the other hand, the fear is that legal rights and justice itself may be denied to many people on the grounds of saving money, particularly in relation to the Legal Services Commission.

The courts have been encouraging parties to settle cases for many years. Three-quarters of financial cases are dealt with by consent, that is, an agreement is reached and the court makes the appropriate (consent) order. This has been called the 'settlement culture' and under the consent order procedure, court approval of the parties' agreement enables them to enjoy relative security and peace of mind, knowing that the agreement cannot be overturned at a later date.

Agreement

5.21　Some couples, whether divorcing or separating after a period of cohabitation, can manage the process without outside intervention. It is sensible, however, to take an agreement concerning finance and/or property to separate solicitors in order to ensure that each individual's interests are addressed and to have the agreement incorporated in a deed or court order.

Negotiation

5.22　Most family lawyers' work involves negotiation. If court proceedings are begun, negotiation can still take place, right up to the door of the court on the day of the hearing. In private cases, the court's emphasis is on obtaining agreement, driven mostly by district judges whose experience as former practitioners has taught them that a court-imposed decision will satisfy neither party.

Mediation

5.23   Mediation is appropriate for issues of finance
and property, as well as for issues relating to children. It
can begin at any stage – before, during and even after
proceedings when, for example, a contact order needs
amending because of a change in circumstances.
Mediators encourage clients to stay in touch with their
legal representatives throughout the mediation process
because mediators do not give legal advice but they can
give information, although it may be difficult for the
impartial observer to tell the difference. Clients are
advised to take any agreement about finance and/or
property to their own solicitors, again to make sure that
their individual interests are being protected. The
concern about mediation is that its emphasis on the
private ordering of disputes without supervision or
inquiry by the courts could be a disadvantage to the less
informed, and therefore less powerful, party. However,
it is the task of the mediator to ensure that this does
not occur. See further **2.88** and **3.39** onwards.

In-court Conciliation and Mediation

5.24   There is a strong Government impetus to make
in-court conciliation and mediation services available so
that they are routinely used for all families in dispute
before a formal court hearing, except in cases involving
allegations of serious harm. A new Private Law
Programme (PLP) is due to make a difference. For its
key features see **3.22**.

Collaborative Law

5.25   Through collaborative law, couples, their lawyers
and other professionals work together in round table
meetings to negotiate agreements to resolve financial
and other issues without the involvement of the courts.
See further **2.16**.

Financial Dispute Resolution

5.26   A financial dispute resolution (FDR)
appointment at court is a well-established part of
financial ancillary relief (ie sorting out financial matters
on divorce) proceedings. The procedure is intended to
reduce delay, facilitate settlements, limit costs incurred
by parties and provide the court with greater and more
effective control over the conduct of the proceedings.

The FDR appointment is for discussion and negotiation and is an important part of the settlement process. The aim of the FDR appointment is for a judge to help couples to reach an agreement on relevant matters of issue between them through discussion in a more informal setting than that of a final trial.

The House of Commons Inquiry

5.27 In 2005 a House of Commons Select Committee conducted an inquiry into family courts and concluded that there must be a clear and unequivocal commitment to remove as many child contact and residency cases as possible from the family court system with more disputes dealt with through mediation. Its report, which followed a 5-month inquiry into whether the family court system was being run effectively, concluded that the courts were not the best place to resolve complex family disputes and should only be used as a last resort. The report stated that in appropriate cases, where safety was not an issue, making most parents attend a compulsory preliminary session with a mediator to assess whether mediation is suitable might help steer people away from the court system.

National Audit Office Report on Low Take Up of Family Mediation

5.28 The National Audit Office (NAO) scrutinises public spending on behalf of Parliament and is totally independent of the Government. It concluded in a report in 2007 that family disputes which are resolved through mediation are cheaper, quicker and, according to academic research, less acrimonious than those that are settled through the courts. Despite these advantages, only some 20% of people who at that time had been funded by legal aid for family breakdown cases (excluding those involving domestic violence) had opted for mediation. Even less in privately funded cases, for example:

- In the period October 2004 to March 2006 some 29,000 people who were funded through legal aid attempted to resolve their family dispute through mediation.

- In the same period 120,000 family disputes involving finances and children were completed through court proceedings or bilateral negotiation between solicitors.

- There were a further 30,000 completed cases settled through the courts that involved domestic violence over 2 years.

The report stated that it was the duty of the solicitor or legal adviser to advise their legally-aided client of the option of mediation in family law cases, although it stated that there was a financial disincentive to do so as it would result in the loss of potential fees.

> 'In response to our survey of recipients of legal aid, 33 per cent said that they had not been made aware by their adviser that mediation was an option. Of those who were not told about mediation, and so did not try it, 42 per cent said they would have been willing to. This represents, potentially, some 14 per cent more cases overall; and even higher rates of take-up might be possible if the option of mediation were better understood by clients.'

The average cost of legal aid in non-mediated cases was estimated in 2007 to be £1,682, compared with £752 for mediated cases, representing an additional annual cost to the taxpayer of some £74 million. Not all cases are suitable for mediation, however, for example, where there has been a history of domestic abuse. Nevertheless, if 14% of the cases that proceeded to court had been resolved through mediation, there would have been resulting savings equivalent to some £10 million a year. The report also stated that mediated cases are quicker to resolve, taking on average 110 days, compared with 435 days for non-mediated cases.

The NAO maintained that in addition to financial savings there were potential benefits for those involved in family breakdown in terms of outcomes that are less acrimonious, quicker, and longer lasting than might otherwise have been achieved. In order to achieve this, the report recommended that the Legal Services Commission should publicise the benefits of this option to the general public so that they are aware of and have confidence in it as a means of resolution, and remove the disincentives to solicitors of recommending this option to their clients.

According to the Chief Executive of National Family Mediation, three things need to happen if mediation is to be properly integrated and used to best effect:

(1) The family procedure rules need to be amended/altered to make sure mediation is considered and used first.

(2) Mediation should be considered for all issues that are presented to the family courts – ancillary relief hearings as well as children's issues. Separating the finances from the children does not promote children's welfare, it undermines it: family money is inextricably linked to the quality of life children experience after family breakdown.

Jane Robey, Chief Executive, National Family Mediation, 'Family Mediation: the Future' Family Law August 2009

(3) The divide between publicly funded and private clients must be eliminated. This will be achieved if the procedures and rules are changed.

Children and Local Authorities

5.29   If the phrase 'resolution of disputes' is taken as meaning the avoidance of court adjudication, then it aptly describes the basic tenet of the Children Act 1989, which is that it is better for the court to make no order at all if that is in the child's best interests. The 1989 Act's principle of non-intervention means that parties should do their best to resolve differences by negotiation and co-operation. The level of co-operation and partnership between parents and local authorities, and the level of services which local authorities are under a duty to provide to children in need, are essential to the successful operation of the 1989 Act.

As regards services to children, authorities are facing high levels of demand for child protection services which limit their capacity to provide family support. The fear of not being able to meet budgetary demands for extended or new services has slowed down the investigation of the level of need. Social services (now called children's services) have to prioritise demands on their resources and the demands of child protection are continuing to outstrip provision for children in need.

The idea that disputes between parents and local authorities about child protection can be negotiated is growing. Meanwhile a children's guardian's investigation is often able to identify areas of agreement and the possibilities for agreement (or at least assent) which do not compromise the child's welfare. For example, a parent may accept that it would be better for a child to live away from home if the child can be placed with relatives rather than with strangers. Consequently, although a care order can only be granted by a court, many proceedings do not result in contested final hearings.

The pre-proceedings protocol (PPP) which was initially drawn up by High Court Family Division judges as an amendment to the public law protocol at the beginning of 2006, has been re-emphasised under The Public Law Outline (see **3.23**). Families should be helped to understand proceedings by means of the local authority:

- giving a simple language document drafted before issue of proceedings to explain local authority concerns to families, especially to older children. In the longer term more could be done to engage families in local authority concerns earlier, in order to avoid proceedings altogether where possible, and alternative care options should be considered pre-proceedings;

- giving parents a list of local panel solicitors and/or local family law firms;

- providing better information for parents and children. Children of sufficient age and understanding who are subject to proceedings should routinely be given detailed information by their social worker about what to expect in language they understand.

Under the Public Law Outline, care proceedings should only be brought after all safe, appropriate alternatives have been explored, eg by:

- following the revised statutory guidance as to best practice with case preparation;

- following The Public Law Outline as to what the court expects of every section 31 application which itself dovetails with the above guidance;

- utilising early interventions to engage parents and find kinship carers; and

- making greater use of Family Group Conferences (see below).

It is an ongoing concern, however, that in order for early intervention/treatment evaluation to succeed, there needs to be a radical increase in the number of available skilled front-line social workers to ensure the effective operation of a proactive problem-solving approach.

Family Group Conferencing

5.30 The family group conference is a growing area of social work practice, which can be a useful tool to avoid the issue of proceedings or can be recommended by the court to take place during the course of proceedings, where appropriate. The family group conference is a decision-making forum that focuses on the welfare of the child. At a family group conference, the wider family (this can include friends), meets and is given information by the relevant agencies on the needs of the child and the reasons why a decision is required. Members of the wider family are given time on their own to make plans and come to a decision that promotes and safeguards the child's welfare. In care proceedings, family group conferences may be helpful:

(a)   in identifying family and community supports, so that it is safe for a child to live with the child's parent(s);

(b)   in identifying a placement in the wider family, if the child cannot live with the child's parent(s);

(c)   where a kinship placement is not possible, allowing the wider family to support the plan for the child.

*Further information on the process is available at: www.frg.org.uk and see **3.46**. See also **2.141–2.144***

DOMESTIC VIOLENCE

5.31   Domestic violence can take many forms. In its narrower sense, it describes the use of threat or physical force against a victim in the form of an assault or battery. But in the context of the family there is also a wider meaning which extends to abuse beyond the more typical instances of physical assaults to include any form of physical, sexual or psychological harassment which seriously affects the well-being of the victim, even if there is no violence in the usual sense. Overhearing any form of domestic violence or serious harassment can also be a form of abuse for family members. Examples of harassment are pestering, shouting, denigration, nuisance phone calls and receiving anonymous letters. The victims of domestic violence, either actual or threatened, have to be made aware of the legal protection available. The multi-agency initiatives on domestic violence which have been set up locally have a responsibility to give out this information.

Domestic Violence and Contact

5.32   Domestic violence frequently arises in contact disputes. It provides an exception to many of the general propositions enunciated about residence and

(e)   a wish to make reparation to the child and work towards the child recognising the inappropriateness of the abuse and the attitude to and treatment of the mother and helping the child to develop appropriate values and attitudes;

(f)   an expression of regret and the showing of some understanding of the impact of their behaviour on their ex-partner in the past and currently;

(g)   indications that the parent seeking contact could reliably sustain contact in all senses.

Without the above, Doctors Sturge and Glaser could not see how the non-resident parent could fully support the child, play a part in undoing some of the harm caused to the child and his whole situation, help the child understand the reality of past events and experiences and fully support the child's current situation and need to move on and develop healthily.

Without (a)–(f) above, there was a significant risk to the child's general well-being and the child's emotional development and contact potentially raised the likelihood of the most serious of the sequelae of children's exposure, directly or indirectly, to domestic violence, namely the increased risk of aggression and abuse in the child generally, the increased risk of the child becoming the perpetrator of domestic violence or becoming involved in domestically abusive relationships and of increased risk of having disturbed inter-personal relationships themselves.

As for respecting the child's wishes, whilst the children's wishes should always be listened to and considered, within the whole context of such wishes the older the child, the more seriously their wishes should be viewed, and the more insulting and discrediting it could be to the child to have them ignored. As a rough rule, they needed to be taken account of at any age; above 10 they carried considerable weight, with 6–10 as an intermediate stage and under 6 they were often indistinguishable in many ways from the wishes of the main carer (assuming normal development). In domestic violence where the child has memories of that abuse, their wishes would not warrant much more weight than in situations where no real reason for the child's resistance appeared to exist.

In addition to the above considerations, which were specific but by no means exclusive to domestic violence matters, all the other evaluations as to how the contact would benefit the child needed to be made. In particular, the question of its purpose needed answering as there was a great difference between contact, direct or indirect, designed to provide information and, in the case of direct contact, direct knowledge of the parent, and contact designed to re-establish, continue or develop a meaningful father–child relationship.

The report should be read in full.

Source:
Sturge and Glaser
'Contact and Domestic
Violence – The
Experts' Report'
[2000] Fam Law 615

Domestic Violence and Safeguarding Children from Harm

5.33 Children may suffer both directly and indirectly if they live in households where there is domestic violence. Domestic violence is likely to have a damaging effect on the health and development of children, and it will often be appropriate for such children to be regarded as children in need. Children living in families where they are exposed to domestic violence have been shown to be at risk for behavioural, emotional, physical, cognitive functioning, attitudinal and long-term developmental problems. Everyone working with women and children should be alert to the frequent inter-relationship between domestic violence and the abuse and neglect of children. There may be serious effects of children witnessing domestic violence, which often result in behavioural issues, absenteeism, ill health, bullying, anti-social behaviour, drug and alcohol misuse, self-harm and psychosocial impacts. Where there is evidence of domestic violence, the implications for any children in the household should be considered, including the possibility that the children may themselves be subject to abuse or may be harmed by witnessing or overhearing the abuse. Conversely, where it is believed that a child is being abused, those involved with the child and family should be alert to the possibility of domestic violence within the family.

The police are often the first point of contact with families in which domestic violence takes place. When responding to incidents of violence, the police should find out whether there are any children living in the household. They should see any children present in the house to assess their immediate safety. There should be arrangements in place between police and children's services, to enable the police to find out whether any such children are the subject of a child protection plan. The police are already required to determine whether any court orders or injunctions are in force in respect of members of the household. It is good practice for the police to notify children's services promptly when they have responded to an incident of domestic violence and it is known that a child is a member of the household.

Children who are experiencing domestic violence may benefit from a range of support and services, and some may need safeguarding from harm. Often, supporting a non-violent parent is likely to be the most effective way of promoting the child's welfare. The police and other agencies have defined powers in criminal and civil law which can be used to help those who are subject to domestic violence. Health visitors and midwives can play a key role in providing support and need access to information shared by the police and children's services. Safe information-sharing protocols are necessary.

There is an extensive range of services for women and children delivered through refuge projects operated by Women's Aid and probation service provision of Women's Safety Workers, for partners of male perpetrators of domestic violence, where they are on a domestic violence treatment programme (in custody or community). These have a vital role in contributing to an inter-agency approach to children where domestic violence is an issue.

Domestic Violence Forums have been set up in many areas, to raise awareness of domestic violence, to promote co-ordination between agencies in preventing and responding to violence, and to encourage the development of services for those who are subjected to violence or suffer its effects. Each Domestic Violence Forum and Local Safeguarding Children Board (LSCB) should have clearly defined links, which should include cross-membership and identifying and working together on areas of common interest. Other work might include developing joint protocols, safe information sharing arrangements and training.

Source:
Working Together
to Safeguard Children
(DOH, 2006)
www.dcsf.gov.uk/
everychildmatters/

Coordinated Action Against Domestic Abuse (CAADA) has recently developed a multi-agency risk identification checklist in collaboration with the Association of Chief Police Officers. This is based on national and international research into domestic murders and 'near misses'. It has been piloted by specialist domestic violence advisors, police, health visitors, midwives, hospital accident and emergency staff, children's centres and probation. It does not seek to replace the existing procedures in relation to the safeguarding of children or the assessment of offenders. However, familiarity with the 24 risk factors on the checklist is perhaps the easiest and simplest way to identify those victims at high risk of harm for all professionals, including those working within the family courts. The checklist and the associated guidance can be downloaded from www.caada.org.uk.

The introduction of Multi Agency Risk Assessment Conferences, or MARACs has also been a step forward. A MARAC is a regular monthly or fortnightly meeting attended by 10–15 different agencies from both the statutory and voluntary sectors. It is designed to facilitate information sharing between these agencies about the highest risk victims in an area and then to create and implement a safety plan for each one. Links should be made with the safeguarding boards in relation to children and vulnerable adults, and to Multi Agency Public Protection Arrangements (MAPPAs) in relation to offenders. The agencies represented are those who would normally come into contact with domestic violence victims namely the police, the primary care trust, the acute trust, children's services, housing, substance misuse services, the local refuge and crucially the independent domestic violence advisors (IDVAs) whose role it is to offer specialist support to these high risk victims. MARAC is a volume process, quite unlike child protection case conferences for example, with between 15–20 cases being reviewed briefly at a typical meeting. The boundaries of the MARAC are usually consistent with a local police division.

CAADA recommends the following measures:

(1) that training for magistrates and the judiciary be updated to include risk identification in relation to domestic abuse;

(2) that MARAC should be put on a statutory footing to ensure that it is adequately resourced and that clear standards are upheld;

(3) that attention is given at a national level to meeting the needs of those children identified at MARAC and who currently get no additional support;

(4) that in 3–5 years time a full MARAC service exists nationally involving about 350 MARACs and approximately 1500 IDVAs. The total cost of this is estimated at £125m for all agencies involved. The cost savings assuming that repeat victimisation is brought down in line with the declines already witnessed would be over £600m.

CAADA is a registered charity which has been responsible for training IDVAs and implementing MARACs since its establishment in 2005.

The National Centre for Domestic Violence (NCDV) is a charitable organisation that assists victims of domestic violence in obtaining emergency injunctions. Established in 2001 as the London Centre for Domestic Violence, it is expanding and seeking more solicitors firms willing to accept its referrals. The NCDV does not employ qualified lawyers and therefore cannot provide professional legal advice or representation. It will speak to the victim initially to establish the background to the case and the victim's financial situation. Where appropriate, it will then contact local firms to find a solicitor willing and able to take on the case as a matter of urgency. Where the victim does not wish to be publicly funded, the NCDV may assist by preparing the application and providing someone to act as a McKenzie friend at the hearing. The NCDV also provides a process serving service, which can assist, where a power of arrest is attached to the order, assisting in drafting and serving on the police, form FL415.

Court Initiatives

5.34 The government is working closely with the judiciary to address issues of information-sharing between courts. The country's first integrated domestic violence court where civil and criminal matters in one case are dealt with in one place by one judge has also been established.

Section 120 of the Adoption and Children Act 2002, which clarifies the definition of harm in the Children Act 1989, came into force in 2005. The definition includes any impairment of the child's health or development as a result of witnessing the ill treatment of another person, such as domestic violence. It is broader than physical violence and includes sexual abuse and forms of treatment which are not physical. It applies to all proceedings where the court applies the 'welfare checklist' including section 4 (parental responsibility) and section 8 (residence and contact) orders.

In 2006 a report by Lord Justice Wall investigated judicial involvement in five cases in which a court order had been obtained for the father to have contact with his children who were then killed by the father. Lord Justice Wall stated that where violence was

Source:
Fam Law – May 2009

NCDV can be contacted on
Tel: 0844 8044 999
www.ncdv.org.uk.

See further:
'Child Homicide Judicial Investigation' [2006] Fam Law 344
www.familylaw.co.uk

directed at the mother but not at the child,
reinforcement needed to be given to the lead provided
by Drs Sturge and Glaser (see above) that it was a
non-sequitur to consider that a father who had a
history of violence to the mother of his children was, at
one and the same time, a good father. The opportunity
should be taken, either in a judgment or a lecture to
make that point, with the concomitant that it needed to
be considered in all cases where there was domestic
violence. That would ensure a more rigorous approach
to safety in such cases.

A revised Practice Direction entitled 'Practice Direction:
Residence and Contact orders: Domestic Violence and
Harm' was issued in January 2009. This Practice
Direction applies to any family proceedings in the High
Court, a county court or a magistrates' court in which
an application is made for a residence order or a
contact order in respect of a child under the Children
Act 1989 ('the 1989 Act') or the Adoption and Children
Act 2002 ('the 2002 Act') or in which any question
arises about residence or about contact between a child
and a parent or other family member. The practice set
out in this Direction is to be followed in any case in
which it is alleged, or there is otherwise reason to
suppose, that the subject child or a party has
experienced domestic violence perpetrated by another
party or that there is a risk of such violence. In these
circumstances, the court must, at all stages of the
proceedings, consider whether domestic violence is
raised as an issue, either by the parties or otherwise,
and if so must:

- identify at the earliest opportunity the factual and
  welfare issues involved;

- consider the nature of any allegation or admission
  of domestic violence and the extent to which any
  domestic violence which is admitted, or which may
  be proved, would be relevant in deciding whether
  to make an order about residence or contact and,
  if so, in what terms;

- give directions to enable the relevant factual and
  welfare issues to be determined expeditiously and
  fairly.

Immediately on receipt of an application for a residence
order or a contact order, or of the acknowledgement of
the application, the court shall send a copy of it,
together with any accompanying documents, to Cafcass
or Cafcass Cymru, as appropriate, to enable Cafcass or
Cafcass Cymru to undertake initial screening in

accordance with their safeguarding policies. The court should determine as soon as possible whether it is necessary to conduct a fact-finding hearing in relation to any disputed allegation of domestic violence before it can proceed to consider any final order(s) for residence or contact. Where the court determines that a finding of fact hearing is not necessary, the order shall record the reasons for that decision. Where the court considers that a fact-finding hearing is necessary, it must give directions to ensure that the matters in issue are determined expeditiously. In its judgment or reasons the court should always make clear how its findings on the issue of domestic violence have influenced its decision on the issue of residence or contact. In particular, where the court has found domestic violence proved but nonetheless makes an order, the court should always explain, whether by way of reference to the welfare checklist or otherwise, why it takes the view that the order which it has made is in the best interests of the child.

The Government announced in March 2009 that victims of domestic violence are to receive extra help and support from 18 new Specialist Domestic Violence Courts. The new courts will be located in Eastern England, East Midlands, London, North East, North West, South West, West Midlands and Yorkshire and Humberside. The government has a target to have a total of 128 courts by 2011. Victims who have given evidence against violent husbands will be allowed to start divorce and child-custody proceedings immediately after giving evidence to a judge. The Specialist Domestic Violence Court programme is to promote a combined approach to tackling domestic violence by the police, the Crown prosecutors, magistrates, courts and probation together with specialist support services for victims, which situates the court and the Criminal Justice System as part of a community-wide response to domestic violence. Key features of the courts include:

- trained and dedicated criminal justice staff with enhanced expertise in dealing with domestic violence, including magistrates specially trained in dealing with domestic violence cases;
- cases clustered on a particular day to enable all agencies to focus their specialist resources;
- tailored support and advice from Independent Domestic Violence Advisers.

As well as specialist domestic violence courts, the government has introduced other measures such as Independent Domestic Violence Advisers, the Forced Marriage Act 2008 (see **5.67**) and trained criminal justice personnel.

Interdisciplinary Approaches to Domestic Violence

Local Children Safeguarding Boards

For more information on Local Safeguarding Children Boards see **3.83**

5.35 One of the roles of Local Children Safeguarding Boards (LCSB) is to promote responsive work to protect children who are abused and neglected within families in the context of domestic violence. LCSBs should link to Domestic Violence Forums either by inviting them to join the LCSB or through some other mechanism. LCSBs should also ensure effective inter-agency training.

Crown Prosecution Service

5.36 The Crown Prosecution Service (CPS) was issued with good practice guidance on domestic violence cases in 2005. The guidance sets out ten points for action, including recommendations for improving partnership with statutory and voluntary agencies and enhancing community engagement to ensure that local agencies and community organisations are better consulted and involved. It provides practical measures to improve the effectiveness of prosecutions, to develop the expertise and training of all prosecutors in domestic violence issues and to support victims and their children as much as possible throughout the case. The document also sets out recommended approaches for working with criminal justice partners to set up and develop specialist domestic violence courts. Two different approaches were piloted in two domestic violence courts in Caerphilly and Croydon. The pilots increased the number of perpetrators brought to justice through increased guilty pleas and convictions, increased the number of domestic violence incidents that resulted in a case going to court and reduced the number of cases lost before trial due to withdrawals and discontinuances. Specialist domestic violence courts were being extended to 25 court centres across England and Wales. A feature of the guidance is interdisciplinary co-operation, namely the CPS:

- working with the police and with equal involvement of broader multi-agency partnerships;

- recognising the need for, and allocating time to establishing, and participating in, operational multi-agency domestic violence partnerships with agreements with statutory and voluntary agencies and developing methods of identifying and tracking cases with ongoing communication;
- developing domestic violence local strategies and action plans with the Local Criminal Justice Boards;
- actively participating in strategic domestic violence fora, locally and regionally;
- actively developing local protocols for inter-agency working including outlining the roles and responsibilities of each agency;
- developing information sharing agreements;
- ensuring, through local partnerships, links to independent domestic violence advisors and any other specialist domestic violence services working with diverse and/or minority communities;
- encouraging appropriate sharing of domestic violence data across partnerships.

See also **2.154**.

The full guidance is available on www.cps.gov.uk

Physical, Emotional and Behavioural Signs of Domestic Violence

5.37

Physical:

- Unexplained burns or bruises, areas of erythema consistent with slaps, multiple injuries in various stages of healing, repeated or chronic injuries.
- Injuries in areas of the body inconsistent with falls, walking into doors or other explanations given.
- Injuries to the breast, chest and abdomen – battered women are 13 times more likely to be injured here and they are common injuries during pregnancies.
- Injuries to face, head or neck.
- Evidence of sexual abuse or frequent gynaecological problems.
- Frequent visits with vague complaints or symptoms.
- Frequent use of pain medications.

- Premature removal of sutures following delivery.

Emotional:

- Feelings of isolation.
- Suicide attempts.
- Panic attacks, anxiety, depression.
- Alcohol or drug abuse.
- Post-traumatic stress reaction/disorder.
- Frequent use of minor tranquillisers.

Behavioural:

- Patient may be frightened, evasive, ashamed or embarrassed.
- Partner accompanies patient, insists on staying close and answers all questions directed at patient.
- Reluctance of patient to speak or disagree.
- Denial or minimisation of violence by partner or patient.

Domestic Violence, Equality and Diversity

5.38 Domestic violence is experienced by women of all races, ages, abilities and sexualities. The following points should be considered.

- The cultural setting in which domestic violence occurs affects the way women can react to it.
- Some women do not speak English as a first language. This is a barrier when seeking and receiving services. Interpreters should be found.
- Some women may have been excluded from dealing with practical matters like housing or social security which may affect their confidence in dealing with these issues.
- Black and minority ethnic women might feel that they have too much to lose by leaving their partners. For instance, religious or cultural beliefs may forbid divorce. However, their community or religion probably does not actually support violence or abuse. Religious and community leaders in all cultures tend to be men and only some speak out against violence. Black and minority ethnic women might be able to find people in their community who will support them.
- Black and other women from minority ethnic communities may be wary of involving the police or other services.

- It is not true to assume that all women from black or minority ethnic communities are recent migrants.

- Migrant women may fear losing their right to stay in this country if they separate from their partners, and they may have been threatened with this. They may also fear that their partner's immigration status might be threatened. They may fear that their partner, having links with another country, may be able to abduct their children to take them abroad.

Some older women may feel that they have coped with abuse for so long that it is not worth making difficult changes; others may be embarrassed about having put up with the abuse for so long and may try to underplay it. The abuser of an older woman may well be an older man. Agencies which offer protection and help may be less willing to believe that an older man could be violent and be reluctant to take action. Older women may experience abuse from a partner who is also the carer. Like women with disabilities, they may fear losing their home, their support, their independence, especially if institutional care is the only option. A woman with disabilities may be dependent upon the abusing or violent man for 'care'. She may also be dependent on the home which may have been specially adapted.

Domestic Violence Helplines

5.39 *National*

The national Freephone 24 hour **National Domestic Violence Helpline**, run in partnership between Women's Aid and Refuge

0808 2000 247

Men's Advice Line

0808 801 0327

Children

The Hideout is a domestic violence website produced by Women's Aid specifically to give advice and information to children.

www.thehideout.org.uk

ChildLine offers a free 24-hour helpline for children and young people who need to talk about any problem they may have.

0800 1111

Compiled by
Thames Valley
Family Justice
Council

www.childline.org.uk/

NSPCC is the leading UK charity specialising in child protection and the prevention of cruelty to children.

0808 800 5000

www.nspcc.org.uk/

Action for Children (formerly National Children's Homes (NCH)) helps over 30,000 of the most vulnerable children and their families in need, through projects nationwide.

www.actionforchildren.org.uk

Barnardo's helps children, young people and their families over the long term to overcome disadvantages and problems such as abuse, homelessness and poverty.

www.barnardos.org.uk/

The **Connexions** service is set up by the government to offer a range of guidance and support for young people from 13 to 19 years of age. Each person gets access to a personal adviser. These advisers are from a range of backgrounds including health, youth work and social welfare and are qualified to help whatever the problem.

www.connexions-direct.com/

Runaway Helpline is a national, free, confidential service, provided by the charity Missing People to provide help for anyone who has run away from home or care, or been forced to leave home.

Freefone: 0808 800 70 70

Text 80234

Email: runaway@missingpeople.org.uk

www.missingpeople.org.uk

Women

Women's Aid is a national federation in England of voluntary sector domestic violence services for women and children escaping domestic violence. This is an extremely extensive website and contains information on many aspects of domestic violence.

Tel: 0808 2000 247

www.womensaid.org.uk/

Welsh Women's Aid offers advice help and support for women in Wales.

Wales Domestic Abuse Helpline

Tel: 0808 80 10 800

www.welshwomensaid.org

Refuge is a national domestic violence charity which supports over 800 women and children on any one day. Refuge provides safe, emergency accommodation through a growing number of refuges throughout the country and offers individual and group counselling for abused women and children, and community based outreach services for women including specialist services for minority ethnic communities.

> www.refuge.org.uk

The Rights of Women works to attain justice and equality for women, by informing, educating and empowering women on their legal rights.

> Tel: 0207 251 6577

> www.rightsofwomen.org.uk/

Rape Crisis Federation Wales and England is a referral service for women who are seeking advice and/ or support around the issues of rape and sexual abuse/assault.

> Email: info@rapecrisis.org.uk

> www.rapecrisis.org.uk

Broken Rainbow is a referral service for lesbians, gay men, bisexuals and transgender people experiencing domestic violence:

> Tel: 07812 644 914

Ethnic Minorities Groups

Imkaan is a national research and policy project, initiated by two sister projects, NAWP and Asian Women's Resource Centre (AWRC) and is currently managed by NAWP.

> Tel: 0207 250 3933

> Email: enquiries@imkaan.org.uk

> www.imkaan.org.uk/pub/

NSPCC Asian Child Protection Helplines

> Bengali-speaking adviser 0800 096 7714

> Gujarati-speaking advisor 0800 096 7715

> Hindi-speaking advisor 0800 096 7716

> Punjabi-speaking advisor 0800 096 7717

> Urdu-speaking advisor 0800 096 7718

> English-speaking Asian adviser 0800 096 7719

> Welsh Helpline Number: 0808 100 2524

Black Association of Women Step Out (BAWSO) works with Black women who have experienced or are experiencing domestic violence.

> Tel: 02920 644633 (Cardiff)
>
> General Information: info@bawso.org.uk
>
> www.bawso.org.uk/

Chinese Information and Advice Centre (CIAC) offers information on family issues domestic violence and immigration.

> Tel: 08453 131 868
>
> Email: info@ciac.co.uk
>
> www.ciac.co.uk/

Immigration Advisory Service can provide advice and information on immigration or asylum issues.

> Tel: 0844 974 4000 (for UK callers only)
>
> www.iasuk.org/

Southall Black Sisters provide advice and emotional support for black and Asian women on domestic violence related issues.

> Helpline: 0208 571 0800
>
> General Enquiries: 020 8571 9595
>
> www.southallblacksisters.org.uk/

The Forced Marriage Unit at the Home Office can provide further advice and guidance on issues of forced marriage.

> www.fco.gov.uk

Men

Survivors UK have a helpline, support groups and counselling for men who have been sexually abused.

UK National helpline: 0845 122 1201

> Office number: 020 7404 6234
>
> Email: info@survivorsuk.org
>
> www.survivorsuk.org

General

The Home Office is the lead government department for domestic violence. The link below to the domestic violence page contains a number of research and information documents about domestic violence and outlines what the government is doing about the problem.

> www.homeoffice.gov.uk/crime-victims/
> reducing-crime/domestic-violence/

'*Loves Me, Loves Me Not*' is a Home Office leaflet available online; it provides general information on domestic violence and where help and support can be found.

www.vslondon.org/publications/loves_me_not.pdf

Domestic Violence Intervention Project (DVIP) is a voluntary sector project and registered charity. The aim of DVIP is to increase the safety of women and children who experience domestic violence by providing a range of diverse services challenging men, supporting women, working in partnership. They run a series of perpetrator programmes and corresponding support services for women.

Tel: 0207 633 9181/020 8741 8020

www.dvip.org/

Victim Support offers information and support to victims of crime, whether or not they have reported the crime to the police.

Helpline 0845 303 0900

www.victimsupport.org/

Just Ask is the website of the Community Legal Service, the first port of call for legal information and help in England and Wales.

0845 345 4 345

www.clsdirect.org.uk/

GLDVP (part of London Action Trust) works to increase safety for survivors of domestic violence, and to hold abusers accountable for their behaviour by providing second-tier support and promoting joint working between direct service providers.

Tel: 020 7785 3860

Email: info@gldvp.org.uk

www.gldvp.org.uk/

Samaritans National Number

08457 90 90 90

www.samaritans.org.uk

Reunite (if child abducted)

Tel: 0116 2556 234

www.reunite.org.uk

24-hour national government helpline

Tel: 020 7035 4848

www.crimereduction.gov.uk/
domesticviolence40.htm

Children's Legal Centre

Tel: 01206 877 910

www.childrenslegalcentre.com

Domestic Violence and Mediation

5.40   Increasing numbers of couples use mediation on separation, dissolution and divorce. This creates two risks:

- that people will experience being pressured into mediation;

- that cases which are inappropriate for mediation, such as cases of domestic violence, will be referred to mediation.

The mediator's code of practice requires that:

'[E]ach participant makes a fully informed and voluntary decision to enter mediation. This requires that each participant is sufficiently informed and has sufficient time to make the decision to attempt mediation after all safety issues including screening for domestic violence have been fully considered.'

College of Mediators
Tel: 01179 047 223
http://www.ukcfmcollegeof
mediators.co.uk/

The definition of domestic violence adopted in the College of Mediators' Code of Practice is as follows:

'The most important factor in domestic violence is the impact of the behaviour as experienced by each/any of the individuals involved. Domestic violence is behaviour that seeks to secure power and control for the abuser and to undermine the safety, security, self-esteem and autonomy of the abused person. Domestic violence contains elements of the use of any or all of physical, sexual, psychological, emotional, verbal or economic intimidation, oppression or coercion.'

All mediators compulsorily screen for domestic violence before mediation can begin. See further **2.88** and **3.39** onwards.

CHILD ABUSE

5.41   As stated in *Working together to Safeguard Children* (DOH, 2006) knowledge and understanding of children's welfare – and how to respond in the best interests of a child to concerns about maltreatment (abuse and neglect) – develops over time, informed by research, experience and the critical scrutiny of practice. Sound professional practice involves making judgments supported by evidence: evidence derived from research and experience about the nature and impact of maltreatment.

Source:
Working Together to Safeguard Children
(DfES, 2006)
www.dcsf.gov.uk/
everychildmatters/

The Impact of Maltreatment on Children

5.42   The sustained maltreatment of children physically, emotionally, sexually or through neglect can have major long-term effects on all aspects of a child's health, development and well-being. The immediate and longer-term impact can include anxiety, depression, substance misuse, eating disorders and self-destructive behaviours. Sustained maltreatment is likely to have a deep impact on the child's self-image and self-esteem, and on his or her future life. Difficulties may extend into adulthood: the experience of long-term abuse may lead to difficulties in forming or sustaining close relationships, or in establishing oneself in work, and to extra difficulties in developing the attitudes and skills which are necessary to be an effective parent, and even an effective member of society.

Source:
Working Together to Safeguard Children
(DfES, 2006)
www.dcsf.gov.uk/
everychildmatters/

It is not only the stressful events of maltreatment that have an impact, but also the context in which they take place. Any potentially abusive incident has to be seen in context to assess the extent of harm to a child and to decide on the most appropriate intervention. Often, it is the interaction between a number of factors which serve to increase the likelihood or level of significant harm. For every child and family, there may be factors that aggravate the harm caused to the child and those that protect against harm. Relevant factors include the individual child's means of coping and adapting, support from a family and social network, and the impact of any interventions. The effects on a child are also influenced by the quality of the family environment at the time of maltreatment, and subsequent life events. The way in which professionals respond also has a significant bearing on subsequent outcomes.

Recognising Abuse

5.43 The main categories of abuse are, in order of frequency:

(1) neglect;

(2) emotional abuse;

(3) physical abuse;

(4) sexual abuse.

Increasingly, there are further categories of abuse coming to public recognition (see below). A child may suffer a range of abuse including, for example, physical and emotional abuse, and an abused child may not fit neatly into a particular category.

Physical Abuse

5.44 Physical abuse can lead directly to neurological damage, physical injuries, disability or – at the extreme – death. Harm may be caused to children both by the abuse itself, and by the abuse taking place in a wider family or institutional context of conflict and aggression. Physical abuse has been linked to aggressive behaviour in children, emotional and behavioural problems, and educational difficulties. Violence is pervasive and the physical abuse of children frequently coexists with domestic violence.

Emotional Abuse

Source:
Working Together to
Safeguard Children
(DfES, 2006)
www.dcsf.gov.uk/
everychildmatters/

5.45 There is increasing evidence of the adverse long-term consequences for children's development where they have been subject to sustained emotional abuse. Emotional abuse has an important impact on a developing child's mental health, behaviour and self-esteem. It can be especially damaging in early childhood. Underlying emotional abuse may be as important, if not more so, than other more visible forms of abuse in terms of its impact on the child. Domestic violence is emotionally abusive in itself. Adult mental health problems and parental substance misuse may be features in families where children are exposed to such abuse.

Neglect

5.46 Neglect can take the form of lack of provision and lack of supervision. Severe neglect of young children has adverse effects on children's ability to form attachments and is associated with major impairment of growth and intellectual development. Persistent neglect can lead to serious impairment of health and development, and long-term difficulties with social functioning, relationships and educational progress. Neglected children may also experience low self esteem, feelings of being unloved and isolated. Neglect can also result, in extreme cases, in death. The impact of neglect varies depending on how long children have been neglected, the children's ages, and the multiplicity of neglectful behaviours children have been experiencing.

Sexual Abuse

5.47   Disturbed behaviour including self-harm, inappropriate sexualised behaviour, depression and a loss of self-esteem, have all been linked to sexual abuse. Its adverse effects may endure into adulthood. The severity of impact on a child is believed to increase the longer abuse continues, the more extensive the abuse, and the older the child. A number of features of sexual abuse have also been linked with severity of impact, including the relationship of the abuser to the child, the extent of premeditation, the degree of threat and coercion, sadism, and bizarre or unusual elements. A child's ability to cope with the experience of sexual abuse, once recognised or disclosed, is strengthened by the support of a non-abusive adult carer who believes the child, helps the child understand the abuse, and is able to offer help and protection. The reactions of practitioners also have an impact on the child's ability to cope with what has happened, and the child's feelings of self worth. A proportion of adults who sexually abuse children have themselves been sexually abused as children. They may also have been exposed as children to domestic violence and discontinuity of care. However, it would be quite wrong to suggest that most children who are sexually abused will inevitably go on to become abusers themselves.

Source:
Working Together to Safeguard Children (DOH, 2006)
www.dcsf.gov.uk/everychildmatters/

Particular Forms of Abuse

Fabricated or Induced Illness

5.48   Concerns may be raised when it is considered that the health or development of a child is likely to be significantly impaired or further impaired by a parent or caregiver who has fabricated or induced illness (formerly known as Munchausen Syndrome by Proxy). Concerns may arise when:

- reported symptoms and signs found on examination are not explained by any medical condition from which the child may be suffering; or

- physical examination and results of medical investigations do not explain reported symptoms and signs; or

- there is an inexplicably poor response to prescribed medication and other treatment; or

- new symptoms are reported on resolution of previous ones; or

- reported symptoms and found signs are not seen to begin in the absence of the caregiver; or

- over time the child repeatedly presents with a range of symptoms; or

- the child's normal activities are being curtailed beyond that which might be expected for any medical disorder from which the child is known to suffer.

In 2002 the government published *Safeguarding Children in Whom Illness is Fabricated or Induced* which provides a national framework within which agencies and professionals at a local level – individually and jointly – draw up and agree their own more detailed ways of working together where illness may be being fabricated or induced in a child. LSCBs should incorporate this guidance into their local procedures for safeguarding and promoting the welfare of children.

Children Abused through Obesity

5.49   The UK has seen dramatic increases in childhood obesity in recent years. Reducing obesity is now one of the government's six overarching priorities in the public health white paper, '*Choosing Health. Healthy Weight, Healthy Lives: A Cross-Government Strategy for England*' – a new £372 million strategy to help everyone lead healthier lives – which was published on 23 January 2008 by Alan Johnson, Health Secretary, and Ed Balls, Secretary of State for Children, Schools and Families. The Government has set itself the ambition of being the first major country to reverse the rising tide of obesity and overweight in the population by ensuring that all individuals are able to maintain a healthy weight. Its initial focus for children is that by 2020 it will have reduced the proportion of overweight and obese children to 2000 levels which target is to be supported by a programme of action to help children and their families have healthy lifestyles. The following cross-government schemes and initiatives to reducing childhood obesity have been announced:

- Healthy Schools programme
- Food in Schools programme (information on TeacherNet)
- School Fruit and Vegetable scheme (information on the DH website)
- Physical Education, School Sport and Club Links programme (information on TeacherNet).

National Child Measurement Programme

5.50 The National Child Measurement Programme is a key part of the Government's work to tackle obesity. The programme aims to record the height and weight of all children in Reception Year and Year 6. This data aims to help Primary Care Trusts (PCTs) plan services to support schools and target resources more effectively, and to provide important data to analyse trends at national and local levels

For more information about the programme, go to the Department of Health website www.dh.gov.uk

Children not Receiving a Suitable Education

5.51 Children not receiving a suitable education are at increased risk of a range of negative outcomes that could have long term damaging consequences for their life chances. For example they are at risk of not attaining the skills and qualifications they need to succeed in life, and are at significant risk of becoming NEET (not in education, employment or training) once they have reached the compulsory school leaving age. They could also be more vulnerable in one way or another. They may be from disadvantaged families (experiencing multiple risks such as poverty, substance misuse, mental ill-health and poor housing), travelling communities, immigrant families, be unaccompanied asylum seeking or trafficked children, or be at risk of neglect or abuse or disengaged from education. Statutory guidance for local authorities was published in January 2009 entitled, *Identifying and Maintaining Contact with Children Missing or At Risk of Going Missing from Education*, is also available from the everychildmatters website.

Children Abused through Prostitution

Source:
Working Together to
Safeguard Children
(DfES, 2006)
www.dcsf.gov.uk/
everychildmatters/

5.52 Children involved in prostitution and other forms of commercial sexual exploitation should be treated primarily as the victims of abuse, and their needs require careful assessment. They are likely to be in need of welfare services and – in many cases – protection under the Children Act 1989. Children involved in prostitution may be difficult to reach, and under very strong pressure to remain in prostitution. Local Safeguarding Children Boards (LSCBs) should actively enquire into the extent to which children are involved in prostitution in the local area. They should not assume that it is not a local issue.

Complex (Organised or Multiple) Abuse

The Child
Exploitation and
Online Protection
Centre
www.thinkuknow.co.uk.

5.53 Complex (organised or multiple) abuse may be defined as abuse involving one or more abusers and a number of children. The abusers concerned may be acting in concert to abuse children, sometimes acting independently, or may be using an institutional framework or position of authority to recruit children for abuse. Complex abuse occurs both as part of a network of abuse across a family or community and within institutions such as residential homes or schools. Such abuse is profoundly traumatic for the children who become involved. Its investigation is time-consuming and demanding work requiring specialist skills from both police and social work staff. Some investigations become extremely complex because of the number of places and people involved and the timescale over which abuse is alleged to have occurred. Cases of children being abused via the use of the internet is also a new form of abuse which agencies are having to address. The Child Exploitation and Online Protection (CEOP) Centre has been set up by the government in order to maximise international links and deliver a holistic approach to combating child sex abuse through the internet (www.ceop.gov.uk). CEOP's website has been designed and written specifically for young people. It contains games and up-to-date information on having fun, staying in control and being safer online as well as details on how to report problems. The website, called 'thinkuknow' can be accessed at: www.thinkuknow.co.uk.

Allegations of Abuse against a Professional, Foster Carer or Volunteer

5.54   Children can be subjected to abuse by those who work with them in any and every setting. All allegations of abuse of children by a professional, staff member, foster carer or volunteer (from LSCB member agencies) should therefore be taken seriously. Other organisations which provide services for children (including day care, leisure, churches, other places of worship and voluntary services) should have a procedure for handling such allegations which is consistent with this guidance and with LSCB procedures. In recent years, there have been a number of widely reported cases of historical abuse, usually of an organised or multiple nature. Such cases have generally come to light after adults have reported abuse that they had experienced when children, while living away from home in settings provided by local authorities, the voluntary sector or independent providers.

NICE Guidance

5.55   In July 2009, the National Institute for Health and Clinical Excellence (NICE) produced a quick reference guide, '*When to Suspect Child Maltreatment*' that summarises the recommendations NICE has made to the NHS. The guide is primarily for all healthcare professionals working in the NHS who work with children and young people. The guidance was developed by the National Collaborating Centre for Women's and Children's Health, which is linked with the Royal College of Obstetricians and Gynaecologists. The Collaborating Centre worked with a group of healthcare professionals (including paediatricians, GPs and child mental health professionals), people affected by maltreatment, and technical staff, who reviewed the evidence and drafted the recommendations. The recommendations were finalised after public consultation.

The guidance in relation to the various different forms of child abuse is divided into two categories under each subheading, according to the level of concern, with recommendations to either 'consider' or 'suspect' maltreatment. It also lists obstacles to the possible identification of child maltreatment in order to alert professionals in relevant circumstances. Such potential barriers include:

- concern about missing a treatable disorder;

Source:
Working Together to Safeguard Children (DOH, 2006)
www.dcsf.gov.uk/everychildmatters/

- healthcare professionals being used to working with parents and carers in the care of children and fear losing a positive relationship with a family already under their care;
- discomfort of disbelieving, thinking ill of, suspecting or wrongly blaming a parent or carer;
- divided duties to adult and child patients and breaching confidentiality;
- an understanding of the reasons why the maltreatment might have occurred, and that there was no intention to harm the child;
- losing control over the child protection process and doubts about its benefits;
- stress;
- personal safety;
- fear of complaints.

The NICE booklet is available on www.nice.org.uk.

CHILDREN'S NEEDS AND ASSESSMENTS

Sources of Stress for Children and Families

5.56 Many families under great stress succeed in bringing up their children in a warm, loving and supportive environment in which each child's needs are met. Sources of stress within families may, however, have a negative impact on a child's health, development and well-being, either directly, or because when experienced during pregnancy it may result in delays in the physical and mental development of infants, or because they affect the capacity of parents to respond to their child's needs. This is particularly so when there is no other significant adult who is able to respond to the child's needs in place of the parents' response.

Undertaking assessments of children and families requires a thorough understanding of the factors which influence children's development: the developmental needs of children; the capacities of parents or caregivers to respond appropriately to those needs; and the impact of wider family and environmental factors on both children's development and parenting capacity. There follows some of the key research findings which should be drawn on when assessing children and families, providing services to meet their identified needs and reviewing whether the planned outcomes for each child have been achieved.

Social Exclusion

5.57   Many of the families who seek help for their children, or about whom others raise concerns about a child's welfare, are multiply disadvantaged. These families may face chronic poverty, social isolation, racism and the problems associated with living in disadvantaged areas, such as high crime, poor housing, childcare, transport and education services, and limited employment opportunities. Many lack a wage earner. Poverty may mean that children live in crowded or unsuitable accommodation, have poor diets, health problems or disability, are vulnerable to accidents, and lack ready access to good educational and leisure opportunities. Racism and racial harassment is an additional source of stress for some families and children. Social exclusion can also have an indirect affect on children through its association with parental depression, learning disability and long term physical health problems.

Domestic Violence

5.58   Prolonged and/or regular exposure to domestic violence can have a serious impact on a child's development and emotional well-being, despite the best efforts of the victim parent to protect the child. Domestic violence has an impact in a number of ways. It can pose a threat to an unborn child, because assaults on pregnant women frequently involve punches or kicks directed at the abdomen, risking injury to both mother and foetus. Older children may also suffer blows during episodes of violence. Children may be greatly distressed by directly or indirectly witnessing the physical and emotional suffering of a parent. Both the physical assaults and psychological abuse suffered by adult victims who experience domestic violence can have a negative impact on their ability to look after their children. The negative impact of domestic violence is exacerbated when: the abuse is combined with drink or drug misuse; children witness the abuse; children are drawn into the abuse or are pressured into concealing the assaults. Children's exposure to parental conflict, even where abuse is not present, can lead to serious anxiety and distress.

Source:
Working Together to
Safeguard Children
(DOH, 2006)
www.dcsf.gov.uk/
everychildmatters/

The Mental Illness of a Parent or Carer

Source:
*Working Together to
Safeguard Children*
(DOH, 2006)
www.dcsf.gov.uk/
everychildmatters/

5.59 Mental illness in a parent or carer does not necessarily have an adverse impact on a child, but it is essential always to assess its implications for each child in the family. Parental illness may markedly restrict children's social and recreational activities. With both mental and physical illness in a parent, children may have caring responsibilities placed upon them inappropriate to their years, leading them to be worried and anxious. If they are depressed, parents may neglect their own and their children's physical and emotional needs. In some circumstances, some forms of mental illness may blunt parents' emotions and feelings, or cause them to behave towards their children in bizarre or violent ways. Unusually, but at the extreme, a child may be at risk of severe injury, profound neglect or even death. A study of 100 reviews of child deaths where abuse and neglect had been a factor in the death, showed clear evidence of parental mental illness in one-third of cases. In addition, postnatal depression can also be linked to both behavioural and physiological problems in the infants of such mothers. The adverse effects on children of parental mental illness are less likely when parental problems are mild, last only a short time, are not associated with family disharmony, and do not result in the family breaking up. Children may also be protected from harm when the other parent or a family member can help respond to the child's needs. Children most at risk of significant harm are those who feature within parental delusions, and children who become targets for parental aggression or rejection, or who are neglected as a result of parental mental illness.

Drug and Alcohol Misuse

5.60 As with mental illness in a parent, it is important not to generalise, or make assumptions about the impact on a child of parental drug and alcohol misuse. Their effects on children are complex and require a thorough assessment. Maternal substance misuse in pregnancy can have serious effects on the health and development of an unborn child, often because of the mother's poor nutrition and lifestyle. Newborn babies may experience withdrawal symptoms which may interfere with the parent/child bonding process. Babies may experience a lack of basic health care and poor stimulation and older children may experience poor school attendance, anxiety about their parents' health and taking on caring roles for siblings. Substance misuse can affect parent's practical caring skills: perceptions, attention to basic physical needs, control of emotion, judgement and attachment to or separation from the child. Some substance misuse may give rise to mental states or behaviour that put children at risk of injury, psychological distress or neglect. Children are particularly vulnerable when parents are withdrawing from drugs. The risk will be greater when the adult's substance misuse is chaotic or otherwise out of control and when both parents are involved.

Some substance misusing parents may find it difficult to give priority to the needs of their children, and finding money for drugs and/or alcohol may reduce the money available to the household to meet basic needs, or may draw families into criminal activities. Children may be at risk of physical harm if drugs and paraphernalia (for example, needles) are not kept safely out of reach. Some children have been killed through inadvertent access to drugs (for example, methadone stored in a fridge). In addition, children may be in danger if they are a passenger in a car whilst a drug/alcohol misusing carer is driving. The children of substance misusing parents are at increased risk of developing alcohol and drug use problems themselves, and of being separated from their parents. Children who start drinking at an early age are at greater risk of unwanted sexual encounters, and injuries through accidents and fighting.

In January 2008 the first family drug and alcohol court (FDAC) in the UK opened in London at Wells Street Family Proceedings Court. It is funded by central government and Camden, Islington and Westminster local authorities and will run until 31 December 2010. The main purpose of FDAC is to find out whether it can improve outcomes for children subject to care proceedings by offering parents with substance misusing problems:

- intensive assessment and support from the specialist court;
- help from parent mentors;
- quicker access to community services;
- better co-ordination between child and adult services.

FDAC is based on a model widely used in the USA. The national US evaluation found that outcomes for parents and children were better when families took part in specialist drug and alcohol courts. Key findings were:

- more children were reunited with their parents;
- quicker decisions were made for out of home care if reunification was not possible;
- there were financial savings on foster care.

The results were attributed to the fact that more parents took up and completed substance misuse treatments than in traditional courts and services. FDAC has been adapted to comply with English law and social care services. The adaptations are based on the findings of an extensive feasibility study. Instead of a normal care proceedings court process, a family entering FDAC will go through a slightly different process. They have the same judge for the whole process with frequent non-lawyer review hearings where they can talk directly to the judges. The court's specialist multi-disciplinary team provided by the Tavistock and Portman NHS Trust Foundation in partnership with the children's charity, Coram Family, provides immediate assessment and support to deal with the substance misuse problems and other difficulties that interfere with their parenting capacity. Parents may be linked with parent mentors who have experienced similar problems.

The Nuffield Foundation and Home Office have funded Brunel University to carry out an independent first stage evaluation of FDAC. The aims are:

- to describe the FDAC pilot and identify set-up and implementation lessons;
- to make comparisons with standard court proceedings involving parental substance misuse, including a comparison of costs; and
- to indicate whether this different approach might lead to better outcomes for children and parents.

A final report is due to be presented to the Nuffield Foundation in July 2010.

Children of Drug Misusing Parents

5.61 The Advisory Council on the Misuse of Drugs' (ACMD) report *Hidden Harm – responding to the needs of children of problem drug users* estimated that there are between 200,000 and 300,000 children of problem drug users in England and Wales, ie 2–3% of all children under the age of 16. The report also concludes that parental problem drug use can and does cause serious harm to children at every age from conception to adulthood. Parental problem drug use is characterised by the use of multiple drugs, often by injection and is strongly associated with economic deprivation and other factors that affect parenting capacity. The adverse consequences for the child are typically multiple and cumulative and will vary according to the child's age of development and other factors about their life experience. Some of the key features of the impact of parental drug misuse are:

- physical and emotional abuse and neglect;
- dangerously inadequate supervision and other inappropriate parenting practices;
- intermittent and permanent separation;
- inadequate accommodation and frequent changes in residence;
- toxic substances in the home;
- interrupted and unsatisfactory education;
- exposure to criminal or other inappropriate adult behaviour.

An appropriate response to these children often requires the close collaboration of a number of agencies including health, maternity services, adult's and children's social care, adult treatment, courts, prisons and probation services.

Source:
Working Together to
Safeguard Children
(DOH, 2006)
www.dcsf.gov.uk/
everychildmatters/

Parental Learning Disability

5.62   Where a parent has a learning disability it is important not to generalise or make assumptions about their parental capacity. Such parents may need support to develop the understanding, resources, skills and experience to meet the needs of their children. Such support is particularly needed where they experience additional stressors such as having a disabled child, domestic violence, poor physical and mental health, substance misuse, social isolation, poor housing, poverty and a history of growing up in care. It is these additional stressors when combined with a learning disability that are most likely to lead to concerns about the care a child or children may receive.

Children of parents with learning disabilities are at increased risk from inherited learning disability and more vulnerable to psychiatric disorders and behavioural problems. From an early age children may assume the responsibility of looking after their parent and in many cases other siblings, one or more of whom may be learning disabled. Unless parents with learning disabilities are comprehensively supported – for example, by a capable non-abusive relative, such as their own parent or partner – their children's health and development is likely to be impaired. A further risk of harm to children arises because mothers with learning disabilities may be attractive targets for men who wish to gain access to children for the purpose of sexually abusing them.

Source:
Working Together to
Safeguard Children
(DOH, 2006)
www.dcsf.gov.uk/
everychildmatters/

A specialist assessment will often be needed.

Child Pornography and the Internet

5.63   The internet has now become a significant tool in the distribution of child pornography. Adults are now using the internet to try to establish contact with children with a view to 'grooming' them for inappropriate or abusive relationships. As part of their role in preventing abuse and neglect, LSCBs should consider activities to raise awareness about the safe use of the internet by children – for example, by distributing information through education staff to parents, in relation to both school and home-based use of computers by children. See **5.53**.

Migrant Children

5.64   Over recent years the number of migrant children in the UK has increased for a variety of reasons, including the expansion of the global economy and incidents of war and conflict. Safeguarding and promoting the welfare of these children must remain paramount with agencies in their dealings with this group. Local agencies should give particular consideration to the following groups.

Child Victims of Trafficking

5.65   There is now an increasing awareness of the prevalent problems of child trafficking both into, out of and within the UK. The organised crime of child trafficking into the UK has become an issue of considerable concern to all professionals with responsibility for the care and protection of children. Many describe it as modern-day slavery, where victims are coerced, deceived or forced into the control of others who seek to profit from their exploitation and suffering. It is clear that all forms of trafficking children are an abuse. Moreover, everyone working or in contact with children and young people has a responsibility to take steps to make sure their welfare is safeguarded and promoted. Approximately 2.4 million people are trafficked world-wide every year – half of whom are children. They are transported across borders and sold like commodities. They experience violence and sexual exploitation. Currently, most trafficked children originate from China, India, the Horn of Africa, Uganda, DRC, Congo, Nigeria, Lithuania, Thailand, Vietnam or Albania. They will have been trafficked into the UK for domestic slavery, sexual abuse, or prostitution. They may have been in the UK for some period of time, hidden within the sex trade, or in a person's private home, or employed in the catering industry, in construction and domestic work. According to a recent UK Home Office report, children trafficked into the UK have been documented within domestic service, catering and manual labour. They are also used for credit card/benefit fraud and illicit activities such as acting as drug mules or tending plants in illegal cannabis farms. They can also be trafficked for illegal adoption where financial gain can be from both the child's parents and the adoptive parents (see the Statutory Guidance for the Adoption and Children Act 2002).

As more cases of child trafficking come to light, with some cases involving UK-born children being trafficked within the UK, it is essential that all professionals who come into contact with children, who may have been trafficked, are fully aware of the background of this activity and know how to apply the procedures for safeguarding the children and meeting the needs of those who have been trafficked.

A guidance document issued in December 2007 entitled *Safeguarding Children who may have been trafficked*, is available from the everychildmatters website and is intended to help agencies and their staff safeguard and promote the welfare of children who may have been trafficked. It is supplementary to, and should be used in conjunction with, the Government's statutory guidance: *Working Together to Safeguard Children*.

As these issues have become more widely publicised, support services have become available, including:

- An NSPCC child trafficking advice and information line.

- The UK Human Trafficking Centre (UKHTC – see http://www.ukhtc.org/index.htm), which aims to tackle trafficking from a victim-centred, human rights perspective.

- The Child Exploitation and Online Protection Centre (CEOP), which was formed to protect children from sexual exploitation arising from the internet (www.ceop.gov.uk see **5.53**).

See www.homeoffice.gov.uk/ documents/human-traffick -action-plan

The Council of Europe Convention on Action against Trafficking in Human Beings (CETS no 197) 2005 came into force on 1 February 2008, and into effect in the UK on 1 April 2009. In addition, the UK Border Agency has launched an *Action Plan on Tackling Human Trafficking.*

Unaccompanied Asylum Seeking Children (UASC)

5.66 According to the UK Border Agency, an UASC is an asylum seeking child under the age of $17\frac{1}{2}$, who is not living with his parent, relative or guardian in the UK. Most UASC are referred to local authorities by the immigration authorities and should be supported by local authorities under either s 17 or 20 of the Children Act 1989, depending on their needs. The vast majority of UASC will have been smuggled or escorted into the country and will not have claimed asylum on their arrival at the port of entry: they may also have been a victim of trafficking. Despite a confident or even hostile appearance, the child or young person may have suffered trauma as a result, and will need sensitive handling. The UK Border Agency's '*Code of Practice for Keeping Children Safe from Harm*' was issued on 6 January 2008 and is designed to apply to the full range of UK Border Agency's activities in relation to children. The Borders, Citizenship and Immigration Act 2009, passed on 21 July 2009 came into force on 2 November 2009, and includes in s 55 a duty regarding the welfare of children, together with an increased focus on the prevention and addressing of child trafficking.

The UK Border Agency's Code of Practice is available and can be downloaded from: www.ind.homeoffice.gov.uk/sitecontent/documents/ aboutus/consultations/closedconsultations/ keepingchildrensafe/ uasc_codeofpractice.pdf?view=Binary.

Forced Marriage

5.67　A forced marriage is a marriage conducted without the full consent of both parties and where duress is a factor. In 2004 the government's definition of domestic violence was extended to include acts perpetrated by extended family members as well as intimate partners. Consequently, acts such as forced marriage and other so-called 'honour crimes' which can include abduction and homicide, can now come under the definition of domestic violence. Many of these acts are committed against children. The Forced Marriage Unit of the Foreign and Commonwealth Office produced guidelines in conjunction with children's social care and the Department for Education and Skills on how to identify and support young people threatened by forced marriage. The Forced Marriage Unit currently deals with approximately 400 cases a year, double the number reported by the Association of Chief Police Officers (ACP0) 5 years ago. The website for the UK Government Forced Marriage Unit is http://www.fco.gov.uk/en/fco-in-action/nationals/forced-marriage-unit.

The Forced Marriage (Civil Protection) Act 2007, which began life as a private member's bill, came into force on 25 November 2008, introducing a new remedy to protect the actual or potential victims of forced marriage: the forced marriage protection order. The legislation inserted a new Part 4A into the Family Law Act 1996.

The Family Law Act 1996 (Forced Marriage) (Relevant Third Party) Order 2009, which came into effect on 1 November 2009 defines a 'relevant third party' for the purpose of applying for a forced marriage protection order. The legislation specifies who is able to make an application on behalf of the victim without the need for leave of the court.

The Forced Marriage (Civil Protection) Act 2007 inserted 19 provisions into the Family Law Act 1996 (FLA 1996) which empower the High Court and the county court to make orders to protect a person from being or who has been forced into a marriage. Section 63(2) of the FLA 1996 provides that 'the person to be protected by the order' or a 'relevant third party' can apply for an order without leave. The 2007 Act did not define a relevant third party as the government wished to refer the matter to consultation (Ministry of

Justice, 2007, Consultation Paper (CP 31/07)). The responses were published in November 2008 (Ministry of Justice, 2008, Responses to the Consultation Paper (CP 31/07)) and in the light of feedback received, the Lord Chancellor exercised his powers under s 63C(7). Article 3 of the order states that a local authority (as defined in article 2) is to be designated a relevant third party, which reflects the views of the majority of respondents to the consultation paper. Most respondents supported specifying local authorities as relevant third parties due to: their proximity to the local community, their expertise in relation to child abuse cases and the protection of vulnerable adults, the multi-agency approach that they adopt in relation to housing, counselling, health, etc and the legal resources that they already have which will enable them to undertake the role. Indeed, all the local authorities that responded to the consultation (10 in total) agreed that they should act as relevant third parties. The designation of local authorities as relevant third parties was therefore to be expected.

Source:
Working Together to
Safeguard Children
(DOH, 2006)
www.dcsf.gov.uk/
everychildmatters/
Fam Law Nov 2009

However, the order does not specify the Secretary of State as a relevant third party, given that s 63C(8) expressly anticipates this. Section 63C(8) was included in the Act to attempt to ensure that the Forced Marriage Unit, which falls under the remit of the Secretary of State but has no independent legal status, could easily apply for protection orders. The Unit, which provides assistance for those at risk of being forced into marriage, was cited as an appropriate 'relevant third party' by several respondents to the Consultation Paper. However, the sole respondent from the Forced Marriage Unit itself was opposed to this proposal due to the fact that the unit lacks 'geographical spread'. The order thus reflects the views of the Unit, rather than the majority of respondents. The Forced Marriage Unit will therefore be in the same position as relatives, friends and teachers who wish to make an application, namely it will have to obtain leave of the court in order to do so.

Assessments

5.68 The term 'assessment' is used repeatedly in child welfare. For example, an 'initial assessment' is a brief assessment of a child referred to local authority children's social care where it is necessary to determine whether the child is in need, the nature of any services required, and whether a further, more detailed core assessment should be undertaken with the child and family. It involves:

- seeing and speaking to the child (according to age and understanding) and family members as appropriate; drawing together and analysing available information from a range of sources (including existing records);
- involving and obtaining relevant information from professionals and others in contact with the child and family.

The initial assessment should determine:

- is this a child in need? (Children Act 1989, s 17);
- is there reasonable cause to suspect that this child is suffering, or is likely to suffer, significant harm? (Children Act 1989, s 47).

Even if the reason for a referral was a concern about abuse or neglect that is not subsequently substantiated, a family may still benefit from support and practical help to promote a child's health and development. Local authority children's social care should then decide on the next course of action, following discussion with the child and family, unless that might place a child at risk of significant harm.

Where it is clear that there should be a police investigation in parallel with a section 47 enquiry, children are often the key, and sometimes the only, source of information about what has happened to them, especially in child sexual abuse cases but also in physical and other forms of abuse. Even initial discussions with children have to be conducted in a way that minimises distress caused and maximises the likelihood that they will provide accurate and complete information.

Whenever there is reasonable cause to suspect that a child is suffering, or is likely to suffer, significant harm, there should be a strategy discussion involving local authority children's social care and the police, and other bodies as appropriate (for example, nursery/school and health), in particular any referring agency.

The Common Assessment Framework – CAF

5.69 The Common Assessment Framework (CAF) is a shared assessment tool used across agencies in England. It can help practitioners develop more of a shared understanding of a child's needs, so they can be met more effectively. It will avoid children and families having to tell and re-tell their story. The CAF is an important tool for early intervention, designed specifically to help practitioners assess needs at an earlier stage and then work with other practitioners and agencies to meet them. The CAF is not for when there are concerns that a child may have been harmed or may be at risk of harm. Everyone wants better lives for children. Most children do well, but some have important disadvantages that currently are only addressed when they become serious. Sometimes their parents know there is a problem but struggle to know how to get help. The aim is to identify these children earlier and help them before things reach crisis point. The most important way of doing this is if everyone whose job involves working with children and families keeps an eye out for their well-being, and is prepared to help if something is going wrong. The CAF was introduced to help practitioners do this. There is also an easy-to-use CAF pre-assessment checklist, which can be used by any practitioner at any time, to help decide whether there should be a common assessment.

The CAF aims to provide a national, more standardised approach to assessing children's needs for services and how they should be met. It introduces a common framework for initial needs assessment that can be used by the whole children's workforce for any child in need of support. When used by all agencies, it will help practitioners to communicate and work together more effectively. It is particularly suitable for use in universal services (such as early childhood services, schools and universal health care), to tackle problems before they become serious.

The CAF aims to provide an evidence based, non-bureaucratic, 'whole child' assessment, drawing on good practice, enabling the practitioner to make a decision about how far they themselves (and the family) can meet the needs and who else needs to be involved. The CAF aims to improve coordination and consistency between assessments, leading to fewer and shorter specialist assessments. It will also inform decisions about whether further specialist assessment is required and if necessary provide information to contribute to it. If the outcome of a common assessment indicates that a referral to targeted or specialist services is appropriate as part of the plan to meet need, then the CAF form can provide the information to back up the referral. As the CAF form will contain much of the evidence necessary for a well informed referral, a detailed referral form is unlikely to be needed. The principles underlying the approach to the CAF are that it is a process supported by a standard form which is:

- holistic;
- focuses on needs and strengths;
- simple and practical;
- empowering and a joint process.

A CAF should only be undertaken if the child or parent agrees, and it cannot guarantee service provision. If a common assessment is refused and concerns remain about the safety or welfare of a child established child protection procedures should be followed without delay.

The *Framework for the Assessment of Children in Need and their Families* provides a systematic basis for collecting and analysing information to support professional judgments about how to help children and families in the best interests of the child. Practitioners should use the framework to gain an understanding of a child's developmental needs; the capacity of parents or caregivers to respond appropriately to those needs, including their capacity to keep the child safe from harm; and the impact of wider family and environmental factors on the parents and child. Each of the three main aspects of the framework – the child's developmental needs; parenting capacity; and wider family and environmental factors – is outlined.

The framework is to be used for the assessment of all children in need, including those where there are concerns that a child may be suffering significant harm. The process of engaging in an assessment should be viewed as being part of the range of services offered to children and families. Use of the framework should provide evidence to help, guide and inform judgments about children's welfare and safety from the first point of contact, through the processes of initial and more detailed core assessments, according to the nature and extent of the child's needs. The provision of appropriate services need not, and should not, wait until the end of the assessment process, but should be determined according to what is required, and when, to promote the welfare and safety of the child.

Evidence about children's developmental progress – and their parents' capacity to respond appropriately to the child's needs within the wider family and environmental context – should underpin judgments about:

- the child's welfare and safety;
- whether, and if so how, to provide help to children and family members;
- what form of intervention will bring about the best possible outcomes for the child;
- what the intended outcomes of intervention are.

Details of the framework are in Appendix 2 of *Working Together to Safeguard Children* (DOH, 2006).

Core Assessments

5.70 The core assessment is the means by which a Children Act 1989, section 47 enquiry is carried out. It should be led by a qualified and experienced social worker. Local authority children's services have lead responsibility for the core assessment. In these circumstances the objective of the local authority's involvement is to determine whether action is required to safeguard and promote the welfare of the child or children who are the subjects of the enquiries. The *Framework for the Assessment of Children in Need and their Families* (see **5.69**) provides the structure for helping to collect and analyse information obtained in the course of section 47 enquiries.

Child Assessment Orders

5.71 Local authority children's services should make all reasonable efforts to persuade parents to cooperate with section 47 enquiries. If, despite these efforts, the parents continue to refuse access to a child for the purpose of establishing basic facts about the child's condition – but concerns about the child's safety are not so urgent as to require an emergency protection order – a local authority may apply to the court for a child assessment order. In these circumstances, the court may direct the parents/caregivers to co-operate with an assessment of the child, the details of which should be specified. The order does not take away the child's own right to refuse to participate in an assessment, for example, a medical examination, so long as the child is of sufficient age and understanding.

For court-ordered assessments during care proceedings see **3.25** and **3.32**.

DELAY

Public Law

5.72   Delay is endemic within the family justice system. The difficulties, particularly in relation to the public law aspects of the Children Act 1989 have been well rehearsed ever since the Booth Report in 1996, followed by the Lord Chancellor's Department Scoping Study on Delay in 2002, the final report on the Judicial Case Management Protocol in 2003, the Finch Report on Delay for the Department for Education and Skills in 2004 and the bringing into force of The Public Law Outline, to name but a few. As Finch concluded, there was no shortage of 'good quality analysis and understanding of challenges faced by the system'. Each of the reports contained data and analysis that pointed to the fact that the major obstacle to the resolution of problems in the system was a lack of appropriate resources in areas ranging from local authority children's services to the courts. The Finch Report, standing near the end of this long line of similar conclusions, identified obstacles that included lack of access by families to easy, early advice and advocacy, a lack of specialist judges, magistrates and court facilities, insufficient specialist lawyers and shortages in trained and experienced Children and Family Courts Advisory and Support Service (Cafcass) professionals. The Finch Report concluded: 'Key to progress will be providing sufficient resources with time to invest'.

At the time of writing, despite the warnings of the Finch Report and the subsequent Public Law Outline, the family justice system is under greater pressure than ever from a lack of appropriate resources.

Court Delay

5.73   When the court determines any question with respect to the upbringing of a child, the welfare of the child must be the court's paramount consideration. Further, the court must have regard to the general principle that delay is likely to prejudice the welfare of the child although planned and purposeful delay may be in the child's interest. The problem of delay in care cases has long been recognised and specifically considered in several reports (see above). The Public Law Outline (PLO) was the latest step taken to bring about (amongst other improvements) a reduction of delay in public law cases. A report by Patricia Jessiman

Source:
BenchMark – July 2009

and Peter Keogh of the National Centre for Social Research and Julia Brophy of the Centre for Family Law and Policy evaluating the Public Law Outline concluded in early 2009 that the early signs were promising, but that the application of the PLO by the judiciary, including magistrates and legal advisers, varied. Some were inflexible in its application to the possible detriment to the case. However, most of the survey's respondents did not feel that using the PLO had speeded up the process. 'Poor' local authority compliance throughout the proceedings was cited as a key cause of delay, and in two of the three areas studied (both in England), there was significant delay in the appointment of a children's guardian. Lack of information, including from experts, police, and the local authority was also a problem and adjournments in the court process were frequent. The report warned that the PLO needed more time to 'bed down'.

Concerns noted back at the time of the introduction of the Protocol in November 2003 still remain today:

- Social services departments continue to be seriously understaffed, suffering both recruitment and retention of staff problems. This critically limits their ability to speed up the pre-application stages in the care process. It also has the effect that, were they to focus more of their precious human resources on the actual litigation stage, their other roles in care, prevention and education would be likely to be compromised.

- Cafcass now has an even more critical shortage of guardians.

- Publicly funded remuneration for the legal profession, needed to reflect the fact that children cases required the full input and co-operation of experienced, specialist practitioners, has been drastically cut.

- More family sitting days are still needed in some areas.

- There is still a shortage of experts in a number of fields, preventing the swift hearing of cases in some areas.

- Judges still have difficulties case managing effectively as the listing arrangements still have real problems in not being able to accommodate the need for continuity or allow for a sensible amount of reading time prior to hearings.

It was hoped that introduction of the Protocol, and then the Public Law Outline, would lead to better use of available resources and so reduction of unnecessary delay. Despite this, however, children cases sometimes call for flexibility and delay. There will always remain cases where there is a need for adapting or prolonging the procedure to fit changing circumstances or allow for constructive delay.

Copies of the Public Law Outline are available from: www.dca.gov.uk.

Other Initiatives

5.74   The introduction of Case Progression Officers (CPOs) was piloted for 12 months in relation to public law Children Act 1989 cases in certain courts and appeared to have a valuable role in progressing case management in the courts concerned. Video conferencing (VC) is being increasingly recognised by the courts and practitioners alike as a technology that can help reduce delay. Judges and advocates have long recognised the importance of allowing witnesses in appropriate cases to give evidence from outside the courtroom and even in some cases outside the precincts of the court. Using VC technology for expert evidence in public law Children Act 1989 cases is one important area where this practice could prove extremely beneficial. Recent studies and reports have shown that a major cause of delay in family cases is the experts being unavailable to give necessary evidence, as they are drawn from an ever decreasing and limited pool of resources. These delays increase costs and can negatively affect the children involved in the cases. The use of VC may provide experts with greater flexibility over when they are required to give evidence and will also mean they have to spend less time travelling to and from court and waiting for cases to be heard. All 53 care centres have been provided with VC equipment.

Guidance on using VC equipment is available on: www.hmcourts-service.gov.uk/infoabout/ video_conferencing/index.htm

Private Law

5.75   Delay has not been as endemic in private law cases concerning children, although there are now concerns as to the difficulties faced by Cafcass in being able to prepare court welfare reports in cases of residence and contact concerning children. Delay has inevitably been caused by the reliance on long reports from Cafcass, too many of which are often the result of an automatic resort to a welfare report when attempts at preliminary negotiation by the parties' lawyers and Cafcass have failed. Even after a report has been submitted there can be further delay in fixing a hearing date, when the matter is usually settled on the basis of the Cafcass officer's recommendation. Cafcass has now proposed a much more focused Cafcass investigation which need not culminate in an over-detailed report – for example, oral presentation of the results of the Cafcass officer's enquiries. The aim of keeping private cases out of court in itself minimises delay and the same approach is now applied to financial matters on divorce. A House of Commons Select Committee Report in 2005 accepted that in child contact cases non-resident parents were frequently disadvantaged because of delays which could affect the outcome of a case as well as a lack of judicial continuity and the failure to enforce court orders. Some aggrieved parents reported to the committee their experiences of delay being used as a tactic. Given the strong animosity between the parties which was common in contested family cases, the committee found it hard to believe that tactical delay was not sometimes used to the advantage of resident parents. However, the courts have a continuing duty to ensure that parties and their legal advisers do not unnecessarily delay proceedings and legal advisers have a professional obligation to avoid unnecessary delay.

Delay is a major factor in breakdowns in contact since it allows positions to become entrenched and for contact arrangements to fail. The judiciary recognised the need for proactive case management which resulted in the President's Private Law Programme (now revised) which attempts to achieve early dispute resolution and, if there is no resolution, to improve the judicial case management of private law cases thereafter (see further **3.22**).

CHILD WITNESSES

5.76   When children are victims of abuse, or witnesses to events, they may need to tell their story and give evidence. There are a range of potential problems with this. Special measures are needed to ensure that they can give the best evidence of which they are capable

and to ensure that their evidence can be fairly
challenged. However, there are still areas which need
attention. In one court recently, despite the fact that
these cases are supposed to be prioritised, children were
kept waiting for 5 hours before they gave evidence. If
there is a young witness, the case must be listed as a
priority.

In December 2004, resident judges were written to
about research that had been carried out by Joyce
Plotnikoff and Richard Woolfson into the experience of
child witnesses who gave evidence in Crown courts. A
further study was carried out between May 2007 and
October 2008. This research is also invaluable to all
professionals working in the family justice system.

Case management is vital and needs to be hands-on.
Children may be frightened or inhibited by a range of
things – the abuser, or someone linked with the abuser,
those in authority, the court process itself, the
possibility of their friends finding out about abuse.
Judges need to be proactive and consider issues such as
whether the case has a high press profile, or an unusual
complication which may have an effect on the child, the
risk of intimidation and whether or not a person might
need to be excluded from the court or courtroom, and
the need to prevent drift which may of itself render the
evidence of the child or young person unreliable. Long
waits for forensic or other evidence may not be
acceptable. It may be possible and preferable for the
young witness to enter and leave the court from a
different entrance. Perhaps it would help the witness to
come to court in advance and see the set up. The person
who attends court with the witness should be the same
person throughout: a change in personnel is a concern
for children.

If the child is to give evidence by video, he or she will
need to refresh their memory of their initial interview,
but preferably not at the same time as the advocates
and the judge, to save them embarrassment and distress.
Young children have a very short concentration span,
possibly half an hour if they are school children, and
will need breaks. They also do not give their best
evidence in the afternoon when they are tired. Cameras
should be set so that the child cannot see the defendant
on the screen. The judge will also have to consider
whether or not it may be appropriate to meet the child:
the advantages of this may be that the child can see the
person they will see on video and the person should

then be less intimidating for the child, and it may give the judge a brief opportunity to form an assessment of the child. Once the child is on video link, he or she should always see the judge's face when the judge is speaking, and whoever is asking questions must ensure that the child understands the questions being asked, not lapsing into adult language, and also not behave in what might appear a bullying or intimidating manner, allowing the child plenty of time to think about the answer.

If the case involves physical or sexual abuse, the questioner must be very careful how the child is asked to describe his or her body. No-one must ask the child to point to the part of the body being referred to: a body map being available can assist. Equally, photographs of the child should not be put to the child witness.

After the hearing, the child should always be thanked for taking their part and arrangement must be made for the child to be told the outcome.

Source:
BenchMark – July 2009

The document, '*Good practice guidance in managing young witness cases and questioning children*' can be downloaded from www.nspcc.org.uk/inform.

ADOPTION AND SPECIAL GUARDIANSHIP

5.77   The Adoption and Children Act 2002 was intended to provide a new approach to adoption to reflect society's views in the twenty-first century as to who should be able to adopt, to offer alternative orders which produce permanency for children and to effect a proper balance between the three sets of interest in the adoption triangle, namely the natural parents, the adoptive parents and the children. The 2002 Act:

(i)   aligns adoption law with the Children Act 1989 by making the child's welfare the paramount consideration in all decisions relating to adoption;

(ii)   provides a new welfare based ground for dispensing with parental consent;

(iii)   abolishes freeing for adoption orders and provides new measures for placement for adoption either with parental consent or under a placement order;

(iv)   overhauls eligibility to apply for adoption orders by enabling single persons, married couples and, for the first time, unmarried couples to apply;

(v)   strengthens the restrictions on arranging adoptions and advertising children for adoption other than through adoption agencies and introduces a new restriction relating to reports;

(vi) widens the range of options for providing permanence for children by amending the Children Act 1989 to introduce a new special guardianship order.

Range of Orders

Special Guardianship

5.78   Courts can make a new type of order for those children who cannot live with their birth parents but for whom adoption is inappropriate. Special guardianship orders do not sever the child's relationship with his birth parents which is preserved. The guardian has responsibility for day-to-day decisions about the child's welfare and is able to exercise parental responsibility to the exclusion of birth parents. However, the birth parents retain some limited rights, e g they have the right to consent or not to an adoption or placement

Extended Residence Orders

5.79   The Children Act 1989 is amended to allow courts to direct that residence orders in favour of someone who is not a parent or guardian can be extended until the child is 18.

Parental responsibility for step-parents

5.80   When a person is married to one of the child's parents (ie a step-parent), parental responsibility can be acquired either by a witnessed parental responsibility agreement or an application to court.

Placement Orders

5.81   Placement orders replace 'freeing orders' under the Adoption Act 1976. The difference between the orders is that the parental responsibility of the natural parents is not extinguished by the making of a placement order, although an adoption agency can decide the extent to which the responsibility is restricted. Consequently the question of the natural parents' consent can be decided at an earlier stage in the proceedings and the local authority can apply for a placement order as soon as it decides that adoption is appropriate.

Adoption Orders

Further information from:
www.adoptchild.co.uk;
www.baaf.org.uk

5.82 The range of people who can make applications for adoption has been extended to include a married or unmarried couple (whether of different sexes or the same sex living in an enduring family relationship) or by a single person, a step-parent or the partner of a child's parent.

DIVERSITY

Race, Ethnicity and Culture

5.83 Children from all cultures are subject to abuse and neglect. All children have a right to grow up safe from harm. In order to make sensitive and informed professional judgments about a child's needs, and parents' capacity to respond to their child's needs, it is important that professionals are sensitive to differing family patterns and lifestyles and to child rearing patterns that vary across different racial, ethnic and cultural groups. Professionals should also be aware of the broader social factors that serve to discriminate against black and minority ethnic people. Working in a multi-racial and multi-cultural society requires professionals and organisations to be committed to equality in meeting the needs of all children and families, and to understand the effects of racial harassment, racial discrimination and institutional racism, as well as cultural misunderstanding or misinterpretation.

The assessment process should maintain a focus on the needs of the individual child. It should always include consideration of the way religious beliefs and cultural traditions in different racial, ethnic and cultural groups influence their values, attitudes and behaviour, and the way in which family and community life is structured and organised. Cultural factors neither explain nor condone acts of omission or commission which place a child at risk of significant harm. Professionals should be aware of and work with the strengths and support systems available within families, ethnic groups and communities, which can be built upon to help safeguard children and promote their welfare.

Professionals should guard against myths and stereotypes – both positive and negative – of black and minority ethnic families. Anxiety about being accused of racist practice should not prevent the necessary action being taken to safeguard and promote a child's welfare. Careful assessment – based on evidence – of a child's needs, and a family's strengths and difficulties, understood in the context of the wider social environment, will help to avoid any distorting effect of these influences on professional judgments.

Children from black and minority ethnic groups (and their parents) are likely to have experienced harassment, racial discrimination and institutional racism. Although racism can cause significant harm it is not, in itself, a category of abuse. The experience of racism is likely to affect the responses of the child and family to assessment and enquiry processes. Failure to consider the effects of racism will undermine efforts to protect children from other forms of significant harm. The effects of racism differ for different communities and individuals, and should not be assumed to be uniform. The specific needs of children of mixed parentage and refugee children should be given attention. In particular, the need for neutral, high quality, gender-appropriate translation or interpretation services should be taken into account when working with children and families whose preferred language is not English. All organisations working with children, including those operating in areas where black and minority ethnic communities are numerically small, should address institutional racism, defined in the Macpherson Inquiry Report on Stephen Lawrence as 'the collective failure by an organisation to provide an appropriate and professional service to people on account of their race, culture and/or religion'.

The Public Law Outline Guide to Case Management in Public Law Proceedings and the accompanying Practice Direction for Experts in Family Proceedings related to Children both address the issue of diversity in relation to court proceedings. In aiming to improve the management of cases, the case management guide now sets out what has to be addressed by courts (and therefore the parties) at each stage of the proceedings as follows:

> 'At each case management stage of the proceedings . . . the court will consider giving directions regarding the obtaining of evidence

about the ethnicity, language, religion and culture of the child and other significant persons involved in the proceedings. The court will subsequently consider the implications of this evidence for the child in the context of the issues in the case.'

In addition, the Practice Direction for Experts makes clear experts should:

'In expressing an opinion take into consideration all of the material facts including any relevant factors arising from ethnic, cultural, religious or linguistic contexts at the time the opinion is expressed, identifying the facts, literature and any other material including research material that the expert has relied upon in forming an opinion.'

See also **5.38**.

Diversity in Court

5.84 It is important to remain vigilant over matters of ethnicity, language, religion, culture, gender and vulnerability in relation to the child, dealings with parents and the family and the issues in each case. Professionals should consider the information needed by the court to address diverse cultural contexts. Local authority solicitors should seek to ensure that applications make clear at an early stage the family's race, language, culture and religion. It is important, in addition to providing the descriptive information, to bring to the court's attention the substantive relevance and significance, if any, of the cultural context in each particular case, and to ensure that any assessments of the family have been conducted in a culturally-appropriate manner. Solicitors for all the parties should consider what directions are necessary to ensure that relevant evidence on culturally diverse contexts is available to the court. Professionals should also be sensitive to the services needed by disabled children and adults. For example:

- consider in advance access to the court room;
- consider additional services that might be offered in the context of the care plan and whether venues for therapeutic services are accessible by the child;
- check that contact venues are suitable for both the child and adults involved.

Any perceived need for special facilities should be made known to the court as soon as possible.

Source:
Law Society's Guide
to Good Practice

CHAPTER SIX

INTERPROFESSIONAL ISSUES

THE NEED TO WORK TOGETHER

6.1 The key skill requirement in multi-agency, inter-disciplinary working is not to be able to think like a professional from a different discipline, but to understand how other professions think and to know the legal and knowledge boundaries within which they work. It also requires a capacity to manage task-related anxiety associated with working with people in distress. Failure to manage that anxiety can erode inter-professional boundaries and impede collaboration between practitioners. Inter-agency work is essential within the family justice system.

In those exceptional cases where a child has died or been seriously injured and there has been some kind of examination of the circumstances leading to the death, the reports have criticised the quality of inter-agency co-operation. First voiced in the Cleveland Report in 1987 (the impetus for the Children Act 1989), the theme was expressed as long ago as 1991 in the Orkney Report:

> 'While there is a general recognition that in cases of child sexual abuse it is important to follow the course of a "joint approach" there is some lack of clarity in the understanding of that principle and how it should operate in practice. Even the terms "co-operation", "collaboration", and "co-ordination" are each open to definition. …. There is rightly a growing understanding that child protection is the business of all the agencies not the monopoly of one. It is plainly not sufficient to define it in terms of a requirement for all agencies to work with the common end of securing the welfare of the child as if all were united as one agency. The distinct statutory functions and duties of the principal agencies, the police and the social work department, have to be recognised and respected. The welfare of the child is the consideration which is to be given priority in resolving any problems of procedure or action. The essence of the joint approach is a full sharing of the information and intentions of each agency

so that the action of one is not prejudiced by any action of the other. It does not imply that all must be involved in any action which must be taken by any one but that there is a synthesis and harmony in the actions of all of them with a view to creating the greatest benefit and the least disturbance to the child whose interests are paramount.'

One particular practical advantage of co-operation is ensuring that tasks such as medical examinations or interviewing, which more than one authority wish to carry out, are arranged and carried out jointly so as to avoid the child being subjected to unnecessary repetition of such experiences. But the co-operation does not end there. There should be the fullest sharing of information and thinking.

Working Together, ever since its publication in 1991 (and in 2006 on its third time of publication) has emphasised joint training and the need for local procedures to standardise the handling of inter-agency issues.

Working Together to Safeguard Children (DfES, 2006) www.dcsf.gov.uk/ everychildmatters

Following the criticism of non-co-operation in the *Climbié Report* in 2003 (see **3.47** and **4.40**), the Children Act 2004 states categorically that it is the responsibility of the Local Safeguarding Children Boards (LSCBs) to ensure that multi-agency training on safeguarding and promoting the welfare of children which meets local needs is provided. The 2004 Act also established the principles which guide the LSCBs' tasks generally, namely that they should be:

For more information about Local Safeguarding Children Boards see **3.83**

- child centred;
- rooted in child development;
- supporting the achievement of the best possible outcomes for children and improving their wellbeing;
- holistic in approach;
- ensuring equality of opportunity;
- involving of children and families;
- building on strengths as well as identifying and addressing difficulties;
- multi/inter-agency in its approach;
- a continuing process, not an event;
- designed to provide the services required and monitor the impact their provision has on a child's developmental progress;
- informed by evidence.

The Public Law Outline and the new statutory guidance for local authorities (see **3.23** onwards) in April 2008, state that stronger relationships between agencies are vital and that inter-agency working remains a key area for improvement. They re-affirm the ongoing measures to address these issues, such as the establishment of the Local Family Justice Councils (see **1.15**).

They also state that there is scope to improve the extent to which the many agencies working within the child care proceedings system interact in terms of process improvements, resource management and working culture. It is suggested that further work looking at how greater use of joint targets and funds across agencies might encourage joint planning and shared priorities (ie pooling budget resources rather than sharing a single budget):

> 'That will address the issue flagged above that any improvements to the system must be holistic to avoid merely shifting resource issues from one agency to another. Pooled budgets would have a long-term impact and are more likely to be used to enhance qualitative value while maintaining costs. Their impact is likely to be indirect, through the creation of attitudes where constructive cost reduction proposals are more likely to arise.'

However, this was quickly followed by the news of the tragic case of Baby Peter later in 2008 which brought about yet further criticism of poor interagency working. The Government remains committed to improvements in this area. The *Every Child Matters: Change for Children* programme sets out a model for change with integration at every level. It also sets out how services for children and young people need to be coordinated and built around their needs.

The Children's plan: Building brighter futures (December 2007) described the Government's vision of a system-wide reform to the way services for children and young people work together. It aimed to provide services that made more sense to the parents, children and young people using them, for whom professional boundaries can appear arbitrary and frustrating, by locating services under one roof in the places people visit frequently. *Building brighter futures: Next steps for the children's workforce* (April 2008) reiterated the importance for everyone working with children, young people and families to: understand the difference they can make to children and young people's outcomes;

know how they need to work with other professionals to ensure that services are integrated and personalised to respond to the needs and strengths of individual children; and have the skills, knowledge and expertise to do their job to world-class standards. In May 2008, *Making It Happen* was published to support the development and implementation of more effective front-line integrated working practice across the children's workforce.

Alongside the publication of *Building brighter futures*, the Government set up an Expert Group of workforce champions to ensure that the experience of people who work with children, young people and families directly informs the development and production of a long term strategy for development of a world class children's workforce to be published in the autumn of 2008. It is hoped that Children's Trusts will, by 2010, have in place high quality arrangements for early intervention for children and young people with additional needs. The Expert Group was to consider:

- how we develop and build consensus around a vision for integrated working and ensure accountability for delivery of that vision;
- how we support Children's Trusts to meet the 2010 expectation;
- how we achieve culture change across all children's services, including in schools and health.

The Children's Workforce Development Council is responsible for implementation of integrated working.

The need for inter-disciplinary co-operation has also grown in the private law area. The benefits of mediation in child-centred parental disputes are now well-recognised and the legal profession is confident in recommending clients to mediation in matters of contact, residence and parental responsibility. There is still some reticence amongst lawyers (and judges) to refer couples to mediation in order to resolve financial and property disputes even though children issues and financial issues are often inextricably linked. This resistance is not helped by the fact that children issues are heard in courts under one set of proceedings under the Children Act 1989, while for married persons and same sex registered partners finance and property issues are dealt with in separate 'ancillary relief' proceedings under the Matrimonial Causes Act 1973 and the Civil Partnership Act 2004, respectively.

In August 2009, as part of its Care Proceedings Programme, the Ministry of Justice published a best practice guide for use by all professionals involved with children and families pre-proceedings, and in preparation for applications made under s 31 of the Children Act 1989, entitled '*Preparing for Care and Supervision Proceedings*'. It sets out examples and puts forward suggestions as to how all professionals can work together, valuing and understanding the work and roles of colleagues, and aims to put the needs of the child firmly back at the heart of care proceedings.

The guide is to complement the Statutory Guidance and Public Law Outline but it is not intended to be prescriptive. It has no legal status. However, it describes the processes involved; the respective roles of those involved; tackles some of the most difficult and frequently raised areas of uncertainty; and provides examples of good practice. It is also intended to act as a signpost towards the regulations and Statutory Guidance on specific issues and is one of a range of measures aimed at developing a consistent and practical approach to care proceedings. The guide has the full support of the National Family Justice Board. It is separated into two parts: Chapter 2 covers the pre-proceedings stages up to the point that a CA 1989 section 31 application is issued at court. Chapter 3 looks at the stages from the point that the LA issues a CA 1989 section 31 application through to disposal of the application and conclusion of the proceedings. In particular, its Annexes contain template examples of an 'Immediate Issue Letter', a 'Letter notifying a child about a Pre-Proceedings Meeting', and 'a template list of potential agenda items for a Pre-Proceedings Meeting', which are useful extensions of previous guidance.

THE NEED TO TRAIN AND DEVELOP TOGETHER

The Common Core of Skills and Knowledge for the Children's Workforce (DfES, 2005) www.dcsf.gov.uk/ everychildmatters/

6.2 The impetus of the Children Act 2004 is that those working with children and with adults who are parents or carers must have the knowledge and skills to carry out their own roles, but they must also be able to work effectively with others both within their own agency and across organisational boundaries, best achieved by a combination of single-agency and multi-agency training. Individual agencies are responsible for ensuring that their staff are competent and confident to carry out their responsibilities. The *Common Core of Skills and Knowledge for the Children's Workforce* (DOH, 2005, accessible at www.dcsf.gov.uk/everychildmatters/) sets out six areas of expertise that everyone working with children, young people and families, including those who work as volunteers, need to demonstrate. These are:

(1) effective communication and engagement with children, young people and their families and carers;

(2) child and young person development;

(3) safeguarding and promoting the welfare of the child;

(4) supporting transitions;

(5) multi-agency working;

(6) sharing information.

The Concept of Operations study was established in December 2006 with a remit to investigate the common features of observed effective frontline practice in integrated working, with a focus on the practicalities of how staff worked together on a day-to-day basis. Included in the study was an assessment of the extent to which ICT had helped or hindered integrated working.

Focus interviews were held in 2007 with seven local authorities and their partners. These authorities had been nominated for good practice. Current evaluation literature was reviewed to gather information for the study. The report describes the typical characteristics of effective integrated working, typical structures and processes, and typical interventions found in the nominated areas. It also includes conclusions and recommended next steps. Examples of strategic level documents supporting integrated working, case studies and generic process maps are presented in the appendices of the report, which can be downloaded from the DCSF ('Every Child Matters') website. The two main findings were that:

• integrated working in the areas nominated as good practice was fundamentally based on personal relationships that, although currently effective, may not be sustainable;

• in the areas visited there is general and anecdotal evidence of impact on individual cases; however, it was thought to be too early to measure overall impact on outcomes.

www.dcsf.gov.uk/
everychildmatters

The key conclusion of the study was that integrated working seems to be developing as a two stage process – initially creation of a locally integrated team where effective integrated working is based on strong personal relationships, and the second stage being creation of a fully integrated, sustainable service based on professional relationships, supported by IT tools. The first stage is referred to in the report as implementing 'localised' integrated working and the second stage as mainstreaming integrated working. Further updated guidance is available from the Every Child Matters website.

Training delivered on a multi-agency basis is a highly effective way of promoting a common and shared understanding of the respective roles and responsibilities of different professionals and contributes to effective working relationships. It should create an ethos which values working collaboratively with others, respects diversity (including culture, race and disability), promotes equality, is child-centred and promotes the participation of children and families in the processes. It should help develop and foster:

- a shared understanding of the tasks, processes, principles, roles and responsibilities outlined in national guidance and local arrangements for safeguarding children and promoting their welfare;

- more effective and integrated services at both the strategic and individual case level;

- improved communications between professionals, including a common understanding of key terms, definitions and thresholds for action;

- effective working relationships, including an ability to work in multi-disciplinary groups or teams; and

- sound decision-making based on information sharing, thorough assessment, critical analysis and professional judgment.

Information sharing

6.3 Recognising that most decisions to share information require professional judgment, cross-Government guidance was published in October 2008 with the aim of improving practice by giving practitioners clearer guidance on when and how they can share information legally and professionally about an individual with whom they are in contact. It seeks to provide clarity on the legal framework for practitioners sharing information and give practitioners confidence in making decisions. The guidance, originally published in April 2006, has been brought up-to-date to reflect current policy and extended to cover practitioners working with adults and families as well as those working with children and young people. The guidance is for front-line practitioners who have to make decisions about sharing personal information on a case-by-case basis, and also for managers and advisors who support these practitioners in their decision-making and for others with responsibility for information governance.

The guidance was developed in partnership between the Department for Children Schools and Families (DCSF) with the Department for Communities and Local Government (DCLG) and in consultation with a wide range of practitioner, national organisations and representative bodies and this, as well as other helpful guidance, can be downloaded from the Every Child Matters website.

www.dcsf.gov.uk/
everychildmatters

An Inclusive Curriculum for Continuing Professional Development

6.4   The Family Justice Council has concerned itself with a range of educational matters, particularly relating to the expansion of the inter-disciplinary knowledge base with which a wide range of practitioners need to be familiar. An 'inclusive curriculum' resulted from 3 years' work by representatives from the judiciary, family law barristers and solicitors, child psychiatry, paediatrics, counselling, social work, the magistracy and law and social work academics. This post-qualifying curriculum is for those who work with vulnerable children and families within the court system and lists the broad areas of the curriculum which should be considered for inclusion by anyone designing either single- or multi-disciplinary continuing education for 'family justice professionals' or those who provide a more 'intermittent' service to the courts.

The curriculum is available on www.family-justice-council. org.uk

There follows a summary of the suggested modules. The complete curriculum is available on the Family Justice Council's website at: www.family-justice-council.org.uk – our work – papers drafted by our committees.

Module 1: Frameworks for understanding children and families

1. Child and adolescent development
2. Family relationships and dynamics, parenting patterns
3. Disability and its consequences
4. Children's psychological development and emotional and behavioural difficulties

Module 2: Children, family and human rights legislation; legal and administrative processes

1. The development of the international and UK legal framework to safeguard children's health and well-being
2. The family law system: the role, structure and jurisdiction of the different courts
3. The Human Rights Act 1998 and the UN Convention on the Rights of the Child
4. The Children Act 1989 – public law provisions and its interaction with the Adoption and Children Act 2002 as it concerns looked after children
5. Legal provisions, and the roles and duties of councils with social services responsibilities in respect of children who may be suffering significant harm or who are accommodated, in care or placed for adoption. This will include knowledge about the range of regulations, guidance, performance indicators, standards documents and inspection systems
6. The Children Act 1989 (Parts I and II) – private law provisions
7. The Adoption and Children Act 2002
8. Other ways in which the legislation and the family court might be involved, eg education, homelessness and child abduction
9. The different family court professionals and the settings in which they work, including the voluntary sector and self-help groups – their roles, training, expertise and what each party or colleague might expect of them
10. Practice and procedure in preparation and at court

Module 3: Support and therapy for vulnerable children, their parents and carers

1. Professionals involved in providing support, advocacy and therapy: their role, training, expertise and what other professionals and family members might expect of them

2. Communicating with children

3. Communicating with parents in difficult circumstances

4. Assessment – when and how?

5. Interventions – where, when and by which professional(s)

6. Out-of-home placement as family support or long-term care

LANGUAGE, CONVENTION, CUSTOM AND PRACTICE

6.5 When professionals appear in the family courts dress, demeanour, use of language and clarity of expression are some of the facts upon which first impressions can be based. Stereotyping is, to some extent, an inevitable part of social life but its danger lies in its capacity to obstruct the decision-making process:

> ' . . . if what is being said is valued according to who is saying it, then valuable evidence may be ignored or distorted. Certain professionals (eg doctors and eminent academics) may automatically be accorded more "expert" status simply because of their breadth of knowledge, the fluency of their delivery or their capacity to produce "hard facts". Others, such as foster carers or family centre workers might produce "soft" evidence based on an observation of a particular child in question. In decision-making, however, it is judging the content rather than the performance which matters.'

Source:
Welfare of the Child
(Magistrates
Association, 2000)

It is not only in court but throughout working life that stereotyping inevitably occurs. Professional practices are socially constructed by the context in which professionals work. For example, mediators, who are drawn from many professions and then trained as mediators (eg social workers, lawyers, teachers and doctors), can revert to the particular habits of the profession from which they came when faced with a tricky situation in a mediation session.

Just as professionals find comfort and security in their own cultures of language and custom, so do practices differ geographically, despite the efforts of most professions to work towards national standards. Nowhere is this clearer than in the courts themselves where there are different approaches by different judges and, indeed, by different levels of judges across the country. A lack of judicial continuity in family cases has bedevilled the system for many years but now case management by the courts is a key factor in avoiding delay and ensuring enforcement of proceedings. (See the new Private Law Programme at **3.22** and the Public Law Outline at **3.23**.) The Family Justice Council can, through the Local Family Justice Councils, act as a force for unity of procedures.

National guidelines and codes of practice go a long way towards the standardisation of job descriptions, but it would be impossible to standardise how a job is done because to do so would ignore local pressures and requirements. Nothing is better than joining multi-disciplinary local groups and creating local networks in order to find out the language, conventions, customs and practices of other professionals. The Local Family Justice Councils are a focal point for all such activities.

Codes of Practice: General

6.6 Familiarisation with one's own professional national standards is essential: an appreciation of those of other professions is a start. Members of a profession have obligations to their clients, to their employers, to colleagues including those in other disciplines, and to society in general. These duties are contained in each profession's code of practice.

Social Workers

6.7 Local authorities work with limited resources, and children's services budgets do not expand to meet the needs arising. Limited resources have to be rationed between different clients and a priority system has to be put in place. Social workers are not independent but are employees within a bureaucracy. Social care departments establish systems and procedures for decision-making which limit the discretion social workers have.

Social Work Codes of Practice

6.8 The first UK-wide codes of practice for social care workers and employers were launched in 2002. Produced by the General Social Care Council (GSCC) one code provides a clear guide for all those who work in social care, setting out the standards of practice and conduct workers should meet. The other is a code for employers.

Section 62 of the Care Standards Act 2000 requires the GSCC to produce the codes and to keep them under review. The codes were developed following extensive consultation with social care workers, service users and carers in 2002. The codes mean that, for the first time, the social care sector has similar regulation to doctors and nurses. Registered social care workers who breach the codes could be removed from the Social Care Register.

Source: General Social Care Council www.gscc.org.uk

Over time, it is expected that employers will introduce code compliance as a contractual requirement for all their staff. If an employer feels an issue brings a worker's registration into question, a registered social care worker can be referred to the GSCC, which will investigate and consider whether their case should be heard at a conduct hearing. The Commission for Social Care Inspection (CSCI) takes the Code of Practice for Social Care Employers into account when enforcing care standards.

The code states that social care workers must:

- protect the rights and promote the interests of service users and carers;
- strive to establish and maintain the trust and confidence of service users and carers;
- promote the independence of service users while protecting them as far as possible from danger or harm;
- respect the rights of service users whilst seeking to ensure that their behaviour does not harm themselves or other people;
- uphold public trust and confidence in social care services; and
- be accountable for the quality of their work and take responsibility for maintaining and improving their knowledge and skills.

The essential points of the Code are as follows:

1　As a social care worker, you must protect the rights and promote the interests of service users and carers.

This includes:

1.1　Treating each person as an individual;

1.2　Respecting and, where appropriate, promoting the individual views and wishes of both service users and carers;

1.3　Supporting service users' rights to control their lives and make informed choices about the services they receive;

1.4　Respecting and maintaining the dignity and privacy of service users;

1.5　Promoting equal opportunities for service users and carers; and

1.6　Respecting diversity and different cultures and values.

2　As a social care worker, you must strive to establish and maintain the trust and confidence of service users and carers.

This includes:

2.1　Being honest and trustworthy;

2.2　Communicating in an appropriate, open, accurate and straightforward way;

2.3　Respecting confidential information and clearly explaining agency policies about confidentiality to service users and carers;

2.4　Being reliable and dependable;

2.5　Honouring work commitments, agreements and arrangements and, when it is not possible to do so, explaining why to service users and carers;

2.6　Declaring issues that might create conflicts of interest and making sure that they do not influence your judgement or practice; and

2.7　Adhering to policies and procedures about accepting gifts and money from service users and carers.

3　As a social care worker, you must promote the independence of service users while protecting them as far as possible from danger or harm.

This includes:

3.1 Promoting the independence of service users and assisting them to understand and exercise their rights;

3.2 Using established processes and procedures to challenge and report dangerous, abusive, discriminatory or exploitative behaviour and practice;

3.3 Following practice and procedures designed to keep you and other people safe from violent and abusive behaviour at work;

3.4 Bringing to the attention of your employer or the appropriate authority resource or operational difficulties that might get in the way of the delivery of safe care;

3.5 Informing your employer or an appropriate authority where the practice of colleagues may be unsafe or adversely affecting standards of care;

3.6 Complying with employers' health and safety policies, including those relating to substance abuse;

3.7 Helping service users and carers to make complaints, taking complaints seriously and responding to them or passing them to the appropriate person; and

3.8 Recognising and using responsibly the power that comes from your work with service users and carers.

4   As a social care worker, you must respect the rights of service users while seeking to ensure that their behaviour does not harm themselves or other people.

This includes:

4.1 Recognising that service users have the right to take risks and helping them to identify and manage potential and actual risks to themselves and others;

4.2 Following risk assessment policies and procedures to assess whether the behaviour of service users presents a risk of harm to themselves or others;

4.3 Taking necessary steps to minimise the risks of service users from doing actual or potential harm to themselves or other people; and

4.4 Ensuring that relevant colleagues and agencies are informed about the outcomes and implications of risk assessments.

5 As a social care worker, you must uphold public trust and confidence in social care services.

In particular you must not:

5.1 Abuse, neglect or harm service users, carers or colleagues;

5.2 Exploit service users, carers or colleagues in any way;

5.3 Abuse the trust of service users and carers or the access you have to personal information about them or to their property, home or workplace;

5.4 Form inappropriate personal relationships with service users;

5.5 Discriminate unlawfully or unjustifiably against service users, carers or colleagues;

5.6 Condone any unlawful or unjustifiable discrimination by service users, carers or colleagues;

5.7 Put yourself or other people at unnecessary risk; or

5.8 Behave in a way, in work or outside work, which would call into question your suitability to work in social care services.

6 As a social care worker, you must be accountable for the quality of your work and take responsibility for maintaining and improving your knowledge and skills.

This includes:

6.1 Meeting relevant standards of practice and working in a lawful, safe and effective way;

6.2 Maintaining clear and accurate records as required by procedures established for your work;

6.3 Informing your employer or the appropriate authority about any personal difficulties that might affect your ability to do your job competently and safely;

6.4 Seeking assistance from your employer or the appropriate authority if you do not feel able or adequately prepared to carry out any aspect of your work, or you are not sure about how to proceed in a work matter;

6.5 Working openly and co-operatively with colleagues and treating them with respect;

6.6 Recognising that you remain responsible for the work that you have delegated to other workers;

6.7 Recognising and respecting the roles and expertise of workers from other agencies and working in partnership with them; and

6.8 Undertaking relevant training to maintain and improve your knowledge and skills and contributing to the learning and development of others.

The full GSCC Codes of Conduct can be viewed on www.gscc.org.uk.

GSCC Code of Conduct www.gscc.org.uk

Lawyers

6.9 A solicitor's and barrister's prime duty is to the client. While lawyers have a duty not to mislead the court, their main duty is to carry out the client's instructions. Fulfilling this duty is easier in an adversarial system where there are two opposing sides and each lawyer can be confident in looking after his own client's interests in the knowledge that another lawyer can look after those of the opponent. In theory however, the general approach to family law should be non-adversarial, or 'inquisitorial'.

Barristers

6.10 Barristers are usually self-employed and play a valuable role in the legal system as independent advocates or consultants. They are regulated by the Bar Standards Board, the independent regulatory board of the General Council of the Bar. The BSB publishes its own Code of Conduct and also has a complaints system.

The Code of Conduct is lengthy and can be checked online or be downloaded. Fundamental Principles to which barristers must adhere include not:

(a) engaging in conduct whether in pursuit of his profession or otherwise which is:

    (i) dishonest or otherwise discreditable to a barrister;

    (ii)   prejudicial to the administration of justice; or

    (iii) likely to diminish public confidence in the legal profession or the administration of justice or otherwise bring the legal profession into disrepute;

(b)   engaging directly or indirectly in any occupation if his association with that occupation may adversely affect the reputation of the Bar or in the case of a practising barrister prejudice his ability to attend properly to his practice.

A barrister has an overriding duty to the court to act with independence in the interests of justice: he/she must assist the court in the administration of justice and must not deceive or knowingly or recklessly mislead the court. Amongst other matters, he/she must promote and protect fearlessly and by all proper and lawful means the lay client's best interests and do so without regard to his/her own interests or to any consequences to him/herself or to any other person (including any professional client or other intermediary or another barrister).

In family proceedings, barristers also have the same duty as solicitors to the Legal Services Commission to ensure that public money is not wasted. Barristers cannot be instructed directly by a lay client in family proceedings, but must be instructed by solicitors.

Bar Council
Tel: 020 7242 0082
www.barcouncil.org.uk

(For more detail including about the barristers' Code of Conduct see **2.19**.)

Solicitors

6.11   Solicitors are the first point of contact for people who wish to engage the services of a lawyer. Solicitors work as employees of a firm of solicitors (see further **2.2**). Practice rule 1 of the *Guide to the Professional Conduct of Solicitors* (by the Law Society) states:

    'A solicitor shall not do anything in the course of practising as a solicitor which compromises or impairs any of the following:

- the solicitor's independence or integrity;

- a person's freedom to instruct a solicitor of his or her choice;

- the solicitor's duty to act in the best interests of the client;

- the good repute of the solicitor or the solicitor's profession;

- the solicitor's proper standard of work;
- the solicitor's duty to the court.'

The Law Society's Family Law Protocol

6.12   The Family Law Protocol is the Law Society's definitive guide to best practice in private law cases with which all solicitors practising family law in England and Wales should comply. The Protocol was written by the Law Society's Family Law Committee with the active support and close involvement of the (then) Lord Chancellor's Department, the (then) Solicitors' Family Law Association and the Legal Services Commission. Consultation was also undertaken to ensure that the views of practitioners and other interested parties were taken into account. Written in a clear, accessible style and appended by other relevant guidance, the Protocol offers practical advice to encourage a non-adversarial approach and effective and timely resolution of disputes. The protocol is intended to:

- encourage a constructive and conciliatory approach to the resolution of family disputes;
- encourage the narrowing of the issues in dispute, and the effective and timely resolution of disputes;
- endeavour to minimise any risks to the parties and/or the children and to alert the client to treat safety as a primary concern;
- have regard to the interests of the children and long-term family relationships;
- endeavour to ensure that costs are not unreasonably incurred.

A second edition of the Family Law Protocol was published in 2006. This edition has been produced (as was the first) by the Law Society in consultation with Resolution, the Legal Services Commission and the Department for Constitutional Affairs. The redrafting of the Protocol has enabled amendments to be made to accommodate changes in the way that family law is practised and changes in the law itself.

The Family Law Protocol can be found on www.lawsociety.org.uk/documents/downloads/ . . ./ familylawprotocol.pdf

Resolution's Code of Practice

6.13   This Code of Practice is designed to establish the principles of a constructive approach to family law

The Law Society
Tel: 020 7242 1222
www.lawsociety.org.uk

Family Law
Protocol
www.flp.lawsociety.org.uk

Resolution
Tel: 01689 820272
www.resolution.org.uk

matters. The Code is not a straitjacket, but Resolution members must adhere to the Code unless the law, professional rules or clear client instructions contradict it. The Code has been incorporated in the Law Society's Family Law Protocol and is the standard to which all family solicitors are expected to adhere.

The Code can be found on www.resolution.org.uk.

The Law Society's Good Practice in Child Care Cases

Law Society
Tel: 020 7242 1222
www.lawsociety.org.uk

6.14 For solicitors acting in public law Children Act cases, including those acting for children, the relevant guidance is the Law Society's Good Practice in Child Care Cases. It is a collection of concise good practice guidelines for all solicitors acting in public law Children Act cases, whether they are acting for a local authority, a parent, a child or another party. The guidance:

- sets out the general principles that need to be considered by all solicitors, whichever party they act for;

- includes common issues that need to be considered by all solicitors involved in public law Children Act proceedings;

- deals in particular with the role of solicitors acting for local authority clients;

- deals with matters to be considered when instructed by children or children's guardians;

- outlines the approach to be taken by solicitors when acting for parents and other adult parties;

- covers good practice in relation to other aspects of public law children cases, including adoption.

The first five parts have been written with care order applications in mind, but are intended to be of general assistance with client and professional relationships and the aspects of conduct covered are also relevant for other types of public law proceedings. The guidance also covers confidentiality issues, competence of the child and child's access to documents. The appendices include the Law Society's guidance on acting in the absence of a children's guardian (including the Practice Note on the same issue published on 25 August 2009 and temporarily replacing Appendix 8 of the guidance), and guidance issued jointly by the Law Society's Children Law Sub-committee and Cafcass on the working relationship between Children Panel solicitors and children's guardians. The aims of the guide are:

(1) To accompany the Law Society's Family Law Protocol, which does not cover public law cases involving children.

(2) To provide supportive guidance on the conduct of cases and the particular approach required for less experienced practitioners who are not yet members of the Law Society's Children Panel, and an aide-mémoire for more experienced practitioners.

(3) To ensure the highest standards of representation for children and their families affected by public law Children Act proceedings, addressing the needs of the client.

(4) To complement, but not duplicate, the Protocol for Judicial Case Management in Public Law Children Act Cases.

The guidance can be found on www.lawsociety.org.uk. This should be read in conjunction with the Law Society's Acting in the absence of a children's guardian which replaces Annex 8 of the 2004 Law Society Guide to Good Practice.

Cafcass Officers

6.15 Cafcass stands for the Children and Family Court Advisory Support Service. Cafcass is independent of the courts, social services, education and health authorities and all similar agencies. Cafcass operates within the law set by Parliament and under the rules and directions of the family courts. In carrying out their duties, Cafcass officers must have regard to the principles of the Children Act 1989 that children are generally best looked after within the family with both parents playing a full part without resort to legal proceedings, that the concept of parental responsibility is promoted and that the welfare of the child is the paramount consideration. They must also observe the principles of minimum intervention and minimum delay. The primary objective of all Cafcass family court welfare work is to assist the court, and their various reports filed in family proceedings usually carry significant weight.

The duties of children's guardians are laid down in court rules. Guardians come mostly from a social work and/or Cafcass officer background, and therefore will bring to the job the ethics and practices they have learnt and used in their previous work.

In 2009, requests for reports from Cafcass rose to record levels in both public and private children cases,

CAFCASS CYMRU
Tel: 02920 647979 (Cardiff)/
01352 744537/744538 (National Office, Mold)
Email: cafcasscymru@wales.gsi.gov.uk
www.wales.gov.uk/cafcasscymru

resulting in a serious backlog of work developing for Cafcass and extreme delays occurring in the procurement of Cafcass reports in these cases. As a result, on 11 August 2009 the President of the Family Division issued interim guidance for England on the allocation of Cafcass guardians in public law care proceedings as a matter of emergency to assist in reducing the mounting delays in the allocation of guardians in public law care proceedings and the production of reports in private law cases by Cafcass in England. This temporary arrangement provided for short term local agreements which were to include the allocation of duty guardians to advise on cases as necessary. The interim guidance was not a Practice Direction but was intended instead to create a framework for local arrangements as the best method of achieving necessary improvements to assist Cafcass to deliver its services. It was to put in place measures aimed at addressing the backlog of work which had developed whilst preventing backlogs arising in respect of new work in a planned and time limited way: a temporary solution to help in an emergency situation. The guidance was intended to cease to have effect on 31 March 2010 at which point it was expected that the backlog will have been substantially reduced. Discussions involving key bodies within the same time frame were to take place with a view to identifying how to achieve the enduring elimination of backlogs.

The President made clear in the guidance that it was to be recognised that, to the extent that the measures proposed might involve children's solicitors taking on case management tasks which had hitherto been regarded as functions of Cafcass the courts would have to proceed with caution and by consent, having satisfied themselves that the solicitors understood and accepted what was required of them within the public funding arrangements which applied to them. The full interim guidance for England can be downloaded from the free Family Law website: www.familylaw.co.uk/newswatch. The President's interim guidance for Wales published on 14 August 2009 is also available there. Separate guidance as to the implementation of the President's interim guidance for England specifically as relating to London Family Courts (as approved by Mr Justice Hedley, Family Division Liaison Judge for London) was subsequently published on 9 October 2009.

Subsequent to the publication of the interim guidance, Cafcass then published on its website its operating priorities to be effective until March 2010, setting out its reasoning behind the new priorities and the detail on how they were to be implemented. Many of the measures were attempts to reduce the backlog of cases including:

- freeing up Cafcass court staff to take 'snapshot' reviews of pending cases rather than full section 7 reports;

- cases not needing to be audited before closure;

- open cases, whether public or private, to be categorised as either active or 'watching brief' cases by agreement with the courts;

- cases that Cafcass think are lower priority to be notified to the judiciary.

A core part of the priorities was that all cases were to undergo a 'safeguarding analysis' though the definition of safeguarding remained 'a broad one, in line with our National Standards and Safeguarding Framework'. The agency stated that it would only be able to offer a 'safe minimum service' and the 'previous extent of planned work in long-running cases will only be possible in a limited number of the most exceptional cases'.

In September 2009, Community Care reported that Cafcass was to cut 70 jobs in an attempt to balance its books for 2009. The Government subsequently announced in its Children, Schools and Families Bill its plans to amend section 41 of the Children Act 1989 to appoint Cafcass the organisation rather than a named practitioner, to carry out the role and functions of the children's guardian. That was immediately challenged in October 2009 by a range of stakeholder organisations which grouped together to form the Interdisciplinary Alliance for Children which at the same time was voicing concerns about the government's proposals to permit media access to written evidence and reporting of the 'substance' of children cases. The Government withdrew its section 41 plans in the face of strong opposition from all sides.

At the time of writing, these issues remain live and unresolved, with professionals dealing with children cases expressed serious concerns. How matters develop during this period of crisis remains to be seen.

See further **2.55–2.85**.

Families and Relationships Green Paper

6.16 On 20 January 2010 the Government announced, as part of the cross-government Families and Relationships Green Paper published by the Department for Children, Schools and Families, a fundamental review of the family justice system. The Government stated that the review is to be undertaken by an expert panel made up of independent and government representatives to be appointed 'in the coming weeks', which will consider wider perspectives from a range of people involved in or experiencing the family justice system and which will include possible calls for evidence, focus groups and formal consultation as part of its work. It is to report back in 2011.

The following are amongst the proposals in the Paper:

- to improve flexible working for parents and family friendly employment rights;
- to review the family justice system to look at the best methods for avoiding confrontational court hearings;
- to consider making it compulsory for privately-funded clients of the family justice system to use mediation before having child access disputes heard in court – bringing it into line with the current system covering families represented by legal aid;
- to work with the Family Mediation Council to build on existing accreditation schemes for mediators;
- to give grandparents more recognition, improved legal rights for access and a dedicated website
- to consider additional rights for fathers including encouraging them to get more involved in their child's birth and up-bringing, including publishing a new 'Dad's Guide' to give to all new fathers.

Whether these new proposals will resolve the current crisis being experienced in the family justice system sufficiently, or in time, will become apparent soon enough.

Mediators

6.17 Mediators come from various professional backgrounds and will inevitably bring the culture of those professions to the job. In the days when mediators co-mediated, it was an excellent opportunity for the professions to pick up each other's language, conventions, custom and practice. Also, inter-professional mediators were generally trained together, which was another source of appreciation of different practices. To make mediation cheaper, and therefore more accessible to the clients, sole mediation is the norm, so one opportunity for learning from the practices of different professions has been lost. It would be a pity if the professions retreated into their own training ghettos and completely closed the door on each other.

The College of Mediators (previously known as UKCFM) has a Code of Practice which covers:

www.collegeofmediators.co.uk

(1) the scope of mediation;

(2) voluntary participation;

(3) neutrality;

(4) impartiality;

(5) independence and conflicts of interest;

(6) privilege and legal proceedings;

(7) welfare of children;

(8) abuse within the family;

(9) qualifications and training;

(10) the conduct of mediation.

The College has also published policies on domestic violence and children in mediation. All these documents can be viewed on www.collegeofmediators.co.uk.

The Family Mediation Council is also developing a Code, see www.familymediationcouncil.org.uk.

The Medical Profession

Guidance from the Ethics Department of the British Medical Association (BMA, June 2004)

6.18 Where doctors have concerns about a child who may be at risk of abuse or neglect, it is essential that these concerns are acted upon, in accordance with the guidance in this note, or other local and national protocols. The best interests of the child or children involved must guide decision-making at all times. Where suspicions of abuse or neglect have been raised, doctors must ensure that their concerns, and the actions they have either taken, or intend to take, including any discussion with colleagues or professionals in other agencies, are clearly recorded in the child or children's

British Medical Association
Tel: 0300 123 1233
www.bma.org.uk

medical record. Where doctors have raised concerns about a child with colleagues or with other agencies and no action is regarded as necessary, doctors must ensure that all individual concerns have been properly recognised and responded to. When working with children who may be at risk of neglect or abuse, doctors should judge each case on its merits, taking into consideration the likely degree of risk to the child or children involved. Disclosure of information between professionals from different agencies should always take place within an established system and be subject to a recognised protocol. This guidance applies equally to both information about children who may be subject to abuse, as well as to information about third parties, such as adults who may pose a threat to a child.

General Principles

6.19

- In child protection cases, a doctor's chief responsibility is to the well-being of the child or children concerned, therefore where a child is at risk of serious harm, the interests of the child override those of parents or carers.

- All doctors working with children, parents and other adults in contact with children should be able to recognise, and know how to act upon, signs that a child may be at risk of any form of abuse or neglect, not only in a home environment, but also in residential and other institutions.

- Efforts should be made to include children and young people in decisions which closely affect them. The views and wishes of children should therefore be listened to and respected according to their competence and the level of their understanding. In some cases translation services suitable for young people may be needed.

- Wherever possible, the involvement and support of those who have parental responsibility for, or regular care of, a child should be encouraged, insofar as this is in keeping with promoting the best interests of the child or children concerned. Older children and young people may have their own views about parental involvement.

- When concerns about deliberate harm to children or young people have been raised, doctors must keep clear, accurate, comprehensive and contemporaneous notes.

- All doctors working with children, parents and other adults in contact with children must be aware of, and have access at their place of work to, their local Area Child Protection Committee's Child Protection Procedure manual.

A tool kit has been available since 2009 to all subscribers to the BMA to provide a brief and accessible guide to doctors' responsibilities in child protection cases in England and Wales. The toolkit does not aim to be comprehensive, but rather to act as a prompt for doctors where they believe that a child may be at risk of neglect or abuse, and the focus of the tool kit is on safeguarding, particularly in relation to children who are at risk of significant harm. It is designed more for a general audience of health professionals than those with specific management responsibilities or child protection expertise. The tool kit contains a series of separate cards that highlight different aspects of the child protection process such as basic principles, definitions of abuse and neglect, responding to initial concerns and participation in statutory child protection procedures.

The General Medical Council's guidance

6.20   The GMC also emphasises the importance of listening to the patient, but gives specific advice about young patients who lack the ability to give valid and unpressured consent to disclosure.

General Medical Council
Tel: 0845 357 8001
Email: gmc@gmc-uk.org
www.gmc-uk.org

> 'If you believe a patient to be a victim of neglect or physical, sexual or emotional abuse and that the patient cannot give or withhold consent to disclosure, you should give information promptly to an appropriate responsible person or statutory agency, where you believe that the disclosure is in the patient's best interests. You should usually inform the patient that you intend to disclose the information before doing so. Such circumstances may arise in relation to children, where concerns about possible abuse need to be shared with other agencies such as social services. Where appropriate you should inform those with parental responsibility about the disclosure. If, for any reason, you believe that disclosure of information is not in the best interests of an abused or neglected patient, you must still be prepared to justify your decision.'

BMA guidance

British Medical
Association (BMA)
Tel: 0300 123 1233
www.bma.org.uk

6.21   As a result of the *Climbié* inquiry (see **3.47**, **4.40**
and **6.1**), the government published revised guidance for
all professionals directly involved in child protection,
What to do if you're Worried a Child is being Abused.
The BMA developed the guidance note in order to
highlight the particular ethical responsibilities that
doctors have when working with children who may be
at risk of harm or neglect. It aimed to augment and
expand upon the government's guidance, and was based
in part on enquiries to the BMA's Ethics Department
from doctors. Doctors and health care workers who
require more detailed clinical information about
assessing the needs of vulnerable children should refer
at the outset to the government's publication *Framework
for the Assessment of Children in Need and their
Families* (see **5.41**).

CODES OF PRACTICE: CONFIDENTIALITY

6.22   The legal system has developed rules about
confidentiality and disclosure (see **4.41** onwards). The
professions also have their own rules, or codes of
practice. There will always be a conflict between
encouraging people to be frank and open while at the
same time facing up to the consequences of such
frankness. Where there are good grounds for concern
about the safety of a child or other person, a
confidence will always be broken. Below is set out the
relevant advice taken from professional guidances.

Solicitors Acting for Children

6.23   When acting for any child, the duty of
confidentiality exists as it does for the adult client. This
duty always exists, save in the exceptional circumstances
summarised below. The child client should be made
aware of the duty of confidentiality and when and how
the solicitor's duty of confidentiality may be breached
in appropriate circumstances. This should also be
explained, if possible, to any younger, less mature child
in an appropriate way and according to his level of
understanding, after consultation with the children's
guardian.

Where a children's guardian is appointed, it is
important for solicitors to ensure that the mature child
consents to information being given to the children's

guardian (who is not a client). Even if no potential conflict exists, consent should still be obtained.

What any child tells his solicitor is subject to the solicitor's duty of confidentiality. The child should be advised, as appropriate (in practice this is likely to apply to the mature child), that if the child wants a discussion to be confidential it should be with the child's solicitor, subject to the exceptions below applying. What the child tells the children's guardian is not confidential. However, if, for example, the child will only tell the solicitor with whom he wants to live, and asks for this not to be disclosed, the solicitor should explain to the child that the child's views will not be known if the child insists on confidentiality. If the child's solicitor finds himself to be in conflict with the children's guardian, the duty of confidentiality is owed to the client (ie the child). No information should be disclosed to the children's guardian, or any other person, without the child's consent, unless an exception to the solicitor's duty of confidentiality applies.

It may be necessary to breach confidentiality in relation to a child against the child client's wishes:

(a) Where the child reveals information which indicates continuing sexual or other physical abuse, but refuses to allow disclosure of such information, the solicitor must consider whether the threat to the child's life or health, both mental and physical, is sufficiently serious to justify a breach of the duty of confidentiality.

(b) There is a duty to disclose experts' reports obtained in the course of proceedings even if adverse.

(c) In relation to disclosure of adverse material not obtained within the course of proceedings, in exceptional cases to do otherwise would breach the solicitor's duty not to mislead the court.

(d) Where the solicitor is summoned as a witness or subpoenaed, the court may direct the solicitor to disclose documentation or divulge information.

However, solicitors should always bear in mind that they owe a duty of confidentiality to their clients and may have to justify any breach of that duty to their professional body.

Source:
Good Practice in Child Care Cases (Law Society, 2004) and Guide to Good Practice (Law Society, 2004)

Law Society Guidance on Circumstances which Override Confidentiality Generally

6.24   The duty to keep a client's confidences can be overridden in certain exceptional circumstances.

(1)   The duty of confidentiality does not apply to information acquired by a solicitor where he is being used by the client to facilitate the commission of a crime or fraud, because that is not within the scope of a professional retainer. If the solicitor becomes suspicious about a client's activities, the solicitor should normally assess the situation in the light of the client's explanations and the solicitor's professional judgment.

(2)   Express consent by a client to disclosure of information relating to his affairs overrides any duty of confidentiality, as does consent by the personal representatives of a deceased client.

(3)   A solicitor may reveal confidential information to the extent that he believes necessary to prevent the client or a third party committing a criminal act that the solicitor believes on reasonable grounds is likely to result in serious bodily harm.

(4)   There may be exceptional circumstances involving children where a solicitor should consider revealing confidential information to an appropriate authority. This may be where the child is the client and the child reveals information which indicates continuing sexual or other physical abuse but refuses to allow disclosure of such information. Similarly, there may be situations where an adult discloses abuse either by himself or by another adult against a child but refuses to allow any disclosure. The solicitor must consider whether the threat to the child's life or health, both mental and physical, is sufficiently serious to justify a breach of the duty of confidentiality.

(5)   In proceedings under the Children Act 1989, solicitors are under a duty to reveal experts' reports commissioned for the purposes of proceedings, as these reports are not privileged. The position in relation to voluntary disclosure of other documents or solicitor/client communications is uncertain. Clearly advocates are under a duty not to mislead the court. Therefore, if an advocate has certain knowledge which he realises is adverse to the client's case, the solicitor

may be extremely limited in what can be stated in the client's favour. In this situation, the solicitor should seek the client's agreement for full voluntary disclosure for three reasons:

(i)   the matters the client wants to hide will probably emerge anyway;

(ii)   the solicitor will be able to do a better job for the client if all the relevant information is presented to the court;

(iii)   if the information is not voluntarily disclosed, the solicitor may be severely criticised by the court.

If the client refuses to give the solicitor authority to disclose the relevant information, the solicitor is entitled to refuse to continue to act for the client if to do so will place the solicitor in breach of his obligations to the court.

Source:
Guide to the Professional Conduct of Solicitors (Law Society, 1999, www.guide-on-line.lawsociety.org.uk)

Medical Confidentiality

6.25   Medical confidentiality is now generally respected for children long before the age of legal responsibility and probably from the age of about 12 providing they have full understanding and there is no information relevant to a criminal investigation (see **4.14** for a description of the *Gillick* case and children's rights). The status of being a parent gives some strong entitlement to information about the child but it does not override the right of the mature child to confidentiality. Even with younger children, parents have an obligation (which is an aspect of parental responsibility), to treat information about their child's health as confidential.

Competent patients may apply for access to their own records, or may authorise a third party, such as their lawyer, to do so on their behalf. Parents may have access to their child's records if this is in the child's best interests and not contrary to a competent child's wishes. People appointed by a court to manage the affairs of mentally incapacitated adults may have access to information necessary to fulfil their function. The main exemptions are that information must not be disclosed if it:

•   is likely to cause serious physical or mental harm to the patient or another person; or

- relates to a third party who has not given consent for disclosure (where that third party is not a health professional who has cared for the patient).

Children's Guardians and Cafcass Officers

6.26 See **4.41** onwards.

Local Authorities

General Social Care
Council
Tel: 0845 070 0630
www.gscc.org.uk

6.27 For the General Social Care Council codes of practice on confidentiality see **6.8**.

The British Association of Social Workers' (BASW) code of ethics states, as regards privacy, confidentiality and records, that social workers will:

a. Respect service users' rights to a relationship of trust, to privacy, reliability and confidentiality and to the responsible use of information obtained from or about them.

b. Observe the principle that information given for one purpose may not be used for a different purpose without the permission of the informant.

c. Consult service users about their preferences in respect of the use of information relating to them.

d. Divulge confidential information only with the consent of the service user or informant, except where there is clear evidence of serious risk to the service user, worker, other persons or the community, or in other circumstances judged exceptional on the basis of professional consideration and consultation, limiting any such breach of confidence to the needs of the situation at the time.

e. Offer counselling as appropriate throughout the process of a service user's access to records.

f. Ensure, so far as it is in their power, that records, whether manual or electronic, are stored securely, are protected from unauthorised access, and are not transferred, manually or electronically, to locations where access may not be satisfactorily controlled.

g. Record information impartially and accurately, recording only relevant matters and specifying the source of information.

h.   The sharing of records across agencies and professions, and within a multi-purpose agency, is subject to ethical requirements in respect of privacy and confidentiality. Service users have a right of access to all information recorded about them, subject only to the preservation of other persons' rights to privacy and confidentiality.

British Association
of Social Workers
Tel: 0121 622 3911
www.basw.co.uk

For government guidance on information sharing see **4.41** onwards.

For the full BASW Code of Ethics see www.basw.co.uk.

For guidance on information sharing see **4.39–4.44**.

Mediation

6.28   Confidentiality is essential if there is to be full and frank discussion within the mediation process. The promise of confidentiality by the mediator is not absolute and cannot prevent the disclosure of information in the exceptional situation where there is substantial risk to the life, health or safety of children, the parties or anyone else. See further the College of Mediators Code of Practice at www.collegeofmediators.co.uk and Policies and Standards and the Family Mediation Code of Practice at www.familymediationcouncil.org.uk.

RECORD-KEEPING, DOCUMENTS AND EVIDENCE

6.29   Every agency in which staff work with children has to have a policy on record-keeping which includes giving all children and parents access to records. Records have to be accurate and clear and contain all the information known to the agency about the child and family. Records need to reflect all the work which is being done by the workers within the agency and should also indicate working arrangements with staff in other agencies.

There must be best practice in recording information on social care files based on key principles of partnership, openness and accuracy. Social care departments should have a policy framework that expresses the values and principles underpinning recording practice. There should be a statement of purpose of recording, definition of documents to be routinely copied to users, statements of access, public information on social care department policy and practice and agreements on information provided by other agencies. All personal data must be adequate, relevant and not excessive for the purpose for which it is held, kept up to date and not kept for longer than is necessary for its purpose.

Child Protection Register/Child Protection Plans

6.30 Prior to 1 April 2008, every local authority had to maintain a central register which listed all the children in its area considered to be suffering from or likely to suffer from significant harm and for whom there was a child protection plan. The plans were reviewed every 6 months. The register recorded, amongst other things, the names of the child's social worker, GP, health visitor and school. Names of known or alleged abusers were entered on the register with caution and only when there is a direct link with the child. The register had no statutory force: it was a management tool which recorded the fact that a child has been abused or was at risk. Access to the register was restricted to those professionals who were offering services direct to the child. There had to be careful control over access to the information since there was normally little or no judicial check on what the register contained, although the placing of a person's name on the register could be reviewed, in exceptional circumstances, by the courts.

In *Working Together to Safeguard Children* (2006), the Government announced that the maintenance of a separate child protection register would be phased out by 1 April 2008. The functionality of the register was replaced by the Integrated Children's System (ICS) and, more specifically, through the existence of a child protection plan. Each child whose name was on the child protection register then became the subject of a child protection plan (see paragraphs 5.93–5.100 in *Working Together*). New cases which would have been added to the register then became the subject of a child protection plan. When cases were de-registered, their child protection plans came to an end.

Documents as Evidence

6.31 Evidence in court consists of oral evidence as well as other categories of evidence: documentary (which includes audio and video tapes and photographs) and real. Reports and written statements are, by definition, documentary evidence. See further **4.74–4.78**.

Access to Records by Children's Guardians

6.32   Section 42 of the Children Act 1989 gives the guardians the right to have access to the records of, or held by, the local authority in relation to a child and compiled in connection with any function of the social services committee under the Local Authority Social Services Act 1970. It does not extend to records held by the Crown Prosecution Service (CPS). The reasoning is that if the guardian puts material from the CPS records in the report it would come to the attention of all the parties. The only thing the local authority and guardian can do is go to court and apply for leave for the records to be disclosed. In practice, arrangements can be entered into at a local level to allow guardians access to CPS files or, alternatively, to disclose files to the local authority so as to permit inspection by the guardian. Such local protocols are of great benefit in that they facilitate rather than hamper a guardian's investigations.

The Guardian's Analysis (Report)

6.33   The guardian's 'analysis' or report is a confidential document and the confidentiality lies with the court, not with the maker of the report, so court leave must be given to disclose the report to those who are not parties to the proceedings. The confidentiality continues after the conclusion of the hearing; therefore, if a local authority wishes to reveal a report's contents to the police or if the police wish to see a report, leave of the court will be required.

Child's Access to Documents held by Solicitor

6.34   The solicitor is generally under a duty to allow all clients, including child clients, unfettered access to any relevant documentary evidence which the solicitor holds, save where such evidence would adversely affect the client's physical or mental condition. Generally, as a matter of good practice, there may be exceptional cases, such as serious child sexual abuse, when the nature of the document is such that it would be inappropriate for clients to be sent a copy of the document.

When representing a child, solicitors should be particularly careful about showing documents to their client. Where solicitors are instructed by a children's guardian, they should discuss sending any documentation, and requests for documentation made by the child, with the children's guardian. If in any doubt as to whether a document should be disclosed to a child giving direct instructions, the solicitor should seek the opinion of the children's guardian or another professional involved in the case. Ultimately, directions can be sought from the court as to non-disclosure.

Source:
Guide to Good Practice
(Law Society, 2004)

Care should be exercised before copies of documents are given to child clients to keep. It is likely to be inappropriate to send a child client copies of documentation through the post. It is likely to be more appropriate to visit the child and talk the child through the documentation. Solicitors acting for a child should be aware that if a local authority holds personal information about their client, the child has a right of access to that information unless an exception applies. There are similar regulations that give a right of access to education and health records.

RISK MANAGEMENT

6.35   There is practice guidance and information about a range of mechanisms that are available when managing people who have been identified as presenting a risk or potential risk of harm to children. Areas covered include:

- collaborative working between organisations and agencies to identify and manage people who present a risk of harm to children;

- the Multi-agency Public Protection Arrangements (MAPPA) which enable agencies to work together when dealing with people who require a greater degree of resources to manage the risk of harm they present to the public; and

- other processes and mechanisms for working with people who present a risk to children.

Independent Safeguarding Authority

6.36   Following the murders of Jessica Chapman and Holly Wells by Ian Huntley (a school caretaker) in 2002, the *Bichard Inquiry* was commissioned. One of the issues this Inquiry looked at was the way employers recruit people to work with children and vulnerable adults. It asked whether the way employers check the background of job applicants was reliable enough. It also asked whether employers should be responsible for deciding whether a job applicant can be safely employed. The Inquiry's recommendations led to the Safeguarding Vulnerable Groups Act 2006, which recognised the need for a single agency to vet all individuals who want to work or volunteer with vulnerable people.

On 31 March 2008, the ISA was created to fulfil this role across England, Wales and Northern Ireland (Scotland is developing its own similar system, which will work closely with the ISA), and to help prevent unsuitable people from working with children and vulnerable adults. On 20 January 2009, ISA assumed responsibility for making such decisions. From 13 March 2009, the ISA also assumed responsibility for making barring decisions previously made by the Department of Health, Social Services and Public Safety (DHSSPS) under the Protection of Children and Vulnerable Adults (Northern Ireland) Order 2003 (POCVA) and the Department of Education (DE) under the Prohibition from Teaching or Working with Children Regulations (Northern Ireland) 2007 (Unsuitable Persons Regulations).

The ISA works in partnership with the Criminal Records Bureau (CRB), which gathers relevant information on every person who wants to work or volunteer with vulnerable people. Applicants to the ISA are assessed using data gathered by the Criminal Records Bureau (CRB), including relevant criminal convictions, cautions, police intelligence and other appropriate sources. Using this information, the ISA decides on a case-by-case basis whether each person is suited to this work. The ISA securely stores information about people's ISA status for employers and voluntary organisations to use when they are recruiting. Only applicants who are judged not to pose a risk to vulnerable people can be ISA-registered, and employers who work with vulnerable people will only be allowed to recruit people who are ISA-registered.

The ISA operates independently of individual government ministers, including the Secretary of State, who was previously in charge of making discretionary barring decisions. Such decisions are now to be taken by the ISA's board of public appointees. As a

Non-Departmental Public Body (NDPB), the ISA has certain statutory responsibilities and its effectiveness and efficiency are closely scrutinised by government and stakeholders. It must report annually to Parliament and its operations – including decisions on barring – must be seen to be fair, open and transparent.

On 12 October 2009, the ISA assumed responsibilities for referrals and barring decisions under the terms of the Safeguarding Vulnerable Groups Act (2006), according to the Vetting and Barring Scheme (see below).

Employers in the education sector in England and Wales have ceased to make misconduct referrals to the Department for Children, Schools and Families (DCSF). Misconduct referrals on teachers (ie not child-protection related) now go to the relevant General Teaching Council (GTC). The addresses for referrals to the GTC are:

General Teaching Council for England,
Whittington House,
19-30 Alfred Place,
London
WC1E 7EA

General Teaching Council for Wales,
4th Floor, Southgate House,
Wood Street,
Cardiff
CF10 1EW

Independent
Safeguarding Authority:
Tel: 0300 123 1111
www.isa-gov.org.uk

Automatic barring of those newly convicted or cautioned for specified more serious offences (which used only to happen under List 99 – see below) was extended to include both the workforces from which persons are barred by current schemes; employers, regulatory bodies, supervisory bodies and local authorities have a duty to respond to requests from the ISA for further information, where that information is already held (for education employers in Northern Ireland, misconduct referrals, which are not child protection related, should continue to be made to the Department of Education).

6.37 Full guidance for England and Wales on how to refer an individual to (the former) List 99, PoCA or

PoVA, taking account of these changes, can be found on the DCSF and DH websites at:
http://publications.teachernet.gov.uk/
eOrderingDownload/PoCA.doc (PoCA)
http://www.everychildmatters.gov.uk/_files/
AE53C8F9D7AEB1B23E403514A6C1B17D.pdf (For List 99 – Paragraphs 12.33 to 12.36)
http://www.dh.gov.uk/en/SocialCare/
Deliveringadultsocialcare/Vulnerableadults/index.htm
(PoVA)

6.38 Full guidance for Northern Ireland on how to refer an individual to the POCVA and Unsuitable Person's Lists, taking account of these changes, can be found on the DHSSPS website at:
http://www.dhsspsni.gov.uk/child_protection_guidance.

To refer an individual to the ISA, or if you have a query about any existing questions or queries about the Vetting and Barring Scheme or the role of the ISA, you can call their contact centre on 0300 123 1111, or email info@vbs-info.org.uk.

Source:
www.isa-gov.org.uk

The Vetting and Barring Scheme (VBS)

6.39 Over the past 5 years CRB (Criminal Records Bureau) checks prevented around 98,000 unsuitable people from working with children and vulnerable adults. Research suggested that employers recognised the importance of CRB checks to the protection of children and vulnerable adults. The Vetting and Barring Scheme was set up as a result of the *Bichard Inquiry*, which followed the Soham Murders, and recommended that all those who work with vulnerable groups should be registered. The *Bichard Inquiry* was followed by a full public consultation and legislation in the Safeguarding Vulnerable Groups Act 2006.

The new Vetting and Barring Scheme (VBS) was launched on 12 October 2009 with individuals being able to become ISA-Registered from 26 July 2010. On 12 October 2009 the three current barring lists (POCA, POVA and List 99) were replaced by two new barred lists and from 26 July 2010 applicants can start to apply for ISA registration. The Online ISA-registration service will be introduced at the same time, and individuals must submit an application to the CRB to become ISA-registered.

The VBS is a partnership of the CRB, ISA and Access NI. CRB is responsible for the application and monitoring elements of the scheme, and ISA is responsible for the decision making and maintenance of two barred lists for England and Wales and Northern Ireland covering the children's and vulnerable adults' sectors. The two new Barred Lists replaced the Protection of Children Act (PoCA) List (see below), List 99 (see below) and the Protection of Vulnerable Adults (PoVA) List in England and Wales, and the Disqualification from Working with Children (DWC) List, the Unsuitable Persons List (UP List) and the Disqualification from Working with Vulnerable Adults (DWVA) List.

The VBS is designed to ensure that anyone who presents a known risk to vulnerable groups is prevented from working with them and is an additional recruitment tool. It is not a guarantee that an individual is suitable for a particular position. The VBS was set up to enhance the protection afforded to these vulnerable groups. When used together, a CRB and ISA-registration check should provide employers with a most comprehensive vetting and checking service. There was extensive media coverage at the time that the safeguards of the VBS came into place in October 2009.

The Vetting and Barring Scheme, replacing the former barring schemes, is the most inclusive and largest system of its kind in the world. Barring decisions will be taken by Independent Experts. For the purpose of the scheme both paid employees and volunteers are subject to the same implications, restrictions and obligations – except in terms of the application fee (free for volunteers to register). Once the scheme has been fully implemented, it will mean that anyone who wants to work or volunteer with children or vulnerable adults in 'Regulated Activity' will be required to be registered with the ISA.

A barred person will be committing an offence should they seek employment or a volunteering opportunity in Regulated Activity. It will be an offence for any person to commence Regulated Activity without first being ISA-registered. It will be an offence for an employer to hire a person in Regulated Activity without first confirming their ISA registration. Employers, personnel suppliers and other statutory, business and public organisations have a legal duty to refer appropriate information to ISA. Anyone with a legitimate interest will be able to check a person's registration status online. Those with a legitimate interest who have registered this interest will be informed if an employee becomes de-registered from the scheme. Eventually, it is anticipated that 11.3 million people will become ISA-registered over a 5-year period from 26 July 2010. Parents will now be able to check that the individuals they employ in a private capacity as tutors, nannies, carers or in other regulated activity are registered with ISA, using the same online check as an employer. (However, there is no duty on parents to do this; they will not face legal penalties for failing to check.) NB: an individual who is barred is still not permitted to undertake this kind of Regulated Activity.

Making an application to register

6.40   Those people who are applying to work or volunteer with children or vulnerable adults will have to apply to be ISA-registered via the CRB on the application form provided. For individuals undertaking paid employment, the registration will incur a one-off fee of £64 (£58 in Northern Ireland). Volunteers will have to apply in the same way as an employee; however, they will not be charged for registering. Individuals may still be required by their employers to obtain a CRB check to check suitability for their actual job and duties.

The initial vetting process

6.41   Any relevant information from the police or referrals from other sources, such as previous employers or professional bodies, will be passed to ISA for consideration. ISA will use all relevant information to decide whether the applicant should be placed on a Barred List. If there is no information the CRB will inform the applicant that they are ISA-registered.

Individuals placed on the ISA Barred Lists will have the right to make representations against the decision and also to the Care Standards Tribunal, except where they have committed a serious offence.

Continuous monitoring

6.42   All ISA-registered individuals will be subject to continuous monitoring. This means that an ISA decision not to bar them could be reviewed in the light of new police or referral information. Where this happens ISA will notify the employer or service provider concerned, wherever they have registered an interest.

Online checking

6.43 Subsequent employers or service providers will be able to check an individual's status online free of charge. In most cases they will also be able to seek Enhanced Disclosure (which will contain information on any criminal records) from the CRB. As is currently the case, certain employers will be required to obtain an Enhanced Disclosure

From 26 July 2010, all new entrants to roles working regularly with vulnerable groups and those switching jobs to a new provider within these sectors in England, Wales and Northern Ireland, will be able to become ISA-registered and join the scheme. Individuals will be able to apply for ISA-registration and/or a CRB check on one new application form.

When a person becomes ISA-registered they will be continuously monitored and their status reassessed against any new relevant information which becomes available. Employers can also 'subscribe to' an individual's ISA-registration status and be informed if that status changes.

It will not be a legal requirement to register new entrants or those changing roles from 26 July 2010, so it is hoped that there will be no disruption to normal recruitment over the traditionally busy summer period. The legal requirement for employees to become ISA-registered, and employers to check their status will come into force in November 2010.

There are two phases to the launch of the Vetting and Barring Scheme in order that all elements of the scheme can be properly designed and tested before they are implemented. As the scheme was developed, there was a need to reassess certain aspects of its delivery and, to ensure these vital additions work, these too need to be properly designed, piloted and tested.

More information on ISA and VBS can be obtained by calling 0300 123 1111 or by visiting the ISA website at www.isa-gov.org.uk, or www.crb.gov.uk/faqs/vetting_and_barring_scheme.

Collaborative Working

6.44   The Children Act 1989 recognised that the identification and investigation of child abuse together with the protection and support of victims and their families requires multi-agency collaboration. This has rightly focused on the child and the supporting parent/carer. As part of that protection, action has been taken, usually by the police and social service, to prosecute known offenders or control their access to vulnerable children. This work, whilst successful in addressing the safety of particular victims has not always acknowledged the on-going risk of harm that an individual perpetrator may present to other children in the future.

On 15 September 2008, a 12-month Home Office pilot, the *Keeping Children Safe* pilot, was launched in four sites where parents, carers and guardians could formally ask the police to tell them if a person has a record for child sexual offences. The *Keeping Children Safe* pilot was set up to fulfil Action 4 of the Review of the protection of children from sex offenders, which is to:

> 'Pilot a process where members of the public can register their child-protection interest in a named individual. Where this individual has convictions for child sexual offences and is considered a risk, there is a presumption that this information will be disclosed to the relevant member of the public.'

The purpose of the pilot was to test the effectiveness of giving parents, carers and guardians a more formal mechanism for requesting information about people that are involved in their family life, specifically if they are concerned that a person is a child sexual offender. During the pilot, the authorities were to consider the request and decide whether it is appropriate, under the circumstances, for any disclosure to be made. The pilot was set up because the majority of child sexual offenders are known to their victims. They are often a member of the family, a friend of the victim, or a friend of the victim's family, with only 20% of offences carried out by strangers. The aim of the pilot was to keep children safer, and was carried out by Hampshire Constabulary, Cambridgeshire Constabulary, Warwickshire Police and Cleveland Police, managed in association with the Ministry of Justice (MOJ), the Department for Children, Schools and Family (DCSF) and the Association of Chief Police Officers (ACPO), with advice from the National Society for the Prevention of Cruelty to Children (NSPCC), the National Children's Home (NCH), Barnardos, Sara Payne and the Lucy Faithfull Foundation's 'Stop It Now!' project. The pilot areas were Cambridgeshire (Northern Division including Peterborough and surrounding villages) Cleveland (Stockton BCU), Hampshire (Southampton OCU) and Warwickshire (force-wide).

The results of the pilot were to be reviewed and then a decision taken as to whether to roll the pilot out nationally. The review would consider whether the service increased protection for children and young people from child sexual offenders, public interest and take-up of the service, the impact that providing this service has on local police forces and the impact of the pilot in the overall management of child sexual offenders. An overview of the *Keeping Children Safe* pilot, *Keeping Children Safe*, is available from the Home Office.

Risk to Children

Source:
www.homeoffice.gov.uk

6.45   The term 'Schedule One offender' and 'Schedule One offence' was commonly used for anyone convicted of an offence against a child listed in Schedule One to the Children and Young Person's Act 1933. However, a conviction for an offence in Schedule One did not trigger any statutory requirement in relation to child protection issues and inclusion on the schedule was determined solely by the age of the victim and offence for which the offender was sentenced and not by an assessment of future risk of harm to children. Therefore the term 'Schedule One offender' is no longer used. It has been replaced with the term 'Risk to Children'. This clearly indicates that the person has been identified as presenting a risk or potential risk of harm to children.

MAPPA

For more information about MAPPA see www.probation.homeoffice.gov.uk

6.46   MAPPA stands for Multi-Agency Public Protection Arrangements. It is the process through which the Police, Probation and Prison Services work together with other agencies to manage the risks posed by violent and sexual offenders living in the community in order to protect the public. MAPPA began operating in April 2001. This body places a duty on the police and the National Probation Service to assess and manage risks posed by offenders in every community in England and Wales. In the most serious cases MAPPA can recommend increased police monitoring, special steps to protect victims and the use of closely supervised accommodation. The work of the MAPPAs is available to the public in the form of the MAPPA annual report published jointly by the NPS and the Prison Service.

There are three categories of violent and sexual offenders who are managed through MAPPA:

- *Registered sexual offenders* are required to notify the police of their name, address and personal details, under the terms of the Sexual Offences Act 2003. The length of time for which an offender is required to register with the police can be any period between 12 months to life, depending on the age of the offender, the age of the victim and the nature of the offence and sentence they received.

- *Violent offenders* who have been sentenced to 12 months or more in custody or to detention in hospital and who are now living in the community subject to Probation supervision. This Category also includes a small number of people who have been disqualified from working with children.

- *Other dangerous offenders* who have committed an offence in the past and who are considered to pose a risk of serious harm to the public.

Offenders do not attend MAPP meetings but they are usually told about the meeting and the decisions made. All MAPPA offenders are assessed to establish the level of risk of harm they pose to the public. Risk management plans are then worked out for each offender to manage those risks. MAPPA allows agencies to assess and manage offenders on a multi-agency basis by working together, sharing information and meeting, as necessary, to ensure that effective plans are put in place.

There are three levels of MAPPA management. They are mainly based upon the level of multi-agency co-operation required with higher risk the level of risk of harm they pose to the public. Risk management plans are then worked out for each offender to manage those risks.

MAPPA allows agencies to assess and manage offenders on a multi-agency basis by working together, sharing information and meeting, as necessary, to ensure that effective plans are put in place. Offenders will be moved up and down levels, as appropriate.

- *Level 1* – Ordinary agency management is for offenders who can be managed by one or two agencies (eg police and/or probation). It will involve sharing information about the offender with other agencies, if necessary and appropriate.

- *Level 2* – Active multi-agency management is for offenders where the ongoing involvement of several agencies is needed to manage the offender. Once at level 2, there will be regular Multi-Agency Public Protection (MAPP) meetings about the offender.

- *Level 3* – Same arrangements as level 2 but cases qualifying for level 3 tend to be more demanding on resources and require the involvement of senior people from the agencies, who can authorise the use of extra resources, for example, surveillance on an offender or emergency accommodation.

While MAPPA will not address the concerns of further serious harm posed by all perpetrators of child abuse, its purpose is to focus on convicted sexual and violent offenders returning to and in the community. The development of national databases should significantly enhance the capability to track offenders who move between communities and across organisational boundaries.

Offending Behaviour Programmes

6.47 Rehabilitation of offenders is the best guarantee of long-term public protection. A range of treatment programmes have been 'tried and tested' at a national level, which have been developed or commissioned by the prison and probation service. Examples include, Sex Offender Treatment Programmes, programmes for offenders convicted of internet sexually related offences, and for perpetrators of domestic violence.

Disqualification from Working with Children

6.48 The Criminal Justice and Court Services Act (CJCSA) 2000, as amended by the Criminal Justice Act 2003, provides for people to be disqualified from working with children. A person is disqualified by either:

- a disqualification order, made by the Crown Court when a person is convicted for an offence against a child (under 18) listed in Sch 4 to the CJCSA 2000. Schedule 4 includes sexual offences, violent offences and offences of selling Class A drugs to a child; or
- being included in a permanent capacity on the list of people who are unsuitable to work with children that is kept under s 1 of the Protection of Children Act 1999; or
- being included on a Barred List (formerly the DfES List 99) (see **6.39**) on the ground of being unsuitable to work with children.

Criminal Records Bureau

6.49   The Criminal Records Bureau (CRB) is an executive agency of the Home Office. The CRB's disclosure service aims to help employers make safer recruitment decisions by identifying candidates who may be unsuitable for certain types of work. Employers should ask successful candidates to apply to the CRB for a standard or enhanced disclosure, depending on the duties of the particular position or job involved. Further information, including details of how to apply for disclosures, is available at www.crb.gov.uk. (See also above, the VBS).

The Sex Offenders Register

6.50   The notification requirements of Part 2 of the Sexual Offences Act 2003 (known as the Sex Offenders Register) are an automatic requirement on offenders who receive a conviction or caution for certain sexual offences. The notification requirements are intended to ensure that the police are informed of the whereabouts of offenders in the community. The notification requirements do not bar offenders from certain types of employment, from being alone with children etc. There are currently no plans to introduce automatic disclosure about child sexual offenders in this country.

Sex offender orders have been in force since 1 December 1998. A sex offender order can help prevent further offences before they are committed, and provide an important tool for the police and other agencies in the very difficult job they face of managing sex offenders in the community. They carry the requirement to register under the Sex Offenders Act 1997. The sex offender order is a new civil order which can be applied for by the police against any sex offender whose behaviour in the community gives the police reasonable cause for concern that an order is necessary to protect the public from serious harm from him. There is no test of seriousness in respect of the actual behaviour, which has to be considered only in terms of its relevance to the risk of future offending. The minimum duration for an order is 5 years. The prohibitions in the order must be such as are necessary to protect the public from serious harm from the defendant. The lower age limit is 10, which is the criminal age of consent, but where the defendant is under the age of 18, an application for an order should only be considered exceptionally. The orders are intended to fill a gap in the provisions available to protect the public from risk from sex offenders. Breach of an order without reasonable excuse is a criminal offence triable either way with a maximum penalty on indictment of 5 years in prison.

Helplines

6.51 If individuals are worried that their child might be at risk from a child sexual offender, there are various routes of enquiry that are available. They can contact their local police and speak to someone at their local police station, or if they think that the child is in immediate danger, they should call 999.

To find out more about what to look out for, they can contact the Stop It Now! Helpline (080 8100 0900). This is a confidential freephone helpline, operating from 9am to 9pm Monday to Thursday and from 9am to 7pm on Friday, for people worried about their own sexual thoughts and feelings towards children or the sexual behaviour of others, for parents and carers of young people with sexually worrying behaviour and for professionals needing help with difficult cases.

If individuals are worried about a child's safety or welfare or need help or advice, they can call the NSPCC Child Protection Helpline (080 8800 5000). To receive help and advice within 24 hours via email, email the NSPCC at help@nspcc.org.uk (from Northern Ireland: talk@nspcc.org.uk).

- Textphone: 080 0056 0566
- Asian helpline service in English: 080 0096 7719

- Bengali/Sylheti: 080 0096 7714
- Gujarati: 080 0096 7715
- Hindi: 080 0096 7716
- Punjabi: 080 0096 7717
- Urdu: 080 0096 7718

The NSPCC Helpline is a confidential and free service open 24 hours a day, seven days a week.

For information about staying safe online, individuals can visit 'thinkuknow' (www.thinkuknow.co.uk), the online safety centre of the Child Exploitation and Online Protection Centre (CEOP), which provides advice and tips for children and adults.

Further guidance can be downloaded from the Home Office website (www.homeoffice.gov.uk).

CLOSURE

6.52   Closure for lawyers means the ending of the case. Their relationship with clients ends because proceedings are over, but first solicitors should consider, with the children's guardian, when the children's guardian is giving instructions, the best way of advising the child of the outcome. The solicitor should ensure that he remains accessible to the child and is sympathetic yet professional. Over-dependence by either the child or solicitor on the other should be discouraged.

It should, however, be noted that some children may wish to keep in touch with their solicitor from time to time. Care should always be exercised in such a situation because the solicitor–client relationship has ended, and continued communication might compromise the solicitor's future representation of that child in any future or subsequent proceedings. It is important that the solicitor prepares the child for the end of the relationship and begins telling the child, before the end of the case, that the solicitor's role will shortly be over. When the solicitor's role is over, solicitors should ensure, through the children's guardian if more appropriate, that the child:

(a)   has access to information about the local authority's responsibilities to the child;

(b)   is aware of the right to complain about matters concerning the child's welfare in care, if appropriate, and may make further applications to the court.

Source:
Guide to Good Practice
(Law Society, 2004)

This should be done in person and confirmed by letter to which the child could refer at a later stage. It is important, however, not to undermine the child's relationship with his carers or the re-establishment of family relationships which may have been under pressure during the course of proceedings.

The Children Act 1989 states that an order should be made only if it is better than making no order at all. The emphasis now is on the negotiation and mediation of issues within families and, if the local authority becomes involved, to promote the upbringing by their families of children who are in need. There are no neat beginnings and endings to the intervention of professionals in family situations. Family situations are messy, and although it is necessary to try to impose some external system in order to protect the vulnerable members of those families, in most cases professionals and families have to settle for 'good enough' outcomes.

While adults may be fairly clear that a case is over, or intervention has ended, that might not be the experience for children. Children are often aware of something going on but may not be given clear explanations of the issues either by their parents or by the professionals they meet because of the legal proceedings. This is an issue in both public and private law family proceedings. Child parties do not always have full access to court papers. Whether or not they are parties to proceedings, children rarely attend court. Nevertheless, they may be extremely anxious about the process and desperate to know the outcome and the implications for them.

On divorce, many children are never given a clear explanation of what has happened and can sometimes end up blaming themselves. It is the parents' responsibility to try to make sure this does not happen but they may well need the help of mediators, lawyers or Cafcass officers to prevent this. Where the local authority is involved and proceedings are brought, the most suitable person to keep the child informed is the guardian or child's solicitor. What the child needs, from someone, is a full and clear explanation appropriate to his age and understanding. Professionals should always clarify between themselves and, when appropriate, with parents or carers the issue of who will give children the necessary explanations.

Private Family Issues

Outcomes

6.53   Once an agreement is reached between parents about their children, or a court order is imposed, the mediators, lawyers and judges fade away leaving the parents with a result which they have to manage alone. Even if they find a way of doing this, children have a tendency to grow up and make up their own minds about who they want to live with or who they want to see. Unless children are at risk, it is best for divorcing and separating parents to resolve their own problems.

Enforcement

6.54   The enforcement of financial settlements after divorce is beyond the scope of this book. Most financial settlements are successfully negotiated and negotiated agreements generally stick. There will always be people who, dissatisfied with a court order, will resist paying up, but they are in a distinct minority. The lesson which has to be learned from the lax enforcement of child maintenance, and indeed from the low levels of such maintenance orders, in the past, is now embodied in the shape of the Child Support Agency (CSA) and the new Child Maintenance and Enforcement Commission (C-MEC) – see **3.100**). C-MEC represents a new approach (see www.cmoptions.org) and is expected to take over the CSA's functions although the full transition process is likely to extend until at least 2014 (see **3.100**).

For the enforcement of residence and contact orders see **5.18**.

Public Law

After the care order is made

6.55   The making of a care order may end the court's involvement but, for the local authority, it merely changes the basis on which it looks after the child. The local authority's obligations are set out in the Children Act 1989 and regulations. Amongst these is the duty continually to review the care provided for the child, including such matters as health care, contact and legal status. Reviews must form part of an ongoing, continuous planning process and must take place within one month of when the child began to be looked after, within 3 months of that review and then continually within 6 months of each subsequent review.

Section 118 of the Adoption and Children Act 2002 inserted into s 26 of the Children Act 1989 a requirement for local authorities to appoint IROs to review cases and their care plans as necessary. The requirements are also applied to voluntary organisations by virtue of s 59(4) and (5) of the Children Act 1989, and are applied to persons providing private children's homes (but only in cases where the child is not placed by a local authority or voluntary organisation) by virtue of para 10 of Sch 6 to the Children Act 1989.

Section 26(2)(e) of the Children Act 1989 (requirement to consider discharge of a care order) encompasses a review of the care plan and revision as necessary. Looked after and accommodated children are to have a care plan drawn up and reviewed in a similar fashion. The local authorities must now appoint a reviewing officer whose functions will be to participate in the review process, monitor the local authority's functions in respect of the review and refer the case to Cafcass if the reviewer 'considers it appropriate to do so'. The independent reviewing officer is to be a person of a 'prescribed description' as set out in the relevant regulations (see Review of Children's Cases (Amendment) (England) Regulations 2004 (SI 2004/1419), Review of Children's Cases (Amendment) (Wales) Regulations 2004 (SI 2004/1449), and regulation 37 of the Adoption Agencies Regulations 2005 (SI 2005/389)). In November 2004, Cafcass published a Practice Note on cases referred to them by IROs in which the respective roles of the IRO and Cafcass are set out:

The IRO role is to improve care planning and decision making for looked after children and therefore to make an important contribution to the consistency of the local authority's approach to planning for the children in its care. Review meetings must be efficiently chaired by the IRO. They will have a particular responsibility to make sure that the review and care planning process takes full account of the views of the child, their relatives and others close to them so that they are enabled to make a meaningful contribution to reviews of plans for the child's care. The IRO will have a crucial role in ensuring that looked after children are properly safeguarded wherever they live and that care plans are effective and are actioned within an appropriate timescale that takes account of the child's needs and understanding.

Cases should only be referred by IROs to Cafcass as a matter of last resort.

In November 2009 a Care Planning Placement and Case Review Regulations Consultation was launched, the purpose of which is to gather views on the draft Care Planning Placement and Case Review Regulations (England) 2010 and related guidance. As a result of the new duties inserted into the Children Act 1989 by the Children and Young Persons Act 2008 and a prior commitment to revise the entire suite of Children Act 1989 Regulations and guidance the Department for Children, Schools and Families (DCSF) is embarking on a programme of work to revise, strengthen, update and streamline regulations and guidance under the Children Act 1989. The first set of documents for consultation consists of:

- new Care Planning, Placement and Case Review Regulations and statutory guidance;
- guidance on the new sufficiency duty in the new s 22G;
- practice guidance on short break care;
- the role of independent reviewing officers (the IRO Handbook) statutory guidance; and
- statutory guidance on the new sufficiency duty for local authorities

As a result of the new regulations there will be consequential revocations and amendments to other regulations as set out in Schedule 9 to the Care Planning, Placement and Case Review Regulations.

In particular, the Children and Young Persons Act 2008 introduced significant changes to the independent reviewing officers (IRO) role and function. The intention is that the changes to the statutory framework will enable the IRO to have a more effective independent oversight of the child's case. The consultation version of *The IRO Handbook* provides statutory guidance addressed to each IRO about how they should discharge their distinct responsibilities to looked after children. The guidance replaces the 2004 *Independent Reviewing Officers Guidance* and should be read in conjunction with the Care Planning, Placement and Case Review (England) Regulations 2010 ('the Care Planning Regulations'), which in turn revoke the Review of Children's Cases Regulations 1991. The consultation closes on 8 February 2010.The IRO handbook and all the consultation documents are available on: http://www.dcsf.gov.uk/consultations/index.cfm?action= consultationDetails&consultationId =1678&external=no&menu=1.

Contact

6.56 There is a presumption that it is in the child's interests to have contact with the child's parents and the care plan should always address this matter. Even if there is no question of the child returning to the family, it might be appropriate for some form of contact to be maintained. Children need to keep a sense of who they are and where they come from, and may want to resume some family relationships when they are adults. The local authority must get a court order if it wants to stop all contact with a parent or other named person, but this should not stop contact continuing with grandparents, brothers or sisters.

Adoption

6.57 An adoption order severs all legal ties with the birth family and confers parental rights and responsibilities on the new adoptive family. The birth parents no longer have any legal rights over the child and they are not entitled to claim the child back. The child becomes a full member of the adoptive family; the child takes their surname and assumes the same rights and privileges as if he had been born to that family, including the right of inheritance.

Although Children Act 1989 contact provisions do not apply once a child is authorised to be placed for adoption, contact is firmly on the agenda. Under the new Adoption and Children Act 2002, while a child is authorised to be placed for adoption (or has been placed when under 6 weeks old) the court may make a contact order on the application of the child, the agency, or any parent, guardian or relative, as well as a number of others with an interest and may also make an order of its own initiative when making a placement order. During its planning for adoption the agency, too, is required to consider the question of contact and the adoption panel may give advice on the matter. There is no presumption in favour of contact. Each case has to be considered individually in the light of the child's welfare. Once a match with prospective adopters is under consideration, their views too must be ascertained.

For contact post adoption, there is no particular reason to suppose that the courts will be any more inclined than hitherto to impose a section 8 contact order against the wishes of the adopters, but the requirement for the court to consider whether there should be arrangements for contact, and to obtain the views of the parties on existing or proposed arrangements, will ensure that the issue is at least addressed.

See further **5.77**.

Special Guardianship

6.58   Another option for permanence in placement for the child is under a Special Guardianship order (SGO), an option which was created by s 115 of and Schedule III to the Adoption and Children Act 2002 and s 14A–14G which were inserted into the Children Act 1989. An SGO gives the Special Guardian Parental Responsibility (PR) for the child, but the birth parents remain the child's parents and retain their own PR. But the Special Guardian's PR can override the birth parents' PR (unlike the PR held by a holder of a Residence order), and the Special Guardian does not always need to consult the parents when making decisions about day-to-day matters. A Special Guardianship order can be made for a non-relative. Local authorities are required to make arrangements to provide support services to Special Guardians, for example to provide financial support or mediation with regard to contact issues. (See the Special Guardianship Regulations 2005, SI 2005/1109.) Special Guardianship orders may be particularly suitable for:

- older children with strong ties to birth parents/family;
- children from abroad/unaccompanied asylum seeking children;
- prospective permanent carers who cannot accept adoption for religious/cultural reasons.

The differences between Special Guardianship and Adoption is that the Special Guardian will make all day-to-day decisions about the child, but he/she must consult the child's parents regarding a proposed change of the child's surname, or if he/she would like to live abroad with the child for over 3 months, or to consider adoption of the child. Direct contact with the birth family may well continue under an SGO, and previously looked-after children are entitled to receive leaving care provision under an SGO. An SGO lasts formally until the child is 18, but the role of a Special Guardian is expected to last for life. The court can make a Special Guardianship Order even if no application for one has been made.

Closure of Social Services Interventions

6.59 Many cases never get to court. Social services may investigate allegations of child abuse and decisions may then be made to take the case no further, but the way in which families leave the system is seldom tidy. Many allegations of child abuse are not substantiated: they are neither proved nor disproved. Professionals struggle to communicate confidence and certainty to the family. While erring on the side of caution and leaving the child registered may cause distress to parents, professionals risk media criticism and even legal challenge should precipitate de-registration from a child protection plan be followed by serious re-abuse.

To many parents the idea of 'opening' and 'closing' a case has the flavour of the police station and court, rather than the surgery or clinic. Professionals are taught to tolerate a degree of confusion, to manage probability and possibility and to keep emotional distance. Parents, however, want to know when an investigation is open and closed. Parents need clarity – both at the beginning (to know that their child is highly unlikely to be taken away) and at the end (to know whether the accusation is proven, disproved or still in doubt).

Ending Orders

6.60 The local authority, the child, or anyone with parental responsibility for the child can apply for the discharge of a care order. They can also apply for the substitution of a supervision order. The court can discharge the care order and make a residence order to someone else, including a foster parent. Family support may continue at the request of family members under the provisions of Part III of the Children Act 1989 if it is considered that the child is still a 'child in need', as will often be the case.

The Children (Leaving Care) Act 2000 amends and extends the duties in the Children Act 1989 to ensure that young people are looked after until they are ready to leave care, properly prepared for independence and receive appropriate support thereafter.

Health and Medical Services

6.61   For doctors, the closure of cases is rarely an issue in any long-term sense. Patients are discharged from a single consultation or series of consultations in relation to a particular illness episode. Open access or access via the patient's GP or via accident and emergency services at hospital is usually available. However, where there has been a court case neither the court nor the expert witness would (in the normal course of events) hear anything more of a case once it was completed. The lawyers would generally wish to disengage themselves from further involvement, but the clinician and the local authority (as appropriate) remain in touch with the participants.

TITLES PUBLISHED BY *FAMILY LAW*

Reference Books

Adoption and Special Guardianship: A Permanency Handbook (HHJ John Mitchell, 2009)

Adoption: The Modern Law (Caroline Bridge and HHJ Heather Swindells QC, 2003)

Adoption: The Modern Procedure (HHJ Heather Swindells QC and Clive Heaton QC, 2006)

Adult Psychiatry in Family and Child Law (B Mahendra, 2006)

Ancillary Relief Handbook (Roger Bird, 7th edn, 2009)

Bankruptcy and Divorce: A Practical Guide for the Family Lawyer (M Barker, S Calhaem, J Middleton and G Schofield, 3rd edn, 2010)

Child Abuse (Christina Lyon et al, 3rd edn, 2003)

Child Care and Adoption Law: A Practical Guide (The Hon Mr Justice McFarlane and Madeleine Reardon, 2nd edn, 2010)

Child Case Management Practice (The Hon Mr Justice Ryder, Iain Goldrein QC et al, 2009)

Child Maintenance: The New Law (Roger Bird and David Burrows, 2009)

Children Act Private Law Proceedings: A Handbook (HHJ John Mitchell, 2nd edn, 2006)

Children Law: An Interdisciplinary Handbook (Charles Prest and HHJ Stephen Wildblood QC, 2005)

Children: The Modern Law (Andrew Bainham, 3rd edn, 2005)

Civil Partnership: The New Law (Mark Harper, Martin Downs, Katharine Landells, Gerald Wilson, 2005)

Cohabitation: Law, Practice and Precedents (District Judge Helen Wood, Denzil Lush, David Bishop and Ashley Murray, 4th edn, 2009)

Contact: The New Deal (Piers Pressdee QC, John Vater, Frances Judd QC, and The Hon Mr Justice Jonathan Baker, 2006)

Continuing Evolution of Family Law, The (Gillian Douglas and Nigel Lowe, 2009)

Domestic Violence: Law and Practice (Roger Bird, 5th edn, 2006)

Durable Solutions (The Rt Hon Lord Justice Thorpe et al, 2006)

Family Law Case Library: Children (Charles Prest and HHJ Stephen Wildblood QC, 2008)

Family Law Case Library: Finance (Charles Prest, Mark Saunders, HHJ Stephen Wildblood QC and Claire Wills-Goldingham, 2008)

Family Psychiatric Practice: A Guide for Lawyers (B Mahendra, 2010)

Family Law: Tips & Traps – Hints, Help and Specimen Orders (HHJ Clive Million, 2009)

Family Mediation: Past Present and Future (John Westcott et al, 2004)

Finance on Family Breakdown for Low Income Families (David Burrows, Helen Conway and John Eames, 2006)

Forced Marriage: A Special Bulletin (Clive Heaton QC, Louise McCallum and Razia Jogi, 2009)

Handbook for Expert Witnesses in Children Act Cases, A (The Rt Hon Lord Justice Wall, 2nd edn, 2007)

Hearing the Children (The Rt Hon Lord Justice Thorpe et al, 2004)

Human Fertilisation and Embryology: The New Law (Dewinder Birk, 2009)

Integrating Diversity (The Rt Hon Lord Justice Thorpe et al, 2008)

International Movement of Children: Law, Practice and Procedure (HHJ Mark Everall QC, Nigel Lowe and Michael Nicholls QC, 2003)

International Trust and Divorce Litigation (Mark Harper, Dawn Goodman, Paul Matthews and Patrick Hamlin, 2007)

Matrimonial Costs (HHJ Martin Cardinal and District Judge Simon Middleton, 2nd edn, 2007)

Media Access to the Family Courts: A Guide to the New Rules and their Application (Iain Goldrein QC, 2009)

Mental Capacity: The New Law (District Judge Gordon Ashton, Penny Letts, Laurence Oates and Martin Terrell, 2006)

Mental Health: The New Law (Phil Fennell, 2007)

Mental Health and Family Law (The Rt Hon Lord Justice Thorpe et al, 2010)

Model Letters for Family Lawyers (Mark Harper, Lisa Fabian Lustigman and Andrea Woelke, 3rd edn, 2006)

New Ancillary Relief Costs Regime: A Special Bulletin (David Burrows, 2006)

New Brussels II Regulation, The, A Supplement to International Movement of Children (HHJ Mark Everall QC, Nigel Lowe and Michael Nicholls QC, 2005)

Pension Sharing in Practice: A Special Bulletin (David Salter, 2nd edn, 2003)

Practical Guide to Family Proceedings, A (District Judge Robert Blomfield, Helen Brooks et al, 4th edn, 2009)

Practical Guide to International Family Law, A (D Hodson et al, 2008)

Psychology in Family and Child Law (C Van Rooyen and B Mahendra, 2007)

Public Law Outline, The, The Court Companion: A Special Bulletin (Piers Pressdee QC, John Vater, Frances Judd QC, and The Hon Mr Justice Jonathan Baker, 2008)

Re-rooted Lives: Inter-disciplinary work within the Family Justice System (Prof Judith Trowell and Carola Thorpe, 2nd edn, 2007)

Social Work Decision-Making: A Guide for Childcare Lawyers (E Isaacs and C Shepherd, 2008)

Stack v Dowden: Co-Ownership of Property by Unmarried Parties: A Special Bulletin (David Burrows and Nicholas Orr, 2007)

Unlocking Matrimonial Assets on Divorce (Simon Sugar and Andrzej Bojarski, 2nd edn, 2009)

Looseleaf Works

Emergency Remedies in the Family Courts (Her Honour J Nazreen Pearce, His Honour Nigel Fricker QC et al)

Family Law Precedents Service (Roger Bird, David Salter et al)

Hershman and McFarlane: Children Law and Practice (The late David Hershman QC and The Hon Mr Justice McFarlane)

Matrimonial Property and Finance (Peter Duckworth)

Journals

Child and Family Law Quarterly

Family Law

International Family Law

USEFUL CONTACTS: TELEPHONE NUMBERS AND WEBSITES

A

Academy of Medical Royal Colleges
Tel: 020 7408 2244
www.aomrc.org.uk

Action for Children (formerly National Children's Homes)
Tel: 0300 123 2112
www.actionforchildren.org.uk

Action for Sick Children
Helpline: 0800 0744 519
www.actionforsickchildren.org

Action for Sick Children (Scotland)
Tel: 0131 553 6553
www.actionforsickchildren.org

Action for Sick Children (Wales)
Tel: 01792 205227
www.actionforsickchildren.org

Adoption and Fostering Information Line
Tel: 0800 783 4086
www.adoption.org.uk

Adoption Law and Guidance
www.dfes.gov.uk/adoption/lawandguidance/

Adoption Register for England and Wales
Tel: 0870 750 2173
www.adoptionregister.org.uk

Adoption UK
Helpline: 0844 848 7900
www.adoptionuk.com

Advice Now (advice on family law)
www.advicenow.org.uk

AIRE Centre (assists in bringing cases before the European Court of Human Rights)
Tel: 020 7831 3850
www.airecentre.org

Alcohol Concern
Tel: 020 7264 0510
www.alcoholconcern.org.uk

Association for all Speech-Impaired Children (AFASIC)
Helpline: 0845 355 5577
www.afasic.org.uk

Association for Child and Adolescent Mental Health
Tel: 020 7403 7458
www.acamh.org.uk

Association for Spina Bifida and Hydrocephalus (ASBAH)
Tel: 01733 555988
www.asbah.org

Association of Chief Police Officers
Tel: 020 7227 3434
www.acpo.police.uk

Association of Child Psychotherapists
Tel: 020 8458 1609
www.childpsychotherapy.org.uk

Association of Directors of Adult Social Services
Tel: 020 7072 7433
www.adass.org.uk

Association of Directors of Children's Services
Tel: 0161 838 5757
www.adcs.org.uk

Association of District Judges
www.judiciary.gov.uk

Association of Family Therapists(AFT)
Tel: 01925 444414
www.aft.org.uk

Association of Forensic Physicians
www.apsweb.org.uk

Association of Lawyers for Children (ALC)
020 8224 7071
www.alc.org.uk

Asthma UK
Advice line: 0800 121 62 44
www.asthma.org.uk

B

Bar Council
Tel: 020 7242 0082
www.barcouncil.org.uk

Barnardo's
Tel: 020 8550 8822
www.barnardos.org.uk

British Association for Adoption and Fostering (BAAF)
Tel: 020 7421 2600
www.baaf.org.uk

British Association for Early Childhood Education
Tel: 020 7539 5400
www.early-education.org.uk

British Association for the Study and Prevention of Child Abuse and Neglect (BASPCAN)
Tel: 01904 613605
www.baspcan.org.uk

British Association of Community Child Health
Tel: 020 7092 6083/6084
www.bacch.org.uk

British Association of Psychotherapists
Tel: 020 8452 9823
www.bap-pychotherapy.org

British Association of Social Workers (BASW)
Tel: 0121 622 3911
www.basw.co.uk

British Dyslexia Association
Helpline: 0845 251 9002
www.bdadyslexia.org.uk

British Epilepsy Association
Helpline: 0808 800 5050
www.epilepsy.org.uk

British Medical Association (BMA)
Tel: 020 7387 4499
www.bma.org.uk

British Psychological Society
Tel: 0116 254 9568
www.bps.org.uk

Brittle Bone Society
Tel: 01382 204446
Helpline: 08000 282459
www.brittlebone.org

C

Cafcass
Tel: 020 7510 7000
www.cafcass.gov.uk

CAFCASS CYMRU
Tel: 01978 368479
www.wales.gov.uk

Care Quality Commission
Tel: 03000 616161
www.cqc.org.uk

Cellmark (DNA Testing)
Tel: 01235 528000
www.cellmark.co.uk

Central Office of Information
Tel: 020 7928 2345
www.coi.gov.uk

Centre for Policy on Ageing
Tel: 020 7553 6500
www.cpa.org.uk

Chartered Institute of Linguists
www.iol.org.uk

Child Accident Prevention Trust
Tel: 020 7608 3828
www.capt.org.uk

Child Concern
Tel: 0161 832 8113
www.childconcern.org.uk

Child Growth Foundation
Tel: 020 8995 0257
www.childgrowthfoundation.org

ChildLine
Tel: 020 7650 3200
Helpline: 0800 1111
www.childline.org.uk

Child Poverty Action Group
Advice line: 020 7833 4627
www.cpag.org.uk

Child Protection Special Interest Group (CPSIG)
Tel: 020 7092 6083
www.cpsig.org.uk

Child Support Agency
Tel: 08457 133133
www.csa.gov.uk

Children England
www.ncvcco.org

Children Living with Inherited Metabolic Diseases (CLIMB)
Tel: 0800 652 3181
www.climb.org.uk

Children's Commissioner for England – 11 MILLION
Tel: 0844 8009 113
www.11million.org.uk

Children's Commissioner for Scotland
Tel: 0131 558 3733
www.sccyp.org.uk

Children's Commissioner for Wales
Tel: 01792 765600/01492 523333
www.childcom.org.uk

Children's Legal Centre
Tel: 01206 872466
www.childrenslegalcentre.com

Children's Rights Officers and Advocates (CROA)
Tel: 01773 820100
www.croa.org.uk

Children's Society
Tel: 0845 300 1128
www.the-childrens-society.org.uk

Citizens Advice Bureau (CAB)
CAB Advice Guide
www.adviceguide.org.uk

College of Mediators
Tel: 01179 047 223
www.collegeofmediators.co.uk

Commission for Local Administration in England
(Local Government Ombudsman)
Tel: 0845 602 1983
www.lgo.org.uk

Commission for Local Administration in Wales
(Local Government Ombudsman)
Tel: 01656 641150
www.lgo.org.uk

Commission for Maintenance and Enforcement (C-MEC)
Children and Family Court Advisory and Support Service
www.cmoptions.org

Commission for Racial Equality
Tel: 020 7939 0000
www.cre.gov.uk

Community Legal Advice
Tel: 0845 345 4 345
www.communitylegaladvice.org.uk

Consortium of Voluntary Adoption Agencies
www.cvaa.org.uk

Contact a Family
Tel: 020 7608 8700
Helpline: 0808 808 3555
www.cafamily.org.uk

Council for Disabled Children
National Children's Bureau
Tel: 020 7843 1900
www.ncb.org.uk

Council of Europe
Office of the Secretary General
Tel: 0033 88 41 20 00
www.coe.int

Courts and court offices

The Supreme Court
Tel: 020 7960 1500

Royal Courts of Justice
Tel: 020 7947 6000

Court of Appeal Civil Division
Tel: 020 7947 7882

High Court of Justice: Family Division
Tel: 020 7947 6540

Principal Registry
Tel: 020 7947 6000

For court addresses generally:

HM Courts Service
Tel: 020 7189 2000 or 0845 456 8770
www.hmcourts-service.gov.uk

For filing Parental Responsibility agreements:

Family Administration Branch
Children Section
Principal Registry of the Family Division
Tel: 020 7947 6000

Criminal Injuries Compensation Authority
Helpline: 0800 358 3601
www.cica.gov.uk

Criminal Records Bureau (CRB)
Tel: 0870 90 90 811
www.crb.homeoffice.gov.uk

Crown Prosecution Service (CPS)
Tel: 020 7796 8000
www.cps.gov.uk

Cry-sis Support Group
BM Cry-sis
Helpline: 0845 122 8669
www.cry-sis.org.uk

D

Daycare Trust
Tel: 020 7840 3350
Helpline: 0845 872 6251
www.daycaretrust.org.uk

Delia Venables Website: (legal links and searches)
www.venables.co.uk

Department for Children, Schools and Families
www.dcsf.gov.uk

Department of Health
Tel: 020 7210 4850
www.dh.gov.uk

Diabetes UK
Careline: 0845 120 2960
www.diabetes.org.uk

Disabled Living Foundation (DLF)
Helpline: 0845 130 9177
www.dlf.org.uk

Down's Syndrome Association
Tel: 0845 230 0372
www.downs-syndrome.org.uk

Drugscope
Tel: 020 7520 7550
www.drugscope.org.uk

Dyslexia Action
Tel: 01784 222300
www.dyslexiaaction.org.uk

E

Economic and Social Research Council
www.esrc.ac.uk

Every Child Matters
www.dcsf.gov.uk/everychildmatters/

Expert Witness Institute
Tel: 0870 366 6367
www.ewi.org.uk

F

Faculty of Forensic and Legal Medicine
www.fflm.ac.uk

Families Need Fathers
Tel: 020 7613 5060
Helpline: 0300 0300 363
www.fnf.org.uk

Family and Parenting Institute
Tel: 020 7424 3460
www.nfpi.org.uk

Family Justice Council
Tel: 020 7947 7333
www.family-justice-council.org.uk

Family Law Bar Association
Tel: 020 7242 1289
www.flba.co.uk

Family Law Newswatch (information on family law)
www.familylaw.co.uk

Family Mediation Council
www.familymediationcouncil.org.uk

Family Mediation Helpline
Helpline: 0845 6026627
www.familymediationhelpline.co.uk

Family Mediators Association
Tel: 0117 946 7180
www.adrgroup.co.uk

Family Rights Group
020 7923 2628
www.frg.org.uk

Fathers Institute
Tel: 0845 634 1328
www.fatherhoodinstitute.org

Foreign and Commonwealth Office
Tel: 020 7008 1111
www.fco.gov.uk

Foreign and Commonwealth Office's Community Liaison Unit
Tel: 020 7008 0230

Foreign and Commonwealth Office Forced Marriage Unit
Tel: 020 7008 0151
www.fco.gov.uk

Fostering Network
Tel: 020 7620 6400
www.fostering.net

Foundation for the Study of Infant Deaths
Helpline: 020 7233 2090
www.fsid.org.uk

G

General Medical Council
www.gmc-uk.org

General Register Office (England & Wales)
www.gro.gov.uk

General Register Office for Scotland
www.gro-scotland.gov.uk

General Social Care Council
Tel: 020 7397 5100
www.gscc.org.uk

Gingerbread (for lone parents and their children)
Helpline: 0800 018 4318
www.gingerbread.org.uk

Government Information
www.direct.gov.uk

Grandparents Apart
Tel: 0141 882 5658
www.grandparentsapart.co.uk

Grandparents Association
Tel: 01279 428040
www.grandparents-association.org.uk

Grandparents Consortium
BeGrand.net

H

The Haemophilia Society
Helpline: 0800 018 6068
www.haemophilia.org.uk

Her Majesty's Council of Circuit Judges
www.judiciary.gov.uk

Her Majesty's Courts Service
Tel: 020 7189 2000 or 0845 456 8770
www.hmcourts-service.gov.uk

Her Majesty's Inspectorate of Constabulary for England and Wales (HMIC)
020 7035 2004
www.hmic.gov.uk

Her Majesty's Inspectorate of Court Administration (HMICA)
Tel: 0113 394 3900
www.hmica.gov.uk

Home Office
www.homeoffice.gov.uk

Home Office: UK Border Agency
www.ind.homeoffice.gov.uk

Home-Start UK
Freephone: 0800 068 6368
www.home-start.org.uk

Hyperactive Children's Support Group
Tel: 01243 539966
www.hacsg.org.uk

I

Identity and Passport Service (To put a stop on a passport being issued to a child)
Tel: 0300 222 0000
www.ips.gov.uk

Independent Safeguarding Authority
Tel: 0300 123 1111
www.isa-gov.org.uk

Institute of Family Therapy
Tel: 020 7391 9150
www.ift.org.uk

Intercountry Adoption Centre (formerly Overseas Adoption Helpline)
Advice line: 0870 516 8742
www.icacentre.org.uk

International Child Abduction and Contact Unit (ICACU)
Tel: 020 7911 7047
www.officialsolicitor.gov.uk

Invalid Children's Aid Nationwide (ICAN)
Tel: 0845 225 4071
www.ican.org.uk

J

Joseph Rowntree Foundation
Tel: 01904 629241
www.jrf.org.uk

Judicial Studies Board (JSB)
www.jsboard.co.uk

Judiciary of England and Wales
www.judiciary.gov.uk

Justices' Clerks Society
Tel: 0151 255 0790
www.jc-society.co.uk

L

Laboratory of the Government Chemist (LGC)
Tel: 020 8943 7000
www.lgc.co.uk

Law Commission for England and Wales
Tel: 020 7453 1220
www.lawcom.gov.uk

Law Commission for Scotland
Tel: 0131 668 2131
www.scotlawcom.gov.uk

Law Society
Tel: 020 7242 1222
www.lawsociety.org.uk

Law Society of Northern Ireland
Tel: 028 9023 1614
www.lawsoc-ni.org

Law Society of Scotland
Tel: 0131 226 7411
www.lawscot.org.uk

Legal Services Commission
Head Office
Tel: 020 7759 0000
www.legalservices.gov.uk

Leverhulme Trust
Tel: 020 7042 9873
www.leverhulme.org.uk

Local Family Justice Councils
Contact the Family Justice Council (see above) or see full contact list at **1.23**

Local Government Ombudsman
Tel: 020 7915 3210
www.lgo.org.uk

Lone Parent Helpline
Tel: 0808 802 0925 (England and Wales)
0808 801 0323 (Scotland)
www.loneparenthelpline.info

M

Magistrates' Association
Tel: 020 7387 2353
www.magistrates-association.org.uk

Marriage Advice
www.2-in-2-1.co.uk

Medical Research Council
Tel: 020 7636 5422
www.mrc.ac.uk

Mind (National Association for Mental Health)
Tel: 020 8519 2122
Info line: 0845 766 0163
www.mind.org.uk

Ministry of Justice (formerly Department for Constitutional
Affairs/Lord Chancellor's Department)
www.justice.gov.uk

N

NAGALRO (Professional Association for Children's Guardians and Children
and Family Reporters and Independent Social Workers)
Tel: 01372 818504
www.nagalro.com

Napo (Trade Union and Professional Association for Family Court and
Probation Staff)
Tel: 020 7223 4887
www.napo.org.uk

National Assembly for Wales
www.wales.gov.uk

National Association for Gifted Children
Tel: 0845 450 0295
www.nagcbritain.org.uk

National Association for Mental Health (see Mind)

National Association of Child Contact Centres
Tel: 0870 770 3269
www.naccc.org.uk

National Childbirth Trust (NCT)
Enquiry line: 0870 444 8707
www.nct.org.uk

NCB (National Children's Bureau)
Tel: 020 7843 6000
www.ncb.org.uk

National Childminding Association (NCMA)
Tel: 0845 880 0044
www.ncma.org.uk

National Deaf Children's Society (NDCS)
Helpline: 0808 800 8880
www.ndcs.org.uk

National Eczema Society (NES)
Helpline: 0870 241 3604
www.eczema.org

National Family Mediation
Tel: 0117 904 2825
www.nfm.org.uk

National Health Service (NHS)
www.nhs.uk

NHS Wales
www.wales.nhs.uk

NHS Scotland
www.show.scot.nhs.uk

Northern Ireland – Health and Social Services Executive
www.northernireland.gov.uk

National Organisation for the Counselling of Adoptees and Parents
(NORCAP)
Helpline: 01865 875000
www.norcap.org.uk

National Society for the Prevention of Cruelty to Children (NSPCC)
Helpline: 0808 800 5000
www.nspcc.org.uk

National Youth Advocacy Service (NYAS)
Tel: 0151 649 8700
www.nyas.net

Nuffield Foundation
Tel: 020 7631 0566
www.nuffieldorganisation.org

Nursing and Midwifery Council
Tel: 020 7637 7181
www.nmc-uk.org

O

Office for National Statistics
Tel: 0845 601 3034
www.statistics.gov.uk

Official Solicitor to the Supreme Court
Tel: 020 7911 7127
www.officialsolicitor.gov.uk

Office of Public Sector Information
www.opsi.gov.uk

OFSTED (Inspection of Cafcass)
Tel: 08456 404045
www.ofsted.gov.uk

One Plus One (relationship research)
Tel: 020 7553 9530
www.oneplusone.org.uk

P

Parent Network Scotland
Tel: 0141 948 0022
www.parentnetworkscotland.org.uk

Parentline Plus (formerly Parent Network)
Helpline: 0808 800 2222
www.parentlineplus.org.uk

Post-Adoption Centre
Advice line: 020 7284 5879
www.postadoptioncentre.org.uk

Pre-School Learning Alliance
Tel: 020 7697 2500
www.pre-school.org.uk

R

Relate
Tel: 0845 456 1310
www.relate.org.uk

Resolution (formerly Solicitors Family Law Association)
Tel: 01689 820272
www.resolution.org.uk

Reunite
International Child Abduction Centre
Advice line: 0116 2556 234
www.reunite.org

Rights of Women
www.rightsofwomen.org.uk

Royal Association for Disability and Rehabilitation (RADAR)
Tel: 020 7250 3222
www.radar.org.uk

Royal College of General Practitioners
Tel: 0845 4564041
www.rcgp.org.uk

Royal College of Midwives
Tel: 020 7312 3535
www.rcm.org.uk

Royal College of Paediatrics and Child Health
Tel: 020 7307 5600
www.rcpch.ac.uk

Royal College of Physicians
Tel: 020 7935 1174
www.rcplondon.ac.uk

Royal College of Psychiatrists
Tel: 020 7235 2351
www.rcpsych.ac.uk

Royal College of Radiologists
Tel: 020 7636 4432
www.rcr.org.uk

Royal National Institute for Deaf People (RNID)
Helpline: 0808 808 0123
www.rnid.org.uk

Royal National Institute of the Blind (RNIB)
Helpline: 0845 766 9999
www.rnib.org.uk

Royal Society for the Prevention of Accidents (RoSPA)
Tel: 0121 248 2000
www.rospa.com

S

Scope
Helpline: 0808 800 3333
www.scope.org.uk

Scottish Adoption Association
Tel: 0131 553 5060
www.scottishadoption.org

Scotland's Commissioner for Children and Young People
Young Persons Freephone: 0800 019 1179
www.sccyp.org

Social Care Institute for Excellence
Tel: 020 7089 6840
www.scie.org.uk

Society of Legal Scholars (formerly SPTL)
Tel: 023 8059 4039
www.legalscholars.ac.uk

Stationery Office (formerly HMSO)
www.tso.co.uk

T

Tavistock Centre for Couple Relationships
Tel: 020 7380 1975
www.tccr.org.uk

U

UK Council for Psychotherapy (UKCP)
Tel: 020 7014 9955
www.psychotherapy.org.uk

V

Victim Support
Supportline: 0845 30 30 900
www.victimsupport.org.uk

W

Wales – National Assembly for Wales
www.wales.gov.uk

Welsh Women's Aid
Helpline: 0808 8010 800
www.welshwomensaid.org

Who Cares? Trust
(promotes the interests of children and young people in public care)
Tel: 020 7251 3117
www.thewhocarestrust.org.uk

Women's Aid
Tel: 0117 944 4411
Helpline: 0808 2000 247
www.womensaid.org.uk

Y

Young Minds
Parents Helpline: 0808 802 5544
www.youngminds.org.uk

Websites that have been specifically designed for children and young people

www.cafcass.gov.uk

www.carelaw.org.uk

www.cf.ac.uk/claws/kids

www.funkydragon.org

www.itsnotyourfault.org

www.childline.org.uk

INDEX

References are to paragraph numbers.